THE UNFORTUNATE CAPTAIN PEIRCE

Halsewell sinking by R. Smirke (detail)
© *National Maritime Museum, Greenwich, London*

The Unfortunate Captain Peirce

AND THE WRECK OF THE
Halsewell, EAST INDIAMAN

A Life and Death
in the Maritime Service of the East India Company

Philip Browne

THE HOBNOB PRESS
2015

First published in the United Kingdom in 2015

by The Hobnob Press, 30c Deverill Road Trading Estate, Sutton Veny, Warminster BA12 7BZ
www.hobnobpress.co.uk

British Library Cataloguing in Publication Data
A catalogue record for this book is available from the British Library

ISBN 978-1-906978-32-7

Typeset in Adobe Garamond Pro 11/14 pt. Typesetting and origination by John Chandler. Cover design by Chris Browne.

Printed by Lightning Source

Contents

Part Three: 'A Freezing horror' The wreck of the Halsewell, 1786

Part Four: 'Of widow'd consort and of orphan'd child' 1786-1791

Part Five: 'Friends in India'

To Jean Sutton

Illustrations and Figures

The illustrations in this book are reproduced by kind permision of the following institutions and individuals:

Het Scheepvartmuseum, Amsterdam:
p.236, Het fregat Zr. Ms. Ijssel onder moodtuig lenzende (A4750) by J.C. Schotel

National Maritime Museum, Greenwich, London:
Front cover, The Wreck of the Halsewell 1786 (F8256) by Thomas Stothard; p.22, The Indiaman 'Royal George' in three Positions in the Downs (BHC4171) by Francis Holman; p.48, Madras Landing (PZ0219) by C. Hunt; p.59, Shipping off Saint Helena (BHC1926) by Adam Callander; p.77, The European Factories at Canton, China (PZ7195) by William Daniell; p.105, Fort St George on the Coromandel Coast (PAD1845) by Jan Van Ryne; p.125, East Indiamen in a Gale (BHC1029) by Charles Brooking; p.149, Falmouth 1752 (J8710) by unknown; p.198, Madras Embarking (PZ0220) by C. Hunt; p.214, Capt [Richard] Pierce (PAD2961) etched by Isaac Cruikshank; p. 221, Society at Sea, Recreation of the Company aboard the Halsewell (PAG7004) by Robert Dodd; p.232, Sailors in a Storm (PAH7353) by Thomas Stothard; p.243, The Loss of the Halsewell (PAH7421) by Robert Dodd; p.245, The Wreck of the Halsewell (PAH0504) by Thomas Stothard engraved by Edmund Scott; p.289, The Halsewell East Indiaman (PAH8430) by Robert Smirke & Robert Pollard.

National Portrait Gallery, London:
p.36, Sir Eyre Coote (NPG124) attributed to Henry Morland; p.92, Stringer Lawrence (NPG777) by Thomas Gainsborough; p.292, The Loss of the Halsewell (D13063) engraved by James Gillray after James Northcote.

Somerset County Council:
p.309, Benjamin Hammet held at Old Municipal Buildings, Taunton. Artist unknown.

Yale Center for British Art, Paul Mellon collection:
p.334, Thomas Graham (B1981.25.334) by Thomas Hickey.

Edward Cumming:
from the CD-ROM *Three English East Indiamen Wrecked Off the Dorset Coast.*
p.13, cuff link held at Brewers' Quay Museum, Weymouth; p.241, Winspit cliffs; p.267, a cup from the tea set presented to Mr Garland, held at Langton Matravers museum; p.271 gravestone of Elizabeth Blackburn at Christchurch Priory, photograph by Brian Sutton.

Duke's Fine Art Auctioneers, Dorchester:
p.171, A View of the Hongs of Canton (detail), lot 1390, 23 Sep 2010, by unknown Chinese artist.

J.J. Heath Caldwell:
p.144, John Graham, miniature by unknown artist.

Oxbow Books:
p.166, Jane Paul, later Mrs Templer of Shapwick, by Jean Laurent Mosnier

Photographs by Philip Browne:
p.183, the house formerly known as Walnut Tree House, Kingston-upon-Thames, Surrey; p. 256, cliffs near Winspit, Purbeck, Dorset; p. 326, the mausoleum of Richard Peirce junior in Park Street cemetery, Kolkata.

Anonymous private collection:
p.132, East Indiaman (possibly Halsewell) in the Strait of Malacca by unknown artist.

Maps by Peter Woodward:
p. 45, Figure 1, India; p.71, figure 2, China Seas; p.224, figure 3, the final voyage of the Halsewell; p.258, figure 4, the coast of Purbeck.

Acknowledgements

This book has been a long time coming. I first encountered the *Halsewell* in 1986 when a neighbour of mine announced his intention to go to the Purbeck coast one freezing night in January. Seeing my puzzled look, he explained it was the two-hundredth anniversary of one of the most harrowing shipwrecks in Dorset history and he was going to mark the occasion with a night-time vigil.

At the time I was on a sabbatical from my teaching job and was studying for a diploma in librarianship at the Polytechnic of North London. The course included a module on local history and I had an assignment to write. My neighbour's eccentric behaviour aroused my curiosity. I decided to find out more about the wreck of the *Halsewell* and to use it as the focus of my assignment. The deadline was looming and I could only scratch the surface of the topic but my interest had been awakened and I knew I would revisit the *Halsewell* and her captain again one day.

That idea lay dormant for almost a quarter of a century but in 2010, when I retired from the education service, I knew it was time to reacquaint myself with Captain Peirce. For the last five years I have slowly and methodically uncovered piece after piece of his life and career. What I have discovered has exceeded my expectations and restored to the light a remarkable man whose history has been obscured for too long.

In writing this book, I owe a huge debt of gratitude to the maritime historian, Jean Sutton. Her vast knowledge of the East India Company and its maritime service has helped me to understand the world that Captain Peirce inhabited. She has patiently answered my questions, encouraged me and gently steered me away from rocks and sandbanks. This book is dedicated to her.

Along the way, many others have helped me, too. I am particularly grateful to Margaret Makepeace and the staff at the British Library's APAC room where I have spent many happy hours. Nearer to home, Reg Saville of the Museum at Langton Matravers and Ed Cumming, editor of the CD ROM were also generous with their help. So, too, were Francis Noel-Hudson, Stuart Drabble and Godfrey Hebden.

I corresponded with Richard Daglish and Richard Flemming, two distant relatives of Richard Peirce and would like to thank them for the information they freely shared with me.

I would like to thank my wife, Beth, and my sons, Peter and Christopher, for putting up with Captain Peirce so patiently and for letting me disappear to India for a month on his trail. Christopher deserves particular credit for the cover design.

Several good friends also came to my aid. Dave Martin advised me on how to pitch a book proposal and invited me to write an article for *The Historian* about my research. Richard Wheal read the first draft, asked pertinent questions and challenged my thinking. Paul Lashmar supplied constant encouragement and practical advice. Peter Woodward drew the maps and also pointed me in the direction of Hobnob Press.

Without John Chandler, this book would not exist. Luckily, he saw some merit in it and so my final thanks must go to him and to Hobnob Press for enabling my project to become the book you now have before you. Its shortcomings are mine alone.

Philip Browne

Introduction
by Jean Sutton

The quarryman or shepherd might pause in his work on the Dorset cliffs in dead of winter to watch a succession of full-rigged three-masted ships proceed down Channel, dwarfing the brigs and schooners and the even smaller hoys, smacks and ferries which carried goods and people round the coast. He might wonder if it was a naval squadron, but decide that they were probably East Indiamen, as this was the time of year for the departure of the India fleets. Of the hundreds which left these shores over a period of two hundred and thirty-four years, many met a tragic end in eastern seas: news would filter back to this country several months later, the horror diminished by distance of time and place. Very few Indiamen were wrecked on our shores. Of those, the two most tragic instances occurred on the Dorset coast: the *Earl of Abergavenny* and the *Halsewell*.

The harrowing details of the *Halsewell*'s end have moved many people to write an account, but only Philip Browne's version has successfully reached publication. Not only has he given us a thorough description of her final days and hours, but he describes her captain, Richard Peirce's career and his association with the *Halsewell* from her launch in 1778. Further, he examines the consequences of the wreck and the problems faced by his widow: in this he has broken new ground in the general study of the East India Company's Maritime Service.

Jean Sutton is the author of *Lords of the East: the East India Company and its Ships,* and *The East India Company's Maritime Service 1746–1834: Masters of the Eastern Seas.*

Peirce and Paul Family Pedigree

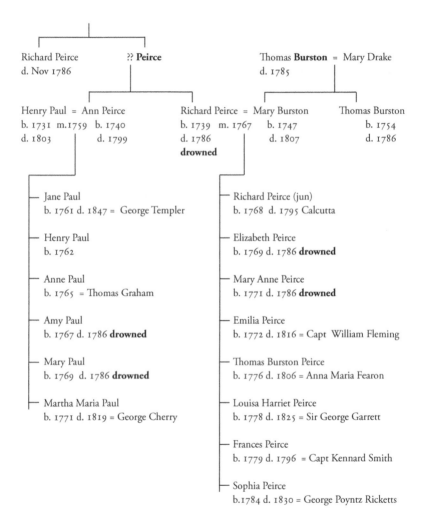

Richard Peirce
d. Nov 1786

?? **Peirce**

Thomas **Burston** = Mary Drake
d. 1785

Henry Paul = Ann Peirce
b. 1731 m.1759 b. 1740
d. 1803   d. 1799

Richard Peirce = Mary Burston
b. 1739 m. 1767 b. 1747
d. 1786   d. 1807
drowned

Thomas Burston
b. 1754
d. 1786

— Jane Paul
  b. 1761 d. 1847 = George Templer

— Henry Paul
  b. 1762

— Anne Paul
  b. 1765 = Thomas Graham

— Amy Paul
  b. 1767 d. 1786 **drowned**

— Mary Paul
  b. 1769 d. 1786 **drowned**

— Martha Maria Paul
  b. 1771 d. 1819 = George Cherry

— Richard Peirce (jun)
  b. 1768 d. 1795 Calcutta

— Elizabeth Peirce
  b. 1769 d. 1786 **drowned**

— Mary Anne Peirce
  b. 1771 d. 1786 **drowned**

— Emilia Peirce
  b. 1772 d. 1816 = Capt William Fleming

— Thomas Burston Peirce
  b. 1776 d. 1806 = Anna Maria Fearon

— Louisa Harriet Peirce
  b. 1778 d. 1825 = Sir George Garrett

— Frances Peirce
  b. 1779 d. 1796 = Capt Kennard Smith

— Sophia Peirce
  b.1784 d. 1830 = George Poyntz Ricketts

PART ONE

'THE FREIGHTED SHIP'

1785

Prologue

Although the temperature outside was below freezing, Richard Peirce had every reason to enjoy an inner glow of well-being. He was commander of the East India Company's ship, *Halsewell*, and his career was approaching a successful conclusion. A few days before Christmas, he would complete the formalities at East India House and then, in January 1786, embark on his final voyage to India. He was already one of the most experienced commanders in the service of the Company. This latest venture, surely, would guarantee his future. On his return, in two years time, he would be able to turn his back on the perils of the sea and devote himself, instead, to the life of an eighteenth-century gentleman with social standing and a 'competent fortune'.

The voyage would be significant for the Peirce family in other ways, too. Richard's eldest daughters, Elizabeth and Mary Ann, were to accompany him as far as Calcutta. Fortunes were being made in Bengal and, with the right social contacts, young ladies like these could hope to find a rich husband there. India would provide them with a lifestyle more exotic and luxurious than any they were likely to enjoy in England.

Perhaps, because the prospects looked so auspicious for his own family, in this season of goodwill, Richard Peirce turned his thoughts to someone less fortunate. In May, that year, he had read in the newspapers of the trial of Samuel Roberts. Richard knew him well. He had served as carpenter's mate during the *Halsewell's* previous voyage and had performed his duties effectively. However, once ashore, Sam had got himself into trouble. A sailor's pay was soon spent and unless he could secure another passage quickly, the temptation was to turn to crime. Spurred on by destitution, Sam Roberts and two others had attempted to steal six pieces of calico from a bleaching yard in Bow. They had been caught and, on the 11th of May at the Old Bailey, Judge Wills had sentenced Sam to fourteen years transportation to

Africa[1]. This was tantamount to a death sentence and Sam's family was distraught. Probably, at the suggestion of Sam himself, they decided to seek assistance from Captain Peirce. They must have regarded him as a compassionate man who might take pity on Sam's plight. They were not mistaken.

On 13 December, in his rooms at 17 Gower Street, Richard Peirce put pen to paper. In the first of two letters to the Judge, he pointed out that Samuel Roberts was not a hardened criminal. 'I have a good opinion of him and believe this the first act of dishonesty'. He confirmed that Sam had served 'soberly, honestly and obediently' on the *Halsewell* and reminded the judge of the hardship such a sentence would bring to Sam's family. He ended the letter with a proposal. In place of this sentence, Richard Peirce offered to re-employ Samuel Roberts for the forthcoming voyage of the *Halsewell*. Samuel Roberts was currently being held at Portsmouth, awaiting transportation. On her way down the Channel, *Halsewell* would put into Portsmouth and pick him up. This would rehabilitate him and be 'the saving of a worthy family from distress'[2].

As the *Halsewell* continued 'her lading' at Gravesend, it was clear that, besides her cargo, she would be carrying the hopes of many people. Yet within a few weeks, these hopes were to be shattered on the Dorset coast, in an event that was to appal and fascinate the nation for years to come. Thereafter, Richard Peirce would be known as 'the unfortunate Captain Peirce'. This book will deal with his career, his success and his final misfortune.

1

Investing in the Future

Mary Peirce understood that, one day, India would claim her two
eldest daughters. Now that day had arrived. On Thursday 1
December 1785, the Directors of the East India Company had given
permission for Eliza and her younger sister, Mary Ann, to 'proceed to
their friends in Bengal'.[1] The girls would sail on the *Halsewell*, the East
Indiaman commanded by their father. This was the news the family
had waited impatiently to hear. At last, the girls' departure was about
to become a bitter-sweet reality.

Mrs Peirce also accepted that two years would have to pass
before she would see her husband again. Then, the safe return of his
ship would signal the successful culmination of his career. If all went
to plan, Richard could retire, a wealthy man, and their financial future
would be secure. As to when she would see her daughters again, Mary
was less certain. It would be several years, at least, and by then both
would be married, perhaps with children of their own. That was the
whole point of it, after all. Despite the raised eyebrows and snide
remarks of some in Kingston society, Mary was convinced they were
doing the right thing.

No doubt, her daughters thought likewise. While they may have
felt some trepidation at the long voyage, it is probably safe to assume
that the two teenaged girls were also excited by what lay ahead. They
would not be the only passengers on the *Halsewell*. A number of other
young ladies would be sailing with them, including their cousins, Amy
and Mary Paul. In the time-honoured phrase, favoured in the minutes
of the Court of Directors, they would all 'proceed to their friends' in
India.[2] Who precisely these 'friends' were, the minutes never disclosed.
However, we do know that amongst those awaiting their arrival in
Calcutta would be Amy and Mary's two older sisters. Both had made
the voyage a few years earlier and were now married to important men

in the Bengal civil service. Anne Paul had accepted a proposal from Thomas Graham of the Revenue Department and Jane had agreed to marry George Templer. It was at the Graham's house in Calcutta that the four young cousins would stay.[3] Also waiting anxiously to see them, would be Eliza and Mary Ann's older brother, Richard.

Three years previously, Richard Peirce junior had sailed to India on his father's ship. At fourteen years of age, he had been recruited as a midshipman but, as soon as the *Halsewell* had reached Calcutta, his father had discharged him on grounds of ill health. Whether or not he was genuinely ill, we cannot be sure.[4] It was a common ploy for captains to appoint, as midshipmen, young protégés who wished to emigrate to India. In this way, they could circumvent the tight Company restrictions on travel to the East.

Once ashore, Richard seems to have made a rapid recovery and soon found employment in a Company office. In doing so, he joined the growing ranks of clerks and others who helped administer the Company's affairs in Bengal. Given the right connections and some oiling of wheels, a Company official could rise to a position where there were rich pickings to be had. The brothers-in-law, Graham and Templer, were good examples. For ambitious young men like these, India was a land of opportunity. And if men could find fortune there, why not women? A rich Company 'servant' was an excellent catch. Eliza Peirce, at seventeen, was already engaged to one and her fifteen-year-old sister and two cousins hoped to follow her lead. They all had the necessary attributes. While Elizabeth displayed exceptional talent at the pianoforte, her younger sister and her cousins were notable for their beauty. With the Grahams to provide introductions and young Richard to chaperone them, they would soon be accepted into Calcutta society where, doubtless, they would attract wealthy suitors.

Although the *Halsewell* would not sail until the New Year, preparations for her departure had already begun. In October 1785, Richard Peirce had been sworn in as her commander, in a formal ceremony at East India House[5]. Then, in early November, Peter Esdaile and William Wells, two of *Halsewell's* owners, had signed the 'charter party'.[6] This was the contract with the East India Company that set out the terms of the voyage. The Company would dictate the ports to be visited and how long should be spent at each one. In return, it would pay the owners an agreed rate to carry the Company's freight. Many decades had elapsed since the East India Company had actually owned its own ships. Instead, the practice of chartering ships had become established. Each East Indiaman was owned by a consortium of investors, under the leadership of a Principal Managing Owner, usually known as 'the ship's husband'. When the *Halsewell* was first launched, in 1778, her principal managing owner had been Mary Peirce's own father, Thomas Burston. He was also Collector of Excise for Surrey and was, therefore, a man of substance. Following Burston's recent death, responsibility for the *Halsewell* had passed to another member of the consortium, Peter Esdaile. The Esdailes were a family of bankers, based in Lombard Street.[7] To be the principal owner of a ship like the *Halsewell* could be extremely lucrative and Peter Esdaile had seen it as a wise business venture.

During November and December 1785, it is likely that Mary Peirce saw little of her husband. The family home was in Kingston-upon-Thames but Richard's work would have kept him in London.[8] Kingston was too far from the city and the waterfront to be convenient so Richard Peirce had rented a place in town. Bloomsbury was being developed and new houses were springing up around Russell Square. It was in this fashionable location that Richard decided to have his base. Letters he wrote in December give his address as 17 Gower Street.[9] While Mary may have joined him there from time to time, her younger children would have required her to remain mostly in Kingston. Until Eliza and Mary Ann departed, there were seven children to be responsible for. All were girls, apart from nine-year-old Thomas, and the youngest, Sophia, was only six months old.[10]

Although the work of preparing the *Halsewell* had been under way since October, Richard Peirce went only occasionally to inspect it. He had more pressing things to do and, in any case, he was not required. The work was the responsibility of a skeleton crew, led by the boatswain and one or two of his officers. After her last voyage, the *Halsewell* had gone for repairs to the Greenland dock in Rotherhithe. Her sails, masts and guns had been removed and work had started on her hull to ensure it remained sound and watertight. Now, with the next voyage looming, the ship had been 'warped', pulled with ropes, out of the dock and guided downstream to Long Reach where a succession of small craft, lighters and hoys, came alongside with stores and equipment. *Halsewell's* masts and rigging had been re-erected and the process of loading and provisioning the ship had begun.

Provided he had competent and reliable officers supervising these operations, Peirce's presence on the ship was unnecessary. He will have been reassured that, at least, his first mate was up to the task. This was Thomas Burston, a man Peirce knew well. The son of the *Halsewell's* late managing owner and younger brother of Mary Peirce, he was, therefore, Richard Peirce's brother-in-law. But, more important than these family ties, Thomas Burston had sailed twice previously on *Halsewell* – once as third mate and, later, as first mate. It was good to have someone like him to rely on. Young Burston would go on, no doubt, to have a successful career as a captain himself, perhaps succeeding Peirce to the command of the *Halsewell*, when the time came.

The other officers had not sailed with Peirce before and, therefore, their true capabilities had yet to be revealed. On Friday 18 November, at India House, Charles Henry Stone had been sworn in as Third Officer and Henry Pilcher as Fourth.[11] Pilcher had formerly served as a lieutenant with the Royal Navy, on the guardship *Scipio*. He came from a good family; his father was 'in the commission of the peace for the County of Kent'.[12] With the temporary suspension of war with France, Royal Navy crews were being laid off. A position on an East Indiaman was an attractive alternative for those with sufficient means and influence. Pilcher was not alone in this respect. In addition to the usual six officers, Peirce had agreed to take James Bremer in a supernumary capacity. Like Pilcher, he, too, had been a lieutenant in the Royal Navy.[13] As for the third mate, Charles Stone, he had transferred from another East Indiaman, the *Berrington*. Less is known about him and for good reason. Circumstances would ensure that the *Halsewell* sailed without him.

In October 1785 another East Indiaman, the *Pigot*, had returned from the East Indies with a cargo that included a 'tyger', a present to King George III from Lord Macartney.[14] Despite this exotic passenger, the *Pigot* had had a troubled voyage. Illness had ravaged the crew and much responsibility had fallen on two of her officers, Henry Meriton, third mate, and John Rogers, fourth mate. Once back in London, good reports of both men must have reached the ears of Captain Peirce. Within a few weeks of his return, Henry Meriton was rewarded with promotion. Joining Stone and Pilcher at East India House, he was sworn in as *Halsewell's* second mate.[15]

One wonders what Richard Peirce's first impressions were of these officers who would serve under him for the next two years. Their performance would be crucial for the efficient and disciplined running of the ship. Peirce will have been aware that while Meriton had performed well during the difficult voyage of the *Pigot*, there were, nonetheless, some doubts concerning his reliability. There had been serious irregularities regarding the loading of the ship. The Company laid down strict rules to ensure that cargo was all accounted for and that pilfering by the 'lumpers' – stevedores who did the loading and unloading – was prevented. On the *Pigot*, these rules had been flouted. On 11 November, Captain Morgan and his chief mate were summoned before the Court of Directors and suspended from the service of the Company. Then, five days later, Henry Meriton was called to appear as well. The Court Minutes record that John Rogers, the fourth mate, was exonerated of any blame but that

> Mr Meriton, the third mate, had absented himself from the ship for six or seven days without leave from the Commanding Officer. Whereupon Mr Meriton was called into Court and reprimanded by the Chairman in the Court's name.[16]

No doubt, Peirce reflected that if Captain Morgan had such scant regard for the regulations, it was hardly surprising that his officers took liberties too. Officers and crew needed to be directed with a firm hand, but not too firmly. There were also dangers in being too autocratic and the newspapers often reported such cases. In recent years, a growing number of seamen had taken officers and captains to court, seeking redress for assault or unlawful imprisonment. These cases had come before Chief Justice Lord Loughborough in the Court of Common Pleas. He was thought to be sympathetic to the sailors who were sometimes brutally treated by those in authority over them. In several well-publicised trials, East India Company commanders had been required to pay out substantial sums in damages. There was a growing concern amongst commanders that sailors might try to take advantage of impressionable juries and bring bogus claims against them.

If, at the start of December, Peirce spent any time at the Jerusalem Coffee House, that favourite haunt of East India Company commanders, the talk would have been of the latest case to come before Lord Loughborough. This time, Captain Johnston was in the dock. His ship, the *Berrington,* had recently returned from India, bearing no less a 'personage' than Warren Hastings, Governor of Bengal. Whether or not the presence of such an illustrious passenger on his ship prompted Captain Johnston to assert his authority with more than usual severity can only be guessed at. What is known is that Johnston flogged one of his seamen, William Douglas. There was nothing out of the ordinary about the flogging of sailors. East India Company commanders did so regularly and it was accepted as the way to punish disobedient crewmen and maintain discipline, but it had to be justified and proportionate. In this case, William Douglas felt he had been unjustly treated. He was sufficiently aggrieved to take Captain Johnston to court where, doubtless, he expected a sympathetic hearing.

On 27 November 1785, the case came before Lord Loughborough at the Guildhall. William Douglas had enlisted a number of witnesses on his behalf but, suddenly, with no explanation, these witnesses declined to testify. Without their testimony, the case collapsed. Lord Loughborough had no alternative but to find Captain Johnston not guilty of assault and to award costs to Douglas.[17] While officers and commanders may have applauded the verdict, this was not the view of ordinary seamen. They were angry and resentful at what they saw as a miscarriage of justice. Had the witnesses been intimidated or bribed to stay silent? If so, the officers must be culpable. Their intervention must have prevented Lord Loughborough from delivering the correct verdict. Nevertheless, he was still thought to be on the side of the ordinary seaman, and officers should remember this. The name of

Lord Loughborough now entered common parlance among mariners. The phrase 'I'll Loughborough you', became a warning with menacing overtones. It indicated not only litigious intent but also a clear challenge to authority. Within a month, men on the *Halsewell* would utter these words to their own officers, invoking the name of Loughborough in a cry of defiance and a declaration of revolt.

2
Completing Her Lading

While *Halsewell* was being got ready for her voyage, Richard Peirce concentrated on what, for him, was the most important part of the whole enterprise. His ship would not only transport goods on behalf of the East India Company; a section of her hold would also carry 'private trade', merchandise that belonged to him personally. It was through trading on his own account, in private commercial dealing, that Peirce expected to make his fortune.

By the 1780s the concept of private trade was well established. For over a century, the Directors of the East India Company had granted to their commanders and officers the privilege of carrying their own personal merchandise on Company ships. This 'indulgence' enabled them to share in the Company's monopoly of trade with the East. On arrival at their destination, their private goods would be sold in the Company's salesroom. The Company would charge commission on the sale but any remaining profit would go to the seller. Although it was officially sanctioned, the privilege of private trade was bound by certain conditions. The Company did not want its employees to be in direct competition with itself so there were restrictions on the type of goods an individual could carry. Since only a proportion of the ship's hold could be set aside for private trade, there also had to be physical limits on the quantity. As commander, Captain Peirce was granted the lion's share – a generous fifty-five tons of personal, private trade.[18]

Without this privilege, Peirce knew that he would never become rich. While they were at sea, East India commanders were paid £10 a month. On his previous voyage to Bengal, Peirce had been away for just under twenty-two months. For this, his wages had been £216-13s-4d, equivalent to roughly £29,000 today.[19] This was barely enough to cover his expenses and so it is hardly surprising that Richard Peirce now focussed his attention on what would be his final opportunity for private trading. But to profit from it, he would have to cater to the demands of the market, both in India and at home.

By 1785, the market in India had grown considerably, reflecting the increasing number of Europeans resident there. An ever-expanding army of civil servants helped to administer the affairs of both the East India Company and its smaller European rivals. In Bombay, the number of white residents amounted to approximately 2,500. Madras, with its large garrison, was twice that size. In both establishments, there were shops, bakeries and taverns catering to European tastes. Madras even enjoyed the services of a portrait-painter and a dancing master. Finally, there was Bengal. Since the India Act of 1784, its status had been raised to chief Presidency, placing it above Bombay and Madras. Calcutta was the seat of government and was where the best career opportunities were to be found. It was home to at least one thousand men from across Europe. Elsewhere, in Bengal, there were five thousand soldiers and at least two thousand other Europeans. Although the influx of women was steadily increasing, by 1785 only a few hundred were resident across all the three Presidencies.[20] Nevertheless, they, like everyone else, yearned for contact with the world they had left behind.

As a result, settlements like Calcutta and Madras offered attractive commercial opportunities to the private trader. Separated from home by thousands of miles of sea and surrounded by an alien way of life, the Company's servants were desperate to maintain their connection with European refinement and culture. They were hungry for the latest fashions and for the trappings of 'civilised' society. As well as clothes, people wanted musical instruments, materials for writing or painting, clocks, jewellery, books and much else besides.

Cufflink retrieved from the Halsewell wreck site.
© *E. Cumming*

In January 1785, Monsieur Blanchard had made the first cross-channel flight in his new hydrogen balloon and subsequently 'balloonomania' had captured the public imagination. Cufflinks bearing an image of Blanchard's balloon were now the height of fashion.[21] Richard Peirce knew that if he invested wisely in products like these, they would command a good price in India.

A second factor, that season, would give Peirce a further commercial advantage. Although the East India Company was planning to send at least forty ships to the East Indies, the *Halsewell* would be one of the first to arrive. There would be a keen demand for Peirce's goods and the price he could charge would be high, but the demand was finite. Commanders arriving later in the season might find that the market for particular items had already been satisfied and their goods could only be sold at a loss or not at all. Private trade was a privilege but it was no guarantee of financial success.

Because very few records have survived, little is known about the private trade that Richard Peirce decided to invest in. However, it is likely to have been worth several thousand pounds. While he may have paid for some of these goods from his own savings, others were acquired on credit. His dealings with Bourne and Hawkins are a case in point.

By 1785, the partnership of Thomas Bourne and John Hawkins had been established for several years. They ran a jewellers and hardware business in Cheapside. They would have seen in the newspapers that the *Halsewell* was destined to arrive in India at the start of the season, so when its commander approached them with a business proposition, they must have recognised a good commercial opportunity. The details of the transaction have not all survived but enough is known to give us an idea. It was agreed that Captain Peirce would carry £1,000 worth of Bourne & Hawkins' goods within his allocated space for private trade.[22] These would be high-end luxury goods, including solid silver shoe buckles set with diamonds. The deal would be on a sale-or-return basis. Peirce would sell the goods in India and no doubt retain a percentage of the profit or take a commission for his trouble. He would incur no financial costs and Bourne & Hawkins would get a better price for their wares in India than they would at home. It was mutually advantageous. With the terms of the contract agreed, all that remained was for the legal paperwork to be completed. Peirce promised to call in at Cheapside to sign the bond before he sailed.

Her masts and sails now in place, the *Halsewell* moved down
the river on 21 November to Gravesend.[23] Accompanying her were the
Ganges and the *Manship*, two other East Indiamen of similar size that
would make the voyage too. On arrival just below Purfleet they found
'riding here' the *Sulivan*, *General Goddard* and the *Kent*.[24] With its
deeper water anchorage, Gravesend Reach was the place where ships
congregated to 'complete their lading'. Now the ship's guns, shot and
powder could be winched aboard and stowed. Water butts were filled
with Thames water and the Company's heavy cargo began to arrive.

Primarily concerned with imports, the East India Company
earned most of its wealth from the sale of the goods it brought
back from the East Indies. The outward voyage was mainly used
for supplying the company's outposts in India. These were not only
concentrated in the three Presidencies but also included smaller
trading posts and 'factories' elsewhere. They all needed supplies of
resources and manpower. The Company was responsible for its own
security and this necessitated a considerable militia. War and disease
regularly decimated their ranks and the Company continuously had
to find fresh replacements. The *Halsewell*, like most East Indiamen,
would be transporting a complement of raw recruits, when she finally
weighed anchor.

As December began, the *Manship*, *Ganges* and *Halsewell*, all
anchored at Gravesend, took on Company cargo. This cargo included
copper and iron hoops but also the 'human lumber'. By 1 December
more than two hundred and fifty recruits to the Company's militia
had gone aboard the three ships. Of these, one hundred and three
were billeted below decks on the *Halsewell*. They were a mixed bunch
– drawn from Ireland, Scotland and all corners of England. Few of
them were taller than five foot six inches and several were as young
as sixteen.[25] Some were accompanied by their wives. All would spend
the next month coming to terms with the darkness, the foul smells
and the restrictions of life on the lower deck of an East Indiaman.
Still untrained and possibly lacking some of their uniform, they were
an unprepossessing sight. Paradoxically, the *Halsewell* was carrying a
large consignment of brand new uniforms but these were not intended
for the Company's recruits. Instead, they were destined for the King's

regular army, the 42nd Royal Highland Regiment of Foot, already stationed in India.[26]

Though we cannot be certain, it would seem that preparations on the *Halsewell* did not go smoothly. The men were uncooperative and angry about something. Was this connected to the outcome of the Douglas vs Johnston court case? Charles Henry Stone had been fifth mate on the *Berrington* and was now promoted to third mate on the *Halsewell*. Some other sailors from the *Berrington* had transferred with him. Were they still angry and resentful about the ruling by Lord Loughborough? Very likely. What is clear is that something infected the crew of the *Halsewell* with a 'want of subordination'. Significantly, their main target seems to have been the third mate. When instructed to extinguish their lights, some sailors threw shot at him. Thomas Burston, as senior officer, struggled to maintain discipline and may even have been assaulted too.[27] By the middle of December, the situation had become so bad that Stone had had enough. Claiming ill-health, he decided to resign. In coming to this decision, he was probably persuaded by Thomas Burston or even by Captain Peirce himself. No commander wants an unhappy crew and, by replacing the third mate, he must have hoped to remove the cause of discontent. Unfortunately, now that discipline had broken down, it would take time to restore. However, the quest for another third mate was quickly resolved. Indeed, the choice may have been influenced by Henry Meriton, for it fell on his former shipmate, John Rogers. The man, who had served well as fourth mate on the *Pigot*, would now occupy the post of third mate on the *Halsewell*.

Once an East Indiaman was fully loaded and ready, the usual practice was to sail to the Downs. This was an area of sheltered water between Deal and the Goodwin Sands where ships would anchor in order to take on their final passengers and to drop their river pilots. During wartime, convoys would form up at the Downs so they could proceed down the Channel under Royal Navy escort. For some reason, on 13 December, the Court of Directors decided to permit the *Halsewell*, *Ganges* and *Manship* to remain at Gravesend for an additional ten days.[28] Presumably this was at the request of their commanders but no explanation is given. Was the loading taking longer than usual for some reason? Could this be a result of the exceptionally cold weather or was it linked to the resignation of Charles Stone? With the date of *Halsewell's* departure fast approaching, we must now turn our attention to her passengers. They would certainly have been on the mind of Richard Peirce. For a commander, the conveyance of passengers was often the second most lucrative aspect of his business, after private trade. The roundhouse, in the stern, and the great cabin were his preserve and could be divided into smaller compartments. People would pay handsomely for these scraps of personal space, particularly if it included eating at the Captain's table. On the homeward voyage from the East, rich merchants or 'nabobs' would pay enormous sums. That very year, Warren Hastings had paid £5,000 for his wife to occupy part of the great cabin, during her return on the *Kent*.[29]

Nobody of the status of Mrs Hastings was intending to sail on the *Halsewell,* but there were one or two potential passengers who could be charged a reasonable sum. Sir George and Lady Staunton had engaged to make the voyage.[30] Previously, Sir George had served in Madras as private secretary to the governor, Lord George Macartney. In 1784, he had played a key role in drafting the Treaty of Mangalore which had brought a temporary halt to the Anglo Mysore war, that long-running struggle with Hyder Ali. In recognition of his contribution, George Staunton had been granted a baronetcy.[31] Now, covered in glory, he planned to rejoin Lord Macartney in India.

Others wishing to sail there included Robert Graham and his wife. Robert Graham had been a partner in the London bank of Mayne and Graham until 1782 when it had suddenly collapsed.[32] Many investors lost their savings and, inevitably, there was much anger. While Mayne's response to the outcry was to commit suicide, his partner opted for a less permanent escape route. He would relocate to Calcutta and join his brother, Thomas. It was through this family connection that Robert Graham was related to the Paul family and, no doubt, was already well known to Captain Peirce. Given that so many passengers on the outward passage would be relatives of his, it is unlikely that Peirce expected to make much profit from this leg of the voyage.

The East India Company took great pains to prevent an influx of the destitute who would place a financial burden on their settlements in the East. Only those who could support themselves were allowed to travel. Consequently, Company regulations required that every passenger was endorsed by two people who would vouch for them and put up £200 as security. This sum was beyond the means of most people and would equate today to about £17,000 The Court of Directors' minutes for 14 December show that the principal managing owner, Peter Esdaile, and Richard Peirce himself, stood security for his two daughters, Eliza and Mary Ann. Richard Peirce also vouched for their cousins, Amy and Mary Paul, as did George Templer. A week later on 21 December, the Court minutes recorded payment of further securities.[33] The £200 for Miss Ann Mansell was deposited by a third member of the Graham family, George Graham, older brother of Thomas and Robert. James Cox, a jeweller, stood security for Mr John George Schultz. The latter had already made his fortune in India but was returning to wind up his affairs and ensure the safe remittance of his wealth back to England. As is so often the case with India, these families were intertwined through a complex web of connections.

The passengers in Captain Peirce's quarters would pass the voyage in relative comfort but there were others who would not. The hundred or so newly recruited company soldiers, some with their wives, would spend most of their time in the dank and fetid conditions of the lower deck. So, too, would other less privileged passengers. Between them, the *Halsewell*, *Ganges* and *Manship* would carry a number of lascars who were to be returned to India.[34] The lascars were a regular feature on East Indiamen. Many were Moslems of Arab descent who had settled on the west coast of India. Others were Hindus from Bengal. Unlike most Indians, lascars had a tradition of seafaring. When it was time for the Company's ships to return to England, their original crews were often very depleted. Disease and desertion had taken their toll, so lascars were recruited to fill the gaps. The understanding was that, having helped to bring the ships home, the lascars would be returned to India at the earliest opportunity. On this occasion, we must assume that the majority were accommodated on *Manship* and *Ganges*. Although one newspaper reported that 'upwards of seventy lascars' sailed on *Halsewell*, this is unlikely.[35] No lascars were listed among the survivors, suggesting that few, if any, were on board.

However, Company records show that a number of other Indians did sail on Peirce's ship.[36] When Europeans returned from India they were often accompanied by their native Indian servants whom they categorised as 'black'. On arrival in England, some of these servants either requested permission to return to India or were simply no longer required. Mary Roza, the Indian servant of General Townsend, was one of at least three 'black' females on board. Another belonged to Laurence Sulivan, the former Company Director who was now on his deathbed. Even George Graham, who had vouched for Ann Mansell, sent away his former servant, Joseph de Gruz.

On 21 December, as the weather worsened, it was time for the final formalities in Leadenhall Street. Dressed ceremonially in their blue cloth coats with black velvet collars and gold braided sleeves, Captain James Williamson of the *Ganges*, Captain Charles Gregorie of the *Manship* and Captain Richard Peirce of the *Halsewell* arrived in front of the imposing façade of India House, accompanied by some of their chief officers. They were ushered into the Court Room and there, in front of two or three Directors, swore the 'usual oath'. This included a promise not to engage in illicit private trading but to keep to the terms of the Charter Party. Immediately after this, John Rogers was sworn in as third mate.[37] The complement of officers on the *Halsewell* was now complete.

Before he left the building, Captain Peirce was invited by the Directors to undertake an additional responsibility. The Company wanted to honour Colonel Cathcart of the Madras Grenadiers with an expensive ceremonial sword. The sword had cost one hundred guineas and was to be presented to Colonel Cathcart in recognition of his courageous gallantry against the French during the siege of Cuddalore. Peirce would be entrusted to convey the sword on the *Halsewell* and to present it to the recipient on arrival in India.[38] Richard Peirce was flattered to be asked and happy to oblige. Locked in its wooden case, the sword would travel with his personal valuables in a secure part of the hold. It was agreed that the sword would be brought to the ship without delay.

For the next ten days, Captain Peirce and his senior officers would be busily tying up any loose ends regarding their own trade. They would need to check that everything had been delivered to the ship and stored safely aboard. For Peirce, this included musical instruments and, from Messrs Reeves & Son in Holborn, crayons, lead pencils, superfine colours and other articles for drawing.[39] He also concluded a deal, with Mr Dickinson of Bond Street, to carry a large number of engravings. The *Morning Chronicle & London Advertiser* reported that these pictures were paid for in full *'by the mere accident of a sportive conversation over a bottle the evening or two before Capt Peirce left London.'*[40] It would seem that Captain Peirce was not averse to an occasional wager. Hardly surprising in one who was about to gamble everything on his private trade. Then on Christmas Eve, he returned to Cheapside to sign the bond with Bourne and Hawkins. With these final transactions completed, Richard Peirce rejoined his family in Kingston-upon-Thames, for the last time.

On Christmas day it snowed.[41] A white Christmas may have added to the atmosphere but, as he stood in front of a blazing fire, with his family gathered around him, one wonders whether Richard Peirce felt any trepidation about what lay ahead. Much depended on this voyage, and yet, despite his long career at sea, Peirce had never taken the precaution of drawing up his will. In this, he differed from most of his fellow commanders and even many humble sailors. It was an extraordinary omission that would cost his widow dear.

By the day after Boxing Day, Captain Peirce was back at his rooms in Gower Street. While the spirit of goodwill to all men remained strong, he wrote a second letter on behalf of Samuel Roberts. As we know, Sam Roberts was a former crew member. He had served on *Halsewell* as carpenter's mate and his captain had been impressed by his honesty and obedience. In May, he had been convicted of stealing calico and he was now incarcerated in a prison hulk at Portsmouth awaiting transportation to Africa. His destination would be a prison settlement on the river Gambia where the climate and disease would quickly carry him off.[42] It is a testament to Richard Peirce's humanity and concern for his men that, even at this eleventh hour, he was prepared to throw Roberts a lifeline. In a final plea to Judge Buller,

Peirce attempted to negotiate a release. He wrote, 'If discharged, I will employ him immediately on board the ship *Halsewell* now at Gravesend on another voyage to India'.[43]

Meanwhile, at Gravesend Reach, the ships were almost ready to depart. On Christmas Eve, the Company recruits on *Halsewell* were mustered for final inspection. George Cooper, resident surgeon at Gravesend, together with each ship's surgeon, checked that the recruits were in a fit state to sail. The voyage would be arduous enough and, if men were already showing signs of illness, they would have to be weeded out before they could pose a health risk to the others. Following the inspection, eight recruits were discharged from *Halsewell*, thirteen from *Ganges* and just one from *Manship*. Mr Dominicus, of the East India Company, then paid the wages to those who remained. There were now ninety-five recruits left on *Halsewell*, under the command of Sgt Thomas Perryman. Of these, only nineteen would survive the voyage.[44]

Nearby, Captain Gregorie went aboard the *Manship*.[45] Then, on Boxing Day, as snow continued to fall heavily, his ship weighed anchor and moved off down river. The same day, Mr Mavor of the Honourable Company came on board the *Ganges* and paid the crew their 'river pay'.[46] This was the equivalent of two months wages paid in advance and was the only money the seamen would receive until the ship had safely returned many months later. It was standard practice and we must assume, therefore, that the crew of the *Halsewell* were also paid.

On Wednesday 28 December, Captain Williamson went aboard the *Ganges*. That afternoon she weighed anchor and, under the direction of a river pilot, began the short journey down river to the stretch known as 'the Hope'. Shortly afterwards, the *Halsewell* followed. At the Hope, both ships stopped again. Traditionally, this was where most passengers chose to come aboard. It was also the last chance to leave the ship before the voyage began in earnest, and the Company's recruits must have been aware of it. That night, four of them decided to desert. Led by one of the oldest – thirty year old John Watts from Sheffield – somehow they made it to shore and disappeared. The Muster Roll records that they had 'run'.[47]

Throughout Thursday there were easterly gales and, by Saturday, the last day of the year, the weather had turned to sleet, combined with

An Indiaman in the Downs, 1779 by Francis Holman
© National Maritime Museum, Greenwich, London

thick fog. The newspapers reported temperatures of fifteen degrees below freezing.[48] It was turning into one of the most severe winters for many years. Even the Thames had started to freeze. At Wapping, a sailor tried to walk across the river on the ice but, halfway over, it cracked and he fell through.[49] At the Hope, in these Arctic conditions, the passengers were waiting to go aboard.

Anyone familiar with the paintings of Robert Dodd or Francis Holman will have in their mind an image of an East Indiamen in full sail, confidently and majestically forging through the waves under a clear sky. The sight that greeted Mary and Eliza Peirce and the other passengers was somewhat different. Shrouded in fog, straining at her anchor in the choppy waters of the estuary, the *Halsewell* must have looked less romantic and reassuring. But, as they were rowed out to the ship, they would not have had time to dwell on this thought. Once alongside the Indiaman, no doubt impatient to escape the sleet and biting wind, the young ladies were quickly helped by the oarsmen onto a bosun's chair which had been lowered to them from the ship. Then, holding tight to the wet ropes, they were winched up the ship's side and swung onto the slippery deck of the *Halsewell*. There, they were welcomed by the familiar faces of Thomas Burston and, of course, Captain Richard Peirce himself. After the briefest of greetings, they were ushered inside to the relative comfort of the roundhouse. Looking about them, they knew this confined space would be their home for many months. They did not know, that in less than a week, it would also be their grave.

PART TWO

'THE HARDY VETERAN'

A CAREER AT SEA

3
An Uncertain Pedigree

The events of the first six days of 1786 would ensure that the name of Captain Peirce became known throughout the land. Not only would his fate be recorded in newspapers, poems and paintings, but his actions, his demeanour, his motives and his very judgement would come under close scrutiny. If he was a tragic figure in the eyes of the nation, there was also a suspicion that this tragedy might have been, at least in part, a result of personal failings. Was the shipwreck simply an act of God or should Peirce shoulder some responsibility for the disaster, too?

Two centuries later, this is still a pertinent question. To answer it with confidence, it is helpful to consider Richard Peirce's previous career. The experiences and events he encountered in the course of many years at sea inevitably shaped the man who now commanded the *Halsewell*. They informed his decision making and influenced his actions. The light, shed by these formative events, helps to reveal the man who would soon face his greatest test.

But when and where does Peirce's story begin? What were his origins? According to a mourning ring, Richard was forty-six when he died.[1] This would indicate that he was born during 1739 but, as yet, very little is known about the family to which he belonged. In fact, only two relatives can be identified with any certainty. Firstly, he had an uncle, also called Richard, who lived in Bath. This uncle rented a house in Gay Street and possibly some other property as well. In his will, he described himself as a gentleman and a member of the Bathonian Society. By 1786, uncle Richard had retired to Taunton where, in November of that year, he died. In his will, he left everything to the widow of 'my nephew, the late Richard Peirce, captain of the *Halsewell*'.[2] From these few facts, we can infer that, since his uncle was called Richard, Captain Peirce's own father must have had a different first name. It was common for firstborn sons to be named after their fathers. If our Richard was named in honour of his uncle, it suggests that he may have had an older brother who took their father's name.

Richard Peirce's sister, Ann, is the only other member of his immediate family we can identify with confidence. She was the mother of Amy and Mary Paul who were to join Peirce's own daughters on that final voyage. In February 1759, Ann Peirce had married Henry Paul in Somerset.[3] He came from West Monkton, a small village, not far from Taunton. Although Ann and Henry were to end their days at Cossington Manor, near Bridgwater, that would not be until the end of the century. Most of their married life seems to have been spent in West Monkton. A few clues, in papers held at the Somerset History Centre, suggest they may have lived at Quantock Farm, just outside the village.[4] Henry seems to have acted as an agent for other more prosperous landowners, organising deliveries of straw, fodder and shipments of Welsh coal through Bridgwater. They also consulted him about the value of their sheep. This suggests the Pauls were of fairly humble status, though in later life their fortunes would change. Together, Henry and Ann Paul had at least six children, five of whom were daughters. Although two would be lost on the *Halsewell*, the other three would make advantageous marriages. Each would marry a man with strong links to India and a rising career. As their children climbed the social ladder, Henry and Ann Paul were able to follow behind.

The fact that both his uncle and sister lived in Somerset might suggest that Richard Peirce also came from the West Country. Although the link is speculative, some circumstantial evidence may help to underpin such a connection. One clue is the presence, on the *Halsewell*, of another resident of West Monkton, Thomas Jeane. Now enlisted as a midshipman,[5] Thomas had sailed previously as Captain Peirce's personal servant or 'guinea pig'.[6] Later, Henry Meriton, would describe Thomas Jeane as being a youth 'under the immediate care' of Captain Peirce. Although the boy's father must have paid for this privilege, it is likely that Peirce already knew the Jeane family. The Rev. John Jeane was rector for the parish of West Monkton and a familiar face to many in the area. Ann Peirce had been married in his church.

The second factor linking Peirce to this part of England is the name of his ship. Although generally spelled *Halsewell*, she was in fact named after Halswell House, the home of Sir Charles Kemeys Tynte.[7] Halswell House is only a few miles north of Taunton and within easy reach of West Monkton. In early newspaper reports, the ship's name is often spelled as *Halswell*. Such a connection makes it likely that Charles Kemeys Tynte was himself a part-owner of the East Indiaman that bore the name of his family seat.

The third connection with Somerset is through a close friend, Benjamin Hammet. Hammet was born in Taunton and later became its Member of Parliament.[8] He and Peirce were friends from 'their earliest years'.[9] If we include their childhood or schooldays in this time frame, it leads us to suppose that Richard Peirce must have grown up in or close to Taunton, but we can draw no firm conclusions; Richard Peirce's actual birthplace remains a mystery. Similar uncertainty surrounds his social origins and place in society.

Broadly, there are two possibilities. Either, Richard Peirce came from a family with sufficient status, wealth and influence to obtain entry into the Company's maritime service or his origins were more humble and other forces opened those doors for him. Given the absence of reliable information, it is worth exploring both possibilities.

Richard Peirce's first recorded post on an East India Company ship was as fifth mate, in 1759.[10] By the time he joined the *Houghton* in November of that year, he was already twenty. If his family were well connected, one would expect that Richard's father would have paid for him to serve as a guinea pig, in the same way as Thomas Jeane's father had. So far, no evidence has emerged to show that this happened. It was in any case, not essential. The first proper rung on the career ladder for officers was as a midshipman and this is how many future captains had their introduction to the sea. However, it would seem that Richard Peirce did not serve as a midshipman either. Anthony Farrington's extensive catalogue of officers and midshipmen makes no mention of him before he joined the *Houghton*. Farrington's work, though, contains a number of inaccuracies and we should not take it as gospel.

If Richard Peirce did, in fact, serve as a midshipman on an Indiaman, he would have incurred considerable expense. The post of midshipman was allocated at the discretion of the captain and money would have to change hands in order to obtain it. Those appointed would have to purchase their uniform, sea chest, sextant and other equipment. They would also require funds to support themselves during the many months abroad. If a midshipman wanted to engage in some personal trading overseas, he would need to raise capital to do so. For all this, a young man would usually look to his family for financial backing. Not surprisingly, therefore, most midshipmen came from the gentry and from families of the better off. Midshipmen were also expected to have had a reasonable level of education. They had to be literate and proficient in mathematics. The calculations essential for accurate navigation were complicated and officers were required to be qualified in them. To become a midshipman necessitated more than basic schooling.

It would seem that Richard Peirce had, also, received a reasonable education. He obtained the required qualifications in navigation and his later career shows him to be a man with an interest in the arts and a considerable library of books. This might suggest that he came from the educated classes. His uncle styled himself as a gentleman so it is reasonable to assume that his father did likewise. Yet Mr Peirce senior is puzzlingly absent. He appears to have left no footprint on history. For there to be no documentary trace of someone from the gentry, or even the middling classes, is very odd. Unless, of course, he did not live in England.

It has been suggested that Richard Peirce's family actually lived in India and that he, himself, may have been born there. It is an attractive theory but there is no evidence to support it. In the 1730s, very few Englishmen in India were accompanied by their English wives and children. Most found the attractions of the local Indian women more than satisfying and many 'natural' mixed race children resulted from these relationships. Those European families that did reside in Madras, Bombay or Bengal were generally associated with the more senior echelons of the East India Company and the military. Many can be identified through surviving Company and church records.

One family in Calcutta does catch the eye. In 1731, a Captain Richard Peirce married Ann Shiers in Calcutta.[11] Over the next decade they had at least four children. Three were sons, the eldest, another Richard, born in 1736, followed by John in 1739 and Thomas in 1745. Soon afterwards, in September 1746, their father, Captain Richard Peirce, died in Calcutta and was buried there. Although clearly members of the same family unit, India Office records spell their names variously as Pearce, Pierce and Peirce. They may, indeed, have been relatives of 'our' Richard Peirce but their first names and dates of birth fall in such a way that they cannot be his immediate family.

Another explanation for the elusiveness of Richard Peirce's father might be that he spent his career at sea. If we follow this line of enquiry, we have to ask if Peirce's father could have been employed in the Company's maritime service, too. An examination of Farrington's catalogue suggests a possible candidate, Captain John Pearse. Between 1747 and 1758, he commanded the *Edgcote* during four voyages to India and China. Could he have been Richard's father?

The fact that the surnames, Pearse and Peirce, sound the same is tantalising but may be a distraction. While newspapers and even the Court of Directors' minutes were prone to spelling people's names inconsistently, Richard Peirce was not. When signing personal letters or the ships' pay books, he always spelled his name as 'Peirce'. His uncle and, later, his two sons did likewise. The transformation to 'Pierce' in the public mind arose after his death and was due to a mistake by those who first wrote about the wreck. It was not of Richard Peirce's doing.

On that basis, we have to reject John Pearse and confine our quest for Richard's relatives only to those people who spelled their surname as 'Peirce'. A search of the National Archive database reveals that, between 1720 and 1786, the wills of at least eighty-five Peirces were proved. By searching for these names in eighteenth century newspapers, it is possible to identify a number of possible candidates to whom Richard Peirce may have been connected.

One such person is Robert Peirce of Brentwood in Essex. He was a merchant with strong trading links to Oporto in Portugal. His first wife was a sister of Josiah Wordsworth who was himself a Director of the East India Company. Robert died in 1748 without, apparently, having had any children of his own.[12] Although he cannot, therefore, be Richard's father, he might be another uncle.

Of the other Peirces who have been identified, some may have had the money but few are likely to have had the necessary influence or 'interest'. Money alone would not secure Richard's entry into the Company's maritime service; 'interest' was the essential factor. Many families sought to obtain a position for their young sons on East Indiamen, so competition for places was usually intense. The posts of midshipmen, junior officers, supernumary officers and 'guinea pigs' were all in the hands of the ships' captains and the managing owners. To gain their patronage, it was essential to have some influence or 'interest' to bring to bear. To be linked by marriage or through an extended family could give an advantage to an applicant. Similarly, the sons of close friends, colleagues or neighbours might be preferred ahead of others. The return of a favour already received could influence a captain's decision, as could hope for a favour yet to be given. It was a time of much mutual back-scratching.

If Richard Peirce's family had sufficient influence to secure patronage, his patron may have been John Durand. He belonged to the class of 'ship's husbands', the powerful middlemen who provided the ships, chartered by the Company. Within this group, John Durand stood out. Between 1761 and 1787, he was to be the managing owner of no fewer than twenty-two ships.[13] Of the dozens of ship's husbands, during this period, only Sir Charles Raymond controlled more. Three of the first four East India Company ships that Richard Peirce is known to have served on were managed by John Durand. This can hardly be a coincidence. It is possible that the Peirce family was already known to Durand and that his influence helped to secure Richard's start on the career ladder. At the very least, he did not object.

With the owners' active or tacit approval, the man who actually appointed Richard Peirce as his fifth mate was Captain Charles Newton. Here too, the forces of 'interest' may have come into play. Within the Company's maritime service, its commanders would sometimes appoint the sons of fellow officers. We cannot rule out the possibility that Richard Peirce's father was well known to Charles Newton and that the latter was happy to assist a colleague by taking on his son.

The conjecture so far has been based on the assumption that Richard Peirce came from a well-connected and affluent family, but that may not have been the case; his origins may have been more humble. If so, this could explain why his family roots remain so difficult to unearth. Although Richard's uncle referred to himself as a gentleman, this was a fairly loose title and many assumed it. On his death, the uncle had little money to bequeath in his will. Richard's sister, Ann, also lived modestly; her husband seeming to be of the yeoman class when they first married. Even Richard Peirce's friend, the eminent banker and alderman, Benjamin Hammet, was said to be the son of a Taunton barber.

If this is the social milieu to which the Peirces belonged, Richard may have served his apprenticeship not on large Indiamen but on vessels a fraction of their size. He could, indeed, have spent several years in the coastal trade. Mostly, these ships plied the south coast between London and the South West, occasionally going to the continent or crossing to Ireland. Throughout the middle of the eighteenth century, a number of coastal vessels were commanded by men called Peirce. In the 1730s, the *Mary* seems to have been based at Exeter. In the mid 1740s, the *Success* and the *Northbrook* visited Weymouth on a regular basis.[14] Weymouth was probably their home port and they may have had family there. If Richard Peirce was the son of one of these men, his earliest experience of the sea would have been along the same Dorset coastline where he would meet his end.

From coastal ships, Richard Peirce could have graduated to those travelling greater distances. Such were the ships of the Baltic trade, transporting timber and other goods from as far away as Russia. Alternatively, across the Atlantic, there was the Newfoundland trade. Ships, operating out of ports like Poole and Dartmouth, brought back enormous catches of salted fish from the fisheries off Nova Scotia. Its seamen were used to long voyages and the challenges of the North Atlantic. In vessels no bigger than 250 tons, they regularly encountered Atlantic storms, thick fogs and even icebergs. On such ships, Peirce could have acquired the practical skills of navigation and seamanship that were now in such demand.

Normally, men from this background had little prospect of employment within the East India Company's maritime service. But by 1759, these were not normal times. The Seven Years War was now at its height and the Royal Navy was desperately short of men and officers. The demands of the war effort so depleted the pool of available seaman that the East India Company was affected too. It had to cast its net wider to find suitable officers. In peace time there would have been a surplus of candidates, now there was a dearth. For a few years, a door opened for capable and experienced seamen to enter a career, normally barred to the lower orders of society. To fill gaps in the ranks of his junior officers, it made sense for an East India Company commander to take on experienced officers, and even captains, from merchant ships. What they lacked in breeding and social class was more than compensated for by the expertise they could offer. The fact that, in 1759, Captain Newton did not appoint a sixth officer on the *Houghton* may indicate that he too had difficulty finding junior officers.[15] Perhaps, this was how Richard Peirce got his break. In any case, it was the start of a career that would propel him to the very top.

4

A Junior Officer

In January 1759, Captain Charles Newton of the *Houghton*, East Indiaman, presented his four senior officers to the Court of Directors at East India House.[16] As Company servants, they were required to take an oath of fidelity. The appointment of fifth and sixth officers was entirely at a captain's discretion and did not need Company approval, so Richard Peirce was not required to attend. His ship, the *Houghton*, had been launched eight years previously and had already undergone two voyages to the East. Although this would be Charles Newton's first time in command, he had been to India three times before. He, therefore, had plenty of experience to draw on. So did his chief mate, Richard Blount, who had served as an officer on four other East Indiamen.[17] The young Peirce now found himself among men who had been toughened by the challenges of long voyages and were knowledgeable about the ways of the East. He would have many months to learn from them before they would arrive in India.

All voyages ran the risk of disaster. Poor navigation, bad weather and even fire could result in ships being lost. However, the maritime world that Richard Peirce was about to enter, now faced another danger. Britain was at war. For much of the eighteenth century, British rivalry with France spilled into open conflict. The latest bout of hostilities was already three years old. Now known as the Seven Years War, this struggle was being fought out on a world stage and India was caught up in it.

From their naval base on the Isle de France (Mauritius) and their trading centre in Pondicherry, the French sought to threaten British trade and influence in the East. Although victory at the Battle of Plassey, in 1757, had largely secured British supremacy in Bengal, further down the coast, at Madras, the situation seemed more precarious. Earlier in the century, the French had overrun the town and the East India

Company feared it might happen again. They requested help from the British Government. It agreed to send fresh troops and military supplies to consolidate British interests in the region. Three East India Company ships were commissioned to carry these reinforcements.

The ships in question were the *Houghton*, the *Stormont* and the *Ajax*. They would sail in convoy, escorted by the Royal Navy. On board would be approximately six hundred men of the newly formed 84th Regiment of Foot. It had been raised by that celebrated war hero, Eyre Coote. Recently promoted to Lieutenant Colonel, Eyre Coote had earned his fame at the Battle of Plassey. He would now command the 84th Regiment which was being sent in instalments to India. This convoy would carry the final contingent of men and Eyre Coote himself would sail on the *Houghton*.

Throughout February 1759, the three East Indiamen lay at Deptford, preparing for the voyage. A few of the *Houghton's* junior officers and a skeleton crew supervised the loading and stowing of cargo. The heavy work was done by the 'lumpers', stevedores who would not sail with the ship. At some time during this month, Richard Peirce had his first experience of exercising authority as an officer of the East India Company. The lumpers were not averse to pilfering and needed to be watched carefully. The ship's journal shows that *Houghton* carried large amounts of metal.[18] On one day the lumpers loaded nearly 1,500 sheets of copper. Another day, more than 1,000 iron bars were winched aboard and stowed below. While cargo was being loaded, some sailors were at work on the masts. Topmasts and yards had to be 'got up' from the deck and then the sails attached. The sailors were experienced at this but the direction of an officer was required to ensure it was carried out efficiently. Although the process was surely familiar to him, Richard Peirce may never have supervised it on so large a ship before. At any one time, there could be as many as a thousand ships on the Thames but most were small. Coastal ships tended to be around one hundred tons and a ship of three or four hundred tons was considered to be large. Through Peirce's eyes, the *Houghton*, at 500 tons, must have looked enormous.

During February, Richard Peirce brought his sea chest on board and moved permanently into his cabin. He may also have brought a washstand and other basic items of furniture, since none was provided. His cabin, like those of his fellow officers, was in steerage, just forward of the area known as the 'great cabin'. It was a small, badly lit space, separated from neighbouring cabins only by canvas sheets, lashed to the deck above and below. Here he would sleep in a sea-cot, suspended by ropes from the deck overhead. Such light as there was came from a small ventilation hole, called a scuttle. The gloom and the nauseating smells of the ship made the cabin suitable for little besides sleeping. Whatever free time Richard Peirce would have, was unlikely to be spent here.

On 3 March, the *Houghton* was ready to move downstream to Gravesend. There she would anchor for three weeks while the ship's provisions, water and more military equipment were taken on board. This included artillery, a howitzer, thousands of shells and cases of hand grenades. Then, when the ship was nearly ready to sail, the private trade was carefully stowed.

As a junior officer, Richard Peirce was entitled to a small amount of space in the hold for his own personal trading goods. We do not know what use he made of it. Lacking funds of his own, Peirce may have looked to a relative or benefactor to lend him money to invest in suitable merchandise. Without such financial backing, a junior officer often had no alternative but to sell his portion of the hold to the captain or one of the senior officers. That way he could offset some of the expenses he would incur during the voyage. It was rare for an officer below the rank of third mate to make a profit. It is likely, therefore, that Richard Peirce sold his space to Captain Newton. Perhaps, he was able to retain some of the payment to spend in India. He knew that private trade was the only route by which he could make his fortune and he must have made every effort not to waste this opportunity.

On Monday 26 March, under the control of a river pilot, the *Houghton* moved down the Thames to Hope Reach. In sight of Tilbury Church, she anchored close to the *Ajax*. The men of the 84th Regiment were already aboard and billeted on the lower deck. Now, at the Hope, their commanding officer, Lieutenant Colonel Coote joined them.[19] However, he would not share a living space with his men. Senior

Sir Eyre Coote. Attributed to Henry Morland.
© National Portrait Gallery, London

Company officials and important passengers like Coote, were allocated
more salubrious accommodation, at the stern of the ship. The most
desirable place was in the roundhouse where Captain Newton was
stationed. It was on the quarterdeck, the uppermost part of the ship,
and was, therefore, well lit and airy. A row of large windows stretched
across the back of the roundhouse and two doors gave access onto the
stern gallery, a balcony that stretched the full width of the stern. It
provided a secluded, sheltered place from which to enjoy the view.

Immediately forward of the roundhouse and opening onto
the quarterdeck was the cuddy. It was about ten feet deep and large
enough to serve as a dining room. It was where Captain Newton and
his senior officers would eat their meals and those passengers who
had paid to eat at the captain's table would join them there. Not
surprisingly, the cuddy and roundhouse would become the focal point

for this select social group. After-dinner conversation, card games and other distractions would help to pass the interminable hours at sea.

Only a small number of privileged passengers could afford cabin space in the roundhouse, so other passengers had to be accommodated elsewhere. Company officials, such as writers and supercargoes, were given the next best option, the great cabin. This was located on the maindeck, directly below the roundhouse. Being nearer the waterline, its windows were fitted with heavy shutters, which had to be closed when the sea was rough. During stormy weather, it could be dark in the great cabin for days on end.

Junior officers were not entitled to dine at Captain Newton's table. Instead, Richard Peirce took his meals, in steerage, at the third mate's mess. Here, Third Officer, William Smith, presided over his subordinate officers and any passengers who, for reasons of social position or lack of funds, did not qualify to eat in the cuddy. The food in the third mate's mess was never as sumptuous as that of the captain's but, in the early stages of a voyage, the company could be convivial and the conversation diverting. Whether it would remain so, after several months at sea, was less certain. Confinement, monotony and boredom often bred ill feeling among passengers, and petty disagreements were a common occurrence. William Smith would need to draw on his diplomatic skills to maintain a harmonious table.

With all preparations completed, the *Houghton* weighed anchor at 8 o'clock on the 26th. By early afternoon, next day, she had reached the Downs. Other ships were waiting there, including *Ajax*, but it was not until Friday 30 March that the order came to proceed towards Spithead. The convoys would form up in the English Channel off Portsmouth. Admiral Cornish with three large warships and one smaller vessel would escort the three Indiamen, *Houghton*, *Ajax* and *Stormont*. Additional ships would sail under the protection of Admiral Boscawen. Viewed from the shoreline, the combined fleet must have been an impressive sight. On the deck of the *Houghton*, Fifth Officer Peirce was surely impressed too, even if he had little time to reflect on it.

On Sunday 15 April, both Admiral Boscawen and Admiral Cornish gave the signal to make sail and the fleet quickly got under way. For Richard Peirce, the routine of life on an East Indiaman now began in earnest.

Every day was divided into periods known as 'watches', with each watch lasting four hours. The sequence began at 8 o'clock in the evening and ran through until 4 o'clock the following afternoon. Then, the period between 4 pm and 8 pm was split into two shorter watches known as the 'dog-watches'. At 8 pm the cycle began again. The insertion of two-hour dog-watches allowed sailors to alternate the pattern of their working day. Those whose watch began at 8 pm would be on duty for a total of fourteen hours out of the next twenty-four, while those who began their watch at midnight would be responsible for only ten hours. By alternating on a daily basis, the workload could be shared fairly.[20]

Officers and men all worked to this cycle, punctuated by the ringing of the ship's bell every half hour. To ensure the smooth running of this system, the crew was divided into two groups – the starboard watch, under the command of the chief mate, and the larboard watch, led by the second mate. The remaining officers were allocated to one or other watch so that at least two officers were on duty at any time. For obvious reasons, a senior, experienced officer would be paired with a junior officer.

As the most junior officer on the *Houghton*, Richard Peirce probably found himself on duty with the chief mate, Richard Blount. The latter was stationed on the quarterdeck, near the ship's wheel, but, as a junior officer, Richard Peirce was responsible for the men forward of the mainmast. Often, the more experienced seamen were stationed in that part of the ship.[21] Amongst the topmen, working out on the yards, were older 'sea-daddies' who would show new guinea pigs the ropes. They would teach them how to 'hand' or shorten sails and how to tie the canvas safely to the yard with gaskets. Men like these had sailed on an Indiaman before; they knew what to do and needed little direction. Although, he had authority over them, Peirce was aware that he too, could learn from such veterans.

From the quarterdeck, Captain Newton or the officer in charge would monitor the progress of the ship. From time to time, when the direction or the strength of the wind altered, they would issue a command to adjust the sails. This was essential if they were to maintain good speed. These commands, delivered by a midshipman to the bosun, were relayed to the barefoot men in the shrouds by the bosun's pipe. A pre-arranged whistle would send them swarming aloft and out along the yards, protected only by their sense of balance. Fifty feet below, other men worked on deck, pulling on ropes, securing them, coiling them, splicing them, unpicking them. Choreographing all this activity was the responsibility of the officers.

Over the following weeks, Richard Peirce also had plenty of time to observe his fellow officers. The fourth mate, John Biddlecomb, he would get to know well. He was a competent officer though it was quickly apparent that he came from a modest background. He was not well connected, nor would he ever secure the patronage that would enable him to purchase a command. Although his career would last another twenty-six years, John Biddlecomb would never rise above the rank of chief mate. In contrast, the second mate, William Smith, and third mate, Benjamin Jones, came from families with influence. In a relatively short time, both would go on to command East Indiamen. Even at this early stage, the difference in their circumstances will not have escaped Richard Peirce. No doubt, he resolved to maximise the profits on his private trade and, on his return, to forge links with those who could further his career.

As he considered his future, Richard Peirce knew that his first priority was to make a success of the here-and-now. He would have to demonstrate to Captain Newton that he was capable of carrying out the duties of a junior officer and was deserving of promotion. At noon each day, Peirce would collect his quadrant from his cabin and join the other officers on the quarterdeck. There they would each measure the angle of the sun and, when they agreed it had reached its zenith, the ship's bell would be rung.[22] This ritual provided an opportunity for Richard Peirce to observe Captain Newton at close quarters. His demeanour, his way of commanding those under him, his priorities and the quirks of his character provided a role model for the young officer to reflect upon.

Although we can only guess at the character of Captain Charles Newton, nonetheless, some hints of his personality can be detected in the *Houghton's* journal. For the most part, the journals of East Indiamen focus on recording the progress of the ship. They describe the weather, estimate the distance sailed each day and give the ship's position in terms of latitude and longitude. They also provide a brief account of the activities of the crew, including punishments inflicted for indiscipline and the death or desertion of seamen. However, human nature being what it is, many captains felt moved to record other information too. The subjective nature of such entries can sometimes open a window onto the preoccupations of their authors.

A reading of the *Houghton's* journal reveals a captain who took pride in maintaining the trim of his ship. This required the weight within the ship to be distributed evenly. If there was too much weight forward of the mainmast, the bows would be depressed and the ship would tend to plough through the waves instead of gliding over them. A ship out of trim would become sluggish, less stable and more difficult to handle. Rather like tuning the engine of a car to get a better performance, Capt Newton regularly tinkered with the weight distribution within the *Houghton*. As food and water was consumed and water butts became empty, the trim of the ship inevitably shifted. On 14 May, Newton wrote in the journal: 'Am endeavouring to find the trim of the ship by bringing her more by the stern.' Then two days later he continued: 'There being more than a half point difference between the fore and after mast, got 2 foremost guns aft abreast of the mast in hopes of the ships sailing better.' It is possible that Capt Lindsay on the *Ajax* was less diligent in this regard. His ship always seemed to lag behind the rest of the fleet and they often had to wait for her to catch up. One senses Charles Newton's impatience in one of his journal entries: 'Shortened sail for the *Ajax*, far astern, which sails very indifferently.'

No doubt, Capt Newton's frustration with these delays was expressed more forcefully on his own quarterdeck and, from time to time, Richard Peirce must have heard him. It was a lesson he would take to heart. Later, as a commander himself, Peirce would ensure that he got the best performance out of his own ship. He would not be the cause of delays as Capt Lindsay had.

After two weeks at sea, the convoy arrived at Madeira where they paused to take on fresh water and fruit. The *Houghton's* journal also records that several 'pipes' of wine were loaded aboard. Each pipe was the equivalent of forty dozen bottles and these had probably been purchased by Captain Newton and his officers. Madeira wine was highly regarded and there was a market for it both in India and in England.[23] We do not know if Richard Peirce took advantage of this opportunity to enhance his private trade but, if his funds allowed, he may well have invested in a few bottles on his own account.

For those aboard the *Houghton*, the stop at Madeira offered a welcome break from the monotony of the sea. A number of seamen had to be sent ashore to supervise the loading of supplies. The distractions of the island proved tempting and, predictably, when it was time to rejoin the ship, some of these men refused to leave. Others, still on the *Houghton*, were keen to join them. In the middle of the night, three sailors stole the ship's yawl and made for the shore. The journal records, 'At daybreak we found her with almost the starboard side stove in on the beach opposite the town.' Although the damaged yawl was recovered, there was no sign of the runaways.

After a week at Madeira, Admiral Cornish was keen to press on and the signal was given to weigh anchor. Eleven of the *Houghton's* crew were missing. The journal recorded: 'At 4 pm weigh'd, the sign being made for some time. There are 11 of our men missing, some refusing to come off as they expected we should not sail till morning.' When ships were in port, crewmen would often 'run'. It was a fact of life and captains were resigned to it. The damage to the ship's yawl was irritating and would take time to repair but the loss of so many men was more worrying. Captain Newton knew that, before reaching India, sickness would probably deplete his crew further. In bad weather, a shortage of manpower could have serious consequences.

After leaving Madeira, the convoy made its way southwest, following the trade winds in a wide arc towards South America. Having crossed the equator and nearing the coast of Brazil, they would then swing southeastward, picking up the westerly trade winds and running before them towards the Cape of Good Hope. To plot their progress, at regular points throughout each day, the officer on duty estimated the current latitude and longitude and chalked the results on the logboard. Meanwhile, every hour, the midshipmen 'heaved the log' to try to measure the ship's speed. One midshipman dropped the log overboard, paying out the knotted line attached to it, so the log could float stationary in the ship's wake. At a given point, his companion turned his half-minute glass timer and watched the sand begin its descent. After thirty seconds precisely, when the sand in the timer was exhausted, time was called. The first midshipman stopped unreeling the line and retrieved the log. By counting the number of knots revealed, it was possible to identify the current speed of the ship and, from this, to calculate the distance travelled in the last hour. In terms of the written record, on an East Indiaman, noon marked the official end of one day and the start of the next. Consequently, at twelve o'clock, each day, the figures would be totalled up and entered in the ship's journal.[24]

Such measurements were essential for calculating the ship's exact position. With a quadrant, latitude could be measured with reasonable accuracy but, without a reliable chronometer on board, it was much more difficult to determine longitude. Captains had to rely on crude dead reckoning, for which the ships speed was a key element. Consequently, ships were often many miles east or west of 'account'. This could prove fatal if they were close to a lee shore, especially at night. When ships sailed 'in company' or passed each other at sea, the captains usually compared notes on their position, calling to each other through long speaking trumpets. It was reassuring to have a second opinion but still no guarantee of accuracy.

Early in the voyage, Captain Newton was concerned that his estimate of their position did not tally with that of Admiral Cornish. He wondered if the *Houghton's* cargo might be to blame: 'Admiral makes 2 degrees more westing than we do which convinces us our compasses have attracted with the Iron beneath.' Given the large margins for error, it is not surprising that captains looked for additional evidence to corroborate their whereabouts. The presence of particular seabirds or seaweed, the kind of sand on the seafloor, even the colour of crabs could provide clues as to their location. Reassured by such manifestations and pulled by the invisible thread of his calculations, Captain Newton hoped to guide the *Houghton* through weeks of empty horizons to her destination thousands of miles away.

Keeping together, the convoy made steady progress, sailing 160 miles on one day. In early June they crossed the equator and by the third week of July they could see the coast of South Africa. Captain Newton continued to ensure that *Houghton* maintained good speed. 'Well up with the Admiral', he wrote one day. 'Ahead of the fleet all night', he recorded, a few days later, with a hint of quiet satisfaction.

Once they had rounded Africa, ships heading for India were directed to take one of two routes. One option was to continue to sail east, until well out into the southern ocean, before turning north towards Ceylon and Madras. The shorter but more dangerous route was to take the so-called 'inner passage' up the Mozambique Channel between Madagascar and Africa. Admiral Cornish was allocated the latter. The convoy would have to avoid hazards in their path, like the large reef, Bassas da India. Its location had not been accurately mapped yet, so they would need to keep a sharp lookout for it. Nonetheless, the inner passage did offer stopping places where fresh supplies and water could be taken on. The rigours of four months at sea was taking its toll and some of the soldiers were already sick.

On 9 August, the *Houghton's* journal recorded that Madagascar had been sighted. The following day, the convoy dropped anchor in St Augustine's Bay, on the southwest side of the island. The bay provided a safe anchorage and was a popular watering place with East Indiamen. On arrival, Colonel Coote and his men disembarked and set up camp. After their long confinement on the *Houghton's* gloomy lower decks, the men of the 84th were hugely relieved to stand on dry land again, in bright, warm sunshine. Their arrival, however, is unlikely to have been welcomed by the local ruler. The sudden appearance of a large body of armed men in his territory made him uneasy. Eyre Coote understood this and recognised the need for a diplomatic gesture. To defuse the situation and to secure the 'king's' goodwill, Coote ordered the regimental band to play for him, while his 'queen' was presented with a pair of embroidered slippers.[25] The ruling family's honour was preserved and the tension evaporated.

Meanwhile, on the *Houghton*, work began to prepare for the next leg of the voyage. It was essential to stock up with fresh meat, fruit and vegetables. Officers went ashore to negotiate the purchase of bullocks. Then shore-parties of seamen had to be supervised while they towed the livestock behind the longboat, out to the ship. Richard Peirce played a role in this. As he did so, he cannot have been oblivious to his surroundings. The lush vegetation, the aromas and the vivid colours of Madagascar delivered a welcome shock to senses, dulled by months at sea.

After three weeks in St Augustine's Bay, Admiral Cornish gave the signal for the fleet to weigh anchor. Coote's men were re-embarked and returned to the gloom of their billets below. A number of them were already sick and showing signs of fever; the environment of Madagascar was not as benign as it may have appeared. Nor, it seemed, was the sea. For several days, there was a large following swell, causing the ships to pitch forward as each wave passed under the stern. If men were seasick, it was worse for the livestock, penned on the deck. Captain Newton wrote, 'Our bullocks has suffered much in the rolling weather we have had this two days past and one died today and were obliged to kill three more in the morning.' The supply of fresh meat would not last long.

Sailing northwards, within a week, they had reached the Comoro Islands, another popular stopping place for East Indiamen. On this occasion they paused for only a day, just long enough to take on more fresh water. By 16 September 1759, the convoy had crossed the equator, and was now averaging one hundred miles a day. On 6 October, a lookout finally spotted land ahead. It was the welcome outline of Cape Comorin, at the southern tip of India, indicating that the voyage was nearly over. They were about to re-enter the world of politics and conflict.

Next day, they passed a ship, outward bound for England. This was the first opportunity to get up-to-date news of the situation in India. Much could have happened in almost a year and it was important to have an idea of the circumstances that awaited them. The news was dramatic. In *Houghton's* journal Captain Newton captured the gist of it: 'Admiral Pocock has had an engagement with the French where the French have had the worst of it. The French have blown up Fort St David and besieged Madras but were obliged to leave it. Visagapatam was retaken by a party from Bengal.'

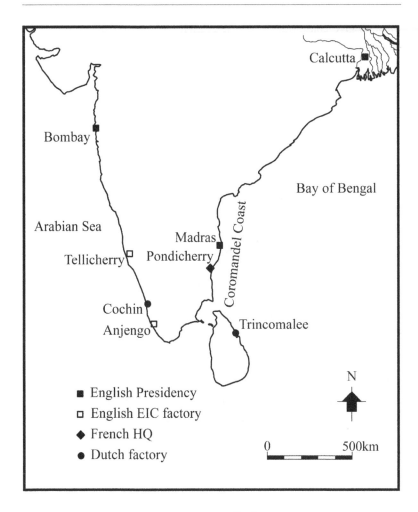

Fig 1. A Map of India

The naval engagement that Captain Newton alluded to had taken place, four weeks previously, just south of Pondicherry. A fleet of eleven French ships, under Admiral Comte d'Ache had been engaged by the seven English ships of Admiral George Pocock. Although it had been a short and fierce engagement, the result was indecisive. The French lost more men but both fleets were equally battered. After d'Ache had been wounded, the French had broken off the fight and withdrawn to Pondicherry. Pocock's ships had been too damaged and slow to give chase but, since the French had conceded control of the sea, Pocock felt entitled to claim victory.

On his flagship, Admiral Cornish must have been relieved at the news. No French fleet would be lying in wait to ambush him and he would have a safe approach to Madras. However, the last leg of the journey seems to have been slow. *Houghton* and the other ships crawled along the Carnatic coast at a snail's pace. On 20 September, they encountered Pocock's fleet. Although victorious, the Admiral was short of men. More than five hundred had been lost in the battle and Pocock was keen to make good the shortfall. The well-manned East Indiamen offered a tempting solution. For the first time, Richard Peirce would witness a practice which plagued the commanders of Indiamen and caused their crews to detest the Navy which protected them.

The Houghton's journal recorded the inevitable: 'In the evening came on board one of Admiral Pocock's lieutents and pressed 12 of our men. 15 were taken from Ajax and 15 from Stormont. At the same time the officer brought orders for me from the Admiral to proceed directly to Fort St George in company with Ajax and Stormont.' Although the French had been chased away at sea, their land forces, under the Comte de Lally, still posed a threat. It was important to get Eyre Coote's men ashore as soon as possible.

5
Dubashes & Pirates

By the end of September 1759, with all three Indiamen anchored safely in Madras roads, Colonel Eyre Coote was preparing to set foot on Indian soil again. On the quarterdeck of the *Houghton*, in full uniform, Richard Peirce and his fellow officers stood to attention. Colonel Coote's departure was a moment of significance and it would be honoured with the necessary formality. East Indiamen always marked the disembarkation of high-ranking passengers with a ceremonial firing of their great guns; the more important the person, the more guns involved. As Captain Newton and Colonel Coote were lowered into a waiting boat, the ship's company gave three cheers. Then with an impressive roar, seventeen of *Houghton's* guns thundered in salute. Nearby, *Ajax* and *Stormont* responded in kind and, for a few moments, the three ships were lost behind a curtain of thick smoke. Those watching from the shore could be in no doubt that a personage of importance was about to arrive.

For two weeks, the three East Indiamen strained at their anchors, a mile or more offshore. There was no harbour to enter, so unloading took time. The soldiers of the 84th Regiment, plus their equipment, had to be ferried to the beach in small local boats. For new arrivals to Madras, this was a memorable experience. A constant succession of large waves broke on the sandy shoreline and the ship's own boats were ill-designed to cope with them. The only alternative was to go ashore in a *masulah* boat. Writing in the 1780s, a new visitor, William Hodges, described these boats as follows:

> A work of curious construction and well designed to withstand the violent shocks of the surf, that breaks here with great violence. They are formed without a keel, flat bottomed and with the sides raised high, and sewed together with the fibres of a cocoa-nut tree,

and caulked with the same material: they are remarkably light and managed with great dexterity by the natives; they are usually attended by two Kattamarans (rafts), paddled by one man each. The intention being that, should the boat be overset by the violence of the surf, the persons in it may be preserved. The boat is driven, as the sailors say, high and dry; and the passengers are landed on a fine sandy beach: and immediately enter the Fort of Madras.[26]

Madras Landing by C. Hunt
© *National Maritime Museum, Greenwich, London*

As soon as the East Indiamen had dropped anchor, an armada of strange craft had come out to greet them. Some were the catamarans, essentially rafts made from three poles tied together, balanced with an outrigger. They sat so low in the water as to be almost invisible. When another traveller, Thomas Twining, first encountered this phenomenon, he thought he was looking at a naked man standing upright on the surface of the sea. In fact, it was a local merchant, wearing only a loincloth, who had come to sell fruit and vegetables from his catamaran.[27]

Other visitors were elegantly dressed in long, white muslin robes, red slippers and impressive turbans. These were the *dubashes*, high-caste Indians, who came aboard to discuss private trade. They offered their services as go-betweens, helping to negotiate with local merchants, to arrange credit and set up deals. The involvement of these middle-men was essential for an officer who intended to remain ashore for any length of time. They acted as interpreters and agents, able to provide '*servants, palanquins, purchase necessaries, exchange money, and transact all domestic affairs.*' Richard Peirce quickly understood that the future success of his own personal trade would rely heavily on the integrity, knowledge and business acumen of any *dubash* he employed.

Captain Newton's eagerness to get onto dry land is not surprising. His orders were to continue to Calcutta and he knew their stay at Madras would not last long. While he could, he wanted to use the opportunity to deal with his own commercial affairs. Over the next few days, the *Houghton's* journal lists the personal possessions that were sent ashore. For the captain, they included bales of canvas, barrels of tar and casks of claret. The purser and senior officers had casks of beer, as well as boxes of stationery and cutlery. As always, there was a demand for all these items from the garrison at Fort St George and the residents of Madras.

Although Richard Peirce's private possessions did not merit an entry in the ship's journal, he may have had a few small items to sell. Even if this was not the case, he was eager to set foot on Indian soil for the first time. From the ship, he could see the squat bastions of Fort St George and the outline of houses stretching along the shoreline. Travellers were often struck by the beauty of this view. William Hodges tried to capture the impact: 'The clear blue, cloudless sky, the polished white buildings, the bright sandy beach, and the dark green sea, present a combination totally new to the eye of an Englishman, just arrived from London, who, accustomed to the sight of rolling masses of clouds floating in a damp atmosphere, cannot but contemplate the difference with delight.' [28] Elated at the prospect of seeing Madras for himself, Richard Peirce descended the ladder on the *Houghton's* side and made the exhilarating journey in a *masulah* boat, through the crashing surf to dry land.

A short walk up the beach led to Fort St George, headquarters of the Madras Presidency and the home of its Governor, George Pigot. Although the East India Company's employees worked there by day, most chose to live elsewhere. Their spacious villas stretched west of the town across Choultry plain. With their long colonnades, open porticos and flat roofs, these buildings had put the impressionable William Hodges in mind of 'a Grecian town in the time of Alexander'. In sharp contrast, a mile north of Fort St George, the local Indian population was confined to an area known as the Black Town. By 1759, its narrow streets were also home to many others. Armenian merchants, Arab traders, Persians, Chinese and less well-off Europeans lived cheek by jowl in what one writer has described as 'a racial and cultural stew pot'.[29] Madras had started to expand.

Despite the growth in their numbers, the confidence of the residents had been shaken by recent events. Less than a year had passed since the last time the French had threatened the city. With fresh troops from France, led by Comte Thomas Arthur Lally, the French had overrun the British garrison at Cuddalore in June 1758. Then with the road open before him, Lally had marched north against Madras. In December his men had arrived, unopposed, in the Black Town and had looted and burned it. Meanwhile, before the first whiff of smoke, most British residents had retreated to the safety of Fort St George. Secure behind its ramparts, the garrison stood firm against Lally's siege for the next six weeks. Then, with the arrival of Admiral Pocock's fleet in February 1759, Lally recognised that his chance to take Madras had passed. Frustrated, he lifted the siege and ordered his soldiers back to Pondicherry. This was the breathless news that the crew of the *Houghton* received, as they approached the Coromandel coast.

Although the threat to Madras had receded for now, the French remained a force to be reckoned with. Lally was an able commander. Like Eyre Coote, he had been born in Ireland but their political allegiances were diametrically opposed. Lally, the son of an Irish Jacobite, had fought for France at Fontenay and had accompanied Charles Edward Stuart ('Bonny Prince Charlie') at the Battle of Falkirk. Colonel Coote, Protestant, Loyalist and now commander of British forces in Madras, was the opponent he would face.

Richard Peirce was undoubtedly aware that he had arrived in India at a time of turmoil. Nonetheless, it was not a matter of great personal concern to him. Like those of his captain, Peirce's priorities were financial. During his short time ashore, he focussed on whatever business he could conduct on his own account. He may also have made some social calls. It is likely that his family or benefactors had provided him with letters of introduction. These would give him access to people with influence and help him to begin the essential process of establishing a network of local contacts.

On 10 November 1759, seventy-five guns on Fort St George fired in salute for the King's birthday. It was also the cue for Richard Peirce and his fellow officers to return to their ship. Two days later, the three East Indiamen weighed anchor and began the next leg of their voyage, across the Bay of Bengal. They were now bound for Calcutta. In the summer, during the southwest monsoon, the distance could be covered in a matter of days but, at this time of year, the prevailing wind was from the northeast and progress was slow. It was Christmas Eve before the *Houghton* finally came to, in Ballasore Road.

The approach to the Hooghly river, in the Ganges delta, was fraught with danger. There were treacherous sand bars to avoid and a local pilot was required to guide the large East Indiamen up the safe western channel. Slowly, they worked their way from the deep-water anchorage at Kedgeree up to Culpee. Although Calcutta was still 50 miles upriver, Culpee was as far as the ships would go. Passengers and cargo would have to be unloaded here and then transported to Calcutta in smaller boats.

If the sight of Madras prompted thoughts of classical Greece, first impressions of Bengal were somewhat different. The waters of the Hooghly were murky and sluggish. On both sides of the estuary, the land was flat and covered in low, thick forest. Another traveller, Thomas Williamson, was unimpressed: 'Very little gratification is offered to the eye by the surrounding scenery', he wrote.[30] There was little incentive to go ashore either. Dangerous tigers roamed the wilderness and mosquitoes were everywhere. Only the occasional break in the jungle revealed the huts of some isolated village: 'No public edifice; no gay villas; no busy hum of men; no crowded wharfs! In fact, I scarcely know a spot more dreary than the debouche of the Hooghly', complained Williamson.

As soon as the *Houghton* was safely anchored at Culpee, Captain Newton left his ship. Private trade again became his overriding concern and he promptly set off for Calcutta. A variety of local craft were available for transport. Those in a hurry might opt for a fast chokey-boat but most passengers preferred the greater comfort of a *budgerow*. These were large boats, with room for luggage, a dining area and an open verandah at the front. There was a place for passengers to hang their sea cots or else to sleep under a canvas awning on the deck. Propelled by, perhaps, a dozen rowers, the heavy budgerows had to wait for the incoming tide to carry them upstream. If travellers left their ships at Kedgeree, the journey to Calcutta in a budgerow could take three days.[31]

Although passengers, including a contingent of soldiers from Madras, soon followed Captain Newton's example, Richard Peirce and the crew would have to stay with the *Houghton* for the time being. The ship needed running repairs. To keep any leaks to a minimum, the caulking between the timbers of her hull should be renewed before another voyage. To this end, five 'black' caulkers came aboard. So too did twenty lascars. So many of the *Houghton's* crew had now succumbed to illness or been pressed by the Navy, that these extra hands were essential to man the ship homewards.

The health of the *Houghton's* crew was not only affected by the climate; their diet probably played its part too. Certainly, there was a problem with some of the ship's meat. Having returned from Calcutta, on 5 January 1760, Captain Newton called his officers together while he inspected the pork. He needed their endorsement for what he was about to do. All agreed that the pork was 'bad, rotten and stinking' and so seven casks of it were thrown overboard. A week later, the officers were summoned again. This time it was decided that a further 25 hogsheads of pork were 'not fit to eat' and so they too went over the side. Despite these measures, the health of the crew continued to decline. But work had to carry on.

Seven French prisoners-of-war, sent from Calcutta, came aboard. Then began the arduous business of loading fresh cargo, five hundred bags of saltpetre. It is no surprise that saltpetre features on the manifest of so many East indiamen during the eighteenth century. It was an essential ingredient in the manufacture of gunpowder and saltpetre from Bengal was of the highest quality; during wartime, the demand was insatiable. By 22 January, the caulkers had finished their work and were discharged. The same day, Captain Newton sent the ship's longboat to Calcutta for the last time with private trade. Was this Richard Peirce's opportunity to see Calcutta, at last? If so, it was a very short visit but long enough for him to form an impression of the place.

After the monotony of the journey upstream, they would, at last, have sighted Garden Reach. This broad expanse of water was where the wealthy of Calcutta were starting to build their elegant mansions. A little further on, on the right bank, was Fort William. Still under construction, this fortress was where the Governor and Council of the Bengal Presidency carried on their business. Here, too, was where the Company's goods for the European market were collected: 'The high quality products of Kazimbazar and Dhaka in the silk belt [...] the famous cotton cloth of Patna and the saltpetre of Bihar.'[32]

Like Madras, Calcutta had recently endured a period of turmoil. It was only three and a half years since Siraj-ud-Daulah, Nawab of Bengal, had captured Fort William and allegedly incarcerated 146 prisoners in the notorious 'black hole of Calcutta'. Despite the memory of this trauma, life and trade continued much as before. If Richard Peirce had any goods to sell, he probably found a ready market for them among the growing European population there. He would also find native merchants willing to offer him credit so that he could purchase merchandise to take back to England. Compared to the scale of Captain Newton's transactions, it may have seemed trivial but it was a start.

On 24 January, while the longboat was still away, Captain Newton gave the order for *Houghton* to move downstream again. This time, the destination was Ingeli, just below Kedgeree, near Saugor Island. The East India Company had a 'factory' at 'Ingellee' and the anchorage, there, was in deeper water. This is where heavy freight could be loaded and unloaded. The ammunition – shot and shells – from England was lowered aboard a Company sloop for transfer to Fort William. In its place, more saltpetre, redwood and, at least three thousand bags of rice were winched onto the *Houghton*. Several 'invalides' were among the passengers who would return to England. These were probably Company servants whose health had suffered so badly in Bengal that only a return to European climes could help them recover. Another person, of greater significance, was on his way home, too. He was Robert Clive. The *Houghton's* journal recorded on 10 February: 'Passed by Col. Clive and family who are going to England. Saluted him with seventeen guns.'

After nearly six weeks at Ingeli, the *Houghton* was ready to depart. But her work in India was not yet done. Before she could begin the 11,000 mile journey back to England, *Houghton* would have to visit the western coast of India. The East India Company had several factories there and, significantly, its Presidency at Bombay. On 3 March, again under the control of a pilot, the ship began to inch its way carefully out of the estuary. The log registered their progress as they passed the marker buoys: 'At noon passd the Buoy of the Broken; at 2 pm Buoy of Barrabulla; half past 12 Buoy of the Fairway.' Then, having dropped the pilot, the *Houghton* moved out into the open waters of the Bay of Bengal. By 5 March, they had passed Point Palmyras and, on Sunday the 9th, Captain Newton summoned the crews for prayers.

It was a requirement, on East Indiamen, for someone, usually the purser, to conduct prayers for the crew every Sunday.[33] On most ships, this was more honoured in the breach than otherwise. According to her journal, the *Houghton* seems to have been an exception. Whether through a sense of duty or his own religious convictions, Captain Newton was diligent in ensuring that Sunday prayers took place on his ship. If Captain Newton was a sincere Christian, it may account for his treatment of his crew. Throughout the entire voyage, there is no record of him punishing a single crew member. It seems he could command his men without resorting to the violence that characterised so many other captains. His was an example that Peirce would later try to emulate.

By the end of March, the *Houghton* had rounded the southern tip of India and was about to turn northwest up the Malabar Coast. A few days later, a lookout spotted the British flag flying on the Company's fort at Anjengo. Standing on a sandspit, fringed by palm trees, this was its most southerly settlement. With no French bases nearby to threaten it, Anjengo was far removed from the political struggles that unsettled the Carnatic and Bengal. For four days, *Houghton* anchored in Anjengo Roads while Company letters were exchanged and supplies delivered. Spices from the area were also taken on board. At some point in the proceedings, Richard Peirce must have gone ashore. Was he impressed by this tranquil paradise, so different from the oppressive climate of the Ganges delta or the jittery atmosphere of Madras? If he was tempted to linger, his stay was soon cut short. On 6 April, *Houghton* weighed anchor and pointed her bow northwards.

At Calicut they stopped only to collect 600 planks of teak. Then in company with a local 'moor' ship the *Fulta Romaina*, they sailed on to Tellicherry. This was where the East India Company had another fortified factory. Like at Anjengo, it was a secure depot in which to store merchandise, gathered from regional markets, ready for transportation onwards. This part of India was renowned for its production of pepper and cardamom but other goods, like betelnut and sandalwood, could be obtained too.

For a week, as the *Houghton's* crew loaded bag after bag of pepper into her hold, their officers used the opportunity for yet more private trading. Goods purchased in Calcutta could be sold here and the money invested in new merchandise. Even if Richard Peirce did not participate in these transactions, he was able to observe his fellow officers and learn how it was done. It was an important part of his education.

After Tellicherry, there was only one more port in India to call at – Bombay. In the early days, Bombay had been the principal base of the East India Company but, in recent decades, its significance had been increasingly overshadowed by Calcutta. Nevertheless, it was one of the three Presidencies with its own Governor and Council. Its trading significance remained considerable and its growing population of Europeans presented a another market for goods from home.

The *Houghton* was now in waters frequented by pirates as well as Arab traders so it was necessary to be prepared for trouble. Ten days out from Tellicherry, Captain Newton feared that it was about to occur. On 29 April 1760, two 'strange sail' were seen, heading towards them. One was identified as a grab and the other as a gallivat; both were behaving suspiciously.[34] As *Houghton* prepared for action, the ships closed to within musket range. It was still not clear if their intentions were hostile, so Captain Newton fired a warning shot. It provoked no response and, for half an hour, the strangers continued to stalk the *Houghton*. Exasperated, Captain Newton ordered a second shot to be fired, this time directly at the grab. It had the desired effect. Both ships quickly hoisted more sail and veered away at full speed.

Nonplussed by the incident, Captain Newton recorded in the journal: 'I do not know what to make of it, their behaviour was very extraordinary. I judge she belonged to the Morrattoes (Marathas). Several white men on board.' Like Captain Newton, we cannot be sure of their intentions. It is possible these ships were from Gheria, the port controlled by the Angria family who were vassals of the Marathas. Raiders from Gheria had a fearsome reputation. They were known to have seized Company shipping before and were said to be afraid of nothing. Those who resisted them would be killed and those who surrendered would be enslaved. This may explain the presence of the white men that Captain Newton saw. Only the wealthy and powerful stood any chance of being ransomed but, unlike with Somali pirates of today, the channels for negotiation were limited. Believing that force was the only language they would understand, a combined Dutch-English fleet, under Admiral Watson, attacked their fortified stronghold in 1756, in an attempt to suppress them.[35] The problem had not gone away, however, and pirates from the region still posed a threat. In this case, they may have been assessing the *Houghton* to see if she was vulnerable to attack. Captain Newton's response must have deterred them and, perhaps, Richard Peirce had come as close to a fight as at any time in his later career.

On 10 May, *Houghton* came to at Bombay. At Madras and Anjengo, she had anchored some way offshore, in the 'road', but at Bombay there was a harbour and even a dry dock where ships could be repaired. For the next six months, this is where the *Houghton* would stay. No sooner had they arrived than three of the French prisoners were sent ashore. Since they had joined the ship in Calcutta they had developed advanced venereal disease. Now, Captain Newton decided they needed treatment. He requested that Governor Permifair send them to hospital to be 'sallivated'.[36]

Despite the length of *Houghton's* stay at Bombay, her ship's journal records very little of what happened there. The anchors and casks of nails, belonging to Captain Newton, were sent ashore to be sold. With some of the proceeds, he invested in forty-five chests of 'cassia', each chest marked with the letters CN. At various times, Richard Peirce went ashore with his fellow officers but their private trade is not recorded. Only the health of the crew features regularly in the journal. Periodically, sick men were sent to the hospital in Bombay. Although several died, others recovered and were able to rejoin the ship. The men's health was not improved by the quality of their food. In June, it was discovered that the replacement salt pork they had loaded in Calcutta was already inedible. Once more, Richard Peirce and his fellow officers were summoned by Captain Newton to inspect the casks. There was no disagreement about the verdict. The pork was so rotten that all but two casks were thrown over the side.

On 22 November 1760, the order finally came to depart. The *Houghton* would sail home in the company of *Stormont* and another East Indiaman, the *Harcourt*. At first, Captain Newton was pleased with his ship. The caulkers had clearly done their work well and the journal records, 'the ship very tight and makes little water.' Soon, however, it became clear that the climate in India had taken its toll. Worms had eaten through the wooden stock of the sheet anchor so that it was unserviceable. Then it was discovered that the wooden shutters on the half-ports were rotten and the carpenter was set to make replacements. This simple task nearly led to disaster. It would seem that the carpenter decided to store the half ports he had made, in the gunroom. To help him see better, the gunner's mate left a candle burning there. The *Houghton's* journal describes what happened next:

A little after 8 am was greatly alarmed by the cry of fire in the ship. Found it to be just within the gunroom door, occasioned by a candle being left there by the gunners mate, among some coats, for half ports just made. Put it out immediately without any more damage: 3 of the coats a little & the end of a chest.

It was a lucky escape. Fire in a wooden ship at sea was greatly feared. It could quickly get out of control and once it had reached the gunpowder store would result in the instant loss of the ship. No doubt, Captain Newton had strong words to say on the matter and the lesson will not have escaped Richard Peirce either.

Even with the help of fresh seamen and some more lascars, the *Houghton's* crew remained very depleted. Several had died in Bombay and others had run. In fact, the *Houghton* was so undermanned that Captain Webber of the *Harcourt* sent over two Company soldiers to help out.

Despite the shortage of crew, Captain Newton continued to take pride in the performance of his ship. Just as on the outward voyage, he was soon complaining that the other ships were lagging behind. By January, they had rounded the Cape and were now in the South Atlantic. Unfortunately, the health of his crew continued to deteriorate. In addition to tropical fevers, the crew were now beginning to succumb to scurvy. On 14 January 1761, Newton wrote, 'Eighteen of our people ill. More complaining daily.' Ten days later, he added, 'Our people very sickly.' Over the next few days, sailors began to die.

The death of a seaman at sea triggered a well-established ritual. Following prayers for his soul, the dead man's body would be weighted and lowered over the side. Then his clothes and any other possessions would be sold 'at the mast' to the highest bidder. The money thus raised was noted in the paybook and would be given to his heirs, on return to England. Many sailors made wills and these make interesting reading. If he was unmarried, a sailor might leave his money to another crewmember and friend. Others would nominate a sweetheart, often citing a tavern as their address. Not surprisingly, the value of the possessions of ordinary seaman was usually pitifully small.[37]

By 1 February, even Mr James Carrick, the surgeon, had succumbed to illness and was unable to treat his patients. 'Our surgeon disabled in both his hands by a fever.' Fortunately, they were now getting close to their next port of call. On 5 February, the three

Shipping off Saint Helena by A. Callander
© *National Maritime Museum, Greenwich, London*

East Indiamen arrived at St Helena. Thanks to its position in the southern Atlantic, St Helena was a highly strategic possession of the British crown. While war continued, there was always a danger that the French might try to snatch it for themselves. Consequently, before a ship could be allowed to approach the island, it had to identify itself beyond any doubt. A top-secret system of signals had been devised by the Admiralty and the East India Company. When the *Delaware*, had arrived a year earlier, she had used a predetermined sequence of flags and musket shots to make herself known to the garrison. Only then could she approach the island in safety.

Captain Newton's journal does not record what signal he used but the three Indiamen clearly received permission to enter the anchorage at James Town. Situated in a lush green valley, with an abundance of fruit trees, James Town was dwarfed by the high mountains all around. From the deck of the ship, it presented an impressive vista.

With so many of his crew unable to work, Captain Newton decided to extend his stay at St Helena. The other two East Indiamen could carry on towards England without him. The *Houghton* would wait until more ships arrived and then would travel back in company with them. Although this delay was frustrating, it was the only solution to the problem of scurvy. It would take time for the men to recover. By 1761, the causes of scurvy had been identified. The rations of Royal Navy crews included lemon juice and limes, yet bizarrely, the commanders of East Indiamen neglected to follow this example. Hidebound by tradition and prejudice, they allowed scurvy to plague their crews for many more years to come.

Over the next sixteen weeks, *Houghton* continued to ride at anchor, with only a skeleton crew on board. While most of the men recuperated ashore, Richard Peirce and his fellow officers had plenty of time to enjoy the island. Together with Captain Newton, they were invited to official social events at the Governor's residence. Governor Hutchinson was used to entertaining. Robert Clive had stopped off on his way home, the previous year, and another member of the Bengal Council was currently staying with him. Charles Manningham had become more than merely a guest; he had recently married the Governor's own daughter.[38] The newly-weds were now anxious to return to England and Captain Newton was happy to accommodate them. Mr and Mrs Manningham would expect to travel in comfort and would be willing to pay handsomely for a share of the roundhouse. Their presence would provide a welcome and unexpected boost to the Captain's income.

On 27 May 1761, in company with the *Royal Duke, Houghton* took her leave from St Helena. After the courtesy of a seven-gun salute, answered by the Fort, the ships made their way out of the bay. The routine of life at sea began once more. Fortunately the weather was good and a steady wind ensured the two ships covered many miles each day. On 8 June they crossed the equator. After more than two years away from home, the wear and tear on Houghton's sails was increasingly apparent. On 14 June, Captain Newton noted: 'Topsail almost to pieces. Thin rags so very bad condemned him'. A few days later, the jib sail split and had to be mended.

None of these problems caused Captain Newton to slacken speed as they raced northwards. Predictably, he soon began to complain again about having to shorten sail so that *Royal Duke* could keep up. Then, as they approached 30 degrees North latitude, the winds died. Day after day it was calm and the ships could make little progress. On 12 July they managed only eight miles. To provide a bit of diversion for his crew, Captain Newton decided to exercise the great guns. *Houghton* carried twenty-six guns and it was important that the crew was practised at loading and firing them. At any stage, they might encounter privateers and they would soon be entering European waters where French naval ships might lie in wait. The worrying encounter in the Arabian Sea had demonstrated the wisdom of being prepared. Although East Indiamen were no match for a determined man-of-war, they could put up a good fight and might deter a lesser opponent.

On 23 July, it suddenly seemed that the guns might have to be fired again, this time in anger. A strange sail was sighted and Captain Newton was instantly on his guard. 'At 4 am saw a sail bearing ESE. Cleard ship immediately and had all hands to their quarters when everything was ready for engaging if she should prove an enemy.' Over the next couple of hours the unidentified ship appeared to be giving chase. Houghton's gun crews waited apprehensively and , once again, Richard Peirce must have wondered if he was going to experience his first sea fight. Then the lookout saw that she was flying British colours. *Houghton's* journal continues the account of what happened:

> She coming up very fast, took in the smallsails and hauled up the mainsail. At 6 she was very near and edging after us, fired a shot to bring us too which we did immediately with our head to the NW. She sent her boat on board, proves to be HM ship the Fame of 74 guns, Hon Capt Byron, commander, bound on a cruize but has taken us under convoy.

Suddenly the enemy had become their protector. There would be no sea battle and they were no longer on their own.

Under escort, the *Houghton* entered the final days of her voyage but her seamen, who had been looking forward to returning home, were now on tenterhooks. Everyone knew that the protection of the Royal Navy came at a price. When they were only a couple of days from Plymouth, their fears were confirmed. A Lieutenant from the *Fame* came on board and began the process of 'pressing' men from

Houghton's crew. More than twenty of them were rounded up and transferred to the warship. This left Captain Newton so short of seamen that there was a doubt about his ability to get his ship safely into harbour. He must have expressed himself in no uncertain terms because the next day Capt Byron relented and allowed twenty-one of them to return, temporarily, 'to assist us up'.

On 2 August, the *Houghton* anchored at last in Plymouth sound. The Purser, Mr Hales, immediately went ashore with two 'packets'. These were secret letters and documents for the Company, sent from India and packaged securely under lock and key. They were to be delivered to the Court of Directors at East India House and it was imperative for them to arrive as quickly as possible. Mr Hales would get to London more quickly by road than by staying with the ship.

Richard Peirce would have to wait a bit longer for his homecoming. On 11 August, *Houghton* weighed anchor and set off up the English Channel. Passing Portland the next day, they arrived in the Downs on the 18th. By Saturday the 22nd they were in Lower Gravesend Reach and by the Monday they had finally reached Deptford. After twenty-nine months, the voyage was finally over.

Arrival at Deptford did not mean that Richard Peirce was free to leave his ship. There was the valuable cargo to be taken care of. Company officials came on board to check the holds before unloading could begin. Then, for three weeks, bags of pepper, cardamom and saltpetre; bales of carmenia wool and Surat 'piece goods'; logs of redwood, all were transferred onto the Company's hoys and lighters, to be taken to the Company's warehouses. Only when this was completed, was fifth mate, Richard Peirce, discharged. On 1 October, he was paid his wages.[39] The Houghton's Receipt Book records the event: 'Received this 1st day of October 1761 by me Richard Pearse (corrected to Peirce) the sum of <u>fifty-two</u> pounds <u>one</u> shilling and <u>one</u> pence being in full for wages, debts and all demand for Services performed on board the ship <u>Houghton</u> Captain <u>Chas Newton</u> commander as <u>fifth mate</u>.' In his own hand, Richard Peirce then added his signature: 'R. Peirce'.

Fifty-two pounds was not a fortune, roughly £9,900 in today's terms, but we have to assume that Richard Peirce had been able to supplement this with some limited private trading.[40] Despite this, taking into account all his expenses, he may still have made an overall loss. However, he will have recognised that, at this stage of his career, the most valuable outcome from the voyage was the experience he had gained. He had visited all the main Company outposts in India, and now had an understanding of how life and business operated there. He had also begun to establish contacts that could be useful in the future.

During the voyage, he had become immersed in the life of an East Indiaman. He had learned to supervise men and work effectively with his fellow officers. He had not disgraced himself but had carried out his duties competently. With help from a patron, he could now seek promotion.

Most important of all, perhaps, Richard Peirce had been able to observe how Captain Newton conducted himself. He had seen a commander who took his responsibilities seriously. Although he may have neglected measures that might have improved their health, Captain Newton was concerned for the spiritual welfare of his crew. He seems to have led them well. After the desertions on Madeira, there had been almost no indiscipline on board. Men respected Captain Newton's authority and no punishments had been necessary. Nevertheless, Charles Newton was no easy-going captain. He was impatient and pushed his ship to perform at its best. He was also acutely aware of his own personal agenda. As soon as he had brought the *Houghton* safely to each destination, Captain Newton had quickly left the ship. In port, private trade was always his priority.

Captain Newton had been a useful role model and Richard Peirce had learned from his example. In the future, he will be seen emulating this practice. But, for now, it was time to take his sea-chest and go ashore.

6

Supercargoes and Sing-songs

The Richard Peirce who strode across London Bridge, in September 1761, was a very different young man from the one who had joined the *Houghton,* two years previously. Now, he was a confident junior officer with business to attend to. The merchandise he had bought in India was already safe in the Company's warehouse at Billiter Lane and would soon go on sale at East India House. After the Company had deducted its commission, the remaining profit would be his.[1]

In the meantime, Richard Peirce looked for new employment. The next season would begin in the new year and the East India Company had already chartered the twenty or so ships that would sail. There was no time to lose but, as it turned out, finding another position was relatively straightforward. A new ship was on the stocks at Wells' dockyard and would soon be launched. Its principal managing owner was none other than John Durand, ship's husband to the *Houghton.* The new ship was to be called the *Horsenden* and her captain would be William Marter. This would be his first command and he would need suitable officers to serve under him. If John Durand recommended someone, William Marter was unlikely to disagree. Although, technically, a captain appointed his crew, most officers were chosen after consultation with the ship's husband.[2] In this case, the husband was a forceful character, with a reputation for getting his own way.[3]

John Durand was favourably disposed towards Richard Peirce. The young man had just completed a successful voyage and Captain Newton had given a good report of him. But there were many other rivals for a position on *Horsenden* and, therefore, some further influence must have worked in Richard Peirce's favour. The nature of the relationship between John Durand and the Peirce family is not known but there surely was one. Within a matter of weeks, it was arranged that Richard Peirce and his colleague, John Biddlecomb, would transfer to the *Horsenden*. Peirce would be promoted from fifth to third mate and Biddlecomb would occupy the rank above. In early November, the *Horsenden* was launched and work began to get her ready for the January deadline. As usual, her officers would be called upon to supervise these preparations. This allowed Richard Peirce only a couple of months before he would have to join his new ship. It would be interesting to know how he spent this time. Did he travel to Somerset to see his sister, his uncle or, perhaps, other relatives? Or was he tempted to remain in London?

The city was in a state of considerable excitement. On 8 September, the young king had married a seventeen-year-old German princess, Charlotte of Mecklenburg-Strelitz. Two weeks later, their joint coronation was due to take place. George II had died almost a year earlier and, on the 22nd, his grandson would ascend to the throne as George III. Half of London was desperate to catch a glimpse of the royal couple as they were carried in sedan chairs to Westminster Hall. The roads quickly became chaotic. Some carriages collided when the nobility, determined to reach Westminster Abbey, tried to force their way through. The coronation was a remarkable spectacle.[4] But, if Richard Peirce was inclined to join the expectant crowds, he also had sound business reasons for staying in the capital.

As Third Officer, his privilege would increase and he would be entitled to more space in the ship's hold.[5] On this voyage, with a larger investment in private trade, he had, at last, the prospect of making a reasonable profit. He was now also a sworn servant of the East India Company. In December, Captain Marter presented his four senior officers at East India House for the Directors' approval.[6] At an official ceremony, they swore an oath of fidelity to the Company and promised to abide by its rules on private trade. These stipulated that officers must itemise, in writing, any goods they wished to carry on the outward voyage. Richard Peirce had duly done so. In January 1762, he and John Biddlecomb both wrote to the Court of Directors seeking permission 'To take with them several particulars therein mentioned on their indulgence in private trade.' These 'particulars' were uncontentious and the Directors raised no objection.[7]

With this in mind, Richard Peirce must have focussed much of his attention on raising the necessary funds. His status as a senior officer, under the Company's protection, would make it easier to obtain credit with London merchants or bankers. No records survive of how Richard Peirce went about funding his investment but one thing is certain. This time, he would be sailing to a different destination and whatever goods he returned with would be determined by this new market.

The destination allocated to *Horsenden* was China. She would be one of only four ships that would sail directly to Canton and would return without stopping at any ports in India. This was significant. Unlike in India, with its growing populations of Europeans, in China, only the Portuguese were allowed a permanent settlement at Macao. Trade between China and Europe was tightly controlled by the Emperor and foreign merchants were permitted to trade only at one designated port, Canton on the Pearl River. Trade was tolerated only through official channels and the movement of foreign merchants was strictly curtailed. Consequently, Richard Peirce would find no market for the sort of domestic goods that were in such demand in Madras or Pondicherry.

Despite these restrictions, a voyage to China was not without its attractions. On the return voyage, officers were permitted to carry a quantity of tea in private trade, With the ever-increasing demand for tea at home, an officer could expect to sell his quota at a good profit. He might also bring back china-ware and silk. Chinese porcelain was still sought after and, in the upper echelons of society, silk continued to be in vogue. There was, therefore, no debate about what to carry on the return journey, but what goods to take out, in the first place?

The Emperor and, by extension, the Chinese people regarded Europeans as less civilised than themselves. They had little interest in or desire for most of the goods that these inferior foreigners wanted to sell. They were prepared to buy flints, which could be used in the production of porcelain, but British manufactured goods held little appeal. The only exceptions to this were the mechanical chiming clocks and other musical 'toys' that the westerners brought with them. The Emperor liked such 'sing-songs' and it is, therefore, unsurprising that his officials desired them, too. A chiming watch or musical box could make an acceptable gift to a superior and, thereby, oil the wheels of patronage and promotion.[8] However, as we will see later, the demand for 'sing-songs' was not without its drawbacks.

There was a further characteristic of the Chinese system that could work to the advantage of European traders. The Chinese valued silver above gold. This meant that tea had to be purchased with silver but also that the Chinese were prepared to trade gold for it. The exchange of currency worked to the advantage of both parties. Not only could the East India Company benefit but so, too, could individuals. Consequently, there was a great incentive to carry as much silver coin as possible on the outward voyage.

An examination of *Horsenden's* log demonstrates this to be the case.[9] On 20 February 1762, twenty chests of Company silver were brought aboard and locked in the bread room where they would be secure. Six days later, a chest of silver coin was received on behalf of Captain Stewart. He was the commander of the *Elizabeth*, one of the other East Indiamen that would sail to China at the same time. Why he chose to transport such a valuable item on *Horsenden* instead of on his own ship is not explained.[10] Meanwhile, Captain Marter had stored twenty-five tons of flints in the hold. Once levelled, they would serve as ballast to steady the ship but, as soon as he reached China, these flints would again become his private trade.[11]

On Friday 26 February, 'Capt Durant (*sic*) the ship's husband' visited *Horsenden,* at the Hope and paid the crew their 'river pay'. To minimise the temptation for sailors to take the money and run, river pay was not issued until a ship was ready to depart. On Sunday morning, *Horsenden* duly weighed anchor and moved downstream. In the Downs, they met up with *Elizabeth* and then, under naval escort, made their way to Portsmouth.

Despite the victories of 1759, the Seven Years War was still dragging on. It would not be safe for a fleet of East Indiamen to sail unprotected during the first part of the voyage. Consequently, for several days, *Horsenden* waited off Spithead while the convoy formed up. It also allowed time to take on board another fourteen sacks of silver coin. At last, on 26 March, the signal was given for the convoy to weigh anchor. Seven East Indiamen would sail together, shepherded by His Majesty's ships, *Arrogant* and *Prince William*.

In rough seas, the fleet made its way southwards, in tight formation. Then, as they reached 40 degrees latitude, on 12 April, it was time for the fleet to separate. Two ships would veer off to Madeira, the naval escort would depart, and *Horsenden*, *Elizabeth*, *Harcourt*, *Hardwick* and *Drake* would continue together. From now on, they would have to fend for themselves.

For the inexperienced Captain Marter, this was a huge responsibility. His brand new ship was more than 110 feet long and 36 feet wide. At 774 tons she was much bigger than the *Houghton*.[12] Captain Marter was answerable to the owners for her safe return and to the Company for carrying out their instructions.

The East India Company's instructions to him, and regulations concerning the voyage, were set out in a number of documents. These had been delivered to him in the sealed 'packet' from the Secret Committee of the Court of Directors. It was not to be opened while they were in convoy. Once the convoy had dispersed, Captain Marter summoned his chief mate, Alexander Jameson, and Second Officer, John Biddlecomb, to the roundhouse. In front of them, he unsealed the 'pacquet' and read his instructions. On his return, he would be called to account if it was suspected he had departed from them.

Although the five East Indiamen endeavoured to keep together, this proved difficult. Within days they had become separated, only *Drake* remaining just visible astern. Then, on 14 April, a strange sail hove into view. At first she was assumed to be the *Elizabeth* but, as she approached, it became clear that she was not. Using the secret Company signal, as instructed in the packet, Captain Marter called on the unknown ship to identify herself. When she failed to do so, he feared the worst. Anxious not to lose his ship on his first voyage, William Marter summoned all hands and cleared his ship for action. Then, to show that he meant business, he fired a 'stern chacer'. This was one of the biggest guns on *Horsenden*, with the greatest range and, as its name suggests, was positioned at the stern. Intended to deter pursuers, it had the desired effect. The unidentified ship immediately veered away and ran up a flag to indicate that she was Dutch. Captain

Marter must have felt relieved to have avoided conflict but the incident underlined the need to be on guard.

For Third Officer, Richard Peirce, life at sea had resumed its normal pattern. In good weather, the ship was easy to handle and few hands were required to go aloft. Instead, the men were kept busy picking oakum, whipping ropes, caulking the quarterdeck and repairing torn sails. As Captain Newton had done, Captain Marter tinkered with the trim of his ship, filling empty water butts with sea water, to 'get the ship by the head'. Meals were eaten at the appointed times: breakfast at eight, dinner at twelve, supper at six. In his capacity as third mate, Richard Peirce now presided over his own officers' mess. This was below deck, in steerage, just forward of his own cabin. A considerable number ate at his table. Whereas *Houghton* had been undermanned, the *Horsenden* seemed almost over-staffed. She carried not only a sixth officer but also no fewer than eleven midshipmen. This was an exceptionally large number and a sign that Captain Marter had decided to cash in, as soon as possible, on the patronage he could now offer.

Whether Richard Peirce profited from this largesse is doubtful. Joining his mess would be the young writers, cadets and any passengers unable to afford the Captain's table. As third mate, he could charge for the food he provided but his guests expected to receive good value for what they paid.[13] Although they ate in the murky gloom of steerage, their fare sometimes rivalled that enjoyed in the cuddy. After Richard Peirce had accounted for his expenses, there was little money left over from the takings. The real advantage lay not in coin but in the prestige and status the third mate's mess conferred on him.

Throughout May and June, the weather was good. Steady winds drove them forward and they passed through the doldrums without delay. On 11 May, *Horsenden* reached the equator. Although Captain Marter makes no mention of it in his journal, the ceremony of crossing the line was celebrated on almost every ship. It was an opportunity for excessive drinking and some boisterous fun on the part of the crew. Commanders felt powerless to prevent it and most were willing to honour the tradition, provided the ceremony did not get out of hand. A member of the crew, dressed as King Neptune supported by several watery acolytes, draped in seaweed, approached the quarterdeck where Captain Marter and his officers waited to receive them. After theatrical salutations had been exchanged, Neptune demanded to know if any on board were entering his kingdom for the first time. He was told the names of those passengers, seamen or officers who had never crossed the equator before.

Now the real fun began. Everyone who had been identified was called upon, in turn, to pay a forfeit, usually in the form of liquor. Those unable or unwilling to pay were handed over to King Neptune for punishment. This usually involved a ducking, either in a barrel of water or by being lowered from the main yard-arm into the sea. In most instances, this was good-humoured horseplay - but not always. An unpopular officer, purser, cook or seaman might be ducked several times and half drowned. On other ships, men had even been known to die. In case the high-jinks on *Horsenden* looked like going too far, Captain Marter was ready to intervene.

After another hundred miles or so, *Horsenden* was clear of the doldrums. Near the Tropic of Capricorn, they altered course to the southeast and picked up the southern trade winds. Now they could make good progress again. On 16 June they estimated they had covered 212 miles in one day. Soon they had passed Cape Laguellas (*Agulhas*) and left the Atlantic. Instead of swinging north to India, past Madagascar, Captain Marter maintained their easterly course out into the Southern Ocean. Here the weather was much more stormy and the seas higher. Accompanied by albatross and sheerwaters, the ship raced before the wind. Even with the minimum of sail, it would sometimes take several men at the wheel to hold the bow steady. Huge following seas would lift *Horsenden's* stern and send her careering ahead into the troughs. If she yawed too much and turned sideways to the waves, she could be lost in a trice. Even if she held her course, there was always a danger of being 'pooped' by a huge wave breaking over the stern, smashing the shutters on the windows and carrying away everything on deck. Like Richard Peirce, Thomas Twining had experienced the Southern Ocean. He described its prodigious waves as 'the Alps of the marine world' and found their 'awful grandeur' exhilarating, terrifying and 'sublime'.[14] Encountering this region for the first time, Peirce must

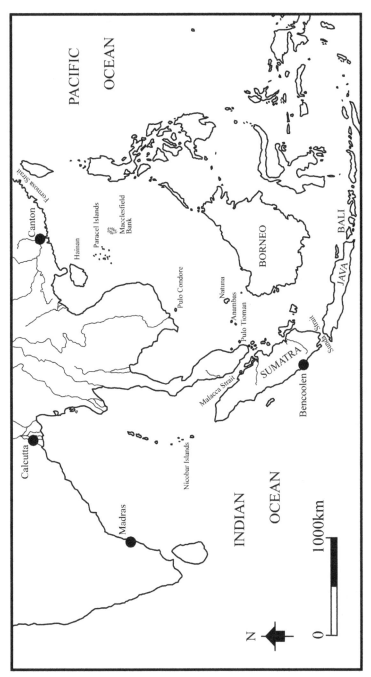

Fig. 2. The China Seas

have been similarly moved. For three weeks, they ran before the wind, harnessing the elements of destruction to achieve speeds of more than ten knots. At times the spray blotted out the sun and only the flash of a white albatross wing showed against the dark sky.

At last, to the relief of her crew, *Horsenden* turned northeast and pointed her bows in the direction of Java and calmer waters. On 23 July, as the lookout scanned the horizon for land, he saw a ship ahead of them. She was going slowly, in the same direction, and he could see she had lost her fore topmast. When they caught up with her, an exchange of Company signals revealed she was the *Harcourt*. They hadn't seen her for two months. Now, in company again, the ships covered the last few hundred miles of open sea.

By 1 August 1762, they were in sight of Krakatoa and the coast of Java. After all those months at sea, Captain Marter was anxious to take on fresh water and supplies. Having negotiated the Sunda Straits between Sumatra and Java, the ships dropped anchor off the Zutphen Islands, to allow the longboat to ferry water and beef from the shore. Another local or 'country' ship was able to supply them with arrack. This strong drink, made from fermented rice or fruit, made a welcome change from the normal beer and grog. Unfortunately, it may also have made the men less amenable to discipline.

It would be important to have a well-disciplined and healthy crew for the next leg of the voyage. Indonesian waters and the South China Seas are hazardous places for a sailing ship. There are many small islands to avoid, the waters are shallow and sand banks can trap the unwary mariner. Concerned for the safety of their ships, Captains Marter and Morrison picked their way slowly northward along the east coast of Sumatra, sounding the depth as they went. At St Nicholas Point, they came upon the *Elizabeth* which they had last seen in May. She too had arrived safely.

Once more the ships paused and Captain Marter used the opportunity to send the carpenter and some men ashore to cut wood. In the afternoon, the pinnace and yawl were dispatched to bring back the fruits of their labour. Both boats returned fully laden but some of the cut wood remained on shore. This time, Captain Marter sent an officer and seven men in the pinnace to gather up what was left. The officer is not identified in the journal but it is possible that he was Richard Peirce. If so, he had a lucky escape.

No sooner had the pinnace approached the shore than the seven sailors turned on the unsuspecting officer and heaved him overboard. Then they made their escape. Fortunately, a local fishing boat was nearby and the boatman saw what was happening. The lucky officer was rescued and word was sent to the *Horsenden*. Captain Marter took immediate action. The second mate, John Biddlecomb, and eight armed officers were dispatched at once to apprehend the deserters. It was 1 pm the following day when they returned. Despite an extensive search, the pinnace had not been found and the deserters remained at large. This kind of thing showed just how fragile the authority of an officer could be. Given half a chance, disaffected seamen might turn on him without warning.

Captain Marter knew that it was important to assert his authority before any more serious incidents could occur. He soon had an opportunity. William Long, emboldened after drinking too much arrack, was insolent and uncooperative. Retribution followed swiftly. A dozen lashes were administered and the unruly seaman was put in irons. It had the desired effect. By the next day, William Long was suitably penitent. Now that he had made his point, Captain Marter could be magnanimous. His journal records, 'Released William Long, he acknowledging himself guilty of a very great crime and promising to behave with sobriety in future.'

These events surely made an impression on Richard Peirce. Seamen were a rough and unpredictable lot, capable of violence at any time. It was important not to alienate them by unfair or unreasonable treatment but, at the same time, they needed to know who was boss. Captain Marter may have been less literate than Captain Newton but he understood this well enough. There would be no more trouble on his ship.

The best way to avoid trouble was to keep the men busy. The next day, 22 August, the *Horsenden, Harcourt* and *Elizabeth* weighed anchor again. Having worked their way up the Sumatran coast, passing landmarks like Monopin Hill and the mouth of the Palamban river, they were soon approaching the islands of Pulo Auro and Pulo

Tioman. Heading north across the South China Sea, they sighted Pulo Condore on 27 August. They were not far from their destination, now. This knowledge may have prompted an uncharacteristic outburst of aesthetic sensibility on the part of Captain Marter. On 2 September *Horsenden's* journal recorded 'At sunset the clouds all round us were so tinged with red that the whole element appeared as fires'.

It was a good omen. *Horsenden* and her companions arrived at the mouth of the Pearl river a few days later. Anchoring near islands called the Ladrones, they fired a gun to attract a Chinese sea-pilot. Often, he was a local fisherman and, speaking no English, would have to use gestures to direct them past various small islands into the safe waters of Macao Roads. There, they could hire an official river-pilot to guide them 65 miles up the Pearl River to Whampoa Roads, the anchorage allocated to them by the Chinese authorities. Although the city of Canton was a further fifteen miles upstream, European ships and their crews were not permitted to proceed beyond Whampoa. Here, two small islands in the river were made available for the men. At the insistence of the Emperor, interaction with ordinary Chinese was kept to a minimum so they would have to remain here, in virtual quarantine, until it was time to depart.

Before he arrived at Whampoa, Richard Peirce knew that China would be very different from India. Nevertheless, the Chinese way of doing things surely made a strong initial impression on him. Their strict protocols and inflexible regulations were alien and often infuriating to Europeans but, over the next two decades, Richard Peirce would learn to work within them. The Company's overriding interest was trade and to achieve this, its representatives would have to conform to the Chinese modus operandi. When in Canton, Peirce would adopt the etiquette and manners expected of him by his Chinese counterparts. Though he would not learn their language, he would become proficient in the pidgin English through which all business was conducted.

On this first encounter, everything seems to have gone smoothly. The river-pilot came aboard and, on 11 September, the process of going upriver to Whampoa began. The Pearl River was a hazardous route for large ships. It was shallow, with powerful currents and strong eddies that could send a ship off course, in an instant. En route, they would have to cross two large sand bars and this could only be done when the tide allowed. Propelled by the current alone, it was difficult to steer the *Horsenden* so, to keep her in the deepest channels, the help of local boats was required. As many as thirty or forty sampans would have to be hired to tow the East Indiaman in the right direction. Others, flying large flags, would be anchored over each sand bar to mark its whereabouts. Progress was determined by the tide, irrespective of whether it was day or night. Even in daylight, co-ordinating so many craft required a sophisticated system of communication. Signals were conveyed by gongs, drum beats and long blasts on conch shells, aided at night by lanterns and torches. To Richard Peirce, it must have seemed a bewildering cacophony but the system clearly worked and that was what mattered.

Meanwhile, the Company's official representative, Alexander Hurria, was impatient to get to Canton. Known as the 'supercargo', he was entrusted with conducting the trade negotiations on behalf of the Company.[15] On the waterfront at Canton, stood the 'factories' of several European nations. During the trading season, the Chinese gave permission for supercargoes to reside there. While the *Horsenden* waited for the tide to carry her over the second bar, Mr Hurria was lowered into the longboat. With the customary mark of respect for supercargoes and to alert the Chinese of his coming, *Horsenden* fired a salute of nine guns.

Once at Whampoa, *Horsenden* anchored a couple of miles from Danes Island. This was where many of the sailors would stay, living in long sheds called 'bankshalls'. When they were not working on the ship, they could while away their time there, playing games and, perhaps, enjoying some *samshu*, the local liquor with its powerful kick. Often crews from other European ships would be in residence too and, inevitably, after too much samshu, fights could break out. This year, only two Danish ships were in evidence. While war continued, the French kept well away and so there was little to provoke Captain Marter's men.

With *Horsenden* riding safely at anchor, Captain Marter prepared to receive an important Chinese official. This was the superintendant of customs for Canton, generally known as 'the Hoppo'.[16] He would formally measure the ship and these measurements would be used to calculate the toll that the Chinese would levy on the *Horsenden*. At the end of their stay, this toll would have to be paid before the Hoppo would grant the permit or *chop* that allowed them to leave. In addition to this, a charge for 'presents' to the Emperor would be demanded. Together, this amounted to a large sum of money, perhaps in excess of £1,000. Before leaving the ship, the Hoppo would also ask to be shown some 'sing-songs'. Taking their cue from the Emperor, senior Chinese officials were keen to get their hands on such novelties. The Hoppo knew that a present of a musical box or chiming clock was a good way to ingratiate himself with his superiors but, for the East India Company, this demand for sing-songs was fast becoming an irritation. If captains did not offer a suitable selection for the Hoppo to choose from, it could lead to ill feeling and result in costly delays. No captain wanted to be held up over some quibble regarding the paperwork but, without permission from the Hoppo, his ship could not leave.

Shortly before the visit by the Hoppo, another Chinese official had come aboard. The wooden licence he wore at his waist identified him as the ship's 'compradore'.[17] He had been allocated to *Horsenden* by the Customs authority and would be responsible for supplying the ship during her stay. He would provide food and water for the crew and such items as wood, tar, paint and nails for the ship, or bundles of bamboo and rattan to use in the hold. All would be delivered on thirty day credit. If additional manpower were needed to empty the hold or with caulking the hull, the compradore would recruit local Chinese labour to assist.[18]

Every day for the next fifteen weeks, the compradore's sampan would come alongside to deliver fruit, vegetables, ducks, pork and even whole cows. Many of these had been obtained from the thousands of sampans that lined the river bank and filled every inlet. From the quarterdeck, Richard Peirce would have been impressed by this floating metropolis where local Chinese lived cheek-by-jowl with their pigs and domestic fowl. He soon learnt that in amongst this confusion of vessels were the 'flower boats', floating brothels that satisfied another appetite of all foreign crews.[19]

With these domestic arrangements in place, Captain Marter's attention switched to commercial priorities. *Horsenden* had carried five chests of treasure belonging to the East India Company and these had to be transported to their factory at Canton. Captain Marter, with his Purser and some of his officers, would accompany the treasure in the chop boat but, first, each chest had to be weighed. On arrival in Canton, the process would be repeated to ensure that none of the precious silver had disappeared en route. Once this important duty had been fulfilled, the captain and his officers could concentrate on their own private trade.

At some point, during the next week or so, Richard Peirce made the journey to Canton himself. This was where business was conducted. Although not as impressive as the first sight of Madras, the waterfront at Canton caught the eye, nonetheless. Small craft scurried about among the larger Chinese junks. Lined along the quayside, facing the river, the European factories formed a striking façade. Each was distinguished by its national flag – Dutch, French, Danish, Swedish and Imperial - but it was immediately evident that the Union flag flew in front of the largest building of all. With its storerooms on the ground floor, the East India Company's factory included a comfortable dining room upstairs, living quarters and a verandah supported on classical columns. The Company's supercargoes would reside in this impressive

The European Factories at Canton by W. Danniell
© *National Maritime Museum, Greenwich, London*

setting throughout the trading season. East India Company captains and senior officers could usually find temporary accommodation there too. It made sense. All trade had to be conducted close to the waterfront. Foreigners were forbidden from entering the walled city of Canton and travel to other parts of China was strictly prohibited. By restricting all movement, the Chinese authorities could keep foreign trade under their tight control.

All Chinese trade with Europeans was conducted through merchants who were members of the Co-Hong. Sometimes described as a guild, this was essentially a cartel which had been granted a monopoly by the Emperor. Europeans were forbidden to deal with other independent Chinese traders and, consequently, the Co-Hong had acquired enormous commercial leverage. An individual member of the Co-Hong was appointed to deal exclusively with the *Horsenden*. This 'security merchant' would agree the price and quantity of tea to be purchased by her supercargo, Mr Hurria.[20] If Richard Peirce wanted to buy tea, as private trade, he too would have to deal with the same security merchant.

The absence of the French in 1762 may have helped to make the Co-Hong more amenable. With fewer ships to sell to, they wanted, perhaps, to avoid any unnecessary disputes. Within days, tea was being packed into lead-lined chests at the factory and ferried down the Pearl River to the waiting East Indiamen. During October and November, more than three thousand chests of tea were brought aboard *Horsenden*. Ninety boxes of porcelain were also loaded, 'some belonging to Captain Marter and his officers.' At home, in England, the demand for willow-pattern was still strong. But, this china-ware was not only a marketable commodity, it also fulfilled a practical function. By placing it under the chests of tea, the tea could be raised off the damp floor of the hold and kept dry. To prevent the cargo from shifting during the voyage, any remaining space in the hold was filled with 'dunnage'. Essentially, this was padding. Sago was poured into the boxes of porcelain and rattan mats were placed between each layer of tea chests.[21] Then, rice, bamboos, canes and whangees were stuffed into every remaining crevice and gap. All this dunnage was regarded as separate from the allowance in private trade but could be sold profitably when the voyage was over.

On 11 January 1763, exactly four months after arriving at Whampoa, it was time for *Horsenden* to depart. She would be in company with four other Indiamen: *Harcourt*, the *Royal Charlotte*, the *Royal Captain* and *True Briton*. As senior commander, the captain of *True Briton* would act as commodore with overall authority. On 20 January, when they were off Pulo Tioman, he summoned all commanders aboard his ship. It was agreed to 'randezvous' at Pulo Auro where they hoped to pick up a Royal Navy escort. After a fruitless wait of four days, no naval ships had appeared. Without their protection, Captain Marter was entitled to open another 'packet': 'Opened my orders from the Secret Committee. To be opened if I did not join His Majesty's ships at Pulo Timoan or Auro.'

Together, the flotilla felt its way gingerly through the waters of Indonesia. They re-passed the familiar landmarks of Monopin Hill, Lucepara Point and Java Head. By 3 February they had sailed through the Sunda Straits and were out into the Indian Ocean. From now on, it was a case of making all speed homewards. *Horsenden* seems to have performed well, progress was good and the men remained biddable and healthy. The only deaths were those of a French prisoner-of-war and John Crowe, the ship's Purser. Still in company, the East Indiamen rounded the Cape, in March, and, on 15 April, arrived at St Helena. Here, they received good news: 'Round Sugar Loaf Point where we took up a boat that informed us that a Treaty of Peace was agreed betwixt Great Britain, France & Spain.' The Seven Years War was at an end and the threat from French naval vessels had gone. They could sail home unmolested.

Two weeks at St Helena allowed time for Richard Peirce to revisit some old haunts. Perhaps he dined again at the Governor's residence and enjoyed conversation with officers from the other Indiamen. This time, with a healthy crew, there was no reason to delay. The supercargoes came aboard to the customary nine gun salute and, then, *Horsenden*, in company with *Harcourt*, *Royal Charlotte* and *True Briton*, weighed anchor and began the final stage of their voyage.

Throughout May and June the weather remained good and the ships worked their way steadily northwards. There was nothing remarkable to report in the ship's journal, other than prodigious quantities of sea-weed. Then on 27 June, at 30 degrees North latitude, they encountered a schooner, which requested urgent assistance: 'AM saw a scooner (*sic*) in the NW under English colours, bore down and spoke her, found her in great distress for water. She had been out from Cadiz 6 weeks and was bound for Boston. Gave her 90 gallons.'

The schooner had clearly been a victim of the doldrums. To have been becalmed like this was potentially fatal, as the plight of the 'the Ancient Mariner' makes clear, and Captain Marter would not have hesitated in coming to their rescue. His act of charity must have relieved the anxiety on the schooner but tension seems to have been rising on *Horsenden,* too. Now that they were almost home, tempers began to fray. On 30 June a fight took place between a quartermaster and one of the seamen. It did not end well: 'At 4 pm departed this life James Snipes seaman of an accidental blow rec'd from James McIntosh Quarter Master in boxing with him. Confined James McIntosh in irons for the above offence in order to bring him home to receive his trial for the same.'

Even if the fight had been a friendly bout between the two, a fatal outcome like this could trigger serious unrest. Once again, Captain Marter had shown he could act decisively. James McIntosh would have to take the consequences. In another few weeks, he would be handed over to the authorities in England.

On 13 July, the man at the masthead saw land to the north which he quickly identified as the headland of Start Point, in Devon. Only two days later, they dropped anchor in the Downs. From there, with a river pilot on board, *Horsenden* worked her way up to Gravesend. A day later, the tide had carried them to Long Reach, opposite Purfleet. For the crew, this was the end of the journey. They had been away for eighteen months but others would take over now and they could be released. The *Horsenden's* journal records this succinctly: 'Discharged the ship's company.' While two surveyors from the Company checked the cargo, lumpers came aboard and began to dismantle the *Horsenden's* guns. By 23 July, the ship had been lightened sufficiently to move again. Now she 'dropped up' to Deptford.

With money in their pockets, at last, the crew quickly disappeared. But not so, Captain Marter and his officers. The tea was still in the ship's hold and so were their precious chests of private trade. Richard Peirce would have to be on hand to ensure that none of his investment went astray. His chests of tea, his china-ware and any other purchases, clearly marked with his initials, would have to be conveyed safely to the Company warehouse and, later, to the salesroom. It was not until 30 August that the last of the private trade had been unloaded.

Now, Richard Peirce could relax and take stock. He had survived another hazardous voyage, he had carried out his duties well, he had encountered the Chinese and, as a result of this experience, he was richer and wiser. His prospects remained good. What he needed now was another voyage and further promotion. Only when he reached the highest rungs of the ladder, would he be able to make the serious money that was his ultimate goal. The time had come to consider his next move.

7
Budgerows & an 'old cock'

IN 1764, as it turned out, the upward trajectory of Richard Peirce's career briefly stalled. Although the East India Company dispatched twenty-three ships that season, a place could not be found for him on any of them. He had no choice but to wait until the following year. For the next twelve months, he would turn this delay to his advantage, developing his contacts within the social circle of ships' husbands, commanders and anyone else whose influence might further his career.

It was probably during this interlude when Peirce first encountered Thomas Burston. Although we do not know precisely when they met, it was a meeting that would have profound consequences. Thomas Burston worked for His Majesty's Excise service. He came from Norfolk but, since 1759, had worked for the Excise Collection in Hertfordshire. In June 1760, he had been elevated to the position of Supervisor of the Watford District. Four years later he was promoted again, this time as Collector of Excise for Salisbury.[1]

Thomas Burston took an interest in the East India Company and, at some point, decided to invest his money in one of its ships. To do so, he joined a consortium of shareholders. Given his subsequent career, it is possible that Burston became a shareholder of one of John Durand's ships and this might explain how he came across Richard Peirce. However, that is speculation. We know nothing for sure about the circumstances of their meeting or, indeed, its date. It could have been as late as 1766 or even 1767. However, one thing is certain. Sooner or later, Richard Peirce met Thomas Burston's daughter, Mary.

The London in which Richard Peirce now found himself had not changed fundamentally in the last two years. During his absence, the excitement prompted by the coronation had been replaced by the more unsettling enthusiasm of the London mob for 'liberty' and its champion, John Wilkes. But even that issue was losing momentum and by the end of 1763, Wilkes had left the country. Although George Grenville had replaced Lord Bute as leader of the government, there had been no major shift in policy. With peace restored, the priority now was to repair the nation's finances. In parliament, the talk was of the Cider Bill and the Sugar Act. Such measures aroused strong feelings among American colonials but Richard Peirce probably gave them little thought. He is more likely to have been interested in the arrival, in April, of another of Durand's ships, the *Earl of Ashburnham*. She was commanded by his namesake, Thomas Pearce, and was carrying an unusual cargo. The *St James Chronicle* reported 'Several wild beasts are brought over in the 'Earl of Ashburnham' and 'Plassey' from the East Indies among which is an elephant and several buffaloes. It is said they are intended as presents to their Majesties.' [2]

During 1764, the Directors of the East India Company began finalising their plans for the fleet of ships to sail the following year. They had already decided to charter the *Pacific*. Although this ship had been launched four years previously, she had not been 'taken up' by the Company until now. Her principal managing owner was John Hyde and her captain would be Charles Barkley. It would be the *Pacific's* maiden voyage and Barkley's first command. Although he had completed a lengthy voyage as chief mate on the *Triton*, he had not been to sea since 1762. He would be the third novice commander that Richard Peirce would serve under.

Like Captains Newton and Marter before him, Charles Barkley gave careful thought to the appointment of his officers. On his first voyage as captain, he would need men who were dependable and capable. He knew that Richard Peirce had acquitted himself well in his previous posts and was ready for promotion. On being approached, Barkley decided to offer Peirce the position of second mate.

The chief mate would be Emerson Tidy. He also brought experience, having already held this rank on another of John Hyde's ships. However, the third and fourth mates had not served as officers on any Company ship before. There was no fifth or sixth officer and only four midshipmen, one of whom was Captain Barkley's own son. [3] Compared to the numbers on *Horsenden*, Barkley would have relatively few senior men to rely on. The success of the voyage would depend to a considerable extent on the performance of Richard Peirce and Emerson Tidy.

Among the rest of the crew, one name stands out. John Coxon was the Purser. Fourteen years later, he would go on to command the *Grosvenor*.[4] The wreck of this ship, in 1782, preceded that of the *Halsewell* but it, too, captured the public's imagination and Coxon's name would become almost as well-known as Peirce's. But that was far in the future. In 1764, both men's thoughts were focused on the voyage they were about to undertake.

The implications of his promotion to second mate were clear to Richard Peirce. His new status would entitle him to sit at the Captain's table where he could mix with the supercargoes and other important passengers. His pay would increase to £4 a month. More significant than either of these things would be the increase in his 'indulgence' for private trade. Now, he was entitled to space in the hold, equivalent to 160 cubic feet or four tons of merchandise.[5] More than ever before, he would need to focus his attention on making the most of this opportunity.

He could boast greater financial credibility now, and merchants were more likely to offer him goods on credit. As ever, the trick was to invest in things which would sell in India at a decent profit. The ship's log records that Captain Barkley's private trade included lead, iron and anchors.[6] The latter would always sell to the captains of local 'country ships' trading between Indian ports and elsewhere in the East. The fourth mate, Mr Fryer, invested in 146 iron bars and 'Mr Emerson' took twenty 'faggots of steel'. There were also chests of coral and the usual cutlery and stationery. Although Richard Peirce is not named specifically, he surely invested in similar things.

In early December 1764, the *Pacific* was moved out of her dock onto the river at Deptford. There, in icy cold weather, work began to load the ballast, erect the masts and rig the ship. The ballast, known as kentledge, consisted of cast iron 'pigs', each weighing between 100 and 300 pounds. Positioned amidships, below the waterline and with most of the weight just forward of the mainmast, the kentledge was then covered in a layer of shingle, into which would be sunk the casks of drinking water. Butts of about one hundred gallons and hogsheads of just over fifty were placed strategically to ensure the ship sat in the water with the best trim.[7] With her cargo of recruits to supply, the *Pacific* may have carried almost 100 tons of fresh water. Whether this could truly be described as drinking water was a moot point. Taken directly from the Thames, it was often 'thick as treacle [...] with a smell you could not stand up against'.[8] No wonder the men preferred their beer and grog.

Meanwhile, above decks the masts were being received. A special vessel, called a 'sheer hulk', came alongside. With its single, sturdy mast acting as a crane, it winched *Pacific's* fifteen ton lower mainmast aboard the Indiaman. Once in position, the rigger secured it with shrouds to the small platforms that projected from the *Pacific's* sides. With all the lower masts in place, the rigger could then proceed to raising the topmasts, the topgallant masts and the yards. Finally the sails could be 'bent' or attached to the yards.

While this work continued high above the deck, the Company's heavy cargo – copper, lead and iron – was stowed in the hold. By 6 January 1765, the ship was ready to move downstream to Gravesend. Here, private trade would be loaded and the East India Company's soldiers would come on board. Perhaps, Richard Peirce was slow in finalising what he would take. As late as 23 January, the Court of Directors considered a joint request from him, the surgeon and from John Coxon, the purser, for 'liberty to carry with them the particulars therein mentioned on their respective indulgence on Private Trade'.[9] Sadly, the record of these 'particulars' has not survived.

From the deck of the *Pacific*, Peirce could see his old ship, the *Horsenden*, anchored nearby. She was sitting very low in the water, suggesting that her hold contained an excessive ballast of flints. Still under the command of Captain Marter, she sailed for Madras on 10 January 1765, in company with Emerson Tidy's former ship, *Albion*. A few days later, word was brought of an accident. While leading the way through the shoals of the Thames Estuary, Captain Marter had suddenly brought *Horsenden* to anchor without signalling to *Albion* that they were in shallow water. Unaware of the danger, *Albion* had carried on and was soon aground on a sandbank. The passengers had had to be taken off and the voyage abandoned. In the subsequent enquiry, the Court of Directors placed the blame squarely on the shoulders of Captain Marter.[10] He had failed to communicate the danger and had acted hastily.

There was a lesson to be learned from this. Since Richard Peirce had left their ships, both his previous commanders had been responsible for serious accidents. In March 1762, Captain Newton was near Spithead, at the start of a new voyage, when *Houghton* had collided with a transport ship, the *Laurel*. Although no lives had been lost, the *Laurel* had been sunk and her owners had taken out a lawsuit against Captain Newton. The stress of the whole situation proved too much for Newton's health and he wrote to the Court of Directors requesting permission to resign his command.[11] While both captains had taught Peirce to make all haste during a voyage, they had now demonstrated the perils of being too hasty. The safety of the ship must always be the overriding consideration.

The loading at Gravesend was taking longer than expected so the Court of Directors agreed to delay the departure of the *Pacific* by a further ten days. Then on 8 February, Captain Barkley presented himself and his senior officers at East India House. The final formalities were completed and the Company packet was handed over. At last, on the 15th, after the crew had been given their river pay, *Pacific* prepared to weigh anchor. She would sail in company with three other Indiamen, the *Granville*, the *Speke* and the *Ponsborne*.

To start with, progress was slow. Battling against headwinds, it took until 6 March to get as far as Portsmouth. Fearing more severe gales, the ships stayed there for over a month. It was not until 14 April 1765 that the voyage began in earnest. A fortnight later, *Pacific* was in sight of Madeira but her companion ships, *Ponsborne* and *Speake,* had disappeared from view. The *Pacific* would have to continue the voyage alone, while life on board her settled into its regular routine. Men picked oakum or knotted rope into gaskets, the carpenter made a new topgallant mast and the caulkers worked in the steerage.

A high priority for Captain Barkley was to maintain a healthy crew. The importance of cleanliness was understood but it was also believed that foul air could cause typhus and perhaps scurvy. The cocktail of waste matter which collected in the bilges – dead rats, cats, faeces, urine, vegetable matter and more – produced a nauseating stench that pervaded the lower decks and was intolerable for the passengers and recruits who could not escape it. The only way to alleviate the stink was to air the ship regularly.

In early May, Captain Barkley ordered the gun deck to be 'smoked'. Small amounts of gunpowder were burnt so the acrid smoke would counteract the pernicious miasma from the bilges. He also ordered all hammocks to be brought on deck where they could be properly aired. Twice more that month, the lower decks were scrubbed with vinegar and hatches were opened to allow fresh air to flow through. Although these measures would be ineffective against both typhus and scurvy, they made life at sea more tolerable and induced a feeling of wellbeing amongst those on board.

Everything was harmonious until they crossed the equator on 23 May. By then, the tedium and confinement of ship-life was making the soldiers irritable. They became increasingly unruly and attempts by Richard Peirce and the other officers to control them merely provoked abuse. This was the point when Captain Barkley needed to assert his authority and be seen to have done so. He rounded up eight of the most troublesome soldiers, charged them with mutinous behaviour and clapped them in irons. The rest of the soldiers got the message and discipline was restored. Three weeks later, one of the soldiers fell overboard. Captain Barkley immediately brought the ship to and ordered the longboat to be lowered. The ship's log records that 'the sea run so very high the boat could not row against it so had the misfortune to loos (*sic*) the man'.[12] The soldiers may have grieved for their lost comrade but they must also have come to realise that Captain Barkley was concerned for their welfare. They gave no more trouble.

By the end of July, *Pacific* had left the South Atlantic and had rounded the Cape. She was nearing Madagascar when a sail was spotted to the southeast. Although war with France had ended, the threat from pirates had not. It was best not to be complacent. The log states 'Got up quarter deck guns and mounted them. The sail we saw proved to be the Trew (*sic*) Britton, Capt Creighton, from England last from Sant Iago where we have hove in'. This was both a relief and an opportunity to share news. *True Briton* reported she had seen the *Speke* at Sant Iago but there was no word of the *Ponsborne* or *Granville*.

As August began, both ships sailed together through the Madagascar channel. They could see St Augustine Bay, where the *Houghton* had stopped in 1759, but Captain Barkley was determined to keep going. Only when they reached Johanna on the 13th, did they drop anchor. They had been continuously at sea for four months. Now the men would have a few days ashore while the ships took on water, wood and supplies. After their confinement on ship, the island must have seemed a paradise to the young soldiers. But, like that of Madagascar, the climate was not as idyllic as it seemed.

Within days of weighing anchor, men began to fall ill. On 5 September, three men died 'very suddenly of strong fever'. On the *True Briton* also, men were sick and 'out of order'. Fortunately, for most, the illness was not fatal. By the 12th, Captain Barkley was able to write 'Soldiers and seamen turning better every day'. With morale lifting, Barkley adjusted the trim of his ship and they pressed on with all speed towards India. Although several more soldiers would die before they would reach Madras, it was not long before they could see land. First the Island of Ceyloan (*sic*) and then the familiar landmarks of Elephant Hill and Fryars Hood. By 1 October, the *Pacific* had dropped anchor in Madras roads, close to three other East Indiamen.

From his position on the quarterdeck, Richard Peirce must have been relieved to see Madras again with the unmistakeable silhouette of Fort St George and, stretching along the shore, the growing number of houses with their white chunam walls. This would be a stop of only a few days but there might be time for a little private trading. Every opportunity had to be seized and it would be surprising if Peirce and his fellow officers did not run the gauntlet of the surf to go ashore.

After barely a fortnight, new and existing passengers had returned to the ship. On Wednesday 16 October, the *Pacific* 'weigh'd and made sail' and, together with another Indiaman, *Admiral Watson*, began the next leg of the voyage to Calcutta. Keeping well clear of the treacherous coastline, the two ships headed east, out into the Bay of Bengal, before swinging north towards the Ganges delta. By the third week, the weather had deteriorated and the winds had increased. On 6

November, *Pacific*'s log recorded 'severe gales' which had damaged her 'ruther' (*sic*). Nevertheless, they maintained their course and a week later had picked up a river pilot. He would guide them past the hazardous sand bars that protruded, like teeth, on either side of the channels leading to the Hooghly river. But even the pilot was not infallible. On the 20th, they struck a sandbank. This could have been disastrous and Richard Peirce must have wondered if he was about to lose his investment. Fortunately, the *Pacific* was not too badly stuck and they were able to winch her off, using the stream anchor and a nine inch hawser. The next day, they anchored safely at Kedgeree. Amongst the other ships riding at anchor was the elusive *Speke*. She had got there first.

Within a day or two of their arrival, the sloop, *Nancy*, appeared. This Company vessel would convey much of the *Pacific*'s cargo upstream to Calcutta. While the crew were busy transferring the contents of the hold, Captain Barkley and his officers could, again, focus their attention on private trading. No doubt they hired a river vessel – a houseboat or *budgerow* – to take them to the city. Five and a half years had passed since Richard Peirce had last seen Calcutta but, in this time, the city had thrived. The Battle of Plassey had restored its position but a more recent event had properly secured it. In October 1764, Company forces under Hector Munro had triumphed at the Battle of Buxar. The defeat they inflicted on the combined armies of the Mughal Emperor and the Nawabs of Bengal and Oudh, was conclusive. From now on, there would be no serious military or economic threat to Calcutta. The East India Company could negotiate from a position of strength and would do so.

Three months earlier, on 16 August, while the crew had been 'watering and wooding' the *Pacific* at Johanna, Robert Lord Clive and Mughal Emperor Shah Alam had signed the Treaty of Allahabad. Under this agreement, Shah Alam granted *diwani* rights to the East India Company. This entitled the Company to collect taxes on behalf of the Emperor from the people of Bengal, Bihar and Orissa. The potential revenue was a staggering £1.7 million. In return, the Company agreed to pay an annual tribute to the Emperor and also to bear the administrative and bureaucratic expense of collecting the tax. After all these costs were met, it was estimated that the Company would be left with a surplus amounting to around £700,000.[13] The significance of this seemed obvious to all. Overnight, the Company had become self-sufficient in funds and, for the foreseeable future, would be able to return a reliable and regular surplus to the Company and the Exchequer in England. Expectations of this bonanza were sky high. It must have seemed to Richard Peirce that he had arrived at a most opportune moment.

Buoyed by a conviction of future prosperity, the expanding population of Calcutta provided a sellers' market for the goods that *Pacific's* officers brought with them. Once his private trade had been converted into rupees, Richard Peirce considered what to do with them. Some he may have deposited at one of the emerging Agency Houses in Calcutta. In return, they would issue him with a Bill of Exchange which the East India Company would honour when he returned to London.

A more likely course of action is that Peirce chose to invest his takings in other goods to bring home. For this he needed the services of people with the right skills and experience. Company officials and other contacts probably put him in touch with Indian middlemen who would help negotiate purchases, act as translators and manage the financial transactions. These were the *gomashtas, banians, munshis* and other essential go-betweens who ensured that the wheels of commerce ran freely. If this process still seemed too daunting and fraught with risk, there was always a safer alternative. Local merchants, free traders and wealthy Company servants were desperate for cargo space on Indiamen. If an officer couldn't purchase enough goods to fill his share of the hold, these bigger fish would pay well for this privilege.

During December 1765 and January 1766, Captain Barkley and his officers may have made the journey between Calcutta and Kedgeree more than once. If they bought cotton or silks, they will have wanted to ensure these were loaded and stored safely on the *Pacific*. Then, as January was ending, the ship moved to Ingeli where she would load Company goods for the return voyage. There would be chests of treasure and bales of cotton but most of the cargo would consist of that essential component of gunpowder, saltpetre. Even in peacetime, the demand remained constant. There were also supplies to be transferred to Madras, including some items intended for its Governor, Robert Palk. Finally, there were a few passengers, Company men returning to England. Among them was Thomas Graham, son of an influential Edinburgh merchant and banker.[14] Like so many Scots, the Grahams had capitalised on the opportunities that followed the Act of Union in 1707 and were making their presence felt in India as well as in London. As we already know, the fortunes of the Graham and Peirce families would also become closely intertwined but, perhaps, it was here, at Ingeli, that the link was first established.

By the middle of February, everything had been loaded and stashed below decks. On the 14th, *Pacific* weighed anchor and headed for the open sea. After two weeks, they were back in Madras roads where the saltpetre was unloaded and replaced by a hundred bales of fabric. The private possessions of Governor Palk were delivered to his house in Fort St George and, we can assume, Captain Barkley and his senior officers called to pay their respects.

Governor Palk was an unusual character.[15] He had begun his career as an Anglican clergyman. In 1747 he became chaplain to Admiral Boscawen and, later, chaplain at Fort St David. There, he had become friends with General Stringer Lawrence, the man credited as founder of the Indian army. In 1752, Lawrence had persuaded Robert Palk to set aside his ecclesiastical duties and become his Paymaster in the Field. Two years later, Palk was involved in peace negotiations with the French and, in 1763, he was appointed Governor of Madras. The transition from religious to civic office was complete.

While seamen in the *Pacific's* hold sweated over saltpetre and bales of cotton, Captain Barkley had a more rewarding task to perform. There would be people in Madras who wanted to return to England and he could accommodate them. Everyone knew travellers had to pay over the odds for a passage home but, if you could secure an important passenger, the profits could be exceptional. As it happened, such a person was staying at Fort St George.

Robert Palk's old friend and mentor, Major General Stringer Lawrence had decided to retire, at last. For many years, he had played a key role in the struggles against the French. He had been an

Stringer Lawrence by Thomas Gainsborough
© *National Portrait Gallery, London*

early champion of Robert Clive and together they had thwarted the ambitions of Francois Dupleix for French dominance of the Carnatic. Later, Stringer Lawrence had fought in tandem with Eyre Coote and, in 1760, the two men had decisively beaten Comte de Lally at the Battle of Wandiwash. It was a setback from which the French would never fully recover.

By 1766, Lawrence's health was failing and he wanted to go home. In another year, he would be seventy. Tubby, irascible and self important, Lawrence was popular, nonetheless, with his men. They admired his toughness and generosity of spirit and referred to him affectionately as the 'Old Cock'.[16] Captain Barkley was delighted to have him aboard his ship. Not only would it be a great honour but a lucrative one, at that. The General would be accompanied by a retinue of 'gentlemen' and army officers, including Colonel Campbell. The entire entourage would pay handsomely to be accommodated in the round house.

Richard Peirce may also have been pleased that the Old Cock would be sailing on the *Pacific*. Over dinner, he could engage the General in conversation about their mutual acquaintance, Eyre Coote. It would help with the process of networking and developing the connections that underpinned success in eighteenth century society. It was essential to be known by people with influence and a celebrated military hero, even a superannuated one, might prove useful one day.

On 4 April 1766, with her passengers aboard and her hold crammed with cotton, redwood and 'sundreys', the *Pacific* set sail from Madras. The weather was fine, the sea was calm and the travellers untroubled by seasickness. Every afternoon at two o'clock, dressed for dinner and seated in strict order of rank, the General and his fellow passengers enjoyed the lavish hospitality of Captain Barkley's table. A succession of meat dishes, curries and pies, accompanied by rice, sauces and pickles, were washed down with ample quantities of wine, beer and coffee. While engaging in polite conversation with his neighbours, Richard Peirce surely kept a careful eye on how the *Pacific's* commander exerted his authority. Tipsy conviviality could easily descend into raucousness and fractiousness but Captain Barkley presided graciously over all, deferred to even by Stringer Lawrence, and decorum was maintained.

8
'Fitly qualified to command'

At the end of July, the *Pacific* reached St Helena and the General and his companions went ashore. To salute their departure and subsequent return, *Pacific* dutifully fired nineteen guns. Also at anchor were two other East Indiamen, the *Clive* and the *Hardwicke*. It was agreed that they would keep company on the final leg of the voyage. Together, they set off on 7 August and sailed northwards. For the rest of August the weather remained good but by September, they began to encounter gales. Several sails split and the sailmaker was kept busy with repairs. By the middle of October they were close to the English Channel. On the 17th they encountered a brig on her way from Virginia to London but Captain Barkley seemed strangely reluctant to follow her. The next day he summoned his officers to a meeting. In the ship's journal, he explained: 'finding the wind hang strong to the SE and a large swell, called a consultation of my officers where it was unanimously agreed that the present condition of the ship so bad it was not proper to enter to the Channel so bore away as per logg.'

The direction that the *Pacific* now took was to the northwest. She would swing round the southwest coast of Ireland and head for the Shannon Estuary and Limerick. It seems a slightly puzzling decision but Captain Barkley had his reasons. It is possible that he, and maybe his officers, had exceeded their permitted allowances in private trade. If they went straight to the Thames, the Company inspectors would be quick to discover any breach of the rules and there would be consequences. In out-of-the-way Limerick, they could sell any excess private trade with far less likelihood of being detected. It was a common ploy and the East India Company directors were wise to it. Any departure from the route stipulated in the charter party or any unnecessary delays were classed as 'demurrage' and would trigger a fine. This probably explains why Captain Barkley was at such pains to justify his actions in the ship's log. By obtaining the unanimous agreement of his officers, it reduced the chances of the finger of suspicion being pointed at him.

As soon as they were at anchor in the Shannon, General Lawrence and his companions disembarked. The salute, as they departed, was restricted to seventeen guns. A few days later, Captain Barkley received a visitor. Lady Inchiquin decided she wanted to be shown around the East Indiamen that had appeared so unexpectedly near her home. A member of the local aristocracy, Lady Inchiquin was married to William O'Brien, the 4th Earl of Inchiquin.[17] His seat was Dromoland Castle in County Clare and his name is forever associated with the great Irish harper, Carolan, who composed a piece in his honour. It is unlikely that Captain Barkley had ever heard of Carolan or, indeed, of Lady Inchiquin. Nevertheless, her arrival was honoured with eleven guns and one hopes she felt suitably gratified.

By the end of October, weather conditions had improved such that Captain Barkley felt he could delay their departure no longer. General Lawrence and 'the other gentlemen' re-embarked to a salute that now merited only fifteen guns. Sometime around 4 November, *Pacific* prepared to sail. She may have put in at Cork for a few days but by 26 November she was in sight of the Scilly Isles. The weather continued to be against them and once again Captain Barkley decided to postpone the run up the English Channel. This time he put into Falmouth. For a further two weeks they would be delayed 'as the weather looking very wild'. It would be almost the end of December 1766 before *Pacific* would finally arrive in the Thames.

With a third successful voyage under his belt, Richard Peirce was eager to reap the rewards from his investments. He had timed his arrival well. The news of the *diwani* had reached London in April and, since then, investors had been intoxicated by prospect of the 'torrent of treasure' that would follow. By December, when Richard Peirce stepped ashore, the price of shares in the East India Company had risen by an extraordinary 33%.[18] In such a heady atmosphere, his private trade must have sold well. Certainly, it was sufficient for him to turn his thoughts to marriage. He was no longer merely a man with prospects, he was becoming a man of substance. Only this can explain why Thomas Burston was prepared to consider him as a potential son-in-law.

Even if Richard Peirce had met Mary Burston before he sailed on the *Pacific*, their courtship did not begin in earnest until after his return. Thomas Burston would not have given his consent until it was clear that Richard Peirce could provide adequately for his daughter. By 1767, these conditions had been met. The East India Company now had a golden future and everyone associated with it hoped to cash in. In May, after the longest meeting in the Company's history, the shareholders had voted to raise the dividend from 10 to 12.5 per cent.[18] Thomas Burston would benefit and, perhaps by now, Richard Peirce had become a shareholder, too.

With a bright future ahead of them, Richard Peirce and Mary Burston were married in London, on Saturday 27 September 1767, at St Dunstans-in-the-East.[19] The witnesses were Robert Rochefort and Richard Peirce. The relationship with the latter witness is not given but it is reasonable to assume this person to be the uncle from Bath. We may also surmise that the bridegroom's own father was not present. In all probability he was already dead. A few days later, several newspapers carried news of the wedding. They reported that Mr Richard Peirce was in the East India service while Miss Burston was the 'only daughter of Thomas Burston Esq., of Lynn in Norfolk'.[20]

Within a few months of the wedding, Mary Peirce was pregnant. Without a permanent home of their own, it seems likely that the couple based themselves with Mary's parents in Norfolk. Mr and Mrs Burston could support their daughter and her baby, especially if Richard had to spend time in London. Now that he was going to be a father, it was essential that Richard Peirce found fresh employment. The logical thing was to seek a position as chief mate but Richard was in a hurry. He hoped to skip that rung of the ladder and go straight to commanding a ship of his own. That he succeeded in doing so was thanks to a combination of the extraordinary times, his own reputation and access to influence.

Following the grant of the *diwani*, the East India Company had to decide what it would do with the revenue it could now collect. Instead of carrying home shiploads of Indian currency, it would use this treasure to buy Indian goods to send back to England. In this way, it hoped to expand its markets and further increase its profits. But such an increase in merchandise would require a larger fleet to transport it. For the next season, the Company would charter an unprecedented thirty-three ships. Amongst them would be the *Earl of Ashburnham*. She was the ship that had brought the cargo of exotic animals from India in 1764. Her captain, Thomas Pearce, now intended to retire and a successor needed to be found. The East India Company's tradition of commands 'in perpetuity' meant that Thomas Pearce could decide who this would be. When making his choice, he would, no doubt, consider the wishes of the ship's husband and the consortium of owners but the ultimate decision would be his. He would also expect a considerable payback. From time to time, the East India Company had tried to outlaw the sale of commands but the practice persisted. A retiring captain could expect to receive several thousand pounds from his successor.

During the eighteenth century, it was common for the command of a ship to be retained within the family. A captain would often pass on his command to his son or to a nephew. It was in this way that dynasties, such as that of the Larkins family, could develop. However, Thomas Pearce had only a daughter and she was married to an antiquarian.[21] In choosing to pass the command to Richard Peirce, Thomas may have been favouring a man from his own extended family but it is much more likely that it was a straightforward financial deal and the similarity in their names was no more than a coincidence.

Although no record survives of the sum that Richard Peirce paid for the command of the *Earl of Ashburnham*, the maritime historian, Jean Sutton, estimates it to have been in the region of £5,000.[22] This was a considerable figure, equivalent to almost 0.75 million pounds in today's terms. It is unlikely that Peirce could have raised so much money unaided but he now had a father-in-law who would have been willing to help. With the future looking so promising for the East India Company, this was a wise investment on the part of Thomas Burston, as much as it was an act of paternal generosity. No doubt, Richard Peirce thought so, too.

Having chosen his successor and agreed terms, Thomas Pearce could now retire to his estate in Essex. It only remained for the

principal managing owner of the *Earl of Ashburnham* to inform the
Court of Directors that his ship had a new commander. John Durand
will have done so promptly, confident that the Directors would not
object. Company regulations stipulated that Commanders must be
over twenty-five years of age and have performed at least one voyage to
the East Indies as chief or second mate.[23] They would only need to be
reassured that Richard Peirce had the requisite experience and was old
enough to command. Their approval was required but, in this case, it
was essentially a formality.

For the remainder of 1767 and the first half of 1768, Richard
and Mary Peirce were able to enjoy their time together. Although,
during much of their married life, they would be separated for years at
a time, these first months of domesticity laid the secure foundations on
which their marriage would stand. Then, at the start of July, Richard
Peirce received the news he had been waiting for. The East India
Company published the list of ships for the next season together with
their 'stations'.[24] His name was printed next to the *Earl of Ashburnham*.
Even better, his ship was destined for Coast and China. Everyone knew
this was a profitable route, involving stops at Madras and Whampoa.
It could have been much worse. A voyage to fever-ridden Benkulen, in
Sumatra, would have yielded almost no profit at all.

Although Peirce's appointment had been reported in the press,
formal confirmation had yet to be completed. On 27 July he would
have to attend at East India House.[25] There, he was informed that the
Directors judged him 'fitly qualified to command' and had approved
his appointment as commander of the *Earl of Ashburnham*. Next, he
and six other captains were called into the Court where, before the
assembled Directors, they were required to take the Oath. As was
customary, they had to promise not to trade to or from India without
the Company's licence. In other words, they would only sail to ports
that they had been instructed to visit and they would not engage in
private trade that exceeded their allowance or included prohibited
items. It was a solemn promise but everyone knew that enforcing it
was difficult. The Chairman 'very particularly cautioned them against
suffering any illicit trade being put on board their respective ships' but
Richard Peirce probably remembered that, only six months previously,

his predecessor had been reprimanded for carrying excess iron. Thomas Pearce had claimed not to have realised his mistake and had got away with no more than a ticking off.

Richard Peirce must have felt relieved to have completed this ritual. The ceremony was the official confirmation that he had achieved his ambition. He was now legally the commander of an East Indiaman. To this status, he soon added another. At the end of the summer, Mary Peirce gave birth to their first child and Richard Peirce became a father. The child was a boy and, as firstborn, he, too, was christened Richard.[26] As the son of an East India Company captain, young Richard's prospects looked good. He would grow up in a family that was well provided for and, in due course, it was expected, he would follow his father's footsteps and find employment within that wider family, the East India Company.

While his son was still only a few weeks old, Richard Peirce turned his attention again to his professional responsibilities. His ship would sail in less than six months and preparations had to begin. Most pressing was the appointment of the crew. In selecting the officers who would serve under him, Peirce probably sought the advice of John Durand. He may also have spoken to the retiring Captain. He already understood the value of having experienced and dependable subordinates who could offer support and good counsel. He had watched Captains Newton, Marter and Barkley, all of whom had grown into the role of commander, before his eyes.

The senior officers who were appointed to the *Earl of Ashburnham* all had appropriate experience. Second mate, John Nail, had already completed two voyages on the *Ashburnham*, beginning his career as Captain Pearce's personal servant. No doubt he came with a good recommendation. The third mate, Rufus Ford, had served in the Royal Navy and was a veteran of the 'Straits trade' before completing two voyages on East Indiamen. The chief mate was Edward Back. Their combined knowledge would be invaluable.

On the *Pacific*, Captain Barkley had been unable to appoint more than four officers. Now that the East India Company's fortunes had revived, there was no shortage of candidates. Richard Peirce was in the enviable position of being able to appoint a fifth and sixth officer as well as five midshipmen. These were all personal appointments and the midshipmen, at least, paid for the privilege. Before his ship had even set sail, Richard Peirce had begun to profit from her.

Throughout the last quarter of 1768, work continued to prepare the *Earl of Ashburnham* for her next voyage. On 26 October, she was warped out of Greenland Dock onto the River.[27] A few days later, Edward Back and Rufus Ford went on board to supervise the loading of the ship. Every week or so, they would alternate with the second and fourth mates. As usual the kentledge, water butts and stores were stowed first. There was spare cordage for the boatswain, spare canvas for the sailmaker, wood for the carpenter, barrels of tar for the caulker and coals for the galley and armourer's forge. Everything that might be needed to repair and maintain the ship had to be carried. By 10 of November, the *Earl of Ashburnham* was ready to move downstream to Gravesend. Now the fifth and sixth mates put in an appearance. As the personal appointments of Richard Peirce, perhaps their selection had taken a little longer and delayed their start.

With the help of the midshipmen, the quartermasters began to stow the private trade. The ship's log records that among the captain's 'indulgence' were thirty-six anchors, other iron work and a quantity of lead. On Saturday 3 December, Captain Peirce went on board his ship for the first time. This was the day his anchors were being loaded so he may have wanted to check their safe arrival. Apart from this, there was no need for him to visit his ship. His officers were in charge and sent regular reports that preparations were proceeding smoothly. In any case, the East India Company was keeping an eye on things, too. Company inspectors or 'waiters' checked that there was enough food for a voyage of seven months and that John Durand and the owners had fulfilled their other obligations. For example, they were required to provide a chest of cutlasses, muskets and other small arms, in case their ship came under attack. In such an event, even the passengers could be called upon to defend her.[28]

As the year came to an end, the Company's soldiers began to embark. There would be more than fifty of them, living below decks for the next six months. At around the same time the livestock was also brought aboard. The living conditions for the animals would be only slightly worse than those of the soldiers, with sheep confined in the longboat and the poultry in hencoops on the poop deck. The racket from the hens was a constant irritation, particularly for passengers living in the roundhouse below.[29] However, on this outward voyage, the *Earl of Ashburnham* would not be carrying many passengers. Only a couple of supercargoes would sit at the Captain's table.

On 29 December 1768, Captain Peirce and several of his fellow commanders paid a last visit to Leadenhall Street.[30] At East India House, they received their final instructions and took formal leave of the Court of Directors. Officially, they were now on their way. In a day or two, *Earl of Ashburnham* would drop downstream to the Hope. Then Richard Peirce would have to say goodbye to Mary and his infant son. It would be the first of many painful partings.

9

Madras Roads to Malacca Straits

The *Earl of Ashburnham* kept well over to the French side of the English Channel as she laboured against a stiff gale. Three days earlier, she had left the Downs in company with two other Indiamen, the *Hampshire* and the *Earl of Lincoln*. Already those ships were lost from view. Perhaps they had chosen a different course but Captain Peirce was happy with his. Cape Barfleur and Cape La Hogue were in his wake and he was now in sight of Finisterre. The worst of the storm seemed to be over but a mountainous swell had taken its place.

Although his ship rolled alarmingly, Captain Peirce was not unduly worried, even when a large sea carried away the jib boom. He had encountered conditions like these before and he was confident that the *Ashburnham* was fundamentally sound. He gave the order for the carpenter to make a replacement boom. The carpenter, Willard Dickinson, was a man that Richard Peirce would come to know well. Uniquely, he would serve under Peirce for three voyages.

Eventually, with the swell subsiding and the weather improving, the *Earl of Ashburnham* picked up speed and sailed south. By 29 January 1769, the island of Madeira was in view. This was a matter of great satisfaction for Peirce. Throughout the previous fortnight, he had worked hard to calculate their exact position. He could be confident about their latitude but estimating longitude was more problematic. The appearance of Madeira confirmed that his calculations had been correct. With scarcely concealed pride, he wrote in the log, 'My acct agrees so well I shall have no occation (*sic*) to correct my long't by Madeira.'[1]

This is the first hint of a theme that runs throughout Richard Peirce's journal entries. He understood the importance of accurate navigation and it was always a matter of personal pride to calculate his position correctly. Like all captains, he would compare his estimate of his position with that of other commanders, when the paths of their respective ships crossed. More often than not, there was a difference of opinion. The log of the *Ashburnham* records some of these encounters but always manages to imply that it is the other commander who has miscalculated.

On 16 March, speaking slowly and enunciating clearly, Peirce communicated via speaking trumpet with Capt Davison of the *Glatton*. He 'makes his observations 18°00' W Long't of London. If he is right we must be 7°12' to the West. This can only be known by our soundings at Hope'. Two days later he encountered the *Cruttenden*, another Indiaman: 'Capt Baker makes us 11°00' East of Tenereef but by the variation I am certain we are much more to the Westward.'

Richard Peirce's confidence was not just a matter of wishful thinking. He used all the techniques available to him. Several times in March and April, he 'lowered down the jolley boat to try the current'. Finding it flowing west-southwest, he factored this drift into his calculations. Another time, he sounded the sea floor and found it to be green mud mixed with sand. What conclusion he drew from this is not recorded but it was traditionally accepted that, in certain places, the content of the seabed could give a rough indication of your whereabouts. Despite his best efforts, even Peirce had to admit he sometimes got it wrong. With so many variables to contend with, there was still a large element of chance. On 2 March, he conceded 'I am 6 miles to southward of my account these 24 hours'. In the vastness of the ocean, being out by six miles does not seem like much, but Peirce knew that, near a coastline and at night, such a mistake could be fatal. He would be painfully reminded of this in 1786.

When not preoccupied with navigation, Richard Peirce concerned himself with the management of the vessel and the welfare of its crew. It seemed to be a contented ship. The sailors gave no trouble, the officers were respected and everyone remained well: 'Our people continue very healthy and not one sick on board. The wheat being all expended give them every morning boild oatmeal with their drams of sugar for breakfast.' The health of his crew mattered. The living areas below decks were fumigated to drive out the noxious vapours and stinks that were thought to cause illness: 'Smoak'd with heated pitch

and burn'd tobacco to preserve the people's health.' Although similar
precautions were taken on all ships, you still get a sense that Peirce
genuinely cared about the men under his command.

Even the weather was benign. In April, the fore-topmast
cracked and had to be lowered so that Willard Dickinson could repair
it. It doesn't seem to have impeded their progress much. That month
they rounded the Cape of Good Hope and turned up the Madagascar
channel. On 20 April, they caught sight of a ship ahead and identified
her as the *Earl of Lincoln*. They hadn't seen her for months but, from
her course, Peirce inferred that she had seen land ahead. Next day, they
saw it too. This meant they were nearing the Comoro islands.

Given that his crew continued to show no signs of scurvy,
Richard Peirce was disinclined to linger. He wanted to press on quickly
to Madras and arrive ahead of as many other Indiamen as possible.
Edward Back and John Nail were probably of a similar mind. They
were only too aware that a late arrival could affect the value of their
private trade.

While the *Earl of Ashburnham* worked herself carefully into
Johanna Bay, the ship's boats were sent ashore in search of livestock. In
their absence, the Indiaman was surrounded by dozens of canoes from
which the locals attempted to sell eggs, fish and a tempting variety of
fruits – pineapples, bananas, oranges and guavas.[2] By next day, the
Ashburnham's boats had returned, laden with bullocks. They would
provide enough fresh meat to see them to Madras. After stopping for
less than two days, Captain Peirce gave the order, on 30 April, to weigh
and make sail.

Eight days later they recrossed the equator. The weather
continued to be fine and, propelled by gentle breezes, they steered out
across the Arabian Sea. Whispering and groaning under her cloud of
canvas, the *Ashburnham's* bow shouldered aside the sparkling water.
At times like this, life on an Indiaman seemed more idyllic than any
other. By the 19th May, they had caught up with the *Triton*. She, too,
was bound for Madras and China but had set off three weeks before
Ashburnham. On his quarterdeck, Peirce must have felt satisfaction
in having overtaken her. It was a vindication of how he managed his
ship and of his navigational skills. He couldn't resist casting doubt on

Captain Elphinstone's calculation of their latitude: 'If he is right we must have had a strong northerly current which is uncommon.'

A week later, they drew level with the *Nottingham*, another Indiamen that had sailed from England before them. *Nottingham* was handicapped by broken topgallant masts and was soon trailing in their wake. On 27 May, the mountains of Ceylon began to creep above the horizon. Soon they could identify those familiar landmarks, the Elephant, Friars Hood and Sugar Loaf Hill. Madras was now only a few days away. For the first time, Richard Peirce would be arriving there in the uniform of an East India Company commander and would be greeted with all the ceremony and deference due to his rank. He wanted to make a good impression and that applied to his ship, too. The gunner was set to painting the 'muzels' of the guns, while sailors replaced or repaired any damaged sails. Then, on the last day of May 1769, in fair weather, the *Earl of Ashburnham* dropped anchor in Madras Roads. The voyage had taken only nineteen weeks and had gone almost without a hitch.

For the next seven weeks, Richard Peirce was able to enjoy Madras society. As captain of an East Indiaman he could expect to be invited to various social gatherings, including dinner with the current

Fort St George, Madras by J. van Ryne
© *National Maritime Museum, Greenwich, London*

Governor, Charles Bourchier. Where he stayed during this time is not known. He may have been a guest in the house of someone he had met on a previous visit, he may have found lodgings in the Fort or, more likely, in the town, nearby. At social functions, in the evenings, Peirce will have quickly sensed that the residents were again in a somewhat jittery state. The previous November, Madras had been threatened with attack. This time, the aggressor was not the French but Hyder Ali, Sultan of Mysore. His reputation as an effective military commander was already widespread and, after several setbacks, the East India Company had learned to take the threat seriously. A mere two months before the arrival of the *Earl of Ashburnham*, they had negotiated an end to hostilities. Hyder Ali had withdrawn his army but he remained a force to be reckoned with. Although Madras was no longer in immediate danger, a sense of insecurity lingered. Perhaps, this added a frisson to the socialising in the evenings.

During the day, there was Company business to be dealt with and, of course, private trade. The latter would necessitate employing a *dubash* to act as translator and help negotiate terms with local merchants. From his previous voyages, Peirce had already gained valuable experience of trading in India but, this time, the stakes were much higher. His privilege in private trade had increased spectacularly. On the *Pacific*, as second officer, he was allowed four tons. Now, as captain, his entitlement rose to more than fifty tons. It was this generous weight allowance that had enabled him to bring the thirty-six anchors that he now hoped to sell.

While Richard Peirce was dealing with affairs on land, the crew continued to labour on board the *Earl of Ashburnham*, riding at anchor in Madras Roads. The Company's ragbag contingent of recruits, plus its cargo of copper and other goods, had to be sent ashore through the perilous surf. Then, when the hold was clear, dozens of bales of cotton were lowered into it. Other crew members were kept busy overhauling the rigging, mending sails and generally preparing the ship for the next leg of her voyage. By the third week of July, the ship was ready to depart. So was the *Triton*, the *Nottingham*, the *Earl of Lincoln* and a fourth Indiaman, the *Plassey*. On Wednesday 19 July, all five ships weighed anchor and set off together. Their next destination was China.

When Richard Peirce had sailed to China on the *Horsenden*, they had gone there direct, without first stopping in India. This had enabled Captain Marter to set a southerly course which had taken them through the Sunda Straits between Sumatra and Java. Given that Madras lies in a higher latitude, that route would not be appropriate this time. Instead, the five East Indiamen would sail across the Bay of Bengal to the Nicobar Islands and then pick their way southeast, through the Straits of Malacca, between Sumatra and the Malay peninsula.

In his classic work, *Trade in the Eastern Seas*, C. Northcote Parkinson wrote disparagingly of the navigational skills of East India Company commanders.[3] Unlike ships of the Royal Navy, East Indiamen stuck to well-beaten tracks, sailing at times when they could count on favourable winds. Its commanders, he argued, had few actual skills but, instead, drew on the accumulated knowledge of their colleagues, shared over dinner or at the Jerusalem Coffee House. While there is some justification for this view, it is not the whole story.

The route that Captain Peirce was about to take was potentially hazardous and he had no personal experience of it. Nevertheless, he was not completely in the dark. East India Company ships had sailed these waters for years and there was much collective wisdom to be drawn on. He would have been equipped with maps, elevations and the commentary of captains who had passed that way before. Nevertheless, there was no justification for complacency. Maps could be inaccurate and features that previous mariners had described were often in the wrong place. There was a need to improve the quality of information; to move from anecdotal wisdom to systematic, scientific recording of coastlines, currents, shoals and weather patterns. Richard Peirce understood this and wanted to play a part.

A week after leaving Madras, the northernmost of the Nicobar Islands was in view. Passing to the east of them, it took only another twelve hours before they could see Pulo Rondo. This small island marked the northwest tip of Sumatra. The five Indiamen now turned east and followed its northern coast as far as Diamond Point. After this, the sea between Sumatra and the Malay shore would start to narrow and become the Malacca Straits. Although the southwest monsoon was at its height, the area was subject to calms. There were also strong currents which could be dangerous, particularly if the wind dropped. Received wisdom was that it was sensible to carry some extra anchors with ten-inch cables. There was good anchoring along the Sumatran side and the additional anchors would help a becalmed ship resist the current. It had been known for ill-prepared ships to be carried from Diamond Point almost the whole way back to Pulo Rondo.[4]

With *Nottingham* leading the way and *Earl of Lincoln* bringing up the rear, the *Ashburnham* sailed southeast along the Sumatran coast. On 29 July, two days after leaving Diamond Point, Pulo Perah was in view. Its steep, forested slopes, enabled this small island to be seen from a considerable distance. It was a reassuring sight. Pulo Perah marked the entrance to the Straits of Malacca.[5]

Once in the Straits, the three ships moved closer to the Malay shore. In his log, Peirce commented on the appearance of Pulo Dinding. Its hills and low shoreline gave the impression of three islands instead of one. On 1 August, they passed the cluster of small islands known as the Sambelans and, a day later, could identify the Long and Round Arroes. These two remarkable rocks, ringed with breakers, were a reminder to be cautious. In sailing round them, Peirce knew he must take care not to stray too close to the Malay shore. As long ago as 1732, predecessors like Captain Tully had warned of a dangerous shoal: 'It may be considered the most dangerous in the straits and should not be approached nearer than 14 or 15 fathoms.'[6] The following morning, taking advantage of the high tide, they skirted this potential hazard. From his quarterdeck, Captain Peirce recorded the view on paper. Experience had taught him the importance of identifying landmarks correctly and he wanted accurate, relief drawings of the islands that would help him and other commanders when they passed this way, in future. By the end of 3 August, as the light faded, they dropped anchor in sight of Parcelar Hill. They were close to the mainland now but, with twenty fathoms of water under them, they could pass the night safely. Next morning, before they sailed south again on another rising tide, Peirce took time to sketch Parcelar Hill's distinctive profile. Later, these drawings would impress the hydrographer, Alexander Dalrymple, and, in 1779, he would publish them as part of a series of plates illustrating the Strait of Malacca.[7] Meanwhile, off the port bow, another significant landmark soon came into view. Cape Rachado, the 'broken cape' named by the Portuguese, was now distinguished by the lighthouse that the Dutch had built many years before. Over the next few days, a pattern was established. The ships would sail on a flood tide but, once it began to ebb, they would drop anchor and wait for it to turn again. This made for slow progress but these were dangerous waters and safety was paramount. Perhaps, Richard Peirce was more cautious than his fellow commanders. As the *Earl of Ashburnham* crept passed Malacca Fort and skirted the Water Islands, the other Indiamen seemed to pull ahead. Soon, they were on their own.

Between 10 and 15 August, the shoreline to the east was dominated by Mount Formosa. Then on the afternoon of the 15th, Peirce could see the island of Pulo Pisang dead ahead. They were now approaching the end of the Malacca Straits and about to enter its trickiest section. There were many small islands to negotiate before they could round Romania Point at the tip of the Malayan peninsula. Only then could they set a course northeast for China.

It took a further five days to complete this stage. On the 19th and 20th, as they felt their way past Barn Island and the smaller Rabbit and Coney Islands, Richard Peirce continued to sketch furiously. He captured Pedro Branco, the memorable Point Cockup, the Bintang Hills and the Strait of Sincapore (*sic*) itself. All this would subsequently find its way into another of Dalrymple's publications, *The Strait of Sincapore*.[8] On 21 August, as Romania Point and Singapore fell away astern, a new set of islands came into view. These were Pulo Auro and Pulo Tioman. Once they, too, had been passed, the ships would be in open water at last. The next waymark to look out for would be Pulo Condore. It was 125 leagues away (375 nautical miles) and sighting would help fix their position and confirm that they were still on course.

With its high, tree-covered mountains, Pulo Condore ought to be visible from a distance of at least forty miles. Nevertheless, finding it was not always straightforward. There were strong easterly currents which could push ships off course. The benign weather with which they had been blessed for so long, briefly deserted them. There were sharp squalls and electric storms. By 28 August, Peirce thought they should be getting close to Pulo Condore. With lightning flashing around his ship, he wrote in the journal: 'Shortened sail in the night & kept a good lookout for Condore but did not see it. By our soundings we are to the eastward of it and if Herbert's Chart is good have a strong easterly current.'

Next day, they looked for the island of Sapata instead. Named by the Portuguese after its shoe-shaped mountain, Sapata should have been easy to identify but it, too, proved elusive. By now Richard Peirce was beginning to doubt the accuracy of Mr Herbert's charts. 'Have lookout for Island Sapata but saw nothing of it. By Mr Herbert's chart we are far to ye W'ward of it but our own soundings off Condore ascertain to us our being to ye E'ward.' Despite his irritation with Mr Herbert, Peirce was soon reassured that he was on the right track. On 1 September, they caught up with the *Earl of Lincoln* and another Indiaman, *Havannah*, sailing in the same direction. Now they could sail in company and arrive in Canton together in a few days time.

10
Entertaining the Hoppo

On Saturday 9 September, they could see St John's Island. This was a good sign. The passage from here to Macao was known to be free of hidden dangers.[9] Keeping together, the three ships made steady progress. By the 14th, they were passing the Grand Ladrone and were only about twenty miles from Macao. At this point the wind died completely and *Earl of Ashburnham* came to a stand still. Their destination was tantalisingly close and Captain Peirce was impatient to reach it. He ordered the longboat to be lowered and to row ahead, carrying the kedge anchor. Once the cable, which attached the anchor to his ship, had been fully paid out, the longboat crew would lower the kedge to the sea-bed. Then, with her seamen labouring at the capstan, *Ashburnham* could be winched closer to where the anchor lay. At that point, the kedge would be raised and the process would begin again. Pulling or warping a ship in this way was hard work and forward momentum was slow but it was better than lying idle. For twelve hours, from noon to midnight, the crew of *Ashburnham* sweated at the task.

At last, a breeze got up and the three east indiamen sailed into Macao Roads. An official Chinese river-pilot now came on board. He was licensed by the Chinese authorities to guide the *Earl of Ashburnham* up the Pearl River to Whampoa. But first he was required to gather information about the ship and her cargo. Only ships intending to trade would be allowed to proceed. The terms of entry and of trade were tightly controlled. From now on, Captain Peirce knew that he and his ship would be under close scrutiny.

It is unlikely that the pilot spoke much English but he will have known the names of essential ropes and sails and have been able to give basic commands. These would then be relayed to the crew by Captain Peirce or one of his officers. Throughout the 16th, *Earl of Ashburnham* spent the day warping across Macao Road until her pilot was satisfied she was in the correct starting place for the Bogue. The Bogue or Bocca Tigris was the point of entry to the Pearl River and also the location of a customs station. Here, two Chinese customs officers would board the *Ashburnham*. They would stay with her until Whampoa, to ensure that none of her cargo was unloaded illegally. They would also check the accuracy of the information provided by the pilot. Only then could the pilot obtain the official permit or 'chop', that allowed them to enter the river. After that progress was quick.

Next day, on a flowing tide, the *Earl of Ashburnham* was guided over both sand bars and, before darkness fell, had come to in Whampoa Roads, next to Danes Island. The pilot and customs officials now departed but the ship remained under supervision. While she lay at anchor, a guard boat was chained to her stern. These guardboats contained Chinese security men, sometimes known as 'longside mandarins'. Their function was to prevent any smuggling of goods onto or off the east indiaman.

The next day, a boat carrying the official 'linguist' came alongside. This person would act as translator and would carry messages between Captain Peirce and the Chinese authorities. He would also keep track of the import and export duties, as well as customs fees incurred by Captain Peirce's ship. Before that, he would organise the formal visit by the Hoppo to measure the ship. Although it scarcely gets a mention in most ships' logs, the visit of the Hoppo was a major event, involving strict protocol and a great deal of ceremony. When he was last at Whampoa, seven years previously, Richard Peirce had been mainly a spectator. This time, as captain, he would be cast in a major role.

While preparations to welcome the Hoppo were under way, other work had to proceed. On Friday 22 September two chop boats arrived. These were the lighters that would convey the cargo to the Company's factory at Canton. All that day, they were loaded with cotton and, by Tuesday, they had returned for more. Every journey to Canton took the chop boats past three toll houses. At each one, the cargo was checked and the permit was marked or 'chopped'. On arrival at Canton, the permit would be handed in to the security merchant. Later, in January, when the ship would be ready to leave, the supercargo would have to ensure that all these tolls had been paid. Only then would the Hoppo issue the Grand Chop that allowed the *Earl of Ashburnham* to sail for home.

Although all cargo had to be carried in chop boats, which incurred tolls, the Chinese agreed to make an exception for supercargoes, captains and their senior officers. The Hoppo understood that they would need to travel back and forth on a regular basis, to check that the loading and unloading was going smoothly. Provided they flew the Company's flag, their service boats would not have to stop at the tollhouses.[10] On 27 September, Peirce took advantage of this arrangement to send 'the longboat to town with the Company's treasure, in the care of Mr Ford'. This was quite a responsibility for the third mate. The Company's silver would pay for the tea they hoped to buy. It was essential that the money arrived safely at the factory.

Soon unloading was in full swing. Redwood, lead, more cotton and, of course, private trade were all sent by chop boat to Canton. Then, on Monday 2 October, the Hoppo appeared. The Company's ships were alerted to his imminent arrival by the loud sounding of a gong. It was on the deck of a large Chinese vessel, escorted by many sampans, that was approaching slowly. This was the cue to begin the reception. First *Earl of Ashburnham* and other ships nearby fired their guns in salute. Then as the Hoppo prepared to come aboard, the ship's band struck up. Like the rest of *Ashburnham's* crew, they were dressed smartly. The officers in their best uniforms.

The Hoppo, himself, was an imposing sight. Wearing a ceremonial blue robe and with an impressively large pearl in his hat, he was attended by the linguist, various officials and the Chinese security merchant from the Co-Hong.[11] Before the measuring of the *Ashburnham* could begin, Captain Peirce delivered a formal speech of welcome. This was duly translated into Chinese and the Hoppo made a speech in reply. Then refreshments were offered; such things as candied

The Hoppo, Puankhequa

fruit or sweetmeats and, of course, red wine. The log of the *Earl of Ashburnham* omits to tell us anything of this but it was not unusual for the ceremony to include some form of entertainment.[12] Some of the crew might be called upon to perform a short theatrical piece or sing a chorus or two. Whether these were polished performances or not we can only guess but they seem to have been part of a fairly well-established ritual.

When this part of the proceedings was complete, the Hoppo mounted a platform, specially constructed for him by the ship's carpenter. From there he could observe the measuring of the ship. Using bamboo canes cut to a precise length or a cord marked at regular intervals, his officials measured the ship for length and breadth at two fixed points. The measurements were taken at head height so as not to be impeded by the animal pens or anything else cluttering the deck. As they were taken, each measurement was called out and written down in Chinese.

Now the focus turned to the security merchant. In front of everyone, he was required to sign a bond, presented to him by the Hoppo. In this, he accepted responsibility for the *Earl of Ashburnham* and her crew. He agreed to ensure that the port fees and import and export duties were collected. If any of *Ashburnham's* men became unruly or committed crimes ashore, the Chinese security merchant would be called to account. It was definitely in his interests to avoid complications of any kind. As official security merchant, he had exclusive rights to the cargo of the *Ashburnham* but, if the Hoppo learned there had been trouble, his monopoly could be taken from him.

Once this official business was out of the way, and with his humour improved by a glass or two of wine, the Hoppo asked to be shown the 'sing-songs'. This had been anticipated so a selection of musical boxes, mirrors and other luxury items were now brought on deck for the Hoppo to inspect. If some curiosity caught the Hoppo's eye, he would indicate to the Security Merchant that he would like it as a present. It was impossible to refuse and the unfortunate merchant had no choice but to buy it for him. Happy with his present, the Hoppo then returned to his own ship. But his work was not yet done. There were other East Indiamen to visit. The *Earl of Lincoln* and the *Havannah* had arrived with the *Earl of Ashburnham* and there were possibly Dutch, French or ships of other nationalities as well. With all the ceremonials, not to mention the red wine, it was tiring work.

A few days after the Hoppo's visit, a boat came alongside to deliver a present from the Emperor. Earlier in the century, these presents had been quite substantial but, now so many European ships were visiting, the presents had diminished in value. *Ashburnham* would probably receive a few sacks of wheat flour and some samshu liquor. If they were lucky, there might also be a cow. About this time, Captain Peirce received another visit from the linguist. He provided a translation of the official measurements of the ship and a table of calculations. The port fee was arrived at by multiplying the length by the breadth of the ship and dividing the result by ten. Various adjustments were made to the fee. To show his support for the trade, the Emperor reduced it by 20%. Then commission was added for the Hoppo and other officials. Finally, an enormous amount was added for a present to the Emperor. This was usually greater than the original sum. The total, priced in silver taels, was then presented to Captain Peirce. There was no point in disputing it. The Chinese used the same formula every year and though the price was high, it was not crippling. The Emperor did not want to drive these foreign merchants away so there would still be a healthy profit for the East India Company.

For four months, the *Earl of Ashburnham* would remain at Whampoa. She would have to wait until the New Year and the northeast monsoon, when the winds would be favourable for the homeward voyage. This allowed plenty of time for the crew to relax and for Peirce and his officers to attend to their own affairs. Richard Peirce was quick to follow his third officer to Canton. Although he would return to check on his ship, from time to time, Peirce always went back to Canton the same day. This is where the supercargoes were based and where private trade had to be conducted. It was the best place to be.

By 24 October, the *Earl of Ashburnham's* hold was completely empty. The ship was now light enough for her to be heeled. This meant tilting her over to one side, as far as possible, so her hull could be 'breamed'. The process involved checking the seams and covering them with pitch so she would remain watertight on the homeward voyage. Once this had been done, the ship was ready to receive her new cargo. Throughout November, hundreds of chests of tea were winched aboard. While other ships came and went, the loading of *Ashburnham* continued. The ship's journal records 'Midshipmen and quartermasters employ'd in the hold. People about the needfull'. It was all going smoothly. Then, four days before Christmas, the first mate disappeared.

Edward Back had gone sailing in the jolly boat with three sailors and one of the young guinea pigs. They had not been seen since. It was unlikely that the first mate would have run but it was possible the sailors might have overpowered him. A more plausible explanation was that they had had an accident. Peirce sent out search parties: 'Sent our boats in search of the jollyboat but could hear nothing of her. Imagine she is overset and they are drown'd.' For several days, the search was maintained. Then on 28 December 1769, the body of a boy was found floating nearby. It was the guinea pig. Two days later, the corpses of Edward Back and one of the sailors were recovered also. Although the crew were staying on Danes Island, the bodies of their deceased shipmates were sent to French Island for burial 'with the usual respect shew'd them'.

The death of Edward Back left Captain Peirce without a first officer. As was customary, he promoted his second officer, John Nail, to fill the vacancy. If Rufus Ford thought that he too would be promoted, he was disappointed. Instead, a new man, Edward Atkinson, was taken on as second mate. He had been third mate on the *Devonshire* and must have come highly recommended.[13] By now the *Earl of Ashburnham* was ready to sail. Her hold was filled with tea, the selling and buying of private trade was almost complete and the monsoon winds were now blowing steadily in the right direction. The security merchant was satisfied that the port fee and all the chop boat tolls had been paid, a river pilot was taken on and the Grand Chop was delivered. It was time to go.

While Captain Peirce and the supercargoes completed their affairs in Canton, the *Earl of Ashburnham* weighed anchor. Dropping downriver, past Danes Island, she almost immediately ran aground. It was not an auspicious start. At high tide, they managed to get her off and clear of the first sand bar. By the evening they could see the pagoda that told them they were close to the second bar. At this point, they wisely dropped anchor to wait for the flood tide. Next day, Thursday 4 January 1770, they set off again. The *Ashburnham*, laden with cargo, was sitting low in the water, but her river-pilot seems to have miscalculated. Even before they reached the second bar, they had got stuck again. By now John Nail must have been feeling uncomfortable. What would Captain Peirce do if his ship had been damaged, in his absence. Fortunately, all was well and, once the tide was at its height, *Ashburnham* floated free. On Friday they passed the second bar in four fathoms of water.

While he waited for the supercargoes and Captain Peirce to return with the last of the private trade, John Nail sent a boat over to the *Devonshire*, anchored nearby. It contained a quantity of beef and pork. Perhaps it was a gesture of thanks to Captain Hore for his kindness in allowing Edward Atkinson to join the *Ashburnham*. Finally, on the 8th, the longboat appeared. In it were Captain Peirce and two of the supercargoes. They were greeted with a salute of eleven guns. A similar reception signalled the arrival of the third supercargo, next day. All that remained was for the Purser to bring the box containing the Company's dispatches from Canton. Once he was aboard, they could go. The *Earl of Lincoln*, the *Havannah* and the *Speke* had already departed.

On 11 January, *Earl of Ashburnham* passed through the Bogue and out of the Pearl River. She dropped her pilot near the Grand Ladrone and made sail for the open sea. Ahead of her lay the Macclesfield bank. This enormous shoal was first discovered by the Indiaman, *Macclesfield*, in 1701 but its exact dimensions were still unclear.[14] Company ships returning from China were directed to take soundings as they approached it. Captain Peirce took these instructions seriously and followed them. The log recorded, 'Brought to and sounded on the Western edge of Macclesfield shoal 42 fathoms. By my account we should have been on the Eastern Part as laid down by Mr Herbert.'

Having fulfilled this duty, Peirce pressed on. Now he was sailing for the Sunda Straits, between Java and Sumatra. This was the quickest way home and the route that *Horsenden* had taken. He could look out for familiar landmarks like Monopin Hill and Lucepara. Passing through the Straits on 29 January, they anchored near Prince's Island. Close by they could see another East Indiaman, clearly in distress. She was the *Henrietta* and had run aground. Richard Peirce was quick to offer assistance. 'Sent longboat with the kedge anchor and two hawsers also the pinnace and all the assistance possible to get her off.' It seems they were successful. The delay also provided an opportunity for the longboat to fetch more water. Then on 3 February, *Earl of Ashburnham* weighed anchor and sailed from Java Head.

En route, Richard Peirce expected to see Christmas Island. Mr Herbert had declared it was only a short distance from Java Head but there was no sign of it. Once again Peirce could not prevent himself from discrediting his bete noir: 'According to Mr Herbert who makes Christmas Island to lie on the Merid of Java Head it ought to bear of us 15 miles only. In the Lincoln 1768 they made Christmas Island to lie 47 miles West of Java Head which if right accounts for us not seeing the island.' What is interesting about this is not so much the inevitable point scoring against Mr Herbert but the fact that Peirce was familiar with the recent findings of the *Lincoln*. Had he discussed this with her captain or examined her journal at East India House? Had this information appeared in a newspaper or pamphlet? It is hardly surprising that Captains would be hungry for the latest data but how Peirce learned of this remains a mystery.

The journey home was as uneventful as the outward voyage. Near the Cape of Good Hope they caught up with the *Osterley*. In May, they stopped for ten days at St Helena. Throughout June and much of July, the two ships kept eachother company. On 21 July, they spotted Lands End and before the end of the first week of August, *Earl of Ashburnham* had tied up in Deptford. Richard Peirce had been away for only seventeen months. By the standards of the time, he had made a rapid return. But, in his absence, things had changed dramatically at home. The baby that he had left behind had now become a toddler. More surprisingly, he discovered there was a second baby. While he had been away, Mary had given birth to a daughter. Richard Peirce was now the father of two children.

11
Diseases, Deserters & Deceivers

The birth of Elizabeth may have come as a surprise to her father but it also presents his biographers with a puzzle. When was she conceived? Mary Peirce gave birth to young Richard sometime between July and September 1768 but, in January 1769, her husband set sail for China. It follows that Mary must have become pregnant with Elizabeth only a matter of months after the birth of her first child. If Elizabeth was conceived at the start of January 1769, she would have been born in September of that year. So far, no record of her baptism has come to light.

Nevertheless, we can be confident that Elizabeth Peirce was born in 1769. After her death, the newspapers would assert that she was the eldest daughter. One newspaper reported her age as sixteen.[1] The inscription on her mourning ring said she was seventeen.[2] The only conclusion we can draw is that, on his return to England, Richard Peirce found his wife to be nursing a four-month-old baby girl.

Another change had occurred while he had been away. Thomas Burston had been appointed Collector of Excise for Surrey and was now living in Kingston-upon-Thames.[3] Doubtless, Mary and her children had moved there, too. This will have been good news for Richard. Kingston was much closer to London and he would have to spend less time away from home. However, he would have been reluctant for his family to live under the roof of his father-in-law for much longer. It was important to find a place of their own and the sensible thing was to rent a house nearby.

Within a short time, a house was found in Norbiton.[4] It was quite substantial and provided an appropriate residence for one of the East India Company's rising stars. Mrs Peirce could now be mistress of her own home and attempt to join the polite society of Kingston and its environs. Although her husband was associated with trade, looked down on by the landed aristocracy, his status and increasing wealth should earn him a prominent place within the growing middle class. However humble his origins, Mary Peirce hoped her husband would become, like her own father, a man of influence and importance.

The business of setting up home with his growing family may have been Richard Peirce's main preoccupation during those first weeks back in England but his responsibility for the *Ashburnham* had not finished yet. Throughout August, her cargo was removed and sent by Company hoy to Company warehouse. So many ships had returned from China that year that soon these warehouses would be groaning with tea. Somewhere, amongst it all, were the tea chests labelled as the private trade of Captain Peirce. Given the amount of tea coming onto the market, would they still sell? If he worried about this, Richard Peirce had, at least, the consolation of his pay. Including the time for unloading the *Earl of Ashburnham*, his service had been calculated as twenty months. As Captain, he now earned £10 a month. At the end of September, the Company paid him £200.[5] He could manage on this for the time being.

Although to all appearances, the economic future of the East India Company still looked rosy, Peirce soon learned that, in his absence, there had been a serious wobble. In May 1769, while he was in Madras, word had finally reached England of the conflict with Hyder Ali, Nawab of Mysore.[6] Anxiety had been further heightened by the news that a French fleet had arrived at Mauritius. The prospect of war in the region had returned and the effect on the Company's share price was immediate. The bubble, which had been created by the heady optimism following the *diwani*, now burst. Within a month, the share price had fallen to £230, a plunge of 16%.[7] A great many wealthy investors had had their fingers badly burnt.

By September 1770, the market had recovered its composure and prices had begun to rally but, in Peirce's lifetime, they would never reach such heights again. Although the threat from Hyder Ali had been contained, other bad news from India was now emerging. Shortly after the *Earl of Ashburnham* had left Madras for Canton, the monsoon rains had failed to arrive. For six months, no rain had fallen in Bengal. The effect of this drought on the rice harvest was easy to predict. Rice would soon be in short supply. Faced with this prospect, the East India Company had begun to buy up large quantities of rice to consolidate its own reserves. Inevitably, this pushed the cost of rice ever higher and, by June 1770, the price had increased forty-fold. Having cornered the market in this way, some East India Company servants exploited the situation to make their fortunes. The impact on the indigenous population, however, was disastrous. Famine broke out across Bengal. There were scenes of unparalleled suffering, with hundreds dying openly in the streets of Calcutta. It is difficult to calculate its true extent but, at the time, Warren Hastings estimated that ten million Bengalis had starved to death. Modern historians have revised this figure downwards but it still stands at well over one million deaths.[8] The effect on the region was devastating.

Once news of this human disaster began to trickle back to England, the reaction of the public was one of outrage. The East India Company found itself castigated in the press for its part in the disaster. In the eyes of many, this was yet another example of the rapacious greed and inhumanity of its employees in India. They seemed more concerned with personal profit than in relieving the suffering of their fellow human beings. Whether or not the Company and its servants took this reproach to heart, it did not deter the Court of Proprietors from boosting the dividend to 12 percent, in September 1770. The following March, they raised it again to 12.5 percent.[9]

Unshaken by events in India, the East India Company dispatched another large fleet in January 1771. It was too soon for the *Earl of Ashburnham* to join it. She would need to spend some months in dry dock, being refitted, before she could go to sea again. Richard Peirce, therefore, set his hopes on a voyage in 1772. In the meantime, he would be able to enjoy a whole year in the company of his wife and children.

In January, Mary Peirce became pregnant for a third time. This child, a second daughter, was born on 24 September 1771. Six weeks later, at Kingston church, she was christened Mary Ann, taking her names from her mother and, perhaps, from her aunt.[10] By then,

Richard Peirce knew that his time at home was coming to an end. In August, the East India Company had published the list of ships they would charter for that season. The number of vessels to be 'taken up' had fallen to twenty-five but among them was to be the *Earl of Ashburnham*. Once again her destinations would be 'Coast and China'.

Towards the end of October, the familiar process of getting the ship ready began once more. At Deptford, rigging and sails were installed and the tedious business of levelling the kentledge was completed. In the middle of November, *Ashburnham* moved to Gravesend to continue receiving her cargo.[11] As usual, some men, including the midshipmen, would work in the hold under the direction of a quartermaster. Others would be employed on various tasks. On 21 November, the *Ashburnham's* log recorded that, 'People employ'd drawing and knotting yarns, making nippers.'[12] One or two officers provided overall supervision. In those early weeks, there was no sign of Captain Peirce and nobody questioned his absence. It was understood that he had his private trade to attend to first.

On 19 November, the first consignment of Company recruits arrived. In theory, they had volunteered for service but many probably did so under the influence of drink. Once aboard, the sober reality of life below decks soon struck home. Two weeks later, eight of them tried to escape. They quickly discovered that, for them, leaving an East Indiaman was not as easy as coming aboard. All eight were apprehended and 'confined'. For the present, they were secure but two would try again before *Ashburnham* set sail.

Captain Peirce went on board his ship, on 9 December. His private trade had already preceded him and, judging from the number of entries in the ship's journal, it would seem that he had invested heavily. Listed among his personal goods are the inevitable anchors, sheets of lead, some jewellery and three cases of saffron. He was probably feeling optimistic. His first voyage in command had gone well and he hoped to repeat its success. He was keen to be on his way. On the 18th he joined two other captains at East India House for the official leaving ceremony but the anticipated order to sail did not follow.[13] While they waited, on Christmas Day, Peirce ordered every man on the *Halsewell* to be served a mug of punch. It was a generous gesture and indicative of his leadership. He understood the importance of gaining the goodwill of his men. A ship always functioned better with a cooperative and well-disposed crew than with one that was cowed and resentful.

Meanwhile, as his own restlessness increased, the patience of *Ashburnham's* owners ran out. On Boxing Day, John Durand wrote to the Directors to express 'the desire of the owners that, as the ship is compleat for the sea, Mr Durand be permitted to sign the Charter party that the ship may be no longer unnecessarily detained.' Richard Peirce was also moved to write to them.[14] He bluntly reminded the Directors that 'the detention of the ship will be attended with great loss to himself and his officers and desiring the Court to grant him relief.' The Directors refused to be hurried and deferred the issue to the following Tuesday. If they thought this delay would be acceptable to John Durand, they had miscalculated. Without waiting for any of the other owners to add their signatures, Durand simply signed the Charter Party by himself. It was a flagrant breach of the rules but Durand did not care. Angered by his effrontery, the Directors recorded that 'Mr Durand had signed tenders for Earl of Ashburnham, Earl of Sandwich & Duke of Grafton without agreement.' In future, they insisted, at least two owners had to put their names to the contract.[15]

Having reasserted their authority, the Directors were willing to release the ship, at last. On 4 January 1772, a Company official came on board to pay the crew their River Pay. Even the recruits understood that this meant the *Ashburnham* was about to sail. That night, two of them tried to escape down the chains at the bow of the ship. Unless they were good swimmers, able to battle the current, they are unlikely to have reached the shore. With succinct detachment, the log recorded them as 'supp'd to be drowned'.

At the Hope, a number of passengers joined the ship. They probably included a supercargo or maybe a newly appointed writer or two. There were also some ladies, perhaps travelling with their husbands or hoping to find one in India. Among these passengers was another individual whose reason for sailing to India was less clear. This was Mr Richard Green. His bearing and style of dress suggested someone of a military background. This impression was reinforced by his servant, a 'common soldier' who acted as valet and secretary.[16] Mr Green was pointedly reticent about his past and his reasons for travelling to India. He let it be known that he was a man of letters and hinted that he was on some confidential business for the Company or, perhaps, even the government. Much of the time, he remained in his cabin working at his papers. His fellow passengers were intrigued but none suspected the truth.

In fact, the mysterious Mr Green was a clergyman who had already achieved a measure of notoriety. In May 1769, he had appeared at the Old Bailey, charged with raping a servant girl.[17] Although the evidence against him looks plausible, he had been acquitted, largely on the basis of character references from his friends. Then, two months later, he featured in the newspapers again. This time, it was for fighting a duel. The Reverend Richard Green was an ardent supporter of John Wilkes and had become embroiled in a political argument with a Captain Douglas, in a coffee house. To settle the matter, they had agreed to meet in Hyde Park. In the ensuing duel, Richard Green had wounded his opponent. However, Capt Douglas was not satisfied with this result. After his wound had been treated at home, he asked for the duel to be fought again. Rev. Green felt that honour had been satisfied and refused. Instead, he took to the newspapers to justify his position. In several letters, he explained how the dispute had arisen and why he did not want to fight Capt Douglas a second time.[18] Once the dust had settled, in 1770, Richard Green had been appointed Chaplain to HMS *Prince of Wales*.[19] This appointment seems to have been shortlived and the circumstances of his departure are not clear. Later, Mr Green would plead financial ruin as the reason for his going to India. Given this colourful background, it is, perhaps, not surprising that the Mr Green on the *Ashburnham* was coy about his past. However, it was not yet the end of his story. It would take another twist when he arrived in Madras.

With his passengers safely aboard, Captain Peirce joined his ship. He had already said goodbye to Mary and the three children in Kingston and was now focussed on what lay ahead. At noon, on 7 January 1772, the *Earl of Ashburnham* weighed anchor and began the slow journey down the Thames Estuary. They had only reached the Nore when an unfortunate accident occurred. Thomas Hartwell was one of the young guinea pigs that Richard Peirce had taken on to serve as his own personal servant. The boy had only been at sea for a matter of hours when he was seen climbing the mizzen-mast. It may have been bravado on his part or he may have been sent but the upshot was that he slipped, fell overboard and was drowned. For the seamen on the *Ashburnham*, this was simply a sad fact of life at sea but, for the other two guinea pigs and the midshipmen, it was a sharp reminder of the perils that they faced.

These perils would soon be brought home to everyone. After leaving the Downs, the weather deteriorated quickly. By the time they had passed Portsmouth, a severe northerly gale was blowing and squalls of hail were lashing the ship. A heavy swell began to push the

East Indiaman in a Gale by C. Brooking
© *National Maritime Museum, Greenwich, London*

Ashburnham southwards. On 19 January, Peirce was concerned to find he was twenty-eight miles further south than his account had suggested. For days, big seas continued, breaking over the deck and causing the ship to roll alarmingly. 'Mountanious sea that makes the ship rowl so deep as often to endanger the masts and makes us ship a great deal of water', he wrote on the 23rd. The loss of a mast would be very serious. Although almost four feet in diameter at its base, the main mast could 'spring' or split along the grain and a sprung mast could snap without warning. A ship, crippled in this way, would be harder to steer and could easily founder if she turned sideways onto a large sea.

On 25 January, they encountered a Dutch ship that had been crippled in a different way. She had lost her rudder. She was clearly in difficulties and her drinking water and provisions were running low. In such dreadful weather conditions, Peirce must have felt tempted to sail past. But he did not. Even though she was a foreign ship, he went to her aid. The log records: 'In the morning supplied them with water and a pipe of brandy, biscuits and stockfish. I sent my cutter with many hands to ship a rudder they had made which they nearly accomplished but were prevented, there being a very large swell.' That night, the *Earl of Ashburnham* stayed near the stricken Dutchman. In the morning, 'I sent the cutter again to know if anything else could be done by us or if they wanted anything more to which the Captain replying in the negative, at 8 I made sail.'

One must resist the temptation to overstate Richard Peirce's role as a 'Good Samaritan' in this episode. The unwritten code of the sea would prompt most captains to go to the help of another ship in difficulties. But in this case, the *Earl of Ashburnham* was experiencing difficulties herself. In these conditions, you get a sense that Richard Peirce did more than the minimum expected of him. It gives us another insight into the character of the man.

The threat from the weather continued unabated. On the 29th, a chain plate broke and the fore-topmast was lost. By now, the continuous rolling of the ship was beginning to loosen the rigging and Peirce began to worry that he might lose his mainmast too. The next day, his concern grew: 'Suddenly increased to a very hard gale which split our mainsail to pieces [...] Rowled so very deep I was in great dread of losing the main mast.' As February began, the weather got no better; only after they had passed the island of Palma did the wind subside, at last.

It is tempting to compare this episode with the events of 1786. In this case, Captain Peirce expresses extreme concern – his ship is taking water and his masts are endangered – but he appears to remain in control. There is no hint of him or his crew giving way to despair. The storm may have been every bit as severe as that of 1786 but, what sets it apart, is that now Peirce's ship was in open sea. There was no lee-shore to fear.

With the improving weather, life on the *Earl of Ashburnham* soon settled into a normal routine. The soldiers were kept occupied with picking oakum. The new fore-topmast was found to be 'sprung' and had to be replaced. Guns were moved around to rebalance the ship. After one of the soldiers died, various measures were taken to limit the spread of infection: 'Washed with vinegar and burnt tobacco to sweeten the ship.'

One day, the lookout thought he had spotted a large rock near the ship. No rocks were marked on the chart so Captain Peirce felt bound to investigate it: 'Saw on lee bow something that at first looked like a rock. Lowered down the jollyboat and found it to be a dead whale. Several sharks with their heads above water where (*sic*) eating of it.' An event like this offered a welcome distraction. During meals at the Captain's table, the passengers may have already exhausted most topics of conversation. Even discussion of the enigmatic Mr Green and speculation about his mission had begun to pall. This novelty would give them something else to talk about.

On 6 March, the *Ashburnham* crossed the equator and two weeks later was in sight of the islands of Trinidada. This archipelago lies almost exactly on longitude thirty degrees west and just over seven hundred miles off the Brazilian coast, near Rio de Janeiro. It was a landmark that East India commanders all looked for and usually prompted a change of course. Now Captain Peirce would instruct the helmsman to turn southeast and head towards the Cape. The crew were in good spirits and, on 6 April, he was pleased to record, 'Our people continue very healthy'. It was tempting fate. Shortly afterwards, the soldiers began to fall ill. By 16 April, he wrote, 'Docters (*sic*) list is very long. Many of the soldiers are ill.' Then the first of those soldiers died. They had reached the Cape by this time so Peirce decided to put into Cape False Bay. The dead man could be buried on land and the ship would be able to take on supplies of fresh water and vegetables. While they lingered, two more soldiers died. By now, illness had spread to the crew as well. Peirce decided to press on before the situation got any worse. They left Cape False Bay on 29 April but even as late as 18 May, the log was recording 'We have many people on the docter's list'.

Sailing up the inner passage, they sighted St Christopher, a small, low, sandy island about forty-five miles off the coast of Madagascar. With his increasing passion for accuracy, Peirce recorded its position: 'At noon the body Island of St Christopher. In making the Island of St Christopher I find an error in my account of 3°:1/45 making it lie this voyage in Longitude 47° 25' whereas by former accounts and the opinions of our best hydrographers it lies only in 0/43:1/40 E of London. I make this voyage as I have done before to be in Lat 17°00 S.'

On board his ship, so many people were now ill, 'some in great danger', that Peirce knew he must stop at the Comoros. On his previous voyage, he had hurried on to Madras, but now it was essential to send the unwell ashore. He decided to anchor just off Johanna, in sight of the mosque they could see peeping over the palm trees. This indicated where the town was and where provisions could be bought. There was always an abundant supply of goats, fowl, coconuts and, significantly, lemons and oranges. Prices were low and many traders would accept payment in cowrie shells.

Ashburnham's journal does not make clear the nature of the illness that was affecting those aboard her. Some may have succumbed to the 'flux', as dysentery was known, but it is more likely that scurvy was the culprit. Writing in 1765, from first-hand experience, James Forbes described its symptoms as progressing from swollen limbs and a sense of 'heaviness', through livid spots, ulcerated gums and foul breath to 'total putrefaction'.[20] The end could come suddenly. Men, working on deck, would sometimes drop down dead without any warning.

Once they were on dry land, with access to fresh fruit and vegetables, the invalids began to recover rapidly. For the soldiers, life on an island like Johanna seemed much more appealing than the uncertain future that awaited them in Madras. When it was time to return to the ship, four were found to have absconded. But, their freedom was shortlived; the longboat was dispatched and the runaways were quickly rounded up. This was the third time that recruits had tried to escape from the *Earl of Ashburnham*. It was a direct challenge to the authority of its captain and Richard Peirce was prepared to respond. Perhaps he remembered what Capt Barkley had done on the *Pacific*.

He ordered that the ringleader, Frank Parry, be given twelve lashes and 'Confined Robert Burne in irons for abusing and threatening the serjant ill'. Compared to the savage punishments handed out by some captains, these men got off relatively lightly. But it was sufficient to make the point, or so Peirce hoped. He was interested in deterring future indiscipline, not in exacting revenge. A week later, it became clear that not all the soldiers had grasped the lesson they were meant to learn. Five of them continued to be defiant, ignoring orders and refusing to pick oakum or carry out any of the menial tasks they were given. This time, Peirce had them put in irons. After twenty-four hours of discomfort, four of the rebels had repented but one proved harder to crack: 'Released 4 of the men from irons but kept the 5th being a very troublesome and mischievous fellow'.

As they left Johanna in their wake, Richard Peirce ordered his men to look out for a shoal, known as the Bassas de Patram but there was no sign of it. In a tone that sounds distinctly testy, he wrote, 'Kept a lookout for Bassas de Patram though it is my opinion there is no such shoal in Longt of Johanna. W. Nicholson should not I think have spoke of this shoal so publickly without having authority for it.' This is quite revealing. It shows that, by now, Richard Peirce was sufficiently confident in his own opinions on matters of navigation, that he became impatient with those, like Mr Nicholson, who held a different view. But was this confidence justified? It may well be. In 1758, Capt Wilson of the *Pitt* had located this shoal well to the east of Comoro. On this issue, at least, it would appear that Mr Nicholson was mistaken.[21]

On 20 June, the high mountains of Ceylon appeared on the horizon. As he approached its coastline, it seems that Richard Peirce decided to make some detailed sketches of it.[22] Some features, like the Friars Hood, were easily identified but an accurate outline of the coast would be of use to other navigators. Alexander Dalrymple had seen his drawings from the previous voyage and perhaps encouraged him. In time, Mr Dalrymple would become the official Hydrographer for the East India Company but, even in 1772, his determination to systematically map the seas was attracting attention. In Richard Peirce, he recognised someone who could support this work.

Under a moderate breeze and enjoying 'delightful weather', the *Earl of Ashburnham* tacked round Ceylon and up the Coromandel coast. On the 25th, she dropped anchor in Madras Roads, her home for the next five weeks. As usual, Captain Peirce was one of the first ashore. While the Company's recalcitrant recruits were being put into one *masulah* boat, Peirce set off, through the breakers, in another. This year, the town was busy. Three naval vessels and, maybe, as many as six Indiamen were anchored in the Roads. It was a great opportunity to meet fellow commanders, to talk shop, to gossip and, perhaps, share snippets of information on the state of the local economy. It was all part of the essential business of networking.

Once ashore, there was the familiar routine to follow. Captain Peirce would have to report to Company offices at Fort St George to confirm that the Company's cargo had been safely delivered and to receive any new instructions. Then he could focus on his private trade. No doubt, his *dubash* had already lined up merchants interested in buying the saffron, lead and other items in the chests marked as his. Also, there was the question of what to buy next. In China, there was always a reliable profit to be made from cotton and redwood and so this would make up the bulk of his investment.

Some time also had to be set aside for social engagements. Chief among them was an invitation to supper with the new Governor, Josias Du Pre, at his residence at Garden House. Captain Peirce and some of his lady passengers would be among the guests but Mr Green had inveigled an invitation too. As soon as the *Ashburnham* had dropped anchor, Mr Green had contacted Capt Ourry, senior captain of the naval squadron, lying in Madras Road. He presented a letter purporting to be from the Admiralty and convinced the Captain that he had further letters for the Governor of Madras from such eminent figures as the Earl of Sandwich and the Duke of Queensbury. Captain Ourry agreed to bring Mr Green to the soiree and introduce him to Governor Du Pre.

At the supper, Mr Green excelled himself. Ignoring the astonished looks of Captain Peirce and the ladies, seated opposite him, Richard Green held forth on politics, name-dropping with abandon. Meanwhile, Governor Du Pre had needed only a few moments to conclude that the letters, which his uninvited guest had delivered, were all fraudulent. The man was clearly an imposter. Out of consideration to the duped Captain Ourry, Mr Green was allowed to finish his supper, oblivious to the fact he had been rumbled. Next day, he was taken to Madras gaol to await trial.[23]

By the end of July, the *Earl of Ashburnham* had completed her business at the Coast and it was time to move on to China. Sadly, they could not wait to discover what Mr Green's fate would be.[24] On the 30th, Captain Peirce gave the order to make sail for Canton. He planned to follow the same course as before, through the Malacca Straits. But no two voyages are ever exactly alike. This time they took a slightly more northerly route. After a week at sea, they could just make out the Nicobar Islands, well to the south. Instead of heading for Sumatra and Diamond Point, the *Ashburnham* maintained her easterly course until the Malay coast came into view. They were in the latitude of Pulo Bouton and the Ladda Islands. Now, Peirce gave the order to turn south, hugging the shore on their port side. By 15 August, they could see Pulo Pinang. It provided a good anchorage. Before the end of the century, the East India Company would secure a base there. It would be renamed as Prince of Wales Island and, after his death, would be where one of Richard Peirce's children would marry. Now, it was a distant landmark, soon to be left behind. On the 20th, Pulo Dinding was identified. One after another, familiar features rose above the horizon. The Sambelongs, Long Arroe, Parcelar Hill, Cape Rachado. Within a week, *Ashburnham* had come to in Malacca Roads.

East Indiaman in the Malacca Strait.
© Private collection.

This was a busy waterway and many ships chose to stop here. The Dutch trading settlement at Malacca town was a good source of supplies and merchandise. Among the ships at anchor, Peirce could see at least four other East Indiamen. The *Fox, Lioness, Norfolk* and *Royal Henry* were all bound for China. For the remainder of the voyage to Canton, Captain Peirce would endeavour to sail in their company. Local country ships would join them from time to time. These waters were treacherous and there was safety in numbers.

While at Malacca, the *Earl of Ashburnham* took on some tin. Then, exactly a month after leaving Madras, she made sail again. Together with the other Indiamen, she continued southeast. The log records the litany of landmarks, a sequence of familiar, old faces. Mount Formosa, Great Carimon, Pulo Pisang, Barn Island, Tree Island, Sincapore. By the time they were rounding the tip of the Malay peninsula, only *Fox* and *Royal Henry* were still with them. Keeping ships together was not easy, particularly with independent-minded commanders, who liked to make their own decisions.

From Singapore, the route to Canton lay northeast across the South China Sea. Having passed Pulo Auro, they looked out for Pulo Condore, just as they had done on the previous voyage. This time they found it. For once, Richard Peirce had to admit that the much-criticised Mr Nicholson had got something right. He agreed that Nicholson's calculation of the position of Pulo Condore was more accurate than that of others. In his log, Peirce justified this conclusion 'by experience of several voyages'.

The Macclesfield Bank was the next feature to be wary of and, by 20 September, they had reached it. Like all good seamen, Peirce looked for clues as to his position and the changing weather. That day he sounded the ocean floor and 'got ground. Fine white sand with small bits of coral rock and some shells'. From this, he concluded that they had strayed to the northwest edge of the Bank. Next day, he observed 'a good number of small land birds about the ship of various kinds from which and of the swell I am led to think there has been a hard gale to the North'. Indicators, like this, helped to build a picture of their situation. In his log, Peirce made some additional observations, comparing his findings with that of other ships, during the southwest monsoon.

By 29 September, the Grand Ladrones were visible. Behind these islands lay the Bogue, guarding the entrance to the Pearl River. They were getting close but progress was slow. Another nine days would have to pass before the river pilot guided them past the Bogue and over the two sand bars. Impatient to get to Canton, Peirce seems to have gone on ahead in the longboat. Passing Whampoa, he found the waterway crowded with other ships. Eleven were British but there were also Danish, French, Dutch, Swedish and a variety of country ships. It was a clear sign that the universal demand for tea was as strong as ever. Trade would be brisk this year and Richard Peirce was keen to secure his share.

While his crew began the work of unbending the sails, lowering the topmasts and yards, even gathering up the hen coops and sending all ashore to the bankshalls, Richard Peirce's private trade was lowered into the waiting sampans. Over several days, a succession of these craft would carry his cotton, redwood, pepper and other goods to the Company's factory at Canton. The Company's own goods would make the same journey and its treasure would be sent under guard, in the longboat. On 9 October, Captain Peirce returned to his ship to prepare for the official visit by the Hoppo. This took place the next day, accompanied by nine gun salutes and all the usual ceremony. There do not appear to have been any complications so we must assume that the Hoppo was satisfied with his 'presents'.

With the formalities completed, Peirce could return to his accommodation at Canton. Here he would dine with the resident supercargoes and the commanders of other East Indiamen. After the isolation of life on board ship, the sociable atmosphere at the factory must have been very welcome. He could now mix with his peers. He may also have enjoyed social contact with his security merchant from the Co-Hong. Although the Emperor did not want the crews of western ships to come into contact with the general population, the interaction between the Co-Hong and the supercargoes sometimes extended beyond a purely commercial relationship. When the diarist, William Hickey, had come to Whampoa, three years earlier, he had enjoyed the lavish hospitality of Puankhequa, one of the most successful of the Chinese merchants. The party had included an impressive fireworks display.[25] A few years later, James Wathen enjoyed a similar experience as one of eighty guests of the merchant Mauk-qua. Although he struggled to use chopsticks, he enjoyed birds' nest soup, 'some fine fish' and a dessert of mandarin oranges. The evening was enlivened by theatricals and music, neither of which appealed to Wathen's European sensibilities. He found the play to be unintelligible, the actors 'strutted and bellowed' and the orchestra was 'harsh and discordant'.[26] Despite Wathen's artisic reservations, it is clear that such social events regularly occurred. It is reasonable to assume, therefore, that Richard Peirce may also have received an invitation, at some point, from the security merchant allocated to his ship.

Meanwhile, at Whampoa, eight new seamen were enlisted. They would replace a similar number that had 'run' at Madras, thus ensuring the *Ashburnham* had a full complement of crew for her return voyage. They joined those working in the hold to clear the ship of all its cargo. The tea that would replace it weighed less than the redwood and lead brought from Madras. To keep the ship stable during the homeward voyage, it was first necessary to load more ballast. Once that had been levelled, crates of Chinese porcelain could be laid on top. Only then would the chests of tea be lowered into the hold. The process began on 5 November. With the ballast *in situ*, more than one hundred crates of china were brought on board. This included some half chests of plate belonging to Peirce and his officers. Among the contents may have been dinner services commissioned for their own personal use but the bulk of the consignment was intended for the home market.

On 16 November, the tea began to arrive and one chopboat after another came alongside *Ashburnham*. The delivery of the tea usually marked the point at which the ship began its preparations for departure. All the paraphernalia of rigging, sails and spars were now collected from the bankshall and returned on board. During December, the crews of the various Indiamen worked hard to sway up masts and bend the sails. It was important to be ready. The northwest monsoon had begun and to miss these seasonal winds would spell commercial disaster.

By the end of December, some ships were anxious to depart. Generously, Richard Peirce sent the longboat with the *Ashburnham's* kedge anchor to help the *Lioness* warp past the other anchored ships. Her departure was soon followed by that of the *Royal Henry* and the *Fox*. On the *Ashburnham*, the sense of urgency began to increase as the loading of tea continued into the third week of January 1773. In the haste to get the cargo aboard, someone must have seen an opportunity to pull a fast one. One of the last chop boats to come alongside was not carrying her full consignment of tea. Perhaps, it had been loaded dishonestly or, perhaps, some tea had been pilfered en route from Canton. Whatever the cause, it did not fool the officer receiving the cargo and he quickly alerted Peirce to the shortfall. The chop boat was immediately commandeered and the five Chinese crewmen were taken into custody. Once the Co-Hong had been alerted to the problem, they would deal with it. It was not in their interests to condone the cheating of foreign merchants. Generally, they were scrupulously honest and Peirce could be confident that the miscreants would suffer the weight of Chinese justice. He would release the boat, hand over the prisoners and receive the appropriate compensation.

As this was being sorted out, the final consignment of cargo was delivered. It consisted of 150 bags of raw silk, plus some bales of nankeen cloth. Predictably, a proportion of the silk was Peirce's private trade. At last, with her hold now full, the *Earl of Ashburnham* cast off from her moorings in Whampoa Roads. On 24 January, she moved down the Pearl River to the second bar where she waited for her captain to rejoin his ship. The cutter was sent to collect him from Canton and four days later he appeared, bringing with him a collection of 'sing-songs'. Presumably, they had been surplus to requirement. Perhaps with so many foreign ships trading that year, the Chinese appetite for such novelties had already been satisfied. No matter. They could always be brought again, on any future voyage to China.

On 1 February, *Ashburnham* made sail and, together with the *Anson*, passed through the Bogue and out of the river. The return voyage to England had begun. Within a week they had passed the Macclesfield shoal but saw no land until the Island of Tioman came into view. From there, they steered towards Sumatra. At the entrance to the Palamban river, they turned to follow the coast, south to the Sunda Straits. Once again, the landmarks of Monopin Hill, Banka Island, Parmasan Hill and St Nicholas Point were recorded in the log, their features now reassuringly familiar. By 21 February, *Ashburnham* was passing through the Straits and in sight of the island of 'Cracatoa', its sleeping volcano, set in a bed of emerald and azure like a benign gemstone.

Then, shadowed by the *Anson*, they set a course for the Cape. For three days in April, they anchored in Table Bay to replenish provisions, and then quickly pressed on towards home. By-passing St Helena, they steered to the northwest for another 800 miles until, on 24 May, they reached Ascension Island. As before, Peirce was in no mood to linger. Pausing only to take on water, he made sail again two days later. In terms of speed the *Ashburnham* was a thoroughbred and now she was on a loose rein. In under than ten weeks, Lands End was visible from the mainmast. On 3 August 1773, the *Earl of Ashburnham* dropped anchor at Gravesend. She had been a lucky ship and a happy one but, after four voyages to the East, her career as an Indiaman was now over. A new ship would have to be built to replace her. As Richard Peirce was lowered down *Ashburnham*'s side for the final time, he may have wondered if his next ship would prove to be so fortunate.

12
A Career Becalmed

At home in Norbiton, Richard Peirce found all his family in good health. In September, Mary Ann would be two years old; young Richard would be five. The children had changed considerably during the eighteen months that he had been away but other things had changed too – and not for the better.

The health of the East India Company itself was now in doubt, and its very future called into question. Its financial wellbeing lay at the root of its problems. In return for a monopoly of trade with the East, the Company had undertaken to pay £400,000 annually to the government. However, the fact was that, for several years, it had failed to do so. The income, which it expected from its import of tea, had fallen well short and the Company found itself with insufficient funds to meet its obligations. In 1767, tea, that cost one shilling to purchase in China, could be sold for four times that price in London.[1] But now the market had virtually collapsed. In England, smuggled tea presented serious competition and, in America, that problem seemed insurmountable. Almost three-quarters of the tea consumed on the other side of the Atlantic was smuggled in from the Dutch. Unable to sell enough tea of its own, the East India Company could no longer generate the profit it needed.

Even before Richard Peirce set sail to China in January 1772, it was obvious that there was a glut of tea in the Company's stores. After the return of the *Earl of Ashburnham* and the rest of that season's fleet, the surplus exceeded 16,000,000 lbs.[2] Now, the warehouses were full to bursting and some tea was beginning to rot. Without a market for its chief product, the East India Company was facing bankruptcy. The effect of such an outcome on the economy as a whole was too dreadful to contemplate. An enterprise of such significance could not be allowed to fail and so the government felt compelled to act.

In its early years, Lord North's administration had adopted a largely laissez-faire approach to policy. However, in the case of the East India Company, they recognised the need for action. It was time for the government to become involved and to sort things out. There were, in fact, a number of issues that required attention, besides the immediate problem of the Company's solvency. A large injection of cash might stave off bankruptcy for a while but such a bailout would not address the underlying lack of profitability. The Company would need to regain its markets, particularly in America where smuggling was draining its lifeblood. In Britain, the efforts of the excise men were ineffective but, in America, they were woefully inadequate. To have any chance of defeating the smuggler, it would be necessary to reconsider the taxation of tea.

There was also the question of the Company's governance. At home, its democratic structure gave shareholders undue influence and this was seen as contributing to its current predicament. Shareholders were more concerned with the size of the dividend than the viability of the Company itself. At the same time, in India, the Company now found itself ruling large swathes of land. It was a responsibility which it was ill-equipped to carry out and which did not sit comfortably alongside its primary function, commercial trading. At some point the constitutional question of who owned Bengal would have to be addressed. Finally, there was the question of corruption.

In June 1772, while Peirce was in Madras, a new play opened at the Haymarket Theatre in London. *The Nabob* was a scathing attack on those who made their fortunes by plundering India and using their ill-gotten gains to buy position and influence in England.[3] The play was a huge success and clearly struck a chord with its English audience. It was widely understood that some of these fortunes had been hastily acquired by extracting 'presents' from local Indian rulers and their officials. Enormous sums of money were being channelled through Company representatives in return for political influence or military support. To many in England, this smacked of extortion or a grubby protection racket. When Horace Walpole declared that 'no man ever went to India with good intentions', everyone knew what he meant. Chief among the culprits was Robert Clive himself. It was clear to the audience of *The Nabob* that, with his 'roupees' and 'jaghires', Lord Clive provided the model for the character of Sir Matthew Mite. Perhaps, Lord North saw the play. In any case, he was in tune with popular opinion when he decided to tackle the question of 'presents' in the legislation he proposed.

Lord North's legislation came before Parliament just as Richard Peirce was arriving back in England. The first element to be passed was a loan to the Company of £1.4 million. This staved off immediate collapse. Wages could be paid and bills of exchange could be honoured. Captain Peirce and his crew would be able to collect their pay. The *Ashburnham's* Pay Book records that on 14 September, Peirce signed for £162-15s-3d, his wages after the usual deductions had been made.[4]

In the second piece of legislation, known as the Regulating Act, North tackled the Company's corporate independence. Anyone holding £500 worth of Company shares had voting rights at Company meetings. The Regulating Act raised this threshold to £1,000. The result was to cut the number of voters by more than half. However, many of those small investors, now disenfranchised, had played little part in directing Company policy. Men like Thomas Burston, John Durand and maybe even Richard Peirce himself will have been above the new threshold. So too were the rich 'nabobs' who returned from India. Ironically, instead of producing greater 'integrity of conduct', the effect of North's bill was to allow a smaller 'cabal' of investors to exert greater control over the Company, in their own interests.

If Richard Peirce regarded the disenfranchising of small shareholders with equanimity, he is unlikely to have felt the same way about another aspect of the Regulating Act. This was a head-on attack on the 'shipping interest' to which his father-in-law aspired and on which Peirce himself was dependent. For years, ships' owners had combined to exert voting influence to drive up freight rates. This was the price per ton at which the Company agreed to charter their ships. It was widely recognised that the 'shipping interest' had pressurised the Company into paying at least one third more than was necessary. They also tried to persuade the Company to take up as many of their ships as possible. Previous attempts to break this cartel had failed but, this time, Lord North was prepared to see it through. Legislation was introduced which limited the tonnage the Company could charter. Only sixteen ships would be required for the following season. Inevitably, this would leave many ships idle, a disastrous scenario for the owners who had invested in them.

The Regulating Act also introduced structural changes to the administration of India. Although Lord North ducked the issue of sovereignty, he introduced a Supreme Council of five members who would run affairs in Bengal. Two of the appointees were men already serving in India, Richard Barwell and the present Governor, Warren Hastings. The latter would become Governor General and would lead the Council. However, three of the Supreme Councillors would be appointed by the government. This was designed to ensure that the state had a majority in decision-making and to keep the Governor General in check.

Alongside the Bengal Council would be a new Supreme Court with Sir Elijah Impey as Chief Justice. He and the three new Councillors would have to travel to India to take up their posts. It was decided that Impey would sail to Calcutta on the *Anson* and the others on the *Earl of Ashburnham*.[5] Richard Peirce may have wished to retain the command but he knew that was unlikely. In October 1773, John Durand had sold the *Ashburnham* on the open market.[6] The advertisement for the sale had praised the ship as 'a remarkable fast sailor', just what was needed for conveying the Councillors to Bengal. The Government had contracted to use her but, with the sale, Peirce's right to command had lapsed. The honour of transporting these important dignitaries would go to someone else. His services were not required.

Finally, while *The Nabob* continued to play to enthusiastic audiences, North's legislation tried to put a stop to Company corruption in India. The receiving of 'presents' was to be banned. Any employee found to have accepted one would be fined double its value and then dismissed from the Company's service. It looked like the end of the road for those who hoped to get rich quick. Easy fortunes would never again be so readily available. But, of course, it was not so simple. In India, many men would still make large amounts of money. They would just have to be less brazen about it and cover their tracks more thoroughly in future. The temptations of India could not be negated so easily.

Meanwhile, for Richard Peirce, the rewards of India and of China were ready for reaping. Although, his chests of tea may have been added to the existing tea mountain, his other private trade probably sold well. The market for porcelain, silk and other eastern desirables was still strong so we can assume that Peirce made a reasonable profit. In addition, his income from trading in Madras and Canton would have been remitted to London, either as Bills of Exchange or in the form of diamonds and other precious stones. He was clearly feeling sufficiently well off to extend his holdings in Kingston. In 1773, soon after his return, he acquired some additional land from a Mr Hollis.[7] It was another step on the way to establishing himself as a man of property.

Although Richard Peirce could live comfortably for a while, the future for East India Company commanders did not look so promising. Unless the trade with America suddenly revived, Lord North's legislation was likely to force early retirement on many of them. Inevitably, they will have discussed this over drinks at the Jerusalem coffee house. There is nothing like a common threat for bringing men together, even such independent-minded men as these. During the autumn of 1773, a number of commanders, including Peirce, decided that some form of collective action was needed. They agreed to form the Society of East India Commanders.[8] Not only would it give them a united voice but also a mechanism for addressing the hardships that they sensed approaching from over the horizon.

The Society of East India Commanders held its inaugural meeting in December 1773 at the Queens Arms Tavern near St Paul's. One of its first actions was to lobby the East India Company over the loss of earnings suffered by its commanders. The sharp reduction in ships 'taken up' in recent years had had a direct impact on those in the Company's maritime service. Without a source of income, many commanders were facing financial ruin. In April 1774, the Society wrote to the Directors requesting that commanders who have been 'thrown out of employment' should be paid an allowance of £200. This should be means tested and paid only to those with less than £6,000 'clear of all encumbrances'.

It is unlikely that Richard Peirce fell into this category. On the basis of the home addresses of the thirty or so subscribers, Jean Sutton has suggested that this was an exclusive group of commanders of substance.[9] They were all willing to subscribe £50 to a fund to help members who got into financial difficulties. Five captains were appointed as trustees. The name of one of them was recorded as 'Rd Pierce'. In the face of the Society's argument and under pressure from the shipping interest, the Directors yielded. The East India Company agreed to pay its unemployed commanders an annual gratuity of £200. This was a clear indication to Peirce that the Society, which he had helped to set up, could make a difference. It felt gratifying and can only have raised his esteem with his fellow commanders.

As 1773 drew to a close, dark clouds continued to gather. On 16 December, men dressed as Mohawk Indians dumped 90,000 lbs of tea in Boston harbour. Earlier that year, parliament had passed the Tea Act. Intended to pull the rug from under the feet of smugglers and get the export of Company tea flowing again to America, it had failed to have the desired effect. The resentment of the colonialists towards British taxation had not been assuaged and, with the Boston Tea Party, events would now take on their own momentum.

Throughout 1774, Richard Peirce must have settled into life in Kingston. No ship had been commissioned 'in the room' of the *Earl of Ashburnham* and, without a replacement, there was no prospect of a command. In April, his former ship sailed for India. *Asburnham,* which began her career by ferrying wild animals, now had the honour of conveying the three parliamentary appointees who would tame the Supreme Council. Six months later, as these Councillors stepped ashore in Calcutta, the latest 'nabob' was preparing to return to England with his fortune.

Since his arrival in Bengal at the age of eighteen, John Graham had done well out of India. In the mid 1760s he had been appointed to the lucrative post of Resident of Midnapore. From there he was promoted to Resident of Burdwan where it was rumoured he had accepted a 'present' of two lakh rupees from the local nawab. In today's terms, that would have been worth around £3.1 million. Even if the figure was exaggerated, it was assumed that, as a revenue expert,

Graham had harvested a good revenue for himself, too. By 1772, when Warren Hastings became Governor, John Graham was Chief at Patna. He was also a member of the Bengal Council. Although at first he appeared to have little in common with the more austere Hastings, John Graham was soon won over. Throughout the fierce infighting that dogged much of Warren Hastings' time as Governor, John Graham would remain a staunch supporter.[10]

By 1774, the Indian climate was taking its toll on John Graham's health. He had accumulated his fortune and now his concern was to live long enough to enjoy it. He decided to return to England. There, he could argue the case for Warren Hastings in the internal politics of the Company while, at the same time, living the life of a gentleman on his Yatton estate in Somerset. It is this Somerset connection which probably brought John Graham into the social sphere of Richard Peirce's sister. Within a decade, one

John Graham.
© JJ Heath Caldwell

of her daughters would marry John Graham's brother, Thomas. This was the same Thomas Graham who had taken a passage on the *Pacific*, eight years earlier. Thus, the ties between the Graham, Paul and Peirce families were long-established and would continue to link them well into the future. However, John Graham would not live to see that. The illness, which he had contracted in India, continued to dog him and in June 1776 he succumbed. The newspapers lamented his 'irreparable loss' and, without any hint of irony, praised him for his clear head and the excellent regulations he had introduced at the Department of Revenue.[11]

In the meantime, Richard Peirce had to content himself with his enforced idleness. We know nothing of how he spent his time but he must surely have encountered Mary's social circle in Kingston. Equally, he will have kept in touch with his own friends. Benjamin Hammet, for example, was doing well. He was a successful London merchant now, married to the daughter of the banker, James Esdaile.[12] In Taunton, his home town, Hammet was playing a key role developing it as a commercial centre. He acquired property and built more. Richard Peirce will have known about this and may have gone to see for himself, especially if he was visiting his sister at West Monkton.

In early Spring 1774, Mary Peirce became pregnant for the fourth time. The baby, a boy, was born at the end of December. Sadly, he only lived a short while. On the 3rd January 1775, Thomas Peirce, 'son of Captain Richard Pearce' (*sic*) was buried at Kingston Church.[13] It was a sad start to a bad year. Across the Atlantic, the political situation had worsened. In April 1775, someone in the Massachusets militia fired 'the shot heard round the world'. The skirmishes at Lexington and Concord were to mark the start of the American War of Independence, a struggle that would dominate the next six and a half years. As it sucked in money, resources and ships, the American War would put the East India Company under great pressure. The prospect of a command for Richard Peirce seemed to recede yet further.

During the spring of 1775, worries about his financial situation prompted Peirce to write to Leadenhall Street. The relief, which he and the other trustees of the Society of East India Commanders had sought for unemployed commanders, Peirce now requested for himself. He duly submitted a 'memorial' to the Directors, describing himself as a commander in the Company's sea service 'render'd unemployed in consequence of the reduction of Company's shipping'.[14] His letter was passed to the Committee of Shipping for a decision.

On 7 June 1775, the committee delivered their verdict. Captain Richard Peirce, late commander of the *Earl of Ashburnham*, should be admitted to an annual allowance of £200, backdated to 14 March 'being 18 months after the said ship was cleared'. This recommendation may also suggest that the Peirces were no longer worth more than the £6,000 threshold for means-testing suitable applicants. It is not clear from Company minutes whether they agreed to waive this requirement or not. Either way, in Kingston, the news must have come as a relief, particularly as domestic expenses continued to increase.

On 20 June 1776, Mary Peirce gave birth again. It was another boy. At his christening, he was named Thomas Burston Peirce.[15] No doubt his grandfather was pleased by the choice of name and his parents hoped, perhaps, that some of Thomas Burston's good fortune would rub off on him too. It would be needed. Richard Peirce's own prospects showed no sign of improving. In fact, he disappears almost totally from the public record. Only the fact that he insured his house for £1,200 in May 1777, confirms his continuing existence.[16] What did he do during this time?

Almost certainly, Richard Peirce lobbied for the construction of a new ship to replace the *Earl of Ashburnham*. In this endeavour, he now had an important ally. Following the sale of the *Ashburnham*, the veteran ship's husband, John Durand, had surrendered his interest in building on that ship's 'bottom'. That controlling interest had been acquired by none other than Thomas Burston.[17] If the East India Company were to charter another ship, Thomas Burston would become its principal managing owner. No doubt, Burston viewed this as a shrewd business move but one wonders if he also saw it as a way of helping his son-in-law. Such an arrangement could only benefit the family as a whole.

During this time, it is possible that Peirce became involved in more philanthropic work. In April, the trustees of Westminster Hospital met at the Kings Arms Tavern for their annual dinner. Among the stewards was Richard Pearce esq.[18] Later, in October, a man of the same name was a founder member of a committee set up to raise money for the relief of Aldbourn.[19] This village in Wiltshire had been devastated by fire and many inhabitants left homeless. For the next six months, the relief committee met periodically at the Rainbow Coffee House, in Cornhill. Of course, this person may not be our Richard but, given the unreliable spelling of his name by the press, we should not rule out the possibility that it is.

Although, for most of 1777, his career prospects continued to stagnate, Richard Peirce's family was about to increase again. By

May of that year, Mary was expecting another baby. She gave birth on the 3rd January 1778 to a third daughter, Louisa Harriet.[20] At the end of the month, the family gathered for her christening at Kingston church. The arrival of another healthy child was a cause for celebration but, by now, there was a further reason for optimism. The fortunes of the East India Company were beginning to recover and, at last, it was looking to increase the number of its ships. Several of its former vessels, including the *Earl of Ashburnham*, had completed their quota of voyages and were now considered by the Company to be worn out. Within the year, at least seven new ships would have to be built.

The replacement of worn out ships was tied in with the system of rotation. This was the arrangement by which ships were chartered or 'taken up' for voyages, in turn. The rota ensured fairness. The owners who had invested heavily in building the East Indiamen knew that their ships would not be idle for too long. Their opportunity for another profitable voyage would come round soon. Even if their ship was wrecked, irreparably damaged or just worn out, the Company agreed to commission a replacement to be built 'on her bottom'. Thus, the cycle could continue. Even when the Company wanted to expand the size of its fleet, it would approach the same cartel of owners to commission additional ships.

On this occasion, Sir Charles Raymond and John Durand secured six of the new contracts.[21] The seventh would go to Durand's protégé and successor, Thomas Burston. By the autumn of 1777, Burston had been given the go-ahead to build on *Ashburnham's* bottom. For Richard Peirce, this news came as a relief. Within a year, he would command an Indiaman again and the interruption of his career would be over.

The construction of this new ship would take about eight months. She would be built at 'Mr Wells' dock in Rotherhithe'.[22] This was the large Greenland Dock which the Wells family had acquired in 1763. John Wells was an experienced builder who had constructed ships for John Durand and other owners, over many years. In fact, two of Durand's new ships, the *Ganges* and the *Walpole*, would be built there at the same time as Burston's. Thomas Burston knew he could rely on Wells to do a good job. But first the money to pay for the ship had to be raised and this involved convening the consortium of investors. The names of these part-owners are not known but many are likely to have been members of the consortium that had owned the *Earl of Ashburnham*. Thomas Burston may have recruited new investors, too, one of whom could have been Sir Charles Kemeys Tynte. His estates were in Somerset and he had tenants in West Monkton. Tynte certainly knew the Paul family and may have known Richard Peirce too.

The choice of name for the new ship reflected this west country connection. The *Public Advertiser* reported that 'she is called the Halswell, from the seat of Sir Charles Kemeys Tynte, bart'.[23] This was a reference to Halswell House near Goathurst in Somerset. In fact, for reasons of their own, the East India Company chose to spell the name 'Halsewell'. It is this form of spelling that would stick and become permanently associated with the wreck.

Having secured his group of financial backers, Thomas Burston now had to ascertain the amount that each part-owner was prepared to invest. During the eighteenth century, it was customary to split the cost of building a new ship into shares of 1/16. Individuals within the consortium would buy one or more shares in return for an equivalent share of the profits from future voyages. As the size of ships grew and the cost of building them rose, so the price of each share increased. In 1767, when *Granby* was built, the cost of a one-sixteenth share was £1,073.[24] *Halsewell's* part-owners must have paid more. The construction of their ship will have come to more than £20,000 and they would also have to fit it out and provide provisions for its first voyage before they could see any return on their investment. However, for most of these men, this was not their only investment. As bankers, merchants and even retired sea captains, a typical part-owner spread his investment across several ships. The perils of the sea made it too risky to invest all your eggs in one basket. Many also took the added precaution of insuring their own shares at the London Assurance House or some other reputable insurance firm. You never knew what misfortune might befall a ship, even a new one like the *Halsewell*.

With their financial commitments agreed, *Halsewell's* owners now formalised their arrangements with legal documents. They signed a bond appointing Thomas Burston as principal managing owner and, in return, he signed a contract in which he promised to carry out his duties as husband of the *Halsewell*. As such, he would have sole charge of the finances. Calling in the share capital when necessary, he would be responsible for paying the shipbuilder, the suppliers of stores and provisions, the advance 'river pay' of the crew and, after each voyage, for presenting the accounts to the owners and declaring the dividends.

Most of these duties lay in the future but Burston's immediate priority was the construction of his ship. Before this work could begin, he had to sign a separate contract with John Wells. This contract with the builder set out the dimensions of the proposed ship and any specific features that had to be included. These were determined by the Company. Although the *Halsewell* would belong to her owners, the East India Company wanted her design to meet their requirements. The contract between Burston and Wells also confirmed the cost of building the ship, expressed as a price per ton. Although the records have been lost, Thomas Burston probably paid at least £12 a ton.[26] Wells would receive his payment in instalments, with an advance of £1,000 as soon as the contract was signed. Two or three subsequent instalments would follow at later stages of the construction.

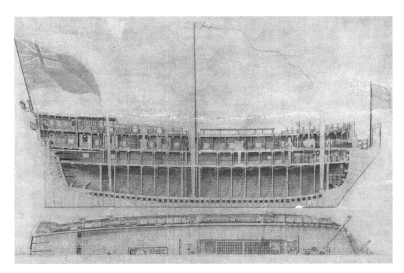

Plans of an Indiaman, 1752.
© *National Maritime Museum, Greenwich, London*

In terms of size, the *Halsewell* would be almost identical to her predecessor. She would weigh 776 tons, a mere one ton lighter than the *Earl of Ashburnham*. The keels of both ships were 112 feet 2.5 inches long, but each ship's full length would extend beyond that to just over 139 feet. In common with other Indiamen, *Halsewell* would have three decks. Her width, at the widest point, would be 36 feet.[27] For the sake of stability, her width needed to be under one-third the length of the keel. The *Earl of Ashburnham* had been praised as 'a remarkable fast sailor' and Thomas Burston must have hoped that, with her similar dimensions, the *Halsewell* would perform equally well.

By the start of 1778, the keel had been laid. Once launched, the keel would be permanently submerged, so it needed to be made from wood that would preserve well in salt water. For this reason, elm was always chosen. The keel would provide the foundation on which the hull would be raised. First the stem and stern posts were attached and then thick floor timbers were laid at right angles across the keel. Next, curved pieces of wood, called futtocks, were attached to the floor. They gave the sides of the ship their distinctive curved shape but they also anchored the frames, which provided the internal structure that strengthened the hull. It was vital that the hull was robust and so it was made almost entirely from oak. With planks four inches thick along its bottom, a ship of *Halsewell's* size would require the wood of at least eight-hundred mature oak trees. Although some oak could be imported, shipbuilders maintained that, for quality, English oak was the best. A requirement of this scale was not always easy to meet. At times of intense shipbuilding by the navy, shortages of wood could occur. The demands of the American War were a case in point and had contributed to the recent reduction in shipbuilding for the East India Company.

Probably by March, the framing was complete and work had begun to attach the outer planking. At this stage, Thomas Burston may have paid a second instalment of about £1,000. With the outer shell in place, work could start to make the hull watertight. Caulkers would seal the gaps between the planks by hammering in oakum. Meanwhile, inside the ship, the knees were being secured to the frame. Knees were single pieces of mature wood that formed a right angle. Their function was to support the deck planking and fix it to the side of the ship. They had been cut from trees where a branch grew at 90 degrees to the trunk. A shape like this was not easy to come by. Even more difficult to find were the V-shaped timbers, called breasthooks, which knitted the bow together, between decks. When such pieces had been acquired, they had to be seasoned before they could be used.

While work was progressing, Thomas Burston will have visited the shipyard, from time to time, to see for himself. As principal managing owner, he was answerable to the other shareholders and also to the Company. The East India Company insisted on good quality materials and standards of construction for the ships they intended to charter. They regularly sent their Surveyor of Shipping to check that all was in order and that any improvements they recommended had been implemented. Inevitably, this must have involved Thomas Burston in discussions in which he felt out of his depth. He was no maritime expert. Unlike John Durand, Burston had never been to sea. He had only a theoretical understanding of how ships functioned and must have relied on his son-in-law for practical expertise. It would be very surprising if Thomas Burston did not bring Richard Peirce with him on inspection visits to Rotherhithe. Peirce would be able to explain some of the more obscure terminology that made up the vocabulary of shipbuilders. His experience of the *Ashburnham* was invaluable and would enable him to gauge the quality of her successor. In any case, Richard Peirce was destined to command her. It would be the first time he would have responsibility for a brand new ship and, naturally, he took a keen interest in her construction.

During the summer of 1778, Thomas Burston undertook one of his most important duties as managing owner, the signing of the Charter Party. This contract between a ship's husband and the Company, set out the terms on which a particular ship would be hired. It stated the rate that the Company would pay the owners for every ton of Company cargo that their ship carried. Fine goods like tea and silk would command a higher freight rate than that paid for 'gruff' or coarse goods such as saltpetre. Naturally, it was in the interest of owners to extract the best freight rates they could. In 1772, the Company was paying £37 per ton for fine goods but a decade later that had risen to just over £47.[28]

The Charter Party, signed by Thomas Burston, also covered other aspects of *Halsewell's* forthcoming voyage. It specified the ports she must go to and the fines that would be incurred if the schedule were not adhered to. This was known as 'demorage' and was intended to deter captains from visiting other ports or lingering in the East Indies, purely for the sake of their own private trade. Either side could be liable to a fine if the ship was unjustifiably delayed. Besides demorage, the charter party also set out what guns the ship would carry, which Company passengers would travel on her and, most importantly, how much private trade would be permitted on board. This would be of particular interest to her captain.

In July 1778, the East India Company published the list of ships it intended to take up for the next season.[29] Among those commanders named as having a 'new ship' was Richard Peirce. It was now a matter of public knowledge. A few days later, Richard Peirce was summoned to India House for a formal meeting with the Directors. He was joined there by three fellow commanders, Burnet Abercromby, Allan Cooper and George Richardson.[30] All four took the oath and were cautioned against breaking the Company's rules, especially regarding private trading. This was the standard procedure but it was also a formal indication that the Company intended to employ these men again. Cooper would command the *Atlas* and Richardson the *Ganges*, already taking shape next to the *Halsewell*. It was not yet clear which ship Abercromby would have but it would be another of John Durand's.

Once the basic structure of *Halsewell's* hull was complete, a number of important fixtures had to be put in. These included the strong timbers which formed the 'steps', a kind of socket which anchored the base of each mast to the keel. Next, the massive capstans had to be fitted into the heart of the ship, with their drums extending up to the main and quarter decks. These were the workhorses that could do the heavy lifting; weighing anchor or hoisting the yards and topmasts. The pumps were also installed, low down in the hull, where water from leaks would collect.

With the basic structure of the hull complete, it was time to finish it off. The frames for the raised sections at the bow and stern were added. Strong timbers were fixed to either side of the bow, to hold the anchors. The rudder was attached and holes cut in the sides for gun ports. Finally the decks were planked with deal. Meanwhile, work continued to ensure the hull remained watertight. After the caulking, a layer of canvas or brown paper, called 'parselling', was stretched over the hull, before being nailed on and covered in tar.

By the middle of August 1778, this work had been completed to everyone's satisfaction and the hull was ready to be launched. This was always a tense moment. Moving the enormous hull from the stocks, which had supported it, into the water, was vital. If the process failed and the hull got stuck, all that previous work would have been for nothing. The reputation of the builder and the investment of the owners would be lost. With so much depending on it, an event of this significance was bound to be a grand affair. On Monday 24th, all the interested parties gathered in Rotherhithe at Mr Wells' shipyard.[31] No doubt, there were speeches and a ceremonial bottle was broken against the ship's bow. Then, Thomas Burston, Richard Peirce and the others watched anxiously as the *Halsewell* slid slowly down her slipway, into the water. At last, she was afloat and the celebrations could begin.

On such occasions, it was customary for the ship's husband to lay on a lavish supper in a local tavern. The consortium of owners would attend and invitations would be issued to other dignitaries, investors and patrons. Speeches would be made and the venture would be toasted regularly and enthusiastically. Eventually, the evening would culminate in a ball, to which the ladies would be invited.[32] It would be surprising if Thomas Burston did not do likewise. His daughter and son-in-law surely felt like dancing. The birth of the *Halsewell* had gone smoothly and the whole family would soon be the richer for it.

13
Punch, Sodomy & the Lash

There was still much work to be done before Richard Peirce's new ship would be ready to sail. For the next six weeks or so, *Halsewell* would float in her wet dock while an army of tradesmen worked on her interior. The furnace for the galley was installed with air pipes to draw off the hot air. Then, as a further precaution against the spread of fire, the tinman insulated the galley with sheets of tin. Meanwhile, in the stern, joiners were busy in the roundhouse, installing partitions, shutters and the doors onto the stern gallery. Nearby, the carver was shaping the woodwork into the intricate design which would decorate *Halsewell's* stern. Above him, on the poop deck, others were attaching the hen coops. These were up to twelve feet long and would house the poultry for the voyage. In the fullness of time, one of the *Halsewell's* hen-coops would perform an even more valuable service.

Deep inside the ship, the caulkers sweated in the darkness. Oakum was hammered into the crevices between each plank and then sealed with melted pitch. Not only the outer hull but every deck and internal lining of the ship had to be made watertight. It was essential that the ship remained as dry as possible, particularly on the lower decks where dry rot posed a real threat. The bread room, for example, was susceptible to damp and needed good ventilation. Elsewhere, in the powder room and sail room, the ravages of damp were also to be resisted.

Work must have proceeded at an impressive pace. Before the end of September, the riggers had 'stepped' the masts and attached the shrouds and stays which held them upright. *Halsewell* had been moved to mooring chains on the river where her ballast, water and sails had been brought aboard. By the start of October, she had dropped downstream to Gravesend to begin loading her cargo.[33] Other new ships were beginning to appear, too. From Perry's dock in Blackwall,

Sir Charles Raymond's three ships, the *Atlas, Earl Talbot* and *Earl of Oxford*, were already on the river. They would soon be joined by the *General Barker* from Adam's yard in Deptford but, in Rotherhithe, it would be another month before *Halsewell's* sister ship, *Ganges*, would be ready for launching. Durand's third ship, the *Walpole*, was even further behind. Worryingly for Burnet Abercromby, it looked like he would now miss the first sailing in the new year.

In Somerset, or more precisely in West Monkton, progress on the *Halsewell* was followed with interest. Ann Paul saw the revival of her brother's career as an opportunity for her own family, too. Her eldest daughter, Jane, was now eighteen and of marriageable age.[34] If only she could travel to India, she would surely make a good match there. It was undoubtedly a seller's market. If he was lucky, a Company official might return to Britain once before the end of his career. In order to secure a British wife, therefore, most men in India were restricted to choosing from the tiny number of women who braved the voyage to come to them. In such circumstances, a plain face or a modest background was of much less consequence.

News of the arrival of another Indiaman with unmarried females on board inevitably spread quickly among the bachelors of Madras or Calcutta. Almost always, these young ladies would stay at the house of a relative or family friend. Parties would be thrown and some of the most eligible local bachelors might be invited. For the rest, their only guarantee of setting eyes on these women was on a Sunday. At St Mary's church in Madras, it was customary for a young lady to be escorted to her pew by a gentleman. During that brief encounter, a few words could be exchanged and, as in supercharged speed-dating, a potential suitor would hope to create a favourable impression. At the church door, a veritable scrum of bachelors would jostle for this opportunity.

Given this level of competition, it is unsurprising that most courtships were perfunctory in the extreme. To insure against the risk of another suitor pipping you to the post, a marriage contract had to be agreed as soon as possible. Proposals of marriage were made almost at once and weddings often followed within a matter of weeks. It has been described as 'a matrimonial bran tub where it was in the interests of both parties to make up their minds quickly – the girls because they did not wish to go home to probable spinsterhood and the men in case someone else seized the prize'.[35]

In the case of Jane Paul, her family already had contacts in Bengal. The Grahams and the Templers were known to them and could be counted upon to look after her. Places on East Indiamen were not easy to come by but, now, Jane's uncle Richard could oblige. A letter was sent to the East India Company requesting permission for Jane to sail on the *Halsewell*. In early November, the Court of Directors considered the application and approved it. All that was required were the customary securities of £200 from two guarantors. William Graham, whose late father, John, had been the friend of Warren Hastings, and William Parry, a linen merchant from London, agreed to put up the money.[36]

By 10 November, *Halsewell* had completed loading at Gravesend and Richard Peirce was anxious to be off. He wrote to the Directors seeking permission to sail for the Downs.[37] He did not want a repetition of the delay that *Ashburnham* had suffered. A hold-up like that could cost him dear in private trade, especially as other Indiamen were beginning to depart. Even *Ganges* had been launched and would be ready soon. In his letter, Peirce asked if he could be excused from the formal business of 'taking his leave' from the Court of Directors. It seems that even the short ride to Leadenhall Street was more than Peirce could tolerate. The Directors would have none of it. Peirce would have to attend in person at East India House, though, as a concession, they did agree that only two directors would need to be present to administer the oath.

The most likely explanation for Peirce's impatience was that he knew this season's Indiamen would be sailing in convoy. In March 1778, the conflict in America had widened and Britain found herself at war with France, as well. Following the defeats of the Seven Years War, the French had brought about great improvements in their navy and it now posed a real threat. It was no longer safe for Indiamen to sail without protection. This year, the convoy would sail from Portsmouth, escorted by the Royal Navy. If *Halsewell* missed their departure, she might not sail at all. There would be no market for

Peirce's private trade and he would lose his investment. It would mean financial ruin. A day or so after attending East India House, Richard Peirce fell ill. It is tempting to speculate that this may have been caused, in part, by stress. After years of idleness ashore, it is understandable that Peirce was impatient to get to sea. He was a man in a hurry, not only for financial reasons but because it was part of his nature. Generally, he enjoyed robust health but whatever laid him low on this occasion was severe enough to confine him to bed. On 18 November, he wrote again to the Directors.[38] This time, he requested permission to stay in town on account of his 'ill health'. His request was granted. The *Halsewell* could sail under the command of the first mate and Peirce could join her at Portsmouth. It would give him an opportunity to recover.

The first mate who took temporary command was John Eastabrooke. Previously, he had served as second mate on *Grenville*. Now, without much warning and with little experience, he found himself in charge of *Halsewell*. Under him, at second mate, was Joseph Garrault. Next came Thomas Burston. Since he had sailed on *Ashburnham* as a humble seaman, Burston had gone to sea twice more. He had served as a midshipman, on *True Briton* and then on *Royal Henry*.[39] Now, he had been elevated to third mate and would, once again, serve under his brother-in-law.

As they waited for the order to sail, last minute work continued on their ship. As late as 19 November, another hearth was being installed and carpenters were busily cutting a scuttle for the funnel to go through. Then on the 28th the pilot came aboard and the Company's representative arrived to dispense the river pay. Next day, *Halsewell* sailed for the Hope where passengers were waiting to embark. Among them would be John Hector Cherry.[40] He had just been appointed a Writer and was on his way to Bengal to take up his post. His family lived in Kent but, in time, they would become linked, via India and marriage, to the Pauls of Somerset.

On 6 December, *Halsewell* weighed anchor again and moved down the estuary towards the Downs. Although she was sailing under the direction of the river pilot, responsibility for discipline and overall command rested with John Eastabrooke. It was not long before his authority was tested. On Wednesday the 9th, the ship's journal recorded: 'At 6 pm the caulker being riotous and refusing his duty and threatening to strike the chief mate, put him in irons.' And there the caulker remained until Saturday, by which time he had become sufficiently contrite: 'On the caulker acknowledging his crime and promising to behave well in future, released him from confinement.' The crew knew their Captain was absent but this incident made it clear to them that his deputy would tolerate no nonsense.

On Boxing Day 1778, *Halsewell* arrived at the Motherbank, off Portsmouth. The fleet was already gathering but Peirce need not have worried. A number of Indiamen were missing and it would be several weeks before late starters, like *Ganges,* would catch up. While *Halsewell* waited, her tradesmen would occupy their time with caulking more of the ship's interior and carrying out other maintenance. It was important to keep the whole crew busy and one popular activity was gunnery practice. On 27 February, they 'exercised the great guns and small arms'. If they were to be attacked by French ships, the crew had to be prepared to respond. When the drum beat to quarters, every man must hurry to his action station. If *Halsewell* were boarded and it came to hand-to-hand fighting, the soldiers, recruits and even the male passengers would be expected to defend her. The routine of preparing for action was deadly serious.

Finally, on 3 March, the *Ganges, Resolution* and *Worcester* arrived together from the Downs. The fleet could now form up in preparation for sailing and it was time for Captain Peirce to rejoin his ship. The delayed departure had worked to Richard Peirce's advantage. It had allowed him to recover from his illness and spend a little more time with his family. Mary was pregnant again and the new baby was due in a couple of months. Nevertheless, the news that the fleet was almost ready to sail was the signal he had been waiting for. Accompanied by Jane Paul and another female passenger, he made his way to Portsmouth and on 6 March 1779 went on board *Halsewell*, at last. They sailed the same day.

The fleet that departed from Portsmouth must have been an impressive sight. In all, there were thirteen Indiamen. Escorting them was Admiral Edward Hughes in his flagship, *Superb*, together with three smaller men-o-war and a sloop. At the same time, another convoy set off for Guinea in West Africa. More naval vessels provided additional protection for the first part of the voyage. Those watching from the shore must surely have been stirred by the sight of so many sail, moving together like a great flock of seabirds towards the horizon.

After nearly six years ashore, to feel the motion of the deck under his feet again prompted feelings of relief and satisfaction in Captain Peirce. The smells of turpentine, tar and freshly-worked oak was a reminder that this was a new ship with a new crew. Only the carpenter, faithful Willard Dickinson, had enlisted for a third voyage. Apart from Thomas Burston, the officers were unknown quantities, though they appeared to have acquitted themselves well in his absence. In addition, there were no fewer than six midshipmen and three personal servants, all selected by Peirce himself.

Below decks, was billeted a contingent of the King's soldiers from the 73rd Regiment of Foot, recently raised by Lord Macleod.[41] These men were Scots highlanders though there were also some Irish within their ranks. Their common tongue would have been Scots Gaelic and few, other than their officers, would have been able to speak English. Within a few days, one of the Highlanders had died. In a desperate attempt to gain his discharge, he had cut off several of his own toes. The ploy had failed, infection had set in and the inevitable result had followed.

The response of the Irish recruits to their circumstances was characteristically different. It would soon be St Patrick's Day and they wanted to celebrate. Captain Peirce agreed to their request: 'Being St Patrick's Day gave the whole on board a tub of punch in consequence of a petition from Irish recruits.' It seems that Peirce had not lost his touch. Gestures like this cost little but were invaluable in gaining the goodwill of those around him. But, not every commander in this convoy could emulate Peirce's talent for man-management. On the *Granby*, relations between Captain Johnston and his contingent of highlanders soon deteriorated. Later, when the soldiers refused to take part in the ceremonies of 'crossing the line', bayonets were drawn and the situation almost deteriorated into full-scale mutiny.[42]

After almost exactly a month, the fleet reached Madeira. Peirce and his passengers went ashore and *Halsewell* was left again under the authority of the first mate. Some of the crew were desperate to go ashore, too and, after a few days, discipline began to break down. When two seamen attempted to leave the ship, they were caught and Eastabrooke had them put in irons. Normally, this would be sufficient to deter the rest but, on this occasion, feelings were running high. That evening, a group of sailors forced their way aft and two of them smashed the lock that secured the prisoners. Realising that the situation had slipped out of his control, John Eastabrooke sent word ashore to his captain. Next morning, Peirce arrived in person. Without hesitation, he ordered the lock breakers to be given two dozen lashes each and the runaways to be confined again. Later that day, these bad apples were transferred to HMS *Nymph*. A spell in a Royal Navy sloop would do them good.

In dealing with this incident, Richard Peirce showed his mettle. Punishment was administered swiftly and publicly, and the rest of the crew were left in no doubt about who was in charge. Like all commanders, Peirce feared the presence of a disaffected cabal. By transferring the troublemakers to another ship, he also ensured that no lingering resentment would contaminate the rest of his crew. If insubordination spread, it would be more difficult to contain later. Much better to nip it in the bud, now.

After three weeks, during which Jane Paul and the other passengers enjoyed the delights of Madeira, it was time for the fleet to weigh anchor. By now, they had been joined by more Royal Navy vessels and several transport ships. Altogether, Admiral Hughes would have in his charge an assortment of more than thirty sailing ships. The next stage of the journey was short. Within a fortnight, they had stopped again, this time at Goree. Lying just off the coast of Senegal, opposite Dakar, this tiny island had recently been evacuated by the French. Colonel Macleod was under secret orders to take possession of it for the Crown and this unexpected detour allowed the fleet to drop off its new garrison.[43]

From Goree, the fleet set a course southwest towards the coast of South America. For the recruits, confined below decks, the tedium of the voyage must have been extreme, although some found ways of dealing with it. After only a few days at sea, one Irish recruit, Dennis McMullen, was found to have died. The log records that his death was 'occasioned as supposed by his taking a quantity of opium'. The recruits evidently relied on more than alcohol to keep their spirits up. It would be interesting to know how McMullen had obtained his opium. Its transportation was forbidden on Company ships. Had it been supplied by a member of the crew? By now, Peirce will have been aware of the simmering unrest on some of the other ships. Opium could render the soldiers more docile and perhaps Peirce was happy to turn a blind eye to it. Where violence against others was concerned, it was a different matter. A few days after McMullen had been buried at sea, another recruit assaulted the sergeant. Without hesitation, Captain Peirce ordered him to be given a dozen lashes.

The progress towards the southern hemisphere was steady but slow. Admiral Hughes was determined to keep his convoy together and this meant sailing at the speed of the slower ships. By the third week of June they were in sight of the island of Trinidada, just off the coast of Brazil from which ships traditionally set their course towards the Cape. Up to this time, the men on *Halsewell* had remained remarkably healthy but towards the end of July scurvy began to appear. On 25 July, the journal recorded: 'We now have 6 seamen and companys soldiers and 8 King's soldiers in the scurvy.' Drinking water was also running low and Peirce put the men on a ration of three pints a day. Fortunately, before the situation could deteriorate any further, they reached the Cape. Having shepherded his charges safely down the Atlantic, Admiral Hughes gave the order to anchor in Table Bay. Here they would remain for another three months.

It is not clear why Admiral Hughes decided to stay at the Cape for so long but his orders were probably to wait for the arrival of more Indiamen. In England, the government was increasingly concerned about the French threat in India and the struggle in Mysore. It wanted to send more troops and supplies. A second convoy of seven ships was intended to carry reinforcements. This convoy included the *Walpole,* which had finally left the Wells shipyard. She would be commanded by Burnet Abercromby, the captain who had been sworn in, alongside Peirce, exactly a year earlier. This convoy had only sailed from

Portsmouth in June. If they travelled as slowly as Admiral Hughes' convoy had done, it could take anything up to another seven months before they reached the Cape.

While they waited, Captain Peirce and his passengers went ashore. After so long at sea, Jane Paul must have been pleased to be back on dry land. The Cape Colony in which they now found themselves was Dutch. At this time, England was at peace with Holland though the situation would change the following year. For now, British visitors were welcome. The diarist, William Hickey, visited the Cape a number of times and found the Dutch settlers to be friendly. Possibly, Richard Peirce found opportunities for some private trading but mostly he will have passed the days in the company of his fellow commanders. It allowed plenty of time to get to know them or to renew old friendships. Perhaps it was at the Cape that he became friendly with John Blackburn of the *Fox*. Six years later, Blackburn's daughter would sail as a passenger on *Halsewell's* final voyage.

Finally, in October, the second convoy arrived at the Cape. It had sailed under Admiral Edwards and had made good time. After a pause to take on supplies, the *Walpole* and five other new arrivals joined seven of the original convoy to form a new fleet, under Admiral Hughes. This time they were escorted by five men-o'-war and one sloop. French vessels were known to be in the Indian Ocean and might strike at the convoy from their base at Isle de France. The convoy needed to be well protected.

As it turned out, no French naval forces were encountered but, instead, an invisible enemy threatened their progress. After less than two weeks at sea, disease had broken out on at least one Indiaman. In such a short time, it cannot have been scurvy and, in view of the speed with which it spread, it must have been highly contagious. The most likely culprit is typhus. By the middle of November, the *Duke of Grafton* was so badly affected that she no longer had enough men capable of working the ship. The only solution was for *Grafton* to be towed by one of her navy escorts. This situation continued throughout December and by January, the crew of *Atlas* had also begun to succumb. On 10 January 1780, *Halsewell's* journal recorded that 120 people on

Atlas were 'inflenced' and she, too, was being towed. With obvious relief, it added 'our people continue very healthy'.

Outbreaks like this brought home to every commander the importance of maintaining a healthy crew. If *Atlas* or *Grafton* had been sailing alone, the impact of such an epidemic would have been catastrophic. It is not surprising that Peirce and his colleagues took such pains to air and fumigate their ships as often as they did.

One other incident on this leg of the voyage deserves a mention. Shortly after sailing from the Cape, two of the company recruits became drunk and were found indulging in 'indecent behaviour'. This term usually implied homosexual activity of some kind and was potentially a very serious matter. Sodomy was a capital offence but, at sea, convictions were rare. For one thing, the almost complete darkness that prevailed below decks meant that little could be seen and witnesses could seldom give convincing evidence. In this case, Captain Peirce must have felt that a lesser punishment was sufficient. The two men were put in irons for a day and then given a dozen lashes to cool their ardour.

14

Dodgy Money & the Macclesfield Bank

On the 18th January 1780, *Halsewell* dropped anchor in Madras Roads. They were a mile off shore and in sight of the flagstaff at Fort St George. The fort acknowledged their arrival with a salute of nine guns, which *Halsewell* duly returned. Next day, Captain Shane led his men to the waiting boats and the disembarkation of the 73rd Regiment began. In kilts of Mackenzie tartan, marching to the skirl of their bagpipes, Macleod's Highlanders presented an extraordinary spectacle to the residents of Madras. Towards the end of the day, they were followed ashore by Captain Peirce and Admiral Hughes, himself. Greeted by a 17-gun salute from the Fort, the arrival of the Admiral was hardly more discreet, though Captain Peirce had to be content with nine.

For some of the *Halsewell's* crew, their arrival at Madras did not start well. As the soldiers were going ashore, a Royal Navy officer, from HMS *Belleisle,* came on board and pressed fifteen of the crew. Peirce could do nothing to stop it. His ship was at anchor, his country was at war and the Royal Navy was short of manpower. The pressing of men was inevitable but it was an irritant, nonetheless. His men would need to be replaced somehow and Peirce might have to make up the shortfall with lascars. However, there was plenty of time. *Halsewell* would remain at Madras for some months and, in the meantime, its captain had more urgent matters to attend to.

First, he had to deliver the packet from Leadenhall Street to the Governor at Fort St George. Governor Du Pre had long departed and the present incumbent was Sir Thomas Rumbold. If ever a man epitomised the piratical, buccaneering qualities of the hated 'nabob', it was Rumbold. While in office he would 'shake the pagoda tree' for all his worth. At this first meeting, Richard Peirce was pleased to inform Governor Rumbold that the Company's own recruits had now disembarked. They were all in good health, and the contingent included one woman and two children, the younger of whom had been born during the voyage.

The safe arrival of more Royal and Company forces was reassuring for the Governor of Madras. Despite appearances, the situation in Madras was not entirely secure. News of the renewal of hostilities with France had reached the Carnatic coast in July 1778. Rumbold had immediately instructed General Hector Munro to march on the French port of Pondicherry. Its defences had fallen into disrepair and it was held by a force of only seven hundred French troops and a similar number of sepoys. A handful of ships under Admiral Tonjoli protected its coastline. After an inconclusive engagement, in August, against ships under Admiral Vernon, the French Admiral decided to withdraw his fleet to Isle de France. Meanwhile, General Munro had assembled an enormous force of twenty thousand men and by the beginning of September the siege of Pondicherry had begun. Despite being hugely outnumbered, the French put up fierce resistance and held out for several weeks but, with no prospect of any reinforcements, the French commander, General de Bellecombe, soon bowed to the inevitable. On 18 October he capitulated.

The fall of Pondicherry removed the only French stronghold capable of threatening Madras. Five months later, British forces captured Mahe. This port on the western, Malabar coast of India, belonged to the French also. Although smaller than Pondicherry, it had strategic importance. For one thing, it was the main gateway through which France could supply their ally, the Sultan of Mysore. He had guaranteed its security. The news that Mahe had been seized by the British was seen by Hyder Ali as a blatant provocation to which he must respond. Throughout the rest of 1779, Hyder Ali began preparations. He put together an alliance with the Nizam of Hyderabad and even with his former enemies the Marathas. Together they would raise an army large enough to confront the British and drive them from the Carnatic. This took time and it would be July 1780, before Hyder Ali was ready to act. Then, with an enormous force of 80,000 men, he marched through the passes of the Eastern Ghats and began laying waste around Arcot. British forces, there, withdrew to their forts and were powerless to intervene.

In January 1780, when Richard Peirce stepped ashore in Madras, this conflict was still seven months away. But the storm clouds were already gathering. *Halsewell* would remain at anchor until June while the atmosphere in Madras grew increasingly fraught. Whether anticipation of trouble ahead was good or bad for private trade is not clear but, as usual, Peirce pressed on with settling his own affairs.

Jane Paul by Jean Mosnier
© *Oxbow Books*

Before the Crown's military stores or the Company's cargo could be unloaded, the private trade of Captain Peirce and his officers had been taken ashore. The process of selling and investing in new goods was one that Peirce was well practised at, by now. Despite the long interval since his last visit, many of his business contacts in Madras were probably still around.

So, too, were some of the friends he had made. Invitations to their houses and to formal receptions at Fort St George allowed Peirce to introduce his niece to Madras society. On Sundays, they attended St Mary's church. Jane was noted for her good looks so competition to escort her to her pew must have been particularly fierce.[44] If Jane enjoyed this attention, she also knew she was bound for Bengal where even more eligible bachelors were waiting to meet her.

On 31 January, the air was rent by a thunderous noise, as Fort St George and every ship in Madras Roads fired twenty-one gun salutes. Remarkably, the reason for this gesture was the opening of a royal letter. The letter in question was from King George III to the local ruler, Mohamed Ali Khan Walejah, Nawab of the Carnatic, and its delivery demanded such pomp. Popularly known as the 'Nabob of Arcot', the Nawab was almost totally dependent on British military protection. Almost half of the Madras army was billeted in one or other of the Nawab's forts. In return for the defence of his territory, the Nabob of Arcot paid the British an enormous sum of money each year. He also spent heavily in maintaining his lavish lifestyle. This included the commissioning of paintings, displaying him in all his opulence. For several years, the Scottish painter, George Willison, had worked for the Nabob and had produced no less than eight portraits of him.[45] In return, the Nabob had rewarded Willison generously. It was said he had received jewels and at least £16,000 in pagodas. Not surprisingly, the ruler of the Carnatic was heavily in debt. His creditors were not only the British government. Many merchants and individuals in Madras claimed that the Nabob owed them money too. The debts of the Nabob of Arcot reached such a scale that they would preoccupy the East India Company and have an impact on British domestic politics for years to come.

Meanwhile, during February and March 1780, the emptying of *Halsewell's* hold continued at a leisurely pace. The Company's copper was removed and replaced by redwood and bales of cotton. In China, the demand for raw cotton was growing steadily. An Imperial edict had instructed farmers to grow more rice and, consequently, the production of cotton had fallen. This shortfall would guarantee a good price for Indian cotton at Canton, and Peirce will have been keen to take his quota in private trade.

While other ships made haste, there appears to have been little urgency on *Halsewell*. On 21 February, *Walpole* and *True Briton* sailed for Bengal. It is likely that Jane Paul was a passenger. Her destination had always been Calcutta but her uncle's ship was intended for China. There was no feasible route overland so the young lady must have sailed this final leg of the journey, under the protection of another East India Company commander. As Jane was departing, *Halsewell's* sister ship, the *Ganges*, was arriving. *Ganges* had already been to Bengal and now was heading home.

Meanwhile, *Halsewell* rode at anchor in Madras Roads, where she would remain until June. Towards the end of that period, three French prisoners-of-war were sent on board, accompanied by Lieutenant Urquhart. The Frenchmen were also officers and, therefore, entitled to be treated with the respect due to their rank. Having given their word not to escape, they would be free to mingle with the other passengers. Lieutenant Urquhart may even have permitted them to retain their swords. United by a common code of honour and gentlemanly behaviour, relations with captured enemy officers was often remarkably relaxed. However, in this instance, it did not extend to their inclusion at Captain Peirce's table. Instead, it was decided that the French officers would be accommodated in the third mate's mess. To cover this additional expense, Captain Peirce gave Thomas Burston an advance of £90, knowing the Company would reimburse him on his return to London.

In the third week of June, Peirce returned to his ship, bringing with him some other passengers. Amongst the travellers was George Willison. He had completed his commissions for the Nawab and was now ready to return home with his fortune. His money, silver pagodas secured in locked chests, would accompany him as far as China. At Canton, he would pay them into the Company's treasury and receive bills of exchange in return. These could be cashed in London.

On 21 June, only a matter of weeks before Hyder Ali began his invasion of the Carnatic, *Halsewell* finally weighed anchor. Together with the *Granby, Earl of Oxford, Earl of Sandwich* and a recent arrival, the *Britannia*, this small fleet put to sea. They were escorted by the *Seahorse*, a twenty-four gun frigate, whose commander was Captain Panton. This was a good choice. Captain Panton was familiar with the route and had been sent by Admiral Vernon, to Canton the previous year. His mission had been to try to recover money owed to the East India Company by merchants of the Co-Hong.[46]

In recent years, the trade between the Co-Hong and the foreign merchants had not always worked to the advantage of the Chinese. In 1774 the Hong merchant Senqua had gone bankrupt, owing a quarter of a million dollars.[47] By 1779 three more were in trouble and the debts of the Co-Hong to foreign merchants was thought to have reached a million dollars. While the East India Company looked to negotiate a settlement by diplomatic means, Admiral Vernon had opted for a more direct approach. The *Seahorse* had carried letters demanding the money. Although, Captain Panton had failed to obtain a meeting with the Emperor's viceroy, his mission was not a complete disaster. He had been encouraged to try again, the following year. This was what he hoped to do now.

Although the Chinese merchants and the Nawab of the Carnatic had their liquidity problems, others, it seems, did not. Since taking up his post as Governor of Madras in 1778, Sir Thomas Rumbold had done very well for himself. His official salary was set at a generous 40,000 pagodas a year, roughly equivalent to £15,000. Not content with this, he had also managed to siphon off huge amounts of public money into his own pocket and, by the time of his resignation, later in 1780, he was said to have amassed a staggering fortune of £200,000. Even by the lax standards of India, corruption on this scale was outrageous and Rumbold would be called to account on his return to England. However, he had covered his tracks well and nothing would be conclusively proved against him. Though he would hold onto his 'obnoxious' fortune, in the eyes of many he exemplified the brazen 'rapacious and peculating despotism' of the hated nabob.[48]

An example of how Thomas Rumbold operated can be seen in case of the *Seahorse* and the Indiamen that sailed with her in 1780. Essentially, it was a money-laundering exercise. Captain Panton agreed to convey chests of silver pagodas, belonging to Rumbold, from Madras to Canton. Later a parliamentary enquiry would discover that this coin was valued at £6,400 and that Panton had been paid 3% for shipping it. By paying his money into the treasury at Canton, Rumbold would be able to remit his fortune to Britain securely while covering his tracks at the same time. His coin would be welcomed by the Council of Supercargoes and no questions would be asked as to how he had obtained it. Since the outbreak of war, the supply of silver from England had almost dried up and a serious cash-flow problem was looming. Without sufficient coin to pay for their purchases, the supercargoes would not be able to buy the tea they wanted. It is hardly surprising, therefore, that they were reluctant to enquire too closely into the source of any money deposited with them.

Exactly one month after leaving Madras, the fleet had reached Malacca. From there, *Seahorse* led her charges carefully down the Straits. Again the litany of landmarks is recorded in *Halsewell's* journal. Mount Formosa on 31 July; Great Carimon on 2 August; Point Romania on the 5th. They passed Pulo Sapata on 15 August and had reached the Macclesfield shoal by the 19th. Ten days later they were off Macao. There was no point in taking the French prisoners to Whampoa, so they were sent ashore to wait at the Portuguese settlement. The *Earl of Oxford*, also carrying French officers, did likewise. While he waited for a river pilot to guide them up to Whampoa, Captain Peirce sent the longboat ahead to deliver the packet to the supercargoes. He then fired thirteen guns in a gesture of thanks and farewell to *Seahorse*. As the naval vessel of a foreign power, the Chinese would not permit her to pass through the Bogue or approach Canton.

At the start of September, *Halsewell* was warped to her anchorage near the upper part of Danes Island. Here she would remain until December while her redwood and cotton was unloaded. On this occasion, the security merchant allocated to the *Halsewell* was called Munqua. He, too, had his debts but it was believed that he was not 'in any immediate distress'.[49] Once *Halsewell's* hold was empty, a disturbing discovery was made. The step, securing the foremast to the hull, was found to have rotted. Unless these timbers were replaced, there was a danger that the mast would fall. This would have to be fixed before *Halsewell* could stow any of the chests of Bohea and Congou tea that the supercargoes had purchased. Under the direction of Willard Dickinson, the carpenters set to work. Deep in the bowels of the ship, this was hot and difficult work. Ventilation was poor and the smell must have been powerful. Combined with the climate and its attendant diseases, the assault on Dickinson's health proved too much.

The English Factory at Canton (detail)
© *Duke's of Dorchester*

On 28 October, he succumbed. Having served under Richard Peirce on more voyages than any other sailor, Willard Dickinson would sail no more. He was buried on French Island. The death of seamen was a common occurrence but it would be surprising if Richard Peirce did not feel this loss more than most.

Throughout November and December, Richard Peirce stayed at the Company's factory in Canton, enjoying the camaraderie of fellow commanders and the hospitality of Munqua. The other factories were quiet this year. Since the outbreak of war, the French had prudently stayed away. Other nations were also sparsely represented and this may explain why Peirce was able to recruit some Danish seamen who were looking for work. If there were any Dutch ships at Whampoa, neither their commanders nor Peirce would have known that Britain was about to declare war on Holland, too. By the time that news arrived, this season's ships had long departed. However, bad news from India may well have reached Peirce's ears before he set sail. In September, Hyder Ali's invading forces had inflicted a humiliating defeat on the British at the battle of Pollilur. The British had suffered 3,000 casualties and their commander, Colonel Baillie had been taken prisoner. Once again, it would require Eyre Coote to rectify the situation but, for now, the British position in Madras looked distinctly precarious.

By early December, repairs to *Halsewell* had been completed, her sides painted with 'varnish of pine and yellow oker' and her hold filled with tea, raw silk and private trade. It was time for Richard Peirce to bank the proceeds of his business deals. On 9 December, he paid the equivalent of £1,730 into the Company treasury and received a 90-days certificate in return. If he presented this document at India House in London, the Company would repay this sum within three months. Next day, with their river pilots aboard, *Halsewell*, *Granby* and *Earl of Sandwich* prepared to unmoor. On the 11th, they cleared the first and second bars in three fathoms of water. Still upriver from the Bogue, they anchored alongside *Britannia* and *Earl of Oxford* to wait for the Grand Chop. This was the permission to depart, only granted by the Hoppo when all customs duties and fees had been paid. Another ten days would have to pass before everything was in order. During this time, Captain Peirce sent a letter to the Directors, via another ship, telling them that he was about to sail. Then, on 29 December 1780, he arrived from the factory at Canton to rejoin his ship. Next morning, the five Indiamen and one country ship made sail, at last. Without a naval escort, they would be led by their most senior commander, known as the commodore. In this case, the commodore was to be Captain Johnston of the *Granby*. Richard Peirce and the other commanders would be expected to follow his instructions.

One can imagine that Richard Peirce was anxious to be home. His private trading in the East had been completed and now he wanted to sell his goods in London. He must also have longed to see his family again. In May 1779, Mary had given birth to another daughter.[50] Word of this had probably reached Peirce already but news was intermittent, at best, and he must have wanted to reassure himself that all was well. Whatever, his personal feelings, Richard Peirce was in no position to hurry. He would have to keep pace with the fleet and, in any case, they still had another important duty to perform, mapping the seabed. Under the prompting of its hydrographer, Alexander Dalrymple, the East India Company was trying to improve the quality and accuracy of the sea charts for this part of the world. The seas from Malaysia to Whampoa were imperfectly known. There were shallows, reefs, rocks and other hazards whose positions were not yet precisely fixed. On their homeward voyage from Whampoa, this season's ships had been instructed to take careful soundings at points along the way.

The first area to examine was the Macclesfield Bank. Although known for many years, its exact extent was still unclear. Alexander Dalrymple had provided Peirce and the others with a chart showing its supposed location. He wanted them to check its southern boundary. On Wednesday 3 January 1781, when they reached a latitude of 15 °15', Commodore Johnston instructed his commanders to take soundings. This was done by sending the longboats ahead of their ships. With a crew of eight men under the command of an officer, each longboat would be able to pause to measure the depth more accurately. Captain Peirce put Thomas Burston in charge of *Halsewell's* longboat. When the third mate reported at the end of the day, Peirce was surprised to learn that they were in at least seventy fathoms of water. On two previous voyages he had located the Bank. Now, he recorded his disappointment in 'not getting ground this day', concluding correctly that Macclesfield Bank must lie further to the north. He passed these findings to the commodore. For the next three days, as they sailed south, the longboats continued to sound the depth, every hour. They found they were in deep water throughout.

By Tuesday 9 January, propelled southwards by an 'amazing current', *Halsewell* was close to the Natunas islands, and approaching 5° north. The longboat, equipped with 'signals, lights and necessaries', was sent ahead, throughout the night, to keep a good lookout. This proved a sensible precaution. At midnight, Thomas Burston signalled that land lay ahead. Daylight revealed it to be Steeple Island and not, as Peirce had first thought, the eastern Natunas. He corrected his log accordingly to 'ye land, agreeable to Mr Dalrymple's chart.' Despite deteriorating weather, the *Halsewell* and *Earl of Sandwich* kept their longboats ahead of the fleet. From Tuesday to Thursday the Indiamen followed under an 'easy sail'. Meanwile, in their open boats, drenched with rain, the men under Thomas Burston were cold and tired, but still the work continued.

As Thursday drew to a close, they were approaching 1 degree north. Still referring to Dalrymple's chart, Captain Peirce looked out for an island called Platte. There was no sign of it. Then around midnight, they saw land ahead. In the moonlight, Peirce sketched its outline, 'a small round island', which he thought must be one of a pair of islands, named by Dalrymple as St Pierre and De Remarque. With the return of daylight on Friday morning, he decided it was the easternmost island and one that he had seen before. Despite the name attributed to it by Dalrymple, Richard Peirce confidently noted in the journal, 'I call it Deanes Island'.

Throughout the weekend, they sailed south of the equator into the Karimata Strait, between Borneo and Sumatra. The wind was freshening again and sharp squalls made life difficult for the boats. On Saturday, *Earl of Sandwich* hoisted in her cutter but the bigger longboats were kept at sea throughout another night. The depths they recorded appeared to be very irregular, fluctuating between sixteen and twenty-five fathoms. On Sunday, another island was visible. Identified by Peirce as Saratou, this must be Serutu Island which lies southwest of Karimata. By now, the crew of *Halsewell's* longboat had had enough. They had been at sea for a considerable time, their supplies were low and they wanted to return. Burston signalled their request and Peirce acceded. However, it was only a temporary respite; the surveying of the seabed was not finished. *Halsewell's* journal recorded: 'gave them a fresh supply of candles, lanthorns & necessary refreshments and sent her ahead again.'

On Monday night, the unsettled weather took another turn for the worse. By now, the gale was strong enough to split *Halsewell's* topsail. In the *Granby*, Commodore Johnston decided to run eastward but on *Halsewell* they neither heard his signal nor saw his lights. As a result, Peirce continued on his present course under an easy sail. When sun rose on Monday morning, there was no sign of *Granby* nor, more worryingly, of any of the longboats. Peirce began to fear the worst: 'I was under much anxiety for the boats as it blew very hard in the night with a large sea.' Immediately, *Halsewell*, *Britannia* and *Sandwich* all hove to, while they scanned the horizon. After some time, an eagle-eyed lookout saw the longboats some distance away to the northwest. They had survived the storm and their relieved captains now summoned them back to their ships.

Having also reunited with the *Granby*, the fleet carried southeast, through the Java Sea, towards the 'Streights of Bally'. On Thursday 18 January, as they approached Bali, Commodore Johnston gave the order for the ships to follow him through the narrow Strait. 'Commodore made signal to close in his wake. I bore down accordingly.' With characteristic thoroughness, Richard Peirce continued to record his surroundings. 'I saw plainly the islands called in Mr Dalrymple's chart Turtle Island and Sunkan Island. Sketches of which I have taken. Coasting along Java I saw a reef off Two Tree Point the particulars of which I mark'd to avoid it in my observations.'

From 19 January the fleet anchored in the straits while their longboats continued to take soundings. The scenery was beautiful and the inhabitants were 'a very friendly and fair-dealing people, as any ever met with in the eastern countries', willing to trade in bullocks, fowls, sago and 'remarkable fine rice'. The crew of another ship, the *Vansittart*, found the natives were fond of red cloth, muskets and knives.

Its captain recorded that 'cheap cutlery is the best and surest article to procure fowls, fruits and anything in the small way'.[51] However, this idyllic place was not without its dangers. 'The tides here set stronger', says the captain of the *Osterley*,' than those I have met with in any other straits, having found them to run 6 knots an hour.' Securely anchored, *Halsewell* and her companions were able to withstand this danger, until the Commodore decided their mapping work was done. Then on 27 January 1781, the order was given to make sail. It was time to go home.

Bali may have seemed like paradise but it hid a danger that could decimate a crew. The ships had been at sea for about two weeks when illness began to affect the sailors. Fever and 'the flux', dysentery, was spreading, not only in *Halsewell*, but in the rest of the fleet, too. When Peirce sent the jollyboat to speak to the commodore, it reported that the *Granby's* crew were 'very sickly'. On 12 February, two of *Halsewell's* youngest crewmen died. They were the servants of the second mate and the gunner. A couple of days after they had been buried at sea, their few possessions were sold 'before the mast'.

By 4 March, a quartermaster had died and sixteen more of *Halsewell's* men were on the sick list, mostly with the flux. The *Granby* reported five deaths, *Earl of Oxford* four. As March continued, two more of *Halsewell's* men would die and it was not until April that the sick list began to reduce, at last. On 24 May, the ships arrived in St Helena Road. Nearly five months had passed since they had left Whampoa and the men were desperate to go ashore. Some became truculent and tensions began to rise. On the 28th, the longboat was sent to pick up fresh water from the island but, having reached dry land, one of the seamen refused to load the longboat for the return journey. He became violent and hit the fourth mate, John Stewart. This could not be tolerated and the man was forcibly returned to the ship to await punishment. Predictably, Captain Peirce was ashore himself but word was sent to him and he reappeared next morning. Henderson was punished with 'two dozen lashes'. Once again, Richard Peirce had stood by his officers. He would not allow their authority to be undermined and discipline would be maintained.

During the last two days of May, work proceeded on getting *Halsewell* ready to put to sea again. The ship was 'heel'd' or tilted over on one side to reveal as much of her hull as possible. To ensure she remained watertight, the men 'Hog'd and scrub'd her & pay'd her Bottom with Pitch and Greese'. While this was going on, the sailmaker worked to repair the sails and dry them. The boatswain overhauled the rigging, the cooper reassembled water casks and the armourer worked at his forge. In such a hive of activity, a busy crew was less likely to become troublesome.

The final leg of the voyage from St Helena to London would take *Halsewell* through European waters where the French might be lying in wait. She would need naval protection. In St Helena Road, other Indiamen were waiting to depart and together they formed a fleet of seventeen ships, escorted by the *Renoun* man-of-war and a sloop, the *Shark*. Laden with tea, cotton and other goods from the east, the total value of this fleet was enormous. Were it to fall into the hands of the enemy, the loss to the East India Company, even to Britain as a whole, would be devastating. Such a fear was not unfounded. In August 1780, while *Halsewell* was approaching Whampoa, the French and Spanish had intercepted an outward-bound fleet, which included five Indiamen. All five East Indiamen and many of the other ships had been taken to Cadiz as prizes and would not be returned. The only consolation was that they had been heading to India and not returning with their holds full.

On 29 July, Captain Henry of the *Renoun* made the signal to the fleet to make sail. It was also the signal for the East India commanders to return to their ships. Captain Peirce went on board the *Halsewell* that morning, bringing with him a female passenger, Mrs Wrangham. Almost certainly, this person was Elizabeth Wrangham, wife of William Wrangham. Since 1760, the Wranghams had lived on St Helena where William had been sent as a writer with the East India Company. Over the years, his career had thrived and, by 1774, Wrangham had been elevated to the St Helena Council. It is highly likely that Richard Peirce had made the acquaintance of the Wranghams during his many stays on the island so it is no surprise that Mrs Wrangham chose to return to Europe on his ship. If indeed, Richard Peirce was a friend of the family, he must also have known Mrs Wrangham's daughter, Amelia. In 1780, Amelia was eighteen and already celebrated for her beauty and unconventional approach to life.[52] Soon she would achieve fame, if not notoriety, breaking the hearts of many men in Bengal. Whether Richard Peirce was susceptible to the attractions of the 'St Helena belle', we can only wonder.

Despite anxieties regarding the French, the voyage home seems to have been largely uneventful. There was, however, a foretaste of what was to come. On *Renoun*, Capt Henry found his ship to be rather under-manned, perhaps as a result of illness amongst his crew. He decided to rectify the situation by pressing sailors from the ships he was escorting. On 10 September, his officers came aboard *Halsewell* and took off three of her seamen. There was nothing Richard Peirce could do to prevent this but he did ensure that one of the three men seized was William Henderson, the sailor he had punished for striking an officer. Peirce was not going to waste this opportunity to rid his ship of another bad apple. However, the pressing of Henderson and his two companions did nothing to reduce tension among the rest of the crew. They knew that the risk of being pressed would increase as they entered home waters. The war with France, Spain and now with Holland had stretched the Royal Navy so that it was desperately short of manpower. The opportunity to pick off the crews from returning merchant ships was too tempting to resist. But for the men on the *Halsewell* and the other Indiamen, such a prospect filled them with dread. They would receive no pay until their ship was safely in the Thames and they were desperate to see the families and friends again. To be pressed now would be a cruel stroke of fate.

By 12 October, the fleet were in sight of Lands End. Over the following week, they worked their way slowly up the Channel and by the 23rd were abreast of Margate. From there, they opted to take the Queen's Channel up the Thames Estuary but progress was painfully slow. The winds were too light and the current was against them. Having got as high as the Pan Land, they were forced to run downstream again and anchor in deeper water. On Sunday 28th, they tried again. This time they got as far as the buoy of the Mouse but had to anchor in eleven fathoms to wait for the tide. This delay was to prove unfortunate.

At noon, a boat carrying two Royal Navy lieutenants came alongside. The men of the *Halsewell* were in no doubt about what they wanted. If the Royal Navy tried to press them, they would resist. The ship's journal records succinctly that 'our men [...] armed themselves'. Faced by such a determined show of force, the two naval officers beat a hasty retreat.

Halsewell's journal is noticeably silent about the role played by Captain Peirce and his officers in this incident. He does not say that he was overpowered by his own crew or that firearms were seized or even that his orders were disobeyed. It is tempting to think that the show of defiance by the crew had his tacit approval. At a human level, Captain Peirce would feel sympathy for men who, for the most part, had served him loyally. At a practical level, he did not want to lose them now. The ship still had to be worked up to Deptford and he and his officers could not do this alone. Nevertheless, the actions of his men could not be treated lightly; there were bound to be consequences.

Early that evening, *Halsewell* weighed anchor and tried to move upstream again. Whether, this was done under Peirce's orders or against his wishes, is not recorded. He and his officers were clearly not held prisoner so, again, we may infer his agreement. Soon they were passing the Nore, the great naval anchorage where several naval vessels were moored. By now the two lieutenants had reported their humiliating treatment aboard *Halsewell* and retribution was about to follow. As *Halsewell* sailed past, she came under fire from several ships.

The seriousness of the situation was not lost on Richard Peirce. He was responsible for returning his ship in one piece, with her cargo intact. *Halsewell's* hold contained not only the Company's tea but also his own investment in private trade, and that of his officers. Nothing must jeopardise that. To ignore these warning shots and to continue to sail past would be to invite destruction. He gave the order to come to and drop anchor. His crew refused to obey. Now they were in open revolt and Peirce had lost control of his ship. The journal describes his predicament: 'Could not bring our ship too the people refusing to clew the sails up or let go the anchor.'

Aware only that the *Halsewell* was still under sail, one naval vessel continued to fire on her. This was the frigate, *Albemarle*, under the command of a young Captain Horatio Nelson. Perhaps it was his officers who had returned empty-handed from *Halsewell* with their tails between their legs. Although not aimed at *Halsewell's* hull, the fire from *Albemarle* began to inflict damage. One shot hit the mainmast, knocking off the 'chick'. Another ripped through the main topsail and several whistled close overhead. Without assistance from the men, Peirce ordered his officers to try to bring *Halsewell* to a stop. One went aloft to release the topsail halyards but found them already ripped by shot. The journal describes how 'at last with difficulty the Chief and 4 Mates let go the Anchor aft'. This had the desired effect. *Halsewell* was brought abruptly to a standstill, with her head facing the shore. The firing stopped and, soon, a boat was seen to be approaching from the *Albemarle*. It contained Captain Nelson himself. If he thought he could be more persuasive than his officers had been, he was to be disappointed. Despite his 'offers to our men', they 'all refused'. Now that they were so close to home and payday, no seaman was prepared to go willingly. Captain Nelson returned to his ship, temporarily defeated. However, the man who would triumph over the French in battle was not going to let merchant seamen get the better of him.

The next morning 'Came on board again Captain Nelson who told the people if they refused serving his Majesty he must bring the Frigate alongside.' This was an ultimatum. If he had to use force, he would. But even then, it took time for some of Peirce's men to accept the inevitable. 'After much trouble and difficulty they got all our people and left only the Foreigners and Servants.' At a stroke, Richard Peirce had lost almost one hundred men. With only a few Danes, lascars and his officers to work the ship, he would be unable to get *Halsewell* to her moorings in London. At 8pm that evening, help materialised when a lieutenant with twenty-four men arrived from the Nore. They would be Peirce's crew for the final stretch of the river.

On Tuesday 30 October, this skeleton crew took *Halsewell* as far as Gravesend Reach. Here, the pilot came on board, bringing with him a dozen more men. However, it was not until Tuesday 6th November 1781 that *Halsewell* finally reached her destination at Deptford. Her journal was delivered to East India House and her hatches, which had remained padlocked, were opened in the presence of a Company official. Now, the lumpers could start their work and the unloading of the ship began. As soon as he was sure his private trade had been transported safely to a Company warehouse, Richard Peirce left the City and set off up the Thames to rejoin his family.

15

Putting Family First

Mary Peirce's happiness at seeing Richard again can scarcely have exceeded that of her father. As ship's husband to the *Halsewell*, Thomas Burston had staked a fortune on her safe return. Now he and his son-in-law could enjoy the proceeds. Not everyone had been so fortunate. One of John Durand's ships, the *General Barker* had returned much earlier in the year, carrying the now retired Governor of Madras. It was reported that Thomas Rumbold had paid Captain Todd the enormous sum of 7,000 guineas for bringing him home.[1] At first, it seemed that this voyage had been a success, too. As soon as they reached the British Isles, Rumbold had disembarked, leaving the *General Barker* to work her way slowly back to the Thames. The ship had sailed as far as the Downs when disaster struck. A severe gale caused *General Barker* to lose her anchors and drove her eastward onto the sands near Ostend. By now, Britain was at war with the Dutch and so the beached Indiamen and all her cargo fell into the hands of the enemy.[2] As an experienced owner, John Durand had taken out adequate insurance but his captain, Alexander Todd, had not been so prudent. Consequently, he had lost his entire investment.

With his own private trade now safe in the Company's warehouse, Richard Peirce presented the bill of exchange he had drawn on the Canton treasury. On 7 November, the Court of Directors approved its payment.[3] Some months later they also agreed to refund the £90 that Peirce had spent on food for his three French prisoners-of-war.[4] The Directors were, evidently, unperturbed by the news that two of these officers had been 'accidently' left behind in Macao. What did concern the Directors, though, was a suspected irregularity in *Halsewell's* paperwork. There had been a delay in handing over the ship's journal and it was February before the Court was satisfied everything was in order. This may simply have been due to a bureaucratic muddle but,

Walnut Tree House, Kingston-upon-Thames
© *Philip Browne*

perhaps explains the Directors' caution when Richard Peirce then presented them with another bill of exchange. This time the amount was £60, drawn on the account of William Wrangham, in St Helena. The intended recipient was a Reverend Bearcroft but he had died intestate. Peirce now requested the money for himself, on the grounds that he was Wrangham's attorney.[5] The Directors referred the request to their Treasury Committee which, after deliberation, they eventually agreed to pay.

By May 1782, Richard Peirce felt financially secure enough to move his family to a much bigger house. He decided to rent Walnut Tree House near the centre of Kingston-upon-Thames. Rated at £80 a year, this was a substantial dwelling and one of the largest in the area.[6] It had been rebuilt in 1756 and belonged to Sir Peregrine Fury who let it to a succession of eminent tenants. Before the arrival of the Peirce family, it had been occupied by the Duke of Atholl.

The house into which the Peirces now moved was a typical Georgian mansion. Its solid, uncompromising exterior lacked ostentation but suggested durability and a no-nonsense outlook that chimed well with its new occupant. Built in fashionable yellow brick and three storeys high, Walnut Tree House was assessed in 1774 as having 56 windows. An octagonal bay on the south front broke the monotony of its façade.

The interior of the house provided a spacious, well-lit and attractive environment for the family to inhabit. Here, Captain Peirce could display the trappings of status. His growing library of books, his porcelain, his pictures, all would proclaim him a man of sensibility and culture. Now in his early forties, he was an experienced commander, respected within the East India Company and confident about his place in society. Walnut Tree House was an appropriate residence for such a person.

The Britain to which Richard Peirce had returned was less confident about its own position in the world. The struggle in America was going badly and much of Europe had sided with the rebels. In November, it became clear that the French Admiral de Grasse had won a tactical victory in Chesapeake Bay over Admiral Thomas Graves. The consequences of this were not difficult to foresee. At Yorktown, without supplies from the sea, Cornwallis's beleaguered army could not hold out for long. Just before Christmas, the news arrived that Cornwallis had surrendered to George Washington. It was a crushing defeat that would shake the whole country.

The loss of the American colonies dealt a severe blow to British self-esteem and, in particular, to its monarch, George III. Perhaps, he would have felt less depressed had he known that, in India, the outlook was more encouraging. In June 1781, the veteran Eyre Coote had finally stopped Hyder Ali in his tracks, soundly defeating his much bigger army at the Battle of Porto Novo. In October, Rumbold's successor, Lord Macartney, had taken up his post as Governor of Madras. His first action was to send General Munro to attack Dutch-held Negapatam. It fell in November 1781, though word would not reach London until the following April. Then, in January 1782, Admiral Edward Hughes ferried an army to attack another Dutch stronghold, on the Island of Ceylon. Trincomalee was of greater strategic significance and, with its capture, it looked for a time as if Britain had defeated her European rivals in Southern India. Ignorant of these successes, the prevailing mood at Court remained one of gloom.

At a personal level, it is doubtful that Richard Peirce shared this pessimism. He had survived six voyages to the East Indies and there was every likelihood that, within a year, he would undertake a seventh. He had prospered and risen in the world. He had a wife and seven children, all of whom enjoyed good health. Of course, he felt positive. Fate had smiled on him and, for a few months, he could harvest the fruits of his success.

It was later said of Richard Peirce that he enjoyed 'the polite arts'. In 1782 he had a brief opportunity to indulge this inclination. If he took Mary to the theatre in those first months after his return, there were many plays to choose from. In December, *School For Scandal* was playing at the Theatre Royal, Drury Lane. For those seeking Shakespeare, there was *Much Ado About Nothing* and *Henry The Fourth* at Covent Garden.[7] Elsewhere, a pantomime of *Robinson Crusoe* satisfied more low-brow tastes, though the theme of shipwreck might have been too close to home for the Peirces to relish. In any case, those who wanted the vicarious thrill of a shipwreck had a much better option available to them. In Leicester Square, the German painter, Philip James De Loutherbourg, had reopened his performance of moving pictures.[8] This primitive version of animation enthralled audiences with sights of erupting volcanoes, the Niagara Falls, rising and setting suns and, most popular of all, a storm at sea. Crowds flocked to marvel at it. Whether Captain Peirce was among them is not known; nor whether he would have been impressed. After all, he had survived the real thing.

In February 1782, *Halsewell* was declared officially empty and towed back to Greenland Dock for a refit.[9] There, she would be thoroughly overhauled and repaired. Those in the know were confident that, next season, the East India Company would send a large fleet to India. There was an urgent need for soldiers to bolster the Madras army in its struggle with Hyder Ali. There was also the fear that the French might capitalise on British difficulties in America by striking once more at India. In such circumstances, a new ship like *Halsewell* could expect to be taken up again.

While Thomas Burston and Richard Peirce waited for word from India House, the shockwaves from the defeat at Yorktown continued to reverberate in London. In March, after a vote of no confidence in his administration, Lord North resigned. He had led the government for twelve years. Now, his successors were faced with the unenviable task of opening peace negotiations with the victorious colonialists and their allies in Europe. A government that has been humiliated is unlikely to feel indulgent towards those it holds responsible for its difficulties. Although Sir Thomas Rumbold could not be blamed for events in America, he was answerable for Madras. In parliament, the prevailing view was that he should have foreseen the onslaught by Hyder Ali and been better prepared to resist it. If Rumbold was to be the scapegoat, then his notorious financial manoeuvrings should come in for scrutiny, too. In 1782, a parliamentary enquiry was launched. Its remit included an investigation into the money that Rumbold had deposited in the treasury at Canton and a number of witnesses were called to give evidence.

Among those summoned to appear before the committee were six East India Company commanders, including Richard Peirce.[10] Although Peirce admitted to carrying the coin of other merchants from Madras, he denied any knowledge of Rumbold's financial dealings or of carrying government funds. However, the captain of the *Granby* was more forthcoming. Under questioning, Capt Johnston revealed that he had been approached by Rumbold's attorneys, two weeks before they sailed. There had been irregularities about the paperwork and he admitted the sum had not been properly recorded in the ship's book. All this strengthened the committee's suspicions that Rumbold had moved large amounts of embezzled silver to Canton but they were unable to pin down conclusive evidence. We have to wonder whether Richard Peirce was complicit in this cover-up or whether he told the truth. We cannot know. However, he would have had little to gain by antagonising a man who, despite his public disgrace, would remain rich and influential for years to come.

Meanwhile, the enquiry continued. Thomas Bevan, who was second in charge of the select committee of supercargoes, complained that East India company employees and free merchants often deposited their money at Canton in the Dutch, French or other foreign treasuries. He went on to explain that, when money was deposited in the Company's own treasury, they never enquired about its source but only recorded the name of the intended recipient. Much of the silver in the treasury came via country ships, which were not the responsibility of the Company's supercargoes. Furthermore, Bevan argued, if the secrecy and discretion afforded to depositors were removed, it could adversely affect the flow of money into Canton and, thus, undermine the Company's purchasing power. Faced with this wall of silence, it was clear the charges of embezzlement against Rumbold would never stick. But, although it could not touch this nabob's fortune, the country still wanted Rumbold's scalp. He was dismissed for incompetence.

The fallout from India and America affected not only politicians. In July, the bank of Mayne & Graham crashed.[11] Its founder, Robert Mayne, was a merchant who had won a succession of government contracts to supply the army in America. His partner in this venture was another merchant, Anthony Bacon, who himself was a business partner of John Durand. The loss of the American colonies meant the end of such lucrative contracts for a tight-knit circle of men like these. For Robert Mayne and Robert Graham, it left their Jermyn Street bank overstretched and its depositors demanding their money. The inevitable collapse of their bank drove Robert Mayne to commit suicide a few weeks later, while Robert Graham simply went to ground.[12] Their bankruptcy will not have escaped the notice of Richard Peirce. Robert Graham was yet another member of the powerful Edinburgh merchant-banking dynasty. His oldest brother was the late John Graham of Yatton and his younger brother, Thomas, was engaged to Richard Peirce's niece. In due course, Robert Graham's own fate would be connected to the *Halsewell*.

In August, as angry investors tried to recover their deposits from Jermyn Street, the Directors of the East India Company published the list of ships for their next outward-bound fleet.[13] A total of eighteen ships were named, ten of which would be destined for 'Coast & Bay' or, in other words, for Madras and Calcutta. The second name on the list was that of the 'Haleswell' (*sic*). For the first time since he became a sea captain, Richard Peirce would not be sent to China. As well as being a more lucrative destination than Canton, a return to Calcutta had other advantages. His eldest son, Richard junior, would soon be fifteen, old enough to start out on a career of his own. It went almost without saying that he would look to the East India Company. A writership in Calcutta would be an excellent first rung of the ladder.

The appointment of writers was an effective way through which Company Directors could exercise patronage. Not surprisingly, they were bombarded with requests from friends, supporters and total strangers, hoping to secure positions for their sons. Over the years, Directors had exercised this patronage rather too liberally. The result was that there was a glut of writers in Bengal with insufficient work to occupy them all. As part of its drive to economise, the Directors were determined to cut back on the number of new appointments. In these circumstances, the chances of young Richard Peirce being offered a writership were negligible and his father knew this. On the other hand, if the young man could go to Calcutta in person, he might have more success and a local patron might be able to secure a position for him.

To travel as a passenger to Bengal was not a realistic option. The Company was strongly opposed to the idea of unemployed men arriving in Calcutta 'on spec.'. In any case, the Directors had already decided that no civilian passengers of any kind would be carried in its ships in 1783.[14] The space would be allocated to the officers of the soldiers that were desperately needed in India. For many would-be travellers, this was a serious obstacle but there was a way round it and Peirce knew how. As captain, he was entitled to appoint his quota of midshipmen. For the forthcoming voyage, Richard Peirce planned to take five midshipmen, one of whom would be his eldest son.

As for his officers, Richard Peirce decided to promote his brother-in-law, Thomas Burston to chief mate. He was now twenty-eight years old and had already performed well as third mate. At second mate was a Scotsman, Ninian Lewis, who had served on the *Walpole*. Following the last-minute withdrawal of the new third mate, the fourth and fifth mates were promoted accordingly. The resulting vacancy at fifth mate was filled by Thomas Lucas, who had previously served as a midshipman on *Halsewell*. William Harris was sixth mate.

For his personal servants, on this voyage, Peirce chose Thomas Hope and Thomas Jeane.[15] The choice of Thomas Jeane is interesting. He came from West Monkton, where Peirce's sister lived, and was surely known to her. Perhaps, his appointment owed something to her influence.

Despite the Company's restrictions on the carrying of passengers to India, it would seem that an exception was made in at least one instance. Or, perhaps, the embargo was simply ignored. The younger sister of Jane Paul now wished to follow in her sibling's footsteps. In July 1782, Anne Paul had reached the age of seventeen.[16] Like her older sister, she was acknowledged to be very beautiful and had already attracted an admirer. Thomas Graham, the brother of the failed banker, Robert, and of John, their former neighbour at Yatton, had declared his affections for Anne. It seemed an ideal match and Anne's father had given his approval. Thomas was highly eligible. With more than a dozen years as a Company servant in Bengal, he was now a Senior Merchant with an important position in the Revenue department.[17] For the marriage to take place, it would be necessary for Anne to sail to India. Once again, the Paul family looked to Captain Peirce to provide the means. Once again, he was happy to oblige. His neice would sail under his protection and could enjoy the company of her first-cousin, Richard, and her neighbour, Thomas Jeane, during the voyage.

In September 1782, the formalities that preceded every voyage began. On the 25th, Peirce and three other commanders attended East India House for the oath taking ceremony.[18] They gave the customary promise to engage only in trading that had been licensed by the Company. The Deputy Chairman 'then warned them that if they should be suspected of illicit trading or 'breaking bulk homeward' they could expect to 'experience the Court's severest resentment'. They had heard it all before.

Soon afterwards, the *Halsewell* emerged from her refit in Greenland Dock and was warped down to Deptford. There she tied up alongside another Indiaman, the *Barwell*. Loading could now begin again. Throughout October and November, a succession of Company lighters came alongside to deliver the heavy cargo that would fill the lower hold of the *Halsewell*. Day after day, consignments of copper,

lead and iron were winched aboard and stowed by the lumpers. In
addition to the Company's own cargo, there were the military supplies
for the King's forces in India. Pitch, tar and cordage for the Navy,
gunpowder for the army and victualling stores for both.

Only when most of this was stowed, did the emphasis shift to
the *Halsewell's* own requirements. Her gun carriages were brought
aboard and her guns mounted. The ship then dropped down to
Gravesend Reach for the next stage of her 'lading'. Cases of small arms
were delivered and then the food and drink that would sustain the
crew. Twenty butts of beer came on 25 November, followed by 204
bags of bread on the 30th. On 8 December, they received 60 casks
of 'split pease' and '50 barrels of flower' (*sic*).[19] From early December,
deliveries of private trade also became a regular feature. Unfortunately,
the exact nature of this trade is not made explicit in the log but we can
assume that Peirce and his officers had done their market research and
had a shrewd idea of what the citizens of Calcutta wanted to buy.

On 11 December 1782, eighteen Company recruits came
aboard and, five days later, received their pay from Mr Dominicus, the
Company official. *Halsewell* would soon be ready to sail. Her livestock
and poultry were penned and twenty-four trusses of fresh hay were
stowed. On Christmas Eve, Captain Peirce arrived, accompanied by
two more officials from the East India Company and by Mr Card,
the river pilot. The crew were given their river pay and Mr Card took
charge of the ship.

For the next few hours, the *Halsewell* was crowded with well-
wishers who had come to see them off. No doubt, Thomas Burston
was there and also Mary Peirce. It was the last time she would see
her midshipman son. Perhaps, Henry and Ann Paul were there too,
having travelled up from Somerset to bid an emotional farewell to
young Anne. With or without the knowledge of the Company, her
luggage was aboard and she would not be going ashore when it was
time to leave. On Christmas Day, after the last of the wellwishers had
left the ship, Captain Peirce gave the order to unmoor and weigh
anchor. Slowly, they sailed to the lower part of the Hope. That night,
at roll call, it became clear that one of the recruits was missing. With
his pay in his pockets, he must have tried to swim for the shore. In the

journal, Captain Peirce concluded 'Having no boat alongside after 10 pm, and none prior to their being mustered, he must have committed the rash act of risquing his life for his escape'. There can be little doubt about the outcome.

On Boxing Day, at high tide, *Halsewell* was able to pass over 'the flats' and into Queen's Channel. Next day, they were in the Downs, where they joined other ships in convoy for Portsmouth. There, on New Years Day 1783, they would congregate, near the Motherbank, and await further orders. On the previous voyage, the delay at Portsmouth had lasted four months. Preparing a convoy took time, so Peirce was resigned to a similar wait. Although peace negotiations were in progress, the war with France had not yet ended and there was no question of East Indiamen sailing alone.

As the days crawled by, Peirce's main priority was to keep his men busy. *Halsewell's* journal records 'People employed about the rigging, drawing and knotting yarns etc. Armourer at his Forge. Tradesmen usefully employed'. An active crew felt purposeful and less inclined to brood or get up to mischief. With the soldiers, it was another matter.

On 23 January, it was found that two more of the Company's recruits had absconded. Unlike their foolhardy colleague, they had not risked a swim but had taken a wherry that was tied up at the bow. Their escape was just in time. Next day, all the recruits and their baggage were transferred to another ship. It had been decided that *Halsewell* would transport the King's soldiers instead. Hammocks were delivered, followed on 26 January by men from the 83rd Regiment of Foot.

Known as the Royal Glasgow Volunteers, this Scottish regiment had been stationed in New York during the American War.[20] They had just returned to Britain and were now to be posted to India. Over the next few days, more officers and a further 90 soldiers were accommodated on *Halsewell*. It appears that, having reached British shores, none of these men were happy at the prospect of being shunted straight on to another foreign outpost. On 6 February, some took matters into their own hands. First, a party of forty-seven 'private soldiers' commandeered a boat and went ashore. On this occasion, they went with their officers' 'approbation' but, later the same day, another 57 men insisted on following them, this time 'against every persuation'. On the 8th, the remaining officers and men also disembarked, leaving Captain Peirce to send their baggage ashore the next day. The explanation for this odd behaviour is probably that news had just arrived that the 83rd Regiment was to be disbanded. Its fighting days were over and it would not sail to India after all. The space, unexpectedly vacated by the Scots, was quickly filled by men from Herefordshire. The 36th Regiment of Foot was also bound for Madras. On the 26 February, an advance party of officers, forty-six men and four women came on board *Halsewell*. Over the next ten days, they were joined by another 112 men and five more women. With such large numbers on board, the space below decks was going to be very cramped and unpleasant. The soldiers' wives would have to endure these conditions too.

On 11 March 1783, *Halsewell* was finally ready to depart. Six other Indiamen had already set off a week earlier and now *Halsewell* would sail with two more. Captain Blackburn in the *Fox* and the *Atlas*, under Captain Cooper, would keep her company but it seems the need for a naval escort had been dispensed with. As the most senior commander of the three, Richard Peirce would, therefore, become Commodore with overall responsibility for keeping the flotilla together and setting the course. At midday, he gave the order to weigh anchor, moved *Halsewell* clear of the other moored ships and then hove to, to wait for *Atlas* and *Fox*. By 5pm, they were in position astern and all three ships set off together.

The responsibility of being commodore was new to Richard Peirce and his entries in *Halsewell's* journal reflect this. It is easy to detect both concern for his charges and impatience with their performance. From the outset, both *Fox* and *Atlas* seem to have lagged behind. By the 14th, *Fox* was so far astern that, despite having gone under 'an easy sail' all night, Peirce had to shorten *Halsewell's* sails further. The following day, he signalled to *Atlas* to catch up but her response did not satisfy him. 'The Atlas goes by the head and carries not so much sail as might be'. By the morning of the 16th, she was hull down, astern: 'Made signal to make more sail and when she hoisted her topsails, made signal to come into my wake.' It was to no avail.

Over the next twenty-four hours, *Fox* and *Atlas* fell further and further behind. On the 18th, 'in the morning could see neither of the two ships our consorts.' It had not been a good start. Despite constantly chivvying them, Captain Peirce had lost contact with both his charges. To make matters worse, the weather was now deteriorating and a squall carried away *Halsewell's* fore topmast.

Navigation was also proving tricky. Always a stickler for accuracy, Richard Peirce found his own estimation of their position to be badly awry. There is a note of incredulity in his journal entry for 25 March: 'For this journal account every day so much to the S'ward of Account very much surprises me. I have never before experienced anything like. I have examined the glasses line but find them exact.' Although it was exasperating to be wrong in one's calculations, the fact was that *Halsewell* had made better progress than expected. She would soon be in sight of the Cape Verde Islands. On the 30 March, having passed west of Boa Vista, *Halsewell* dropped anchor in Praya Bay, on the southern side of Sao Tiago island. This was a pre-determined rendezvous point but no other ships were there: 'Expected to find our consorts but on enquiry find none of the ships have been here.' It seems that, despite his misgivings, Richard Peirce was a better navigator than his colleagues. He had arrived first. Now he would have to wait.

The Cape Verde islands belonged to the Kingdom of Portugal but, compared to the Canaries or Madeira, they held little appeal for the crew of the *Halsewell*. Porto Praya was a shabby and impoverished town with limited opportunities for trading. A cartel of Portuguese controlled the prices of provisions for ships and even the watering arrangements were primitive. The nearest well was almost a mile from the beach and barrels had to be rolled along a special rolling way.[21]

On the last day of March, five Indiamen hove into view but neither the *Fox* nor *Atlas* were among them. While they waited, the *Halsewell's* crew filled empty casks with drinking water and rolled them back to the shore, but all this exertion was not enough to keep the men out of mischief. Some of them took exception to the boatswain, William Bryant, and later that day tried to teach him a lesson. Captain Peirce was quick to respond: 'Punished eight seamen for behaving in a mutinous manner and attempting to take the Boatswain out of his cabin to ill use him.' The retribution had the desired effect and the boatswain was not threatened again.

Impatient to press on without *Fox* and *Atlas*, it was agreed that *Halsewell* would sail in company with *Walpole* and *Bellmont* instead. But even so, there was a delay. Finally, on 4 April, they made sail: 'Joined by Walpole. Kept waiting for her. I take my departure from Port Praya'. For several weeks, progress was good and the ships were able to keep together. On 20 April they crossed the equator and, just over a month later, passed east of 'the meridian of London'. This meant they were south of the Cape of Good Hope. Settled into their routines, the crew of the *Halsewell* performed well and appear to have been content. Only one bizarre episode upset the equilibrium. Two sailors were caught cutting canvas from the sails. What they intended to do with the stolen canvas is not explained but clearly damage to the sails of a sailing ship was a serious offence. At noon, before their assembled comrades, both men were given a dozen lashes.

The coast of Madagascar was seen on 17 June and the ships turned up the Inner Passage along its western edge. Having sailed this stretch many times, Richard Peirce was aware of the potential hazards in his path: 'Kept a good lookout for St Christava as it is generally called but which I call John de Nova, an island covered in trees which I have made 2 voyages to the NW of Sandy Island but saw nothing of it.' This was fortunate because, despite Peirce's confident tone, St Christopher and John de Nova were two different and distinct islands, not far from one another.[22]

From here it was only two days' sail to the Comoro Islands. Dropping anchor off Johanna town, on 23 June, Peirce found two other Indiamen preparing to depart. These were the *Barwell* and *Lord Macartney*. On the latter was the artist, Johan Zoffany, wearing the uniform of a midshipman. Like Richard Peirce junior, Zoffany wanted to travel to Calcutta but his request had been turned down by the Directors. Luckily, he, too, had a benefactor, the powerful ship's husband, Robert Preston, who had found a position for him on one of his ships.[23] Although Zoffany was already beginning to make a name for himself in London, he knew that India offered greater prospects for financial success. The experience of George Willison had not gone unnoticed. Over the next five years, Zoffany would, indeed, earn a good living in India but it is for his artistic achievements there that he is remembered today. After the sinking of the *Halsewell*, some newspapers credited Captain Richard Peirce with having introduced Zoffany to India. This is clearly not true in the literal sense and he is unlikely to have helped the artist with introductions to patrons in Calcutta. Nonetheless, Zoffany may have heard that Willison had sailed on the *Halsewell* and, possibly, approached Peirce for advice, before they left London.

Zoffany was not the only artist sailing to India that season. Charles Smith had previously been Zoffany's studio assistant but was now artist-in-residence on the *Bellmont*.²⁴ This was the ship that had sailed with *Halsewell* from the Cape Verde islands. While they paused at Johanna, Richard Peirce may well have met Smith and been shown some of his work. Possibly, Charles Smith was on hand to sketch the scene when some important visitors came to look round the ships. These were two sons of the 'King' of Johanna, accompanied by their attendants.

Official visits by members of the ruling Sultan's family were acknowledged to be something of a mixed blessing. They had adopted British titles with which they had been mischievously endowed by previous visitors. Some were notoriously light-fingered and had to be watched carefully. When William Hickey had visited the islands on the *Plassey*, the 'Prince of Wales' had been caught red handed, stealing a silver teaspoon from the second mate's cabin while his attendant, the 'Prime Minister,' was attempting to make off with a blanket. Caring nothing for their titles, the ship's officer had administered a horse-whipping to both culprits.²⁵ Fortunately, on this occasion, the royal guests seem to have behaved themselves. Their departure was saluted with seven guns and then the business of loading water and livestock could resume. Before the end of the day, another Indiaman sailed into the bay. It was the *Fox*. Peirce had lost sight of her soon after leaving Portsmouth so it was good to know that his friend, Captain Blackburn, was safe and well.

Later on 25 June, *Halsewell* weighed anchor and set off under an easy sail. Peirce expected *Bellmont* to follow but Capt Gamage was slow to respond. The next day, Peirce's journal records tersely, 'Waiting for Bellmont'. By the 27th, they were properly on their way and Peirce could turn his attention again to matters of navigation. Ahead of them lay the Bassas de Paltram, a hazardous shoal whose exact location was still uncertain. Throughout the night of 30 June, they proceeded cautiously, checking the depth as they went: 'Sounded in the night for Bassas de Paltram tho' I am of the opinion it is much further to the Ewd [...]. It is a concern it is not ascertaind as ships lose much by endeavouring to avoid it.' The dearth of accurate information about the location of hazards was indeed a concern that many shared. This is why the work of Alexander Dalrymple was of such importance. Until it was completed, captains would have to remain vigilant.

On the 17 July, this vigilance was rewarded: 'At 1pm saw island of Kelah. I did not expect to see it so soon. We must have had a strong W'erly current. I reckoned myself 100 miles from it [...] An island surrounded by breakers…a dangerous reef running off to the NE 2 miles.' Of course, this demonstrated that knowing the location of an island was only of limited use if you could not be sure of your own position. Until longitude could be calculated with precision, there would always be a large margin of error. Human fallibility also played a part. On the 26th, as they approached Madras in the dark, the sailor taking soundings was careless. *Halsewell* was much closer to the shore than she should have been: 'At 11 pm the man at the lead giving false soundings, found ourselves inshore. When the man at the lead gave out 12 fathoms immediately hauld off shore and soon saw ships lights.' It was a lucky escape. Next day, as *Halsewell* anchored in Madras Roads, they could see that Admiral Hughes' fleet was also present. It was their lights that had been glowing in the darkness.

The presence of the Royal Navy was reassuring for the citizens of Madras. The previous September, the French Admiral de Suffren had driven the British from Trincomalee and established his own fleet there. It was a secure base from which he could threaten Madras. In June, de Suffren had attacked Hughes' ships while they were off Cuddalore. Both sides had sustained heavy casualties but, although none of his ships were lost, Hughes had been forced to withdraw his fleet to Madras. While the outcome was still doubtful, news arrived from Europe of a preliminary peace treaty between Britain and France. It meant that Hughes and De Suffren would have to suspend hostilities and neither side would win a decisive victory. Or, at least, not yet.

For Admiral Hughes, the immediate priority was to make good the losses of his crews. Peace negotiations might break down and he wanted to be prepared. The arrival of the Indiamen provided him with an ideal source of fresh manpower and, within a few hours, he had pressed thirty of *Halsewell's* men. It was the same familiar predicament but, this time, Peirce's men were in no position to resist. Two days later, the *Seahorse* sent her boat to take off another man. This was the very sloop that had escorted *Halsewell* to China in 1780 but such sentimental ties counted for nothing where pressing men was concerned.

Throughout August 1783, the men of the 36th Regiment and all their military stores were delivered to Fort St George while cordage, cables and provisions were transferred to His Majesty's ships. The official packet was sent to Governor Macartney and Captain Peirce was free to go ashore to attend to his own affairs. This would be his sixth and final visit to Madras. The town, which he now showed to his son, had changed much in the twenty-four years since he first set foot there. Building work had continued within the fort, there were more fine houses on Choultry Plain and Black Town had extended to the north. Despite the recent wars, Richard Peirce could detect a defiant air of prosperity as he introduced his son and neice to Madras society. On Sundays they attended church. Three years previously, Jane Paul had run the gauntlet of eager bachelors at St Mary's church door. Now it was Anne's turn.

For midshipman Peirce, the few weeks spent with his father in Madras were a useful apprenticeship. He could see, at close hand, the interaction between his father, local merchants and the middlemen who acted as translators, money-changers and fixers. With all his years of experience, Captain Peirce could alert his son to the pitfalls and stratagems that might trip up the novice trader and eat away at his profits. Even the elements could conspire against you. This year, the surf, that perennial feature of the Madras shore, was much higher than usual. On 12 August it was too extreme for *Halsewell's* boats, and the

Madras Embarking by C. Hunt.
© *National Maritime Museum, Greenwich, London*

unloading of private trade had to be postponed: 'Sent the longboat to the back of the surf but being so great she returned as no boat could come off.'

On board the *Halsewell*, the usual running repairs continued. The foretopmast was lowered, strengthened and some of its yards were replaced. In Madras Roads, other ships came and went. Two weeks after *Halsewell* had dropped anchor, the *Fox* arrived. Then, singly and in groups, eight other Indiamen weighed anchor and set off for China, marking each departure with thunderous salutes from their guns. This year, *Halsewell* would not be following them. Her next destination was Bengal.

16
Within Sight of the Summit

On 24 August 1783, Captain Peirce, accompanied by passengers, returned to his ship. At one o'clock, the next day, he signalled his intention to sail, with a fifteen gun salute in honour of Admiral Hughes. Then, with the sound of the guns still reverberating in the ears of his passengers, Peirce gave the order to weigh anchor and make sail.

By the end of August, the southwest monsoon was nearly over. It would still provide a following wind but could be unpredictable and stormy. Even with reasonable weather, the voyage to Calcutta could last around two weeks but, this year, the gods were feeling benign. Sailing conditions were ideal and, in a mere eight days, *Halsewell* was in sight of the low-lying land of the Ganges delta. At the entrance to one of the estuaries, three pilot boats could be seen at anchor. After Captain Peirce had given the signal requesting assistance, one of the pilot sloops pulled alongside and Mr Gilbert came aboard. He was an official East India Company pilot and would now take charge of the *Halsewell*. It would be down to him to negotiate the Braces, the dangerous sand bars that flanked the entrance to the Hooghly, and to guide the ship safely to her anchorage at Kedgeree.

It was apparent that the sloop that had delivered Mr Gilbert was missing her fore-topmast. While they waited for next morning's tide, Captain Peirce ordered his carpenter to work through the night to fashion a replacement mast from one of *Halsewell's* spars. It was a considerate gesture and not something every East India commander would have thought to do. By morning, the job was done and the sloop could depart with her foremast restored. That day, 3 September, Mr Gilbert took *Halsewell* over, first, the Western Brace and, then, the Eastern Brace. By noon, they were near 'Saugor' Island.

Although low-lying and unremarkable in appearance, Sagar Island is of immense significance to Hindus. It is deemed to be the place where the holy Ganges meets the open sea of the Bay of Bengal. Every January, thousands of Hindu pilgrims converge on Sagar to bathe in its sacred waters and to visit its temple. Whether this was of any interest to Richard Peirce we do not know but Mr Gilbert may well have mentioned the significance of the place where they now dropped anchor. However, there was no time for any passengers to go ashore and it is unlikely any would have wanted to. Sagar island lies in the area of the delta known as the Sundarbans. It was mosquito-ridden, its forests roamed by tigers and, consequently, not somewhere to linger. Next day, on the incoming tide, *Halsewell* moved upstream to Kedgeree. This was a busy spot. Several country ships were already moored there, and three larger Indiamen, one of which was the *Winterton*. This was her first voyage but, in 1792, the *Winterton* would meet a fate almost as dramatic as that of *Halsewell* when she was wrecked off the coast of Madagascar.

The work of clearing the ship began on 5 September, with the private trade unloaded first. On the 8th, satisfied that his goods were ready to be dispatched, Captain Peirce and Anne Paul boarded the longboat for the journey to Calcutta. The city was fifty miles away and it would take two days to get there. In the meantime, Jane Templer and Thomas Graham waited for news of their arrival.

The Calcutta at which Richard Peirce now arrived had changed just as much as he had. Twenty-three years earlier, he had been a junior officer, starting out on his career. The city had been recovering from the occupation by Siraj-ud-Daulah and was coming to terms with the victory at Plassey. Now the place was thriving. Craft of all sizes crowded the river, some bringing goods from Indiamen in the delta, others unloading produce from further up the Ganges. Overlooking this activity, Fort William exuded authority and power. Its construction had barely begun in 1760 but now it was complete, star-shaped, protected by projecting bastions and ditches and confidently flying the Union Flag. Downstream, along Garden Reach, were new and more elegant houses, reflecting the recent fortunes that had been made. To the east of the Fort lay the Maidan, a large, open, grassy park where Calcutta society would congregate, in their carriages, in the early evening.

Northwards along the river, where St Anne's Church had previously stood, the imposing Writers' Building now dominated. This was the East India Company's administrative centre in Calcutta. It stood next to the Court House and faced the large 'tank' which supplied water to that part of the city. No doubt, Captain Peirce called at the Writers' Building on Company business during his stay. Perhaps, he also enquired if there were any prospects of employment for his son. Only a few streets away, land had been acquired for a new church to be built. Soon, Warren Hastings would lay the foundation stone of St John's Church. Modelled on St Martins-in-the-Fields and containing a 'Last Supper' painted by Zoffany, St John's became the focal point of Anglican worship in Calcutta. There, in just over a decade, two of Richard Peirce's daughters would marry and the funeral of his eldest son would be held. But, oblivious to this, Captain Peirce enjoyed the immediate delights of the city. Its sophisticated society bore no comparison with its provincial, backward and much less affluent counterpart in Madras. Calcutta was, above all, an excellent place to do business. Accompanied by his servant, Thomas Jeane, and perhaps by his son, Captain Peirce would now concentrate on his own affairs.

Meanwhile, at Kedgeree, a week after *Halsewell* had dropped anchor, the *Bellmont* and *Lord Macartney* arrived from Madras. At almost the same time, the first of the Company's sloops appeared and tied up next to *Halsewell*. They would take some cargo upstream to Calcutta and deliver other goods to be taken to England. As the sheets of copper were removed from *Halsewell's* hold, the space was filled with redwood and thousands of bags of saltpetre. While all this was going on, a dozen crewmen were set to work re-caulking the ship. Others picked oakum and the rest were 'employed as necessary'. By 6 October, the task of caulking the lower decks was finished so the Company's Deputy Master Attendant was sent to inspect the work. He 'watered' the deck and 'found it tight'. This was important: too much dampness in the hold and the cargo would spoil.

Next, work began on the outer hull. By pulling on the lower masts to tilt or 'heel' the ship, much of one side of the hull could be exposed. Working as fast as they could, men scraped off any barnacles and seaweed and then 'pay'd' or coated the bottom of the *Halsewell* with pitch and tar. When one side was done, the ship was heeled the other way to reveal her other side. She was now as watertight as possible and the remainder of her cargo could be stowed below.

Meanwhile other Indiamen continued to come and go. On 10 October, *Atlas* and *Pigot* arrived from Madras. Captain Cooper of the *Atlas* had failed to make up time on *Halsewell* and he might now pay the price for his tardiness. He would have to trust that there was still a demand in Calcutta for the items in his private trade. On *Halsewell*, some members of the crew were about to pay a price of a more permanent nature. The unrelenting heat and humidity, the ubiquitous mosquitoes, the unclean water and the inevitable fevers had begun to take their toll. By the third week of October, men of the *Halsewell* had begun to die and, for a while, the mortality rate showed no sign of slowing. On 17 November, so many were sick that twenty-three men were transferred to hospital in Calcutta. The ship's log does not record if one of them was Midshipman Peirce. It is more likely that he had already departed in the longboat with his father and cousin, having no intention of returning. The prevalence of illness amongst the crew provided a plausible reason for his remaining in Calcutta. On the *Lord Macartney*, Midshipman Zoffany had no such excuse for his desertion. He had simply jumped ship and resumed his career as an artist.[26] He was recorded as having 'run'.

For four months, Captain Peirce remained in Calcutta, occasionally dispatching a *burr* downriver with new private trade for *Halsewell*'s hold. Meanwhile, regular reports from his officers kept him informed of progress in loading the ship and the state of her crew. Peirce can have been under no illusions about the shortage of manpower and this prompted the urgent recruitment of lascars. During December, groups of lascars began to arrive at *Halsewell*'s anchorage but some quickly changed their minds about working on her. Maybe, they were worried about the number of sick crewmen or, perhaps, they took exception to Thomas Burston and the other officers. For whatever reason, a substantial number decided not to stay. On 20 December, the ships journal recorded that '17 lascars run in the night'. Over the next few days, four more followed.

Fortunately, there was an ample supply of lascars in Calcutta and more were quickly found. On 5 January 1784, ten lascars came aboard, led by a *tindal*. Four days later another ten appeared. They, too, were accompanied by a *tindal* and a *cassob*. On 15 January, eight 'Portygueze' seaman were added and, finally, six more lascars, with a *serang* and *tindal*, completed the new crew. Despite some language difficulties, the Portuguese would integrate with *Halsewell's* own crew but the lascars would live apart. Whether Muslim or Hindu, they insisted on cooking their own food and eating it separately. In this instance, with names like Mahomet Luffee and Shaikismael, *Halsewell's* lascars were probably all Muslim. Lascars always took their orders from their *serang*, who acted as foreman, overseeing their work and being responsible for their pay and discipline. The role of the *tindal* was equivalent to a petty officer or boatswain's mate. He was subordinate to the *serang* and would direct the work of smaller groups of lascars. The role of the *cassob* or kussab is less clearly defined. In later years, the kussab became associated with deck stores but, in 1784, he was probably a leading deck hand.

Before Captain Peirce could rejoin his ship, there was another event in Calcutta that demanded his attention. On 22 December, he attended the wedding of Anne Paul and Thomas Graham.[27] In a city known for excess, the marriage was marked, no doubt, by lavish celebrations. On his return to England, Captain Peirce would be able to bring the happy news to his sister at West Monkton. Her two eldest daughters were now married to men of fortune in Bengal, an outcome that must have seemed increasingly attractive when Richard Peirce's thoughts turned to his own daughters.

Meanwhile, downriver, as December turned to January, boats continued to deliver more cargo to the *Halsewell*. A Company sloop, *Alexander*, brought bags of saltpetre; the *Fanny*, a snow, brought bales of cotton and a succession of smaller *burrs* delivered water, rice and livestock. On 12 January the first of the passengers' baggage was received on board, followed on the 27th by the passengers themselves. According to *Halsewell's* journal they were a Mr and Mrs Dacres, a Miss Wilding and a Mrs Moore with her children.

From the perspective of Captain Richard Peirce, these were attractive passengers to carry. All were in a position to pay generously for their accommodation. Philip Milner Dacres was a prominent member of Calcutta society where he had lived for over twenty years. He had made his fortune as Collector for Calcutta and had served as a member of the Council.[28] He was now ready to return to England and had sold off those possessions he could not take with him. The *Calcutta Gazette* carried an advertisement for his coach and four horses as well as a chariot and pair.[29] His house, in a fashionable part of Calcutta, near Esplanade Row, had sold for more than 13,000 rupees. The street where it stood would be known for many years as Dacres Lane.

Mr Dacres would be accompanied, on the *Halsewell*, by his wife Rebecca and her sister, Miss Wilding. They may have secured sole occupancy of the roundhouse. However, the other passenger, Mrs Moore, also required comfortable accommodation for herself and her children. She was the wife of Peter Moore, an inveterate opponent of Warren Hastings. In 1782, Moore had been appointed Collector of Calcutta where, like Dacres, he had quickly amassed a fortune.[30] He was now commissioner of police and would follow his wife back to England, a year later. There, he would win a seat in parliament and also give evidence against Hastings during his trial. Through his wife, Sarah, he was brother-in-law to William 'Sylhet' Thackeray, another senior Company official and grandfather of the celebrated novelist. Thackeray had already returned to England and now Sarah Moore and her five children would do likewise. It would be interesting to know if they shared the roundhouse with the Dacres. Travelling in such close proximity to children had its downside. William Hickey had done so once and had found their noisy boisterousness intolerable.[31]

On the same day as these passengers were settling into their new accommodation, an official arrived from Calcutta with the Company's packet. These instructions ordered Captain Peirce to sail in company with two other ships, the *Ceres* and the *Earl Talbot*. Once again, Peirce was appointed commodore. The *Ceres*, under Captain Thomas Price, had in fact sailed from Kedgeree ten days earlier but she would be waiting for *Halsewell*, in the Bay of Bengal. The inclusion of the *Earl Talbot* in his flotilla may have intrigued Peirce. No doubt, he remembered her as one of the new ships built at the same time as *Halsewell*. She belonged to Sir Charles Raymond and had sailed from England in 1782, a full year before *Halsewell*. Her destination had been the Coromandel Coast and China so what she was doing in the Hooghly is not clear. Possibly she had missed the sailing season from Canton and her commander, Robert Taylor, had taken advantage of this setback to visit some other ports. An opportunity for extra-curricular private trading was not to be spurned.

By 3 February, *Halsewell* had reached the open sea. Her river pilot had departed and it was time to rendezvous with *Ceres* and *Talbot*. As commodore, Captain Peirce wanted his two subordinates to be clear about how he intended to proceed. First, the jollyboat was sent to *Ceres* with sailing instructions for Captain Price. Then, a signal was given to *Talbot* to send a boat to collect their instructions. Meanwhile, in light winds and hazy conditions, the three vessels moved slowly down the Bay.

For the next two weeks, 'moderate breezes and fair weather' continued. With little to occupy the crew, Captain Peirce decided to hold 'divine service' on three Sundays in succession. Such regularity was unusual. When the weather was less benign and the crew busier, many Sundays would pass when no service was recorded in the journal. Inevitably, this tranquil weather could not last. By the end of February, the log was recording 'very black and threatening clouds'. For one of the crew, it might have been an omen. On 29 February, the carpenter's first mate died unexpectedly. In the journal, Peirce recorded: 'Committed his body to the deep with the usual ceremony.' The death of the carpenter's first mate created an opening for another member of the crew, Sam Roberts. He now took over the dead man's position and, apparently, carried out his duties effectively. It did not go unnoticed. After the voyage, when Sam Roberts got into trouble, Captain Peirce would not forget him.

The threatening sky soon led to squalls and a 'confused' swell. This worsening weather made it more difficult to keep the flotilla together. By 3 March, Peirce was already expressing concern that *Talbot* was lagging far astern. Just as on the outward voyage, when he had complained over the failure of *Fox* and *Atlas* to keep pace with *Halsewell*, now Richard Peirce began to worry about *Ceres* and *Talbot*. On the 13th, he gave a signal to both ships to 'come into their station'. Not satisfied with her response, he repeated the signal to *Ceres*, a couple of days later. On the 23rd March with a gale threatening, he signalled with a blue light every two hours throughout the night, but neither *Ceres* nor *Talbot* responded. When dawn broke, *Ceres* was so far astern that she was only just visible from the masthead. Despite the factual nature of the record in *Halsewell's* journal, one again detects a mixture of anxiety and impatience in Peirce's entries. It evokes an image of an exasperated mother-hen whose chicks constantly wander off and fail to keep up. On the 24th he wrote 'Made signal for Ceres to make more sail having no topgallant steering sails nor a mizen topgallant sail and a reef in her topsails'. The implication is clear. How can Captain Price possibly hope to keep up, if he fails to deploy the sails properly? Next day, Peirce's worries increased further: 'At 1pm made signal to alter the course which was answerd by Ceres only. The ships keep each so wide makes me fearful of separating. At 4pm made the signal for the ships to move more in my wake which was answerd by Ceres only. At 5pm made to the Talbot a signal to close more in my wake. She did not answer.'

Inevitably, Captain Peirce had to come to terms with the fact that neither of his fellow commanders seemed capable of sailing their ships as efficiently as he could. If they could not sail at *Halsewell's* pace, she would have to adjust to theirs. From now on, Peirce would make this point repeatedly in the journal. 'Ran under topsails until 4 pm waiting for Talbot' and 'Shortened sail for Ceres and Talbot' are typical entries. However, frustratingly slow he may have found this pace, it did have the desired effect of keeping the ships together. From now on the most regular entry is simply 'In company with Ceres and Talbot'.

On 27 April, just as the sun was setting, the coast of Africa finally appeared. They had been at sea for twelve weeks. Someone on the *Talbot* calculated the longitude and Captain Taylor signalled the result to Captain Peirce. This was not the first time they had done so and Peirce seems to have had confidence in their ability to arrive at an accurate figure. It gave him an excuse to indulge in his other preoccupation, disputing the accuracy of sea charts. This time, he wrote 'The Talbot this day at noon made Long'd 31°10' which I believe as the true longitude of this land which is laid too far to the W'd in all the charts.' By 2 May, they were in sight of Cape Talhado. Peirce was pleased to find that it lay in exactly the latitude he had placed it in, fourteen years previously, in the *Earl of Ashburnham*.

The shallow seas between Cape Lagullas and the Cape of Good Hope were notoriously difficult and this year they lived up to expectations. On 4 May, there was a 'mountanious' swell which continued into the next day: 'Swell very high and irregular makes the ship labour very much and destroys our sails by beating them against the masts.' Peirce suspected that the swell indicated they were sailing over the enormous Lagullas Bank which extended for 100 miles towards Cape Town. He took soundings to check and found 'Coarse sand, small red stones, broken shells. By these soundings we must be well on the Bank in this latitude to N'wrd of our account'.

As they came level with False Bay, Captain Peirce decided to seek shelter there so that he could talk face to face with his two subordinates. He summoned Captains Taylor and Price to come aboard *Halsewell*. If they or their passengers hoped for some respite ashore, they would be disappointed. Despite the rough seas, Captain Peirce was in no mood to delay. 'Having no occation (sic) to stop, determined to proceed to Saint Helena' was the terse journal entry for 8 May 1784. There would not even be time to send the body of William Smith ashore for burial. As Third Officer, William James Smith was the most senior of the four crew members who had died since leaving Kedgeree. His position would be taken by Martin Chamberlayne and his body would have to be buried at sea.

Despite more 'mountanious' seas, the three ships pressed on, skirting southern Africa. It would take until the last day of May before St Helena would be reached. That would be too late for another senior member of the crew. The surgeon, Charles Broomfield, had been kept busy tending the sick on this voyage but, now, only days from land, he succumbed, too.

On 1 June, having saluted the fort with seven guns, *Halsewell* dropped anchor and Captain Peirce and his passengers went ashore. They would have two weeks to enjoy the pleasures of St Helena. The island was now peaceful but an event, the previous December, had seriously threatened its tranquillity. A decision had been taken to regularise the drinking habits of the garrison and bring it more into line with practice at Gibraltar and other outposts. The punch houses, which were attached to the soldiers' living quarters, were to be closed and replaced by a single canteen where drinkers would not even be permitted to sit down. This action, plus a restriction on their daily allowance of liquor, had prompted a mutiny by more than two hundred soldiers. At one stage, it looked like they might seize control of the whole island. It had taken prompt action by Major Bazett and a party of loyal soldiers to seize back the artillery, which the rebels had trained on the Governor's residence. Following the loss of their guns, the rebels also lost heart and the mutiny fizzled out. For his part in saving the day, Major Bazett was now enjoying celebrity status on the island.[32]

On 10 June, Major Bazett was invited by Captain Peirce to inspect the *Halsewell*. The entire ship's company was mustered on deck, in their best clothes, and nine guns were fired to welcome the victorious Major aboard. Following the insurrection, ninety-nine soldiers had been condemned to death, although only ten had been actually executed. On this voyage, Captain Peirce had faced no serious challenge to his own authority but Major Bazett's visit offered a salutary reminder to *Halsewell's* crew of the likely outcome of any such action.

On 14 July, as *Halsewell* was preparing to leave, three more East Indiamen sailed into the bay. One of them was the *Fox*. As she rounded Murders Point, she struck a rock and it was soon clear that she had been badly damaged. This was a stark reminder that the most hazardous part of almost every voyage was entering or leaving port. Reacting quickly to *Fox's* distress signals, Richard Peirce sent twenty men in *Halsewell's* longboat to offer assistance. Prompt action saved the day. Damage to the *Fox* was contained and her cargo was saved but Captain Blackburn's ship would not be seaworthy again for some weeks. With barely time to commiserate with his old friend, Captain Peirce now focussed again on his own departure. On the 16th, the *Halsewell, Ceres* and *Earl Talbot* fired farewell salutes and made sail for home.

After only a few days at sea, Richard Peirce's impatience had returned. Once again, *Ceres* and *Talbot* were failing to keep up, despite instructions from their commodore to make more sail. When this did not have the desired effect, Captain Peirce ordered *Halsewell* to sail close to the *Talbot* so he could speak directly to Captain Taylor. He learned that *Talbot* had sprung her foretopmast and this partly explained her sluggishness. Next he closed in on *Ceres*. Her difficulties, it transpired, were more serious:

> Bore down to the Ceres at noon and spoke her. Capt Price informed me that she makes so much water at the wooden ends forward he is obliged to sail large. I desired him therefore to lead and I would follow. Spoke Talbot and informed Capt Taylor of the condition of the Ceres.

Limping along at the pace set by *Ceres*, the three ships sailed northwards. As they entered European waters, they began to encounter a variety of trans-Atlantic vessels. One of them was the *Renoun*, en route from St Kitts to Bristol. She decided to keep them company for the last leg of the journey. On 26 August, 1784, they saw the familiar outline of Start Point. Here, they hove to. The Company packet was sent ashore and a pilot was received in return. Mr Parkman from Portsmouth would now take charge of the *Halsewell* and guide her up to the Downs. With a following wind, this should take only a few days. However, for the passengers, desperate to be on dry land again, that was a delay they were not prepared to tolerate. Next day, as they came past Portland, the three Indiamen paused long enough to lower their boats. That afternoon, a correspondent in Weymouth wrote that 'A number of passengers were landed here out of the said ships, and a great quantity of baggage'. The Dacres, Moores and their fellow travellers had clearly decided to proceed on land. They were only seven miles from Dorchester where the Royal Mail coach called three times a week. If their destination was London, they might have done better to stay with their ships. The very next day, the flotilla had reached the Downs. On *Halsewell*, Mr Parkman would hand over to Mr Huggett, the river pilot, for the passage up the Thames estuary. By 4 September, *Halsewell* had tied up in Deptford, her second voyage completed. She had survived the perils of the sea and there was every likelihood that this voyage would be as profitable as her first.

In Kingston, Mary Peirce's joy at her husband's homecoming may have been tempered by the realisation that her eldest son had remained in Calcutta. However, it probably did not come as a total surprise and it was sugared by the thought of the career opportunities that might now open to him. If Bengal was a door to his advancement why should his sisters not pass through it, too? Elizabeth and Mary Ann would soon be of an age to marry. It is likely that Mrs Peirce already had in mind some suitable candidate for her eldest daughter's hand and perhaps that of her sister, too. During his time at home, Richard Peirce must have often invited colleagues to dine with them at Walnut Tree House and, no doubt, there were others, armed with introductions, who called to pay their respects. Among these men may have been young writers or more senior officials, about to sail for Bengal. The pretty Mary Ann or the musical Elizabeth may have attracted the attention of a bachelor with good prospects. If the attraction was reciprocated, no doubt encouraged by Mary Peirce, an attachment could have resulted and, perhaps, an engagement to marry. Inevitably, the marriage would have to take place in India. Now that Elizabeth was old enough, perhaps, she and Mary Ann could sail east on the *Halsewell's* next voyage.

The prospects of a third voyage for *Halsewell* looked good. The Treaty of Paris had been signed the previous September and peace was now secured. Although Pondicherry had been restored to France once more, she had relinquished Trincomalee and her influence in India was greatly reduced. As a consequence, the outlook for trade was rosy. Despite this, the East India Company still found itself in financial difficulty. The expenses of the Mysore conflict with Hyder Ali and the requirement to honour a growing number of bills of exchange had placed enormous strain on the Company's finances. The direction of Company affairs in India had been dogged by the factional strife within the Bengal Council. The endless recriminations between Warren Hastings and his opponents had exasperated Company directors and politicians alike. Following the fall of Shelburne's administration, Fox had introduced an India Bill to try to sort things out. However, before the legislation could be enacted, the Fox-North administration had itself been dismissed. In December 1783, the government of the country had passed to an administration led by William Pitt and it was his India Bill that had entered the statute book only a few weeks before *Halsewell* had docked at Deptford.

Pitt's India Act of 1784 was to have great significance for British involvement in Indian affairs but its impact on Richard Peirce and his fellow commanders was less dramatic. East India Company directors would continue to charter ships from the usual cartel of owners and the 'shipping interest' would not be seriously threatened, just yet. Likewise, the directors would exercise patronage, as they had for years, through appointments to writerships in India. True, the Act sought to curtail the excessive fortunes and blatant corruption that had persisted, albeit diminished, under Warren Hastings. The well-being of the native Indians was now to be taken seriously and the injustices of the past would not be tolerated. But none of this would have alarmed Richard Peirce. The privilege of private trade had not been abolished and the opportunity to make money had not disappeared. In any case, he was nearing the end of his career as a sea captain. One more voyage should suffice to secure his fortune. Then he would retire from the sea and turn his thoughts to other ventures.

Throughout the remainder of 1784 and all of 1785, Richard Peirce enjoyed the rewards of his latest voyage. He acquired more land, renting from George Hardings and Richard Adams, as well as buying and enclosing part of the southwest corner of Richmond Park. Perhaps, he intended to build there for his retirement.[33] In the meantime, he increased the insurance on his household goods to £800. Included in this sum was £250 for wearing apparel and £200 for 'plate.' His books he valued at £50.[34] Without doubt, Captain Richard Peirce was now a person of substance.

A man in his position might wish to express gratitude for his good fortune by showing concern for those less fortunate. Richard Peirce chose to offer his support to the St Thomas's Hospital in Southwark. In August 1785, having donated £50 to the hospital, he was elected to its Governing Body.[35] As a symbol of office, he was sent the customary green stave. Among his fellow governors were several who had served as Directors of the East India Company and at least one banker, William Esdaile. Richard Peirce was now moving in quite exalted company. Even if his motives were purely philanthropic, it would do no harm to cultivate contacts like these.

At the start of 1785, it looked as if Richard Peirce's time ashore might be swiftly curtailed. In January, several newspapers reported that the Company intended to send four additional ships to China in April. The *Halsewell's* name appeared on the list but, as she had only recently returned to the Greenland dock for repairs, it was soon apparent that she would not be ready in time. This reprieve must have been welcome news for the Peirce family. Mary was pregnant again and the baby was expected in June. It would be good to have the support of her husband, particularly as Mary's own father was not in good health. In fact, Thomas Burston would not live to see the birth of his latest grandchild. His death, in May 1785, meant that Mary would no longer be able to rely on her father while her own husband was away at sea.[36] His death also left the *Halsewell* without its principal managing owner. A new ship's husband would have to be found.

The man with the financial means to take on this role was Peter Esdaile. He was a brother of William and belonged to the family of bankers who operated out of Lombard Street. His sister, Louisa, was married to Richard Peirce's old Taunton friend, Benjamin Hammet. Linked by these ties of friendship and backed by the family bank, Peter Esdaile was the ideal successor to Thomas Burston.[37] With an investor like him, there was every reason for optimism regarding the third voyage of the *Halsewell*. The knowledge that those shrewd financiers, the Esdailes, regarded Captain Peirce as a safe pair of hands would encourage others to follow suit. It would be easier to obtain credit with merchants for the outward investments. Given that Richard Peirce planned to retire from the sea after his next voyage, it was important to maximise the return from this final venture. He would, therefore, extend his credit as much as he dared.

In addition to the financial imperatives of the voyage, there were also closer family issues to consider. If Eliza and Mary Ann were to join their brother in Bengal, this would be the last opportunity for Captain Peirce to accompany and care for them, on the long and difficult voyage. Eliza was barely sixteen and her younger sister only fourteen. Richard and Mary were surely reluctant to send their daughters under the care of another commander while they were still so young. There were also the cousins to consider. Now that her two eldest daughters were in Calcutta, married to Company men, Ann Paul wanted her next two to join them. Once again, she would look to her brother to provide the means. He needed little persuasion. Amy and Mary Paul were two years older than his own daughters and would make ideal companions for them.[38] In all probability, there would be other young ladies making the voyage too. Captain Blackburn was keen for his daughter to go to India and wished her to sail on the ship of his old friend and fellow commander. Before any arrangement with passengers could be entered into, the agreement of the East India Company had to be sought and the financial securities obtained.

During the autumn of 1785, Richard Peirce wrote to the Court of Directors to ask permission for his two eldest daughters to sail with him on the *Halsewell*.[39] He also began to gather his private trade. Merchants, craftsmen and traders were approached, goods were selected, terms were agreed and arrangements were put in place for delivering these items to his ship. It was a process Richard Peirce had followed many times before. This would be the last and he did not want to waste the opportunity. The profit from this voyage would allow him to retire from the sea and would set him up for the next stage of his life. But, as he signed his various deals, did Richard Peirce ask himself if too much was riding on this last throw of the dice?

While he stood poised on this threshold, one wonders if Richard Peirce looked back over his career. How would he have assessed it? Had it fallen short of his own expectations? However critical his own self-assessment may have been, there is no doubt that Captain Peirce had reached the defining moment of his career. The experience of at least twenty-six years in the service of the East India Company had made him the man he now was. More than two hundred years later, we can still get a sense of his character.

His portraits show a thickset man with a bull neck.[40] In profile, he exudes solid dependability but the set of his lips suggests something more. In one picture they seem pursed with impatience or frustration; in another there is a suspicion of a smile. Both may reveal characteristics of Richard Peirce's personality. As a professional

Captain Richard Peirce by I. Cruikshank.
© *National Maritime Museum, Greenwich, London*

seaman, he carried out his responsibilities efficiently and well. He took pride in coaxing the best performance from his ships and they generally sailed faster than those they were 'in company' with. Peirce may have been blessed with competent officers but he directed his ships well. Decisions about adjusting the trim of the ship and how much sail to carry were ultimately his. When other ships failed to keep up, he could not always hide his frustration with them.

For sound commercial reasons, Peirce was always in a hurry to reach his destination. But he was also aware of the risks of being over-hasty. The *Houghton* and *Horsenden* had both been involved in careless accidents and he had seen the *Fox* run aground. He knew that a moment's inattention could lead to disaster. This may explain why Richard Peirce set great store on navigation.

Throughout his career, he questioned the accuracy of his charts and challenged the positions attributed to landmarks and shoals by other navigators. Without any reliable means of estimating longitude, there was plenty of scope for disagreement. Often Peirce expressed irritation with his predecessors' calculations but he was prepared to give credit where he thought it was due. For example, he had confidence in the ability of Captain Taylor to plot their position. Alexander Dalrymple, the East India Company's hydrographer, clearly respected Richard Peirce's judgement. He published Peirce's sketches of the coastline of Ceylon, the Malacca Straits and Singapore and also praised Peirce's observations from other voyages.[41] Perhaps, Richard Peirce's thoroughness and attention to detail was why his ship was one of those selected to help map the Macclesfield Bank.

In order for an East India Company commander to ensure that his ship went safely from A to B, he also had to lead his crew. This drew on a different set of skills. Up to this point, leadership seems to have come naturally to Richard Peirce. He was a good judge of men and selected competent officers. He was by nature affable, not averse to the occasional wager, and well-regarded by his peers. The ordinary seamen seem to have respected him too, and on the whole, his crews appear to have been contented and cooperative. This may have been because they quickly understood that this captain cared for their well-being. We have seen an example of this in the trouble Richard Peirce would take to help the lowly carpenter's mate, Sam Roberts. He was also a man prepared to listen. The request of Irish recruits to be allowed to toast St Patrick's Day did not fall on deaf ears. Richard Peirce clearly enjoyed a drink himself, though he took a firm line on excessive drunkenness, especially when it led to indecent behaviour.

Generally, Richard Peirce seems to have managed his men with a light touch. The brutality which soured the atmosphere on the *Berrington* never infected any of Peirce's voyages. He ordered punishments on only twelve occasions throughout the four voyages under his command. Six of these punishments were for disobedience amongst the Company's recruits – essentially passengers and not members of his crew. A further three punishments were for seamen who had defied his officers while Peirce himself was ashore. Nevertheless, he could assert his authority when trouble needed to be nipped in the bud. On several occasions, men were punished but the floggings were never severe and often it only required the culprits to be confined in irons for a day. However, there was one occasion when his authority appears to have been seriously challenged. When *Halsewell* ignored Nelson's signal to stop, was this because her crew refused to obey the orders of their captain? Perhaps not. The pressing of men from returning Indiamen was not only anathema to the victims, it was also deeply resented by their commanders. Perhaps, Peirce had pre-empted a Nelsonian strategy and turned a blind eye. However, when Nelson showed his intent by firing on *Halsewell*, Peirce responded quickly. The danger to his ship, his men and, most importantly, his cargo, seem to have galvanised him into taking action. Even without the cooperation of the seamen, he ensured that his commands were acted upon. Later, in more challenging circumstances, he would not be so fortunate.

Like all commanders, Captain Peirce was concerned for the health of his men. A ship would not function properly if her crew were incapacitated through illness. On *Ashburnham* and *Halsewell* the diet was probably similar to that on other East Indiamen. There is no evidence that he followed the practice of the Royal Navy in combating scurvy with lemon juice. Peirce's men occasionally suffered from it but it was infectious fevers that posed the greatest threat. While at sea, Peirce followed the normal procedures of airing and fumigating his ship to banish the noxious odours that were thought to encourage disease. Cabins were smoked with tobacco and decks were washed with vinegar. He also kept his men busy. There was nothing unusual in this, either. Idleness at sea could quickly lead to boredom and insubordination. It was sensible to provide the occasional entertainment as a distraction. We know that musicality ran in the Peirce family and that he encouraged music on his ships. *Halsewell* could muster a band and their playing was probably not just confined to harbour. It was conducive to a happy atmosphere as sea also; the sort of atmosphere Richard Peirce hoped would characterise his next and final voyage.

PART THREE

'A FREEZING HORROR'

THE WRECK OF THE *HALSEWELL*, 1786

17
Society at Sea

As the year of 1785 drew to a close, the passengers on the *Halsewell* passed an uncomfortable night in unfamiliar surroundings. Their cramped cabins were dark, damp and bitterly cold. Separated by thin wooden partitions or simply by canvas, each cabin could accommodate only their sea-cot, a trunk and, perhaps, a washstand. Swaying in their cots, suspended from the deck above, the Peirce sisters will have been conscious of the gentle movement of the ship, riding at anchor. Perhaps it lulled them to sleep.

Whether or not the girls slept easily that night, their sleep was interrupted early on the morning of New Year's Day, 1786. Captain Peirce was keen to set sail as soon as it was light. The thump of seaboots on the deck above their heads and the shouting of orders to the crew must have roused Eliza and Mary Ann. In their unheated cabins, they dressed quickly and made their way to the cuddy where they joined the other passengers for breakfast. Sir George and Lady Staunton were not amongst them. At the last minute, they had changed their plans and decided to remain in England.[1] Although their baggage had been loaded already, Mr and Mrs Robert Graham had not come aboard either. Instead, they were en route to Kent and intended to join the ship at Deal.

Despite the bitter weather, the atmosphere at breakfast was probably cheerful. Mr John George Schultz was returning to India and, doubtless, had stories to tell of his experiences there. He had already made his fortune and now wanted to arrange the means of remitting it to England.[2] Among the other young ladies at breakfast were Miss Mary Haggard and Miss Anne Mansell. Both were bound for Madras. Miss Mansell had completed her education in England and was rejoining her family. A few years previously, another member of the Mansell family had attracted notoriety when she had accused the captain of an East Indiaman of raping her. The case had come to trial but the captain had been acquitted. Other crew members and passengers had testified that this Miss Mansell was an outrageous flirt who had propositioned them too.[3] One wonders if anyone at breakfast was aware of the Mansell scandal, as they made polite conversation with Anne. As for Mary Haggard, no scandal was known to attach to her. Her brother was a respectable army officer in Madras and she was going to visit him.[4]

Soon, the Peirce girls hoped to make the acquaintance of others on board. There were a number of interesting young men. The youngest were the 'guinea pigs' who were under the care of Captain Peirce. Thirteen-year-old Charles Webber was the son of the late Admiral Webber. William Cowley was a neighbour from Kingston and Charles Templer was a relative.[5] Amy and Mary Paul's eldest sister, Jane, was married to his brother. There were also the dashing young midshipmen, in their smart uniforms. Thomas Jeane came from West Monkton and was a friend of the Paul family. He had sailed as a guinea pig on *Halsewell's* previous voyage and had performed well. Next there were the brothers, James and William Humphries. Their father was a poor clergyman but someone with influence had persuaded Captain Peirce to take them on. There were also the Scottish lads, McDougal and McManus, with their broad accents. Most important were the senior officers, men like Mr Meriton and Mr Rogers, who helped Captain Peirce to run the ship. The chief officer was Thomas Burston but Mary Ann and Eliza already knew him well. He was their uncle.

Two days previously, on Friday 30 December, the *Ganges* had weighed anchor in Leigh Road and begun to move further down the estuary.[6] It was Saturday 31st before *Halsewell* was ready to follow. For both ships it proved a false start. The weather had now turned to freezing fog and it was soon far too risky for either ship to proceed. That afternoon, having passed the Nore lightship, *Halsewell* dropped anchor within sight of *Ganges*. The pilots of both ships insisted the fog must disperse before they weighed again.

Fortunately, New Year's Day dawned bright and clear. By eight o'clock, as the passengers gathered for breakfast, the two ships were on the move again. Still under the control of their respective pilots, both

Society at Sea by Robert Dodd
© *National Maritime Museum, Greenwich, London*

ships moved cautiously along the coast of north Kent. This stretch, known as 'the flats', was notorious for sand banks and other hazards but, at least, there were two well-signposted routes. On this occasion, the pilots opted for the passage known as the 'Knob-Channel'. Throughout the morning, the log of the *Ganges* catalogued the buoys marking the channel, as they passed each one. The black buoy of the Mouse, the red buoy of the Knob, the buoy of the Shivering Sand, the black buoy of the Girdler, the white buoy of Pan Sand and finally the buoy of Margate Sand. By afternoon, they had rounded North Foreland and were sailing in a southerly direction.

In Meriton and Rogers' *Circumstantial Narrative of the Loss of the Halsewell*, they write that the *Halsewell* 'sailed through the Downs on Sunday the 1st January, 1786'. The journal of the *Ganges* records that the two ships were 'in company' with each other and that they arrived in the Downs at 2.30pm that afternoon. The wind was blowing steadily in a fresh to moderate gale. As they came abreast of Deal, both ships paused. This was the place where they would collect the packet – the box containing the Company's instructions and correspondence for the Council at Bengal. Deal was also a popular boarding point for passengers who wished to delay their departure as long as possible. Without any passengers to collect, *Ganges* waited barely an hour. As soon as her purser had come aboard with the packet, she made sail and departed. *Halsewell* cannot have lingered much longer, even though Captain Peirce was expecting to pick up Mr and Mrs Graham. After communicating with the shore, it became clear that the Grahams had not, in fact, arrived and there was no news of their whereabouts. Consequently, their sea-chests were collected from their cabin and sent ashore.[7] With nothing else to detain her, *Halsewell* set off in pursuit of *Ganges*.

The non-arrival of the Grahams may have puzzled and disappointed Amy and Mary Paul. Robert was the older brother of Thomas Graham, their brother-in-law, with whom they were all intending to stay. At thirty-five, Robert was twice their age. For several years he had been a partner in the London bank of Mayne & Graham, until its collapse in 1782.[8] Now, he proposed to try his luck in the financial arena of the East Indies. For the young ladies, he would have provided a reassuring presence during the long voyage, and his failure to join the ship at Deal was unexpected. Although Captain Peirce could not have known, Robert had missed the rendezvous by only a few hours. His wife had been indisposed and this had delayed their setting off from London. Hampered by the continuing snow, the journey to the Kent coast had taken longer than usual. When they finally reached Deal, their baggage was waiting for them but the *Halsewell* had gone. It would be a lucky escape.

Throughout the rest of Sunday afternoon, the ships made good progress together. At about 4.30pm, while their passengers warmed themselves with hot coffee, they rounded South Foreland and entered the English Channel. Less than an hour later, *Ganges* sent her pilot ashore. He had fulfilled his obligations to guide them through the first part of the voyage and now Captain Williamson felt able to take command of the ship, himself. Captain Peirce, however, decided to keep his pilot on *Halsewell* a little longer. By five o'clock that evening, it was already dark and both ships sailed cautiously down the English Channel under an easy sail.

Although the cold continued to bite, the prospect of supper kept such thoughts at bay. At eight o'clock, the clanging of the bell marked the start of first watch and, for the passengers, signalled that supper was about to be served. They assembled in the cuddy once more. The ship had been their home for two days and, already, the four cousins were becoming familiar with its routines. For supper, there would be at least one warm dish and, probably, some of the leftovers from dinner. The sea was not too turbulent and appetites had been whetted by the pervading chill. Toasts would be drunk, warming the cockles and maintaining a universal sense of optimism. Then there would be card games and music before everyone retired to their seacots. Above their heads, the men on watch would keep them all safe.

By next morning, they were off the Isle of Wight. As dawn broke, the officer in charge could see that *Halsewell* was abreast of Dunnose Head, on its southeast shore.[9] Then the wind died away, leaving an eerie calm. Progress slowed to a crawl, sails hung stiffly from the yards and flakes of snow began to fall. They floated down steadily, agitated into thick flurries when the wind returned in short, sharp squalls. As the snow settled, *Halsewell's* deck became treacherous.

On the quarterdeck, muffled in his greatcoat, epaulettes of snow gracing his shoulders, Captain Peirce was frustrated by these conditions. He was now ready to drop the pilot and he wanted to get nearer to Portsmouth. There was still the issue of Samuel Roberts, the calico thief and former carpenter's mate. He was being held on a prison hulk in Portsmouth harbour, in readiness to be shipped to Africa. It is possible that he had been informed of Richard Peirce's proposal to save him and, if so, Sam will have waited anxiously for his arrival. Finally, at three o'clock on Monday afternoon, a southerly breeze sprang up and *Halsewell* was able to set a course towards Portsmouth.

It was a false start. Before the ship could make much progress, the weather altered again. By early evening, it was snowing hard and the wind had become erratic. It kept changing direction, 'baffling', making it impossible for *Halsewell* to maintain headway. At nine o'clock, with mounting frustration, Peirce decided to postpone the attempt. They would stop for the night and wait for the wind to resolve its indecision. The line revealed eighteen fathoms of water beneath

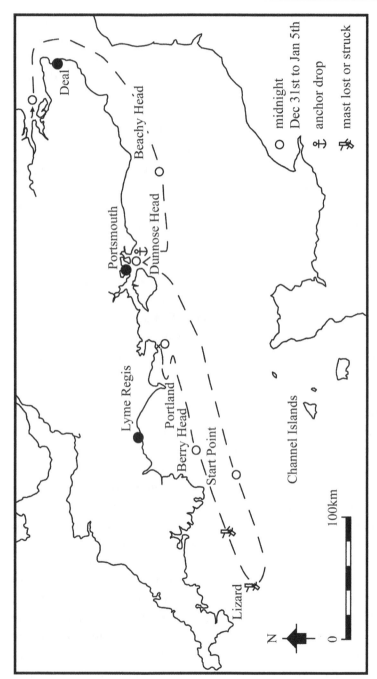

Fig 3. *The Final Voyage of the Halsewell*

them, a safe depth at which to anchor, in normal conditions. But now the times were out of joint. The weather conditions were becoming exceptional and Captain Peirce failed to recognise the implications.

Snow now covered the open deck, and ropes and canvas had frozen hard. If the ship were to remain at anchor, it was imperative to furl the sails but, rigid with ice, these sails now presented a challenge. To furl the sails required sailors aloft. The men would have to move out along the foot ropes to their individual positions on the yards and then, hands clumsy with cold, attempt to gather in the stiff canvas and tie it tightly to the yard. Although it was the larger and more difficult sail to 'hand', the men succeeded in securing the topsail. However, when they tried to furl the smaller mainsail, it proved impossible. The canvas was now so unyielding and heavy, it could not be folded. Although clewed up, the main sail would have to hang like a stiff bag, ballooning at each gust of wind with a crack like a musket shot.

Cold weather of such severity was unusual but it was not unknown. Even in these conditions an experienced crew should have been able to take in all the sails. In worse weather, Captain Cook's crew had done so, in the southern oceans off Antarctica.[10] That they failed to cope on the *Halsewell* suggests that other factors may have come into play. Was the discontent among some crew members still simmering? Did some men refuse to go aloft? If so, did a shortage of manpower delay work on the main sail and contribute to their failure to furl it?

Even with the mainsail flapping in the wind, Captain Peirce hoped the anchor would hold his ship steady until the morning. Then he would reassess the situation. If he had any anxieties about their predicament, doubtless he did his best to conceal them from his daughters and the other ladies. Confined to the great cabin and the cuddy, they will have attempted to pass the time as pleasantly as possible. After a dull day, they may have turned to music to lift their spirits. Young Mr Miller was among the company. The son of the celebrated organist and composer at Doncaster Minster, he was a proficient musician in his own right. His role on *Halsewell* would be to provide musical entertainment, supported by the ship's band. A little musical diversion was just the thing to take people's minds off the miserable weather.

As Monday evening came to a close, Eliza and Mary Ann Peirce withdrew to their cabins to prepare for another night aboard. Teenagers usually sleep soundly but, at four in the morning, the girls may have been aware that something had changed. The *Halsewell* was now rocking more violently. A strong gale had got up from east-northeast and the ship had begun to drag her anchor. *Halsewell* was being pushed steadily towards the Isle of Wight. With no time to winch up the heavy anchor, Captain Peirce gave the order to cut the cable and allow the ship to run clear of the land. The cable, connecting the ship to the anchor, was made of three thick ropes twisted together. Under great tension, it was relatively easy to cut. After a few strokes from a cutlass, it parted with a bang and *Halsewell* was free. Soon, she was running before the wind, down the English Channel. There was no longer any prospect of their reaching Portsmouth. Sam Roberts would not be freed, and now, the pilot on the East Indiaman had become a prisoner, too.

For the pilot, at least, his predicament would be temporary. During the morning of Tuesday 3 January, the lookout spotted another ship ahead. She was a small brig, bound for Dublin. By midday *Halsewell* had caught up with her and, despite the rough conditions, the pilot was transferred. A voyage to Dublin had not been the pilot's original intention but it was preferable to going to India. At least he should get home in a week or two.

During the next few hours, the *Halsewell* ran before the gale. Her stern lifting and falling with every sea, made walking difficult for the passengers. They had not yet learned how to flex their knees to stay in time with the heave of the deck. Lurching, sprawling and grabbing for handholds, many had already succumbed to seasickness. In such a state, most sufferers would retire to their cots. The prospect of food would have lost all appeal and some were already asking themselves why they had ever ventured on such a voyage in the first place.[11] Unable to stagger to the lavatories on the quarter gallery, the passengers made do with the 'easing chairs' or commodes in their cabins. To the vile smells of the ship was now added that of their own vomit.

Then, as Tuesday evening began, the wind started to shift again. It swung round to the south and grew in strength. The officer on duty gave the command to reef some sails, shortening them to reduce the area exposed to the wind. This was a challenge for the men sent aloft. With the masts swaying alarmingly and the ship jolting and juddering, simply holding on took strength and skill. Nevertheless, the reefing was successfully completed. Even before the men had returned to the deck, the storm had worsened. The wind was now howling through the shrouds at strong gale force, gusting at more than fifty miles per hour. The crest of each wave curled and rolled over, trailing behind it dense streaks of foam, like streamers in the wind. With every impact, clouds of spray erupted from *Halsewell's* bows, drenching anyone on her exposed decks.

As the gale muscled and bullied his ship northwards, a fresh concern began to preoccupy Captain Peirce. Was *Halsewell* being pushed too close to the coast of England? It was, of course, pitch dark and no lights were visible from land, so Peirce could not be certain of his position. By now, they were probably sailing across Lyme Bay and he needed no reminding that Chesil Beach lay somewhere to starboard. Too many ships had come to grief on that vast bank of shingle. Perhaps, he also thought of *Ramillies*. In 1760, during a similar storm, a miscalculation had led her to become embayed, near Brixham. Trapped there by a southerly wind, her sheet anchor had failed to save her. When *Ramillies* drove onto the rocks, more than 700 men had died. Captain Peirce understood he must, at all costs, prevent his ship from becoming embayed, too.

Generally, when winds reached gale force, the response on a sailing ship was to reduce sail. This is what they had just done. However, a smaller area of sail inevitably results in slower forward motion and greater sideways drift. Now, it was essential not to be pushed towards the lee shore which lurked unseeen. In order to move further out into the English Channel, Peirce decided the wisest option was to increase sail and to steer as close to the wind as possible. At best, square-rigged ships like *Halsewell* could sail at 70 degrees to the wind. At that angle, she would have been taking the waves on her port bow. Pitching over the wave crests and lurching down into the troughs, it must have reminded Captain Peirce of the 'mountainous seas' he had encountered fourteen years before.[12] Then, he had been 'in dread' for the safety of the mainmast on the *Earl of Ashburnham*. Now, he must have prayed that the *Halsewell's* masts would be equally robust. At ten o'clock, he gave the order to carry more sail.

During the refit, after her previous voyage, *Halsewell* had undergone a number of modifications and improvements. One of these involved the hawseholes, the holes in the ship's bow through which the mooring cables passed. In rough weather, to prevent seawater getting in, each hawsehole was sealed with a conical-shaped canvas bag and then covered with a wooden shield or hawse plug.[13] Traditionally, these plugs were fitted to the outside of the ship but this made them difficult to attach in rough seas. At the dockyard, the decision was made to fit the hawse plugs on the inside instead. This modification should make them easier to operate but, unfortunately, the designer had underestimated the force of the sea. *Halsewell* was now battling in storm conditions with her bow constantly plunging into the waves. Had the plugs been on the outside, these waves would have wedged them ever tighter. Now that they were inside, the waves effortlessly knocked them out of their holes and washed the hawse bags away. With nothing to bar its entry, water began to pour onto the gun deck. There, like a tsunami, it swept aft, soaking hammocks and drenching the Company recruits, huddling in the dark. It carried away trunks and boxes, and poured through the partitions of the cabins in steerage.

This was bad but worse was to follow. Under the continuous battering from the waves, the ship had begun to leak elsewhere. It is possible that her re-caulking had been shoddily done and now oakum was coming loose. Once a ship began 'spitting oakum', her seams would let in water. This was not uncommon. Captain Cook had made the same discovery with the *Resolution*, during his final voyage.[14] However, there may, in fact, have been a more serious structural problem on *Halsewell*. As her masts tilted with each roll of the ship, they put a strain on the shrouds, first on one side, then on the other. These shrouds were attached to either side of the ship through a protruding ledge, called the channel. Consequently, with every wave, there was an alternate pulling and releasing to the ship's side. If the planks, near the shrouds, were not fastened securely, each roll of the ship would cause them to open and close. Every time the planks parted, water would come in.

Whatever the cause, *Halsewell* was shipping water fast and, for several hours, nobody noticed. Checking the level of water in the bottom of the ship should have been a routine task, especially in bad weather. Incredibly, it had been overlooked. When, eventually, somebody went to the hold, it was found to contain seawater to a depth of five feet. A leak of this severity had to be taken seriously. In a turbulent sea, such a quantity of water sloshing about in the bottom of the ship would make her unstable. As the ship rolled, the centre of gravity in the water would always shift to the lower side. The effect of this would be to aggravate both rolling and listing. Soon, *Halsewell* would become unresponsive to the rudder and difficult to manoeuvre. Peirce understood this well and gave the necessary orders.

First, he ordered the pumps to be set to work; essential if they were to reduce the level of water. On *Halsewell*, the pumps were situated at the base of the main mast, in a clear space known as the pump well. At least two vertical wooden cylinders, made of elm, stretched from the well up through the ship to the open deck. Inside each cylinder was a piston, operated by a large lever at the top. Pumps worked by the application of suction and force, raising water from the well to an upper deck where it would drain into the sea. The levers had to be pulled up and down by hand, with several men to each lever. On Nelson's *Victory*, it was said that thirty men could pump 120 tons of water in one hour.[15] Nevertheless, it was strenuous and tiring labour and would require teams of sailors, working in relays, to ensure that pumping continued uninterrupted.

It was also essential to reduce the rate at which the ship was taking in water. If the leak was towards the bow, an obvious way to do this was to sail more slowly. Instead of crashing through the waves under a 'press of sail', they would adjust their speed more appropriately to the weather. The command, therefore, was to haul up both the main sail and main topsail. But, just as on Monday, this proved difficult to carry out. Previously, the cold had been the key factor. Now, storm force winds had been added to the equation. With the masts rolling through an angle of up to sixty degrees, a man could be hurled from the yards into the sea by a sudden gust. It is no surprise that, although they managed to clew up the topsail, the sailors were unable to furl either it or the mainsail.

Again, their failure to complete this essential task may not have been due to the weather alone. It would seem that, when ordered to go aloft, some sailors had simply refused. The men, who earlier had threatened to 'Loughborough' their officers, now ignored their commands and, instead, went below to 'skulk in their hammocks'. The discontent, which had manifested itself in the Thames, now seems to have escalated into open mutiny.[16]

The insubordination of some of his crew presented Captain Peirce with a serious problem. In order to ride out the storm, the ship would have to be worked. Men would have to go aloft. If the sailors were uncooperative, perhaps the soldiers on board would show greater discipline. Later, stories would circulate about how Captain Peirce had been compelled to call on the Company's recruits for help. According to Meriton, some soldiers even climbed the rigging to help with the sails. If this is true, they can have been of little use. Furling a sail, tying it tightly to the yards, required skill, especially in the dark. Despite their courage, the soldiers would not have been able to subdue the struggling canvas. With wind howling like banshees through the shrouds, high above the pitching deck, these men could not hear or understand the commands shouted at them. As midnight came and went, the ship staggered on with her sails still unfurled.

By two in the morning on Wednesday 4 January, the gale had not abated and, despite the pumps, the water in *Halsewell's* hold continued to rise. This was mostly due to the dreadful conditions but insubordination also played a part. The sailors who had declined to go aloft, now refused to take their turn at the pumps. No doubt, Peirce intended to deal with the culprits as soon as he could but, right now, the urgency of the situation required more immediate action. A request was sent to the sergeant in command of the soldiers and a contingent of recruits was pressed into service. At the pumps, only muscle power and stamina was required but even that was in short supply. The recruits were not in great physical condition to start with and they had already become debilitated by cold and seasickness. Eventually, as these men became exhausted, Peirce's own officers stepped up to replace them. It was a sign of how desparate things had become. Faced with this crisis, Peirce now acknowledged that it was futile to continue on their present course. He decided that the only sensible thing was to 'wear' the ship, turning it to the east so they could run before the wind, back up the English Channel. There, they could find a haven where they would shelter. However, it is one thing to make a decision, but, in such appalling weather and with a recalcitrant crew, it was another to carry it out. Unable to work the sails properly and with an increasing weight of water in her hold, the *Halsewell* had become too sluggish to respond. She refused to turn.

For the first time in his career, Captain Peirce was driven to the last resort to save his ship. The weight of masts and sails was impeding the handling of the ship, so a mast would have to be sacrificed. In such circumstances, the standard practice was to cut down the mizzen mast first.[17] Sailors with axes would cut a notch in either side of the mast to determine both where it would break and the direction of its fall. Then others with cutlasses would cut through the thin lanyards that attached the shrouds to the channel on the side of the ship. Without the lateral support of the shrouds, the next roll of the ship would snap the mast where it had been weakened and carry it over the side. Ideally, the mast would be quickly cut free of the ship before it fouled the rudder or damaged the hull. Knowing it meant the abandonment of his voyage and all that rested upon it, Peirce reluctantly gave the order to fell the mizzen mast.

In their sea-cots below deck, the passengers were startled by the crash of the falling mast. The heart-stopping impact of six tons of solid pine hitting the deck above their heads sounded as if some sea demon had set about the ship with a diabolical hammer. Petrified, they waited for the next blow. In the urgency of the moment, it is unlikely that any of the officers had time to explain what had actually happened. In any case, by now, it was obvious to all that they were in great danger. For hours they had listened to the dreadful groaning of the ship's timbers as *Halsewell* rolled and pitched. With every heave, the water in the hold surged towards the bows or the stern in a dull

Sailors in a Storm by Thomas Stothard
© *National Maritime Museum, Greenwich, London*

roar, clearly audible to the recruits on the deck above. It seemed as if the storm was already inside as well as out.

Having reduced the ship to two masts, a second attempt was made to turn *Halsewell* before the wind. It made no difference; the ship still refused to respond. By now, the level of water in the hold had reached seven feet and it was gaining rapidly. The pumps would clearly be inadequate to the task unless they could 'wear' the ship. If things carried on like this much longer, there was a serious risk that *Halsewell* would founder. In this weather, far from shore, that meant certain death for all on board.

Dejected by the failure of his strategy, Peirce summoned his officers to discuss their options. In reality, there was only one thing to do. More extreme surgery was required and another mast would have to be cut down. Sailing with only the fore mast would help to keep the bow before the wind. Then, with the gale at their stern, they would be able to pick up speed. The decision, therefore, was to topple the mainmast. This was a more difficult operation. The entire mainmast, in several sections, was much taller and carried more rope and canvas than the mizzen. As before, it was essential that the whole lot was got clear of the ship. If it remained hanging over the side or became entangled with the fore mast, any hope of manoeuvring the *Halsewell* would be lost.

It was still night time when a team of men set to work. They were probably following the instructions of the coxswain, Jonathan Moreton. On the pitching deck, in almost total darkness, they swung their axes against the thick pine of the mainmast. With the shrouds loose, it began to creak and then, with a loud crack, the mast gave way. Toppling over the side, it dragged a confusion of ropes and canvas with it. Although they tried to scatter when they heard the splintering of wood, not all the men could get away in time. Moreton, and four other men became entangled in the shrouds and either fell or were dragged over the side, into the black maelstrom.[18] Nothing could be done to save them and their cries were soon drowned by the noise of the storm. It was an ominous foretaste of what was to follow.

Although the mast was down, it was still attached to the *Halsewell* and a chaos of rigging, spars and shredded canvas cluttered her deck. It was eight o'clock in the morning, just daylight, before the ship was finally cleared and a third attempt could be made to alter course. At last, with only her foremast left standing, the *Halsewell* began to respond. Slowly, her bow came round until, to everyone's relief, she began to sail before the wind. It probably took several men to hold the wheel steady and maintain her course but, with the wind on her stern, the pressure on *Halsewell's* hull was greatly reduced. At last, her pumps could make a difference.[19] For two more hours, those who were working the pumps continued to labour, no doubt encouraged by the fact that they were winning at last. By ten o'clock, the water level in the hold had fallen by two feet. The strength of the wind had also begun to ease and it seemed the gale was blowing itself out. It would be surprising if the spirits of the ship's officers did not begin to lift, too. The danger of foundering was receding and they were sailing towards harbour. For the passengers, though, there may have been little to cheer about. Although the wind was easing, there was now a heavy swell on the sea, the typical aftermath of a big storm. With the ship rolling and 'labouring' so severely, seasickness continued to afflict demoralised passengers and sodden recruits alike. Inside the great cabin and the roundhouse, it was as dark as on the gundeck. Once the storm had begun, wooden deadlights or shutters had been secured, protecting the large windows but blocking any natural light. Lanterns had to be kept burning constantly. In the stern, the more hardy passengers would have left their cabins for the cuddy where they clung precariously to the chairs cleated to the floor. No one felt like breakfast and none was offered.

Later accounts of the storm have little to say about conditions below deck, on *Halsewell*. Nevertheless we can get a sense of what it might have been like from the survivor of another severe storm. In 1782, the diarist William Hickey was caught in a hurricane in the Indian Ocean. He described how during supper, 'the ship took so desperate a lurch as to tear the table at which we were sitting from its lashings, and the whole party, chairs, dishes, plates and all the etceteras were dashed in one promiscuous heap against the lee side of the cabin.' As the storm increased, Hickey observed that 'not a bureau, chest or trunk but broke loose and was soon demolished, the contents from the quickness and constant splashing from one side to the other of the ship, becoming a perfect paste'.[20] Even in their cabin, Eliza and Mary Ann Peirce will have found little comfort. It had always been cold, now it was also wet. They and the other passengers must surely have understood the truth of Hickey's description of 'a filthy wet bed, in a confined and putrid air, where it is as impossible to think as to breathe freely, the fatigue, the motion, the want of rest and food, give a kind of hysteric sensibility to the frame, which makes it alive to the slightest danger.'[21]

The rolling of the *Halsewell* from side to side not only caused chaos below decks but also put a severe strain on the remaining mast.

Peirce knew this and understood the implications. His ship now had only the fore mast and it was essential to preserve it if they were to reach a safe haven. Like the mainmast, the foremast had additional sections. On top of the fore mast stood the slightly thinner fore topmast. It carried the fore-topsail. These two masts were joined at a point called the fid.[22] This was a point of potential weakness where the two sections could separate. The pressure on this point grew immensely as the mast tilted from side to side with the rolling of the ship.

At around ten o'clock, the inevitable happened. Without warning, the fore topmast suddenly broke free from its fixings and crashed down onto the deck below. As it fell, the splintered wood tore through the fore sail on the lower mast and ripped it to shreds. Instantly, the situation on deck was transformed into one of confusion. In a matter of seconds, *Halsewell* had lost all her sails and was now drifting at the mercy of wind and tide.

Without forward motion, it is impossible to steer a ship. The man at the helm was now powerless to prevent *Halsewell* from 'broaching' or turning sideways to the wind. If that happened, there was a danger that she might be swamped by a large sea or simply capsize. When William Hickey had found himself in a similar situation, his ship had rolled from side to side so violently that, he claimed, half the quarter deck was submerged in water, with each roll.[23] At all costs, *Halsewell* must avoid a similar fate. It was, therefore, imperative to raise a sail of some sort, for only by harnessing the wind could they regain control of the ship.

It probably took an hour to clear the decks and raise a spare foresail on the remaining stump of the fore mast. With the noise of the elements and the flapping of torn canvas, the men strained to hear the commands shouted by the officers through their speaking trumpets. While the wreckage was being jettisoned, Captain Peirce was relieved to see that storm had subsided further and the wind was moving round to the west. By eleven o'clock in the morning, land became visible to the north. It was soon identified as Berry Head, the familiar promontory, near Brixham in Devon. The officer on duty estimated the distance as between 'four and five leagues' or roughly twelve to fifteen miles away. With this information, Peirce could fix their position and calculate the distance to Portsmouth and safety.

Ship under jury rig in a storm by J.C. Schotel
© Het Scheepvartmuseum, Amsterdam

Under only one sail, their progress would be laborious, so it was important to try to raise other canvas as well. This would require the construction of another mast. Like all East Indiamen, *Halsewell* carried spare topmasts as well as yards and spars. It was a regular occurrence for topmasts to become cracked or 'sprung' so removing and replacing them was fairly routine. The obvious thing to do was to erect a temporary or 'jury' mast where the main mast had stood and to use a spare topmast for this purpose. Once this jury mast was in place, a topgallant sail could be raised to act as a miniature main sail. Having succeeded in doing this, Peirce then instructed his crew to repeat the operation by getting up a jury mizzen mast.

As work continued on these tasks throughout Wednesday, *Halsewell* made slow but steady progress eastward. Meriton's account has nothing to say about the passengers at this point so we can only speculate. The worst of the storm was over and some passengers may have felt well enough to take a look on deck. If so, the sight will have shocked them. Gone were all the masts that had towered over them so impressively when they came aboard on Saturday. Instead, they had been replaced with precarious and ramshackle looking structures. It was obvious the ship had suffered a severe battering. Nevertheless, they were now making headway for port and the worst dangers seemed to have passed. Perhaps, with appetites returning, some passengers may have joined Captain Peirce for a cold supper, in the cuddy. Later that night, as they tried to sleep, they must have felt reassured by the thought that, next day, they would reach dry land again.

18
'Gainst the flinty rocks'

Throughout the night, *Halsewell* continued to limp eastward across Lyme Bay. The weather had now turned to freezing fog, so the officer on watch was essentially sailing blind. At 2am the wind began to freshen again, changing direction once more and swinging round to the south. Night turned to morning but visibility remained limited, as 'the weather was very thick'. Then, at around midday, the mist and rain cleared sufficiently for the lookout to spot land. Off to the northeast was the unmistakable sight of Portland Bill and it appeared to be less than nine miles away. This was good news. On their return from the East Indies, Company ships often halted in the lee of Portland. The harbour of Weymouth was sheltered by this great headland and it was a popular place to drop off the purser or any passengers impatient to go ashore. Unfortunately for the *Halsewell*, the break in the weather was short lived and soon the fog closed in again. With no landmarks to guide him, Peirce maintained their course eastward. As the day wore on, the southerly wind grew again in strength until by early evening it had returned to gale force. At 8pm the mist and rain lifted once more and, this time, it was possible to see lights, at least twelve miles away to the northwest. It was obvious to Peirce that this must be Portland lighthouse. Although the Portland lights were somewhat erratically maintained, on a night like this, surely they must have been lit.[24]

If Portland was to the northwest, *Halsewell* had evidently overshot it. Nevertheless, it might still be possible to return there. Peirce gave the order to alter course. Manoeuvering the cumbersome East Indiaman with only its jury masts and few sails was not an easy task but somehow the crew succeeded. With her bow pointing westward again, they began to beat back to Portland. Safety was tantalizingly close but it was soon clear that it was also receding. *Halsewell* was too crippled to make headway against the strong currents and gusting wind. She continued to drift eastward. The realisation that Portland was slipping from their grasp must have come as a demoralising blow. But Captain Peirce was a pragmatist. If the elements made it easier to sail east, then that was the direction they would take. There were other places to shelter and it was better to run for them instead of wasting time on a futile attempt to return to Weymouth. Less than thirty miles away lay the sheltered waters of Studland Bay. If they could get safely past Peverel Point, the situation would be saved. The order was given to turn the ship yet again and to press eastward.

Further down the coast, in the Isle of Purbeck, lies the village of Worth Matravers. Its church and houses are made from purbeck stone, quarried nearby. Even in the eighteenth century, there was much demand for purbeck stone and many quarrymen lived locally. Some residents may also have engaged in smuggling. The notorious Dorset smuggler, Isaac Gulliver, reputedly had a house in the village. On this particular night, most sensible people were indoors. Mr Jones, the clergyman had been so impressed by the weather that he felt moved to record it in the parish records.[25]

Out at sea, for three more hours, *Halsewell* sailed on. Although they were sailing east as fast as they could, the officers on the *Halsewell* knew that the gale was also jostling them relentlessly towards the Dorset coast. Every mariner fears a lee shore and, at eleven o'clock that night, those fears were confirmed. Another clearing in the weather revealed St Alban's Head only a mile and a half to leeward. They were now so close inshore, there was no longer any possibility of getting round Peverel Point into Studland Bay. If they did not act quickly, the gale would drive them onto the rocks.

At once, Captain Peirce gave the order to take in all sail and to drop anchor. The small bower anchor was lowered and the *Halsewell* rode there at a cable's length. The hope was that this anchor would hold the ship until the storm had subsided. It was a situation reminiscent of what had faced them on Monday night, off Portsmouth. Only three days had passed but, for the exhausted passengers and crew, it must have seemed an eternity.

Within an hour, it was apparent that the bower anchor was not up to the task. It had begun to drag and the ship was being driven slowly towards the shore. The biggest anchor that *Halsewell* carried was her sheet anchor. It was intended to be used in emergencies when other anchors were inadequate. This was clearly such an occasion. To lower the sheet anchor and pay out the heavy cable, required many men at the windlass. It was an arduous task but worth the effort if it enabled *Halsewell* to ride out the storm safely. By midnight, the sheet anchor had been lowered.

At first, it seemed to be working and, for two hours, the sheet anchor held the *Halsewell* steady. Then, like the bower, it began to drag. Powered by the relentless sea and wind, *Halsewell* pulled her anchor in a tug-of-war towards the rocks. Perhaps, now, Captain Peirce was reminded of the fate of *Ramillies*. She, too, had leaked badly and lost her masts. There were also striking similarities about their current predicament but they must not share the final outcome. During the eighteenth century, ships in distress would often fire their guns. Now, Captain Peirce gave the order to do so. The booming of the cannons would alert people on shore to their predicament and, if *Halsewell* went aground, they could assist with the rescue.

Through the darkness, Peirce could make out an unbroken line of cliffs. Though he cannot have known her exact position, *Halsewell* was close to a point on the Purbeck coast midway between Winspit and Seacombe. At either end of this stretch, the land falls away to allow small streams to empty into the sea. Anyone coming ashore at either extremity would have the best chance of gaining dry land and escaping. Between these two inlets, the land rises vertically from the sea. Those who approach from seaward are faced with a forbidding wall of rock that rises to a height of 100 feet. This was the prospect that Captain Peirce now surveyed.

Captain Peirce can have been in no doubt that he had run out of options. It was now Friday 6 of January and the next few hours could determine their fate. Up to this point, one must assume that Captain Peirce had been preoccupied almost entirely with his responsibilities as ship's captain. Now, with disaster imminent, his responsibilities as a father and uncle must have intruded upon his thoughts and begun to dominate them. He called some of his officers together, including Henry Meriton. According to the second mate, Captain Peirce asked

Cliffs at Winspit
© E. Cumming

calmly for their assessment of the situation and the probability of saving the young ladies' lives.

Later, when he was safe, Meriton recorded that he had replied to Captain Peirce's question with 'equal calmness and candour'. There was 'little hope', he said. The ship was now 'driving fast' towards the shore and could expect to hit the rocks at any moment. Somebody then suggested lowering the ship's boats but this idea was quickly dismissed as impractical. The storm was still too fierce and the boats would either be swamped or dashed to pieces against the hull of the *Halsewell*. Nevertheless, Peirce was reluctant to abandon this idea entirely. He ordered that the longboat should be reserved for the ladies and the officers, in case there was opportunity to launch it. This plan was to be kept confidential. The longboat was the largest and most seaworthy of *Halsewell's* boats. The rest of the crew would have to take their chances in any other boats that remained intact.

Following this conversation, Richard Peirce left the quarterdeck and went below. For several days and nights he had not slept. Instead, he had spent countless hours on deck trying to manage a crisis that had worsened steadily. Despite his greatcoat, he was cold and wet. Now, he was mentally and physically exhausted. For the next hour or so he appears to have forgotten his concern for the ship and turned his attention instead to the passengers. Accommodated at the stern, they naturally congregated in the roundhouse. Weakened by insomnia, seasickness and lack of food, they, too, were cold, exhausted and frightened. What Peirce said to them has not been recorded but it must have been apparent from his demeanour that they were in great danger.

At about 2am, Captain Peirce withdrew to the cuddy where he was joined, once more, by Henry Meriton. Desperately concerned for his daughters, Peirce was now in a state of extreme anxiety. He 'earnestly' asked his officer if he could find any way of saving Eliza and Mary Ann. There was nothing to be done. Although rudimentary lifejackets made from cork had saved some on the *Ramillies*, they were not routinely carried on East Indiamen. We must assume that none was available on the *Halsewell* and that it was unlikely that any of the young ladies could swim. If the ship were to go to pieces, their only hope would be to hold onto a piece of floating wreckage and pray that the waves would carry them quickly ashore. In the bitterly cold water, their limbs would soon become numb and they would be unable to cling onto any flotsam for long.

Having considered this, Henry Meriton told his captain that he thought their best option was to wait for the morning. If this was their only chance, both men knew it was a perilously slim one. There was nothing more to say and Richard Peirce 'raised his hands in silent and distressful ejaculation'. This eloquent gesture was enough.

Wreck of the Halsewell by Robert Dodd.
© *National Maritime Museum, Greenwich, London*

At almost the same moment, the *Halsewell* hit the rocks. There was a loud crash and the ship lurched violently. Those officers who were standing in the cuddy were thrown off their feet, some banging their heads on the deck above. No-one on board can have been in any doubt about what had just happened. In the roundhouse and in every part of the ship they responded with a 'shriek of horror'.

The violent impact had a galvanising effect on the sailors. Some were still 'skulking' below decks, refusing to work. Now, alerted to the danger, they poured onto the deck in a state of great anxiety, uttering 'frantic exclamations' and imploring the heavens for help. A few, in desperation, even began to climb the flag pole at the stern. In their account, Meriton and Rogers cannot refrain from noting the grim irony of the situation. These were the very same sailors who had refused to carry out the orders of their officers earlier. If they had worked the pumps or carried out their duties on deck when required, they might not have found themselves in such peril now. They had only themselves to blame.

The initial impact was soon followed by more, as each succeeding wave threw the ship against the rocks. She was soon lying broadside to the shore so her sides bore the brunt of the damage. In minutes, the *Halsewell* had 'bulged', her planks separating and allowing the sea to flood onto her lower decks. Her cargo would now be ruined, Colonel Cathcart would never receive his ceremonial sword and the investment of Peirce and his officers would be irretrievably lost.

In response to the desperate entreaties of the crew, Meriton suggested they come over to the side of the ship nearest the shore and take any opportunity to escape that presented itself. It was already too late for concerted action. It was now every man for himself. Later, Meriton would comfort himself with the thought that he had 'provided to the utmost of his power, for the safety of the desponding crew'. Having released the crew from their obligations, Meriton returned to the roundhouse.

The scene that greeted him there was chaotic. The impact with the rocks had thrown everything around. The floor was littered with the wreckage of musical instruments, broken trunks and shattered furniture. The space was also crowded with people, mostly sitting on the deck which shook violently with every wave. Besides the passengers, most of the officers, midshipmen and guinea pigs had gathered there too. Some of the sailors tried to enter as well, looking for lanterns and alcohol, but John Rogers and James Bremer succeeded in keeping them out. However, five additional women had been allowed to join the group. Three were described as 'black' and included the former Indian servants of Laurence Sulivan and General Townsend. The other two were soldiers' wives. Altogether, Meriton estimated, there were now almost fifty people crammed into the roundhouse.

Captain Peirce was sitting on a cot or 'some other moveable' with a daughter on either side of him. Like everyone else in the room, Eliza and Mary Ann were terrified. Peirce alternately pressed each daughter to his 'affectionate bosom' in an attempt to comfort them. Nevertheless, there was an air of resignation about his demeanour and his responsibilities as captain appeared to have been forgotten. While avoiding direct criticism of his commander, Meriton's account presents himself in a better light – quite literally. It was Meriton who gathered up all the glass lanterns he could find and hung them around the roundhouse. He then cut some wax candles into pieces, placed them in the lanterns and lit them. It was a small gesture but, perhaps, the warm light would help to banish the dark terrors that lurked outside. At the very least, it roused Captain Peirce from his apathy.

On becoming aware of Meriton's presence, Captain Peirce asked him again for his assessment of the situation. In the darkness outside, it was difficult to tell but Meriton again expressed hope that the ship would hold together until dawn. Then, in daylight, they would be better able to plan their escape. Comforted by this thought, both men tried to reassure the 'melancholy assembly'. One of the young guinea pigs had let his fears get the better of him and was loudly bewailing the fact that the ship was about to break up. Temporarily regaining his air of authority, Captain Peirce told him to be quiet. The ship might go to pieces but he would not. They would be 'safe enough'.

Peirce's words seem to have had the desired effect. Backed up with further reassurance from Meriton, the 'drooping friends' became

Stothard's Cabin Scene on the Halsewell engraved by Edmund Scott
© National Maritime Museum, Greenwich, London

more composed. Only Miss Mansell continued to have 'hysteric fits' on the floor of the roundhouse.

In the extreme cold, without food or sleep, everyone was feeling the strain. By his own admission, it was the cool headed and observant Henry Meriton who noticed that the young ladies were parched and exhausted. Perhaps, in the short time on board, he had begun to have feelings towards one in particular. Maybe, he wanted to be particularly attentive to Mary Ann. Be that as it may, Meriton went looking for refreshment. He found a basket of oranges and encouraged the Captain's younger daughter to suck the juice. It was an act of kindness and seemed to comfort her.

It is impossible to know how much time had passed since the ship had struck but it is certain that the waves were taking their toll on the *Halsewell*. Her sides had already been breached and the deck was starting to lift and buckle. It was evident to Meriton that the ship could not hold together much longer. He spoke to the chief mate, Thomas Burston, about how they might escape. Burston made it clear that he could not leave his brother-in-law or his young neices. Were he to abandon his 'dear relatives', he feared he would be dismissed from the Service – a disgrace worse than death. Meriton was not bound by such ties so, impelled by a desire for self-preservation, he decided to leave the roundhouse. He went forward to see what state the ship was in. What he saw shocked him.

Halsewell had already broken in two, splitting roughly where her main mast had once stood. The bow section had moved and was further out to sea. It was clear that her stern section would soon disintegrate. Meriton decided there was no time to return to the roundhouse to report to Captain Peirce. In any case, the commander seemed incapable of taking any action. Concern for his children had incapacitated him. On deck, Meriton could see that many of the crew and soldiers had started to abandon ship. They were jumping into the water and trying to reach the shore. The most sensible course of action was to follow them.

The men who had rushed to the ensign flagpole when the ship first hit the rocks had apparently tried to use it as a means of escape. Meriton went to investigate. Up on the poop deck, directly above the roundhouse, he found that the men had unshipped the pole and tried to use it as a bridge to the rocks nearby. It hadn't been long enough or strong enough to bear the men's weight and it now lay snapped in pieces. Through a skylight, Meriton was able to communicate with those still in the roundhouse below. He called for someone to pass a lantern up to him and one of the occupants obliged. This light enabled him to see much better. He noticed a spar that was jutting out from the ship's side in the direction of the cliffs. If this spar reached the rocks, it might provide an escape route. Without informing those in the roundhouse, the second mate decided to try.

Lying down and straddling the spar, Henry Meriton pulled himself slowly forward. When he finally reached the end, he could see that the spar was not actually in contact with the cliff. However, it had stretched far enough: there were rocks directly below. By now, Meriton must have been wet through and numb with cold. Holding onto the slippery spar was difficult and suddenly he felt his grip loosening. Unable to prevent himself, he fell heavily onto the rocks beneath. These rocks were wet and, doubtless, slippery with seaweed. Before Meriton could recover from his fall and get to his feet, a wave arrived and washed him off his rock. Suddenly, he found himself in the freezing sea, swimming for his life.

On board what remained of the *Halsewell*, the occupants of the roundhouse continued to wait, Together, they represented a microcosm of Captain Peirce's world. Around him were his sister's two daughters, his brother-in-law, the son of his friend from West Monkton, a brother-in-law of one of his neices, and the daughter of a fellow commander. There were the guinea pigs under his care, there were merchants and musicians, lascars and Indian servants. And there were crewmen of the kind that he had worked with for over thirty years.

They sat there for about twenty minutes, transfixed by the grinding and cracking noises that grew louder with every shudder of the ship. Eventually, Peirce noticed that Meriton was missing and asked what had become of him. The third mate, John Rogers, replied that Meriton had gone on deck to see what could be done. Just at that moment, there was a loud crash, as an enormous wave broke over the ship. It was clear that anyone on the exposed deck would have been washed overboard. Among the ladies, there was immediate consternation for Meriton's safety. 'Oh poor Meriton, he is drowned: had he staid with us he would have been safe'. Mary Peirce seemed to be especially affected by the thought of his loss. Henry Meriton had shown kindness towards her and concern for her welfare. In contrast with her father, he had displayed confidence and authority at a time of crisis.

To allay their fears, John Rogers now offered to go to look for Meriton. But this only increased their anxiety. What if he shared the same fate? It would be much safer to stay where he was. Rogers knew this was not true and that continuing to wait passively could only have one outcome. The sea had already reached the stump of the mainmast and would soon be upon them. Captain Peirce knew this too. He gave Rogers a nod and stood up. Taking one of the lanterns, the two men left the roundhouse and made their way to the stern gallery. This was the open space or balcony at the very back of the ship from which, in fine weather, it was possible to take the air and enjoy the view. Now, through the gloom, all they could see was the perpendicular wall of black rock.

Just as he had asked Henry Meriton, earlier, Captain Peirce now sought the opinion of John Rogers. Was there any way they could save the girls? From the perspective of the stern gallery, there could only be one answer. Even if they made it alive to the base of the cliff, it was impossible to believe that any of the ladies would be able to climb to the top. Dejected, the two men returned to the roundhouse. The third mate hung up the lantern and the Captain, still wearing his great-coat, resumed his seat between Eliza and Mary. He was visibly upset and struggling to hide his tears. One of his daughters seemed to be on the point of fainting and the other, together with his nieces and some of the other women pressed close to him, clinging to his coat for comfort and reassurance.

This tableau, described by Rogers, is the last sight we have of Captain Peirce. It is a powerful image; a man surrounded by his dependants and the broken remnants of his career, sitting like a rock, resigned to the inevitable. Within a few months, artists would try to recreate the scene. But they had not been there and could only imagine what it had been like. William Hickey, on the other hand, had lived through a similar crisis and knew how it felt to face death in this way. His words give us an insight:

> If we look around the miserable group that surround us no eye beams comfort, no tongue speaks consolation, and when we throw our imagination beyond – to the death-like darkness, the howling blast, the raging and merciless element, expected every moment to become our horrid habitation – surely, surely it is the most terrible of deaths.[26]

To Richard Peirce, the sight of that unbroken wall of rock had seemed just such a death sentence. But, as Meriton was to discover, there was, in fact, a glimmer of hope. At a point opposite the middle of the *Halsewell*, out of sight from the stern gallery, there was a cave. As soon as he had been washed off his rock, the next wave carried Meriton right to the back of it. It was a stroke of fantastic luck. Grabbing a rock that jutted out from the cave wall, Meriton hung on. His hands were numb and he knew that the next wave to break into the cave would dislodge him. He was at the point of letting go when help arrived. Other seamen had found the cave too. They had managed to get a footing and clamber up out of the reach of the sea. One of them leaned down to Meriton and extended his hand to him. This was enough to enable him to get onto a little ledge and, from there, to climb to a shelf of rock, higher up and away from the surf. For the time being, he was out of danger.

On the *Halsewell* the danger was increasing, as she continued to break up. With the realisation that the end was now only minutes away, the solidarity of the group started to disintegrate too. Several of the men began to talk about trying to escape. The surgeon, Mr Clothier, had already gathered some of his most valuable possessions in a bag, which he now tied round his shoulders. Mr Schultz, the merchant, asked Rogers what they should do. This was the prompt the third mate needed. He had served his Captain as best he could but no-one should expect him to go down with the ship. He was entitled to try to save his own life if fate allowed.

'Follow me', he replied. Mr Schultz stood up. A group of men, including the sixth mate and midshipmen, McManus and McDougal did likewise. Rogers led them all to the stern gallery and from there, he and James Bremer, the supernumary officer, climbed up by the upper quarter deck gallery to the poop deck. It was the highest part of the ship and also where the poultry was carried. There were still hen coops attached to the deck. They would float and might provide a means of reaching the shore. Together Rogers and Bremer seized hold of one and cut it free.

As they were doing so, a very heavy sea broke over the ship and poured into the roundhouse. On the poop deck above, despite the howling wind and crashing waves, Rogers could hear the shrieks of the young ladies. The water had now reached them and the roundhouse was collapsing. Holding tightly onto their hen coop, Rogers and Bremer were swept off the poop deck into the sea. So, too, was Mr Clothier and his bag of valuables. He sank at once.

Near the ship but some yards from the shore was a large flat rock, rising just above the level of the water. Later, this would become known as Halsewell Rock. It was against this rock that the hen coop was thrown by the wave. The force of the impact was violent and Rogers and Bremer were 'miserably bruised and hurt'. Despite their injuries, they managed to clamber onto the rock. They were not alone. Another twenty-seven men were already huddled there, just out of reach of the waves. But it would be only a temporary respite. The tide was coming in and the rock would soon be submerged.

From Halsewell Rock, the cave, which now sheltered Meriton, was clearly visible. That was what they would need to aim for. Perhaps, still holding the remnants of their hen coop, Rogers and Bremer abandoned their rock, and attempted to swim to the cave. So did many of their companions. Swimming in such rough seas was extremely difficult and steering a plank or other flotsam was almost impossible. Of the twenty-seven men that Rogers had counted on Halsewell Rock, only about six succeeded in getting to the cave. He and Bremer were lucky. On reaching the cavern, both men were able to scramble up the rocks to one of the ledges above the waves. There, crammed together like bedraggled and half-plucked seabirds, were dozens of men. Rogers spotted his old shipmate, Meriton, and was able to shout congratulations to him. It was impossible to move closer together as there were at least twenty other men squeezed in between. To move would be to risk falling off the narrow shelf, perhaps pulling others with you. On the ledges, there were seamen, soldiers and petty officers. Some were virtually naked and all were wet and cold. They were not out of range of the spray. Below them were the bodies of men who had drowned, died of exhaustion or fallen, trying to climb the walls of the cave. The groans and cries of badly injured men were audible to all.

Through the mouth of the cave, a section of the *Halsewell* could still be seen. Her stern was partly intact and visible above the waves. It was possible that, even now, the people on board might be alive. From their rocky sanctuary, the men watched with anguish and morbid fascination as wave after wave broke against the remnants of the ship. Then, only minutes after Rogers had reached safety, they heard a dreadful sound. In the words of the publisher who embellished Rogers' and Meriton's account 'a universal shriek, which still vibrates in their ears, and, in which the voice of female distress was lamentably distinguishable, announced the dreadful Catastrophe'. These words would send a shiver throughout the nation and the shriek would reverberate in the imagination to this day. In a few moments, nothing more could be seen of the *Halsewell*. She had gone to the 'remorseless deep' and only the sound of the waves could be heard.

The trembling 'wretches', clinging to the sides of the cave, can have been in no doubt about what had just happened. To a greater or lesser extent, they must have been affected by it. Certainly, the author of the *Circumstantial Narrative* saw the dramatic potential of the moment. In two paragraphs of heightened prose, he laments the tragic loss of the beauty and accomplishments of the young passengers whose precious remains now filled a watery grave. 'Great God, how inscrutable are thy judgements!' He imagines the survivors 'hanging about the sides of the horrid cavern' and weeping for themselves and for 'wives, parents, fathers, brothers, sisters,' and then, as an afterthought, perhaps prompted by Meriton, he added, 'perhaps lovers'.

In the dark of the cave, no-one can have known what time it was when *Halsewell* finally vanished. It was probably between four and five o'clock. Meriton and Rogers estimated that another three hours passed before dawn broke. While they waited for daylight, the men in the cave endured torment. Many had suffered injury when the waves had thrown them against the rocks. Most were badly bruised and some had fractured limbs. They were precariously perched on narrow ledges and were severely weakened by cold. Holding onto the side of the cave was tiring and soon exhaustion and hypothermia began to take its toll. One by one, men began to drop. The lucky ones fell into the sea; others landed on the rocks below. For what seemed like hours, the men above had to listen to 'dying groans and gulping exclamations for pity'. It was truly ghastly.

Somehow, the survivors hung on, waiting for daylight. Eventually dawn arrived but it brought little comfort. The true nature of their predicament now became clear. No-one had come to rescue them. The ship's guns, which they had fired repeatedly, had not been heard over the noise of the storm. The *Halsewell* had vanished and anyone walking the cliff top would only have seen wreckage floating over a large area. It would be impossible to pinpoint where she had gone down. From the top of the cliff, the cave was also out of sight; the overhang was too great. Even if someone had been standing there, they could not have seen the men below. It was obvious to the survivors that no one would come to their rescue unless they raised the alarm. To do that, they would have to climb the cliff.

19
'This Horrible Affair'

Several men volunteered to attempt the perilous climb. But, before they could do so, first they had to reach the mouth of the cave. This involved inching carefully along the cave wall to the entrance. To turn the corner, they had to move along a ledge 'scarcely as broad as a man's hand' and, there, they were faced with an almost perpendicular precipice. Today, for properly equipped climbers, in reasonable weather, this is a moderately difficult climb. For the men of the *Halsewell*, it was an enormous challenge. In the darkness, they had to feel their way up at least one hundred feet of wet, slippery and often loose cliff face. Not surprisingly, it proved too much for some. They had survived a night in the cave but now were to die in the attempt to leave it. Incredibly, two men made it to the top. They were the ship's cook and one of the quartermasters, James Thompson.

Having reached the top of the cliff, the men peered through the gloom. They could just make out the fields, blanketed in snow, but could see no sign of any person or habitation. They had no choice but to head inland. They had trudged almost a mile through snow drifts before they saw a light. It probably came from the window of one of the cottages on the edge of Worth Matravers and it must have given them renewed hope. We can only imagine the reaction of the family who responded to the unexpected banging at their door. They would have been confronted by two men, only partially dressed and in a state of great agitation. For a moment, they must have wondered if they were to be attacked by madmen.

Once James Thompson and his companion had explained what had happened, the occupants hurried to rouse their neighbours. Many were quarrymen and a group of them quickly gathered up ropes and started to make their way to the coast. Later, Thompson was to praise the humane treatment he received in the village so we must assume that these men were motivated by humanitarian instincts. However, given the contemporary reputation of coast dwellers, it would be surprising if these instincts were not tempered by thoughts of salvage and plunder. A wrecked East Indiaman could yield unimaginable bounty.

A mile or so away, just east of Worth Matravers, stands Eastington Farm. In 1786 it was the home of Mr Garland. Early that morning, he had received a visit from the Reverend Morgan Jones.[27] The two men were chatting over breakfast when there was a knock at the door. It was someone sent from the village with urgent news. Mr Garland was the agent to the Purbeck Quarries and it is likely that the quarrymen wanted him to be informed. He could authorise the actions they were about to take.

Mr Garland responded at once. He shared the popular perception that local people might be more inclined to kill and plunder survivors than to rescue them. He and the Reverend Jones mounted their horses and set off to look for the wreck. According to a letter that Jones wrote soon afterwards, it was still blowing a gale and there was violent rain and thick fog. The two men seem to have ridden aimlessly along the coast, through deep snowdrifts, for up to three hours without seeing anything. Frustrated, they returned to Worth where they encountered three men in a very distressed state. They found a house where the men could be given shelter and then, taking a guide this time, they set off again to look for the 'fatal spot'.

There, the Rev. Jones was amazed to see a 'horrid, tremendous scene'. The sea ran 'mountains high' and lashed the rocks. The *Halsewell* had completely disintegrated.

> In one place lay her rigging, etc, wound up like the garbage of an animal and rolling to and fro in sullen submission to the imperious waves. In the different recesses of the rocks, a confused heap of boards, broken masts, chests, trunks, and dead bodies, were huddled together, and the face of the water as far as the eye could extend was disfigured with floating carcases, tables, chairs, casks, and parts of every other article in the vessel. I do not think any two boards remained together.[28]

Before either the villagers or these two gentlemen arrived at the coast, other survivors were attempting to escape from the cave. Among them was Henry Meriton. He was following a soldier up the cliff and had almost reached the top. Momentarily, the soldier stopped to rest on a projecting rock. Meriton was immediately below and gripped the same rock with his hands. At this point, the quarrymen arrived. Seeing the soldier almost within reach, they lowered a rope. He took hold of it quickly but, in doing so, dislodged the stone on which he was standing, the same stone that Henry Meriton was clinging to. In a split second, as he felt himself falling, Meriton grabbed the rope, too. Somehow, he managed to hold on. Yet again his luck had held. He was pulled by the quarrymen to the top of the cliff, and finally, to safety.

Now the rescue attempt began in earnest. More quarrymen arrived and more ropes were lowered. Because of the overhang it was impossible to drop them directly into the cave. The men waiting there would all have to make their way out of the cave entrance and round that perilous corner. For the quarrymen above, it was also dangerous. They had to take care not to be pulled over the edge of the cliff and so a safety mechanism was devised. Three pairs of iron bars were hammered into the ground. Two ropes were attached to them and the other ends tied around the waists of two quarrymen. This enabled them to stand safely at the very edge of the cliff. Another rope was passed between them to hold onto. Once they felt secure, the men began to lower a longer rope, with a noose, down to the entrance of the cave. The wind was still blowing hard off the sea and sometimes it blew the dangling rope into the cave itself.

By mid-morning, Mr Garland and Mr Jones had taken over supervision of the rescue operation and, one by one, men were hauled up the cliff. Not all attempts ended in success. James Bremer, who had shared the hen-coop with John Rogers in their escape from the *Halsewell*, was an early victim. Either through exhaustion or confusion, he failed to tie the rope securely. When he was just short of the cliff top, the rope came undone. Before the horrified gaze of the rescuers, he dropped straight downwards and was killed instantly on the rocks below.

He was not the only one to die like this. Other men, through cold, weakness or 'perturbation of mind', failed to make the ascent.

Cliffs at Winspit
© *Philip Browne*

Like Bremer, they were either dashed on the rocks or plunged into the waves and drowned. One case was particularly harrowing. A young drummer boy with the recruits fell as he was being rescued. He landed in the sea and was quickly carried out by the backwash from the waves. Although he was a strong swimmer, the current took him further from the shore. For a long time, the men watched him struggling bravely, until at last, worn out, the young man sank beneath the waves.

Worse was to follow. Not all the men had tried to climb the cliff. A group of approximately thirty waited on a large rock near the bottom. Perhaps they were injured or too frightened to attempt the ascent. While they waited anxiously for their turn on the rope, the tide had turned too. It was now coming in again. To his horror, Rev. Jones saw a large wave break over the rock, sweeping the men effortlessly into the sea.

Throughout the day, the rescue efforts continued. For the quarrymen, it was hard graft, hauling so many people up the cliff. They quickly became cold and tired and the work seemed never-ending. Someone arrived with two casks of spirits. This was much more appealing and there was a real possibility that the quarrymen would abandon their labour and drink the lot. Only the intervention of Mr Garland and the clergyman prevented disaster. The liquor was rationed and work resumed.

There were still at least twenty men in the cave. By continuing to dangle the rope in front of the opening, a further eighteen men were brought up. Most were unconscious by the time they reached the top. Three were found to be dead but the rest were revived with judicious doses of cherry brandy and gingerbread. The survivors were then helped across the fields to Eastington House. For two of them, this last effort was too much. At a stile, half way to Worth Matravers, a lascar died of his wounds. Thereafter, it was known as Black Man's Stile.[29]

Once they were all mustered, a head count was carried out. There were found to be seventy-four survivors. This was less than one third of those who had embarked on the *Halsewell* in the Thames. Miraculously, one more survivor was to be added to the list. William Trenton, a soldier, remained in the cave for a second night and was finally rescued on the morning of Saturday 7 of January. As a feat of endurance, it was remarkable.

Although the rescue operation was now ended, the trauma for rescuers and rescued would continue. In his letter, written shortly afterwards, Rev Morgan Jones admitted, 'I have not yet recovered from the shock I felt at this horrible affair.'[30]

With no more people to rescue, attention now focused on the saved. The unexpected arrival of more than seventy people placed an

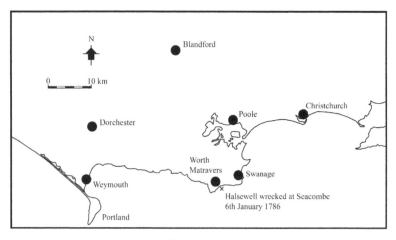

Fig 4. The Coast of Purbeck.

enormous burden on the resources of a small village. Most of these men needed clothing and all needed food. By now, the Rector of Wareham, Rev. George Ryves Hawker, was helping to co-ordinate local support but, at best, this could only provide temporary relief. The ultimate source of assistance for most survivors would have to be their employer, the East India Company. It was essential, therefore, to inform East India House of the disaster as soon as possible.

As the senior surviving officers, it was the duty of Henry Meriton and John Rogers to deliver the news to the Company directors in London. With financial help from Mr Garland and on horses that were provided for them, the officers set off on Saturday morning. At first they rode north towards Blandford Forum. Apart from Christchurch, Blandford was the nearest town of any size. It also lay astride the main route between London and Exeter. The Royal Mail coach passed along it regularly and the road ought be clear. After all the recent snow, there was no telling what state other roads would be in.

Meriton and Rogers had another reason for travelling via towns and larger settlements. They wanted to alert the inhabitants to what was coming. The other survivors would be following behind, but more slowly and on foot. The arrival of a large group of ragged and impoverished men in a town or village would prompt fear and suspicion. They might even be met with hostility. By warning people on the route about the disaster, they would have time to prepare for the arrival of the other survivors. It was a wise precaution.

On Sunday morning, the main body of survivors began the twenty-mile walk to Blandford. Thanks to Meriton and Rogers, they were greeted with great kindness. The landlord of the Crown Inn provided a meal for the men and then presented each of them with half-a-crown. Given the numbers of men, this was an exceptionally generous act. It did not go unrecognised. Rogers and Meriton referred to it in their 'Circumstantial Narrative'[31] but, before this was published, a newspaper had also learned of the story. On Thursday 26 January, the General Evening Post reported that the landlord of the White Hart Inn

> invited them all into his house, lighted fires in the Assembly-room for them, being the largest in the house, provided them hot provisions, put them all to bed, and in the morning, after having provided to each such raiment as could be obtained, he gave them a good breakfast, a slice of meat and bread and a dram a-piece, put half a crown into the hand of each of them and sent them forward for London.[32]

The only doubt about this is the identity of the inn. Both establishments existed but to which the credit is due is unclear. Perhaps, the landlords acted together.

Fortified by their stay at Blandford, the men now split into parties of five or six. By travelling like this, in smaller groups, they were more likely to be offered shelter and food during the hundred miles that lay ahead to London. Meanwhile, Meriton and Rogers had completed their journey in just over twenty-four hours. Just before noon on 8 January they arrived at India House. It was a Sunday and the directors were probably at home. Perhaps, they were sent for. Meanwhile, the second and third officers spoke to whoever was on duty, giving their account of the events of the previous week, in as much detail as they could.

Having done so, Henry Meriton made his way to the Jerusalem Coffee House nearby. There, he knew he was likely to encounter captains and officers from the Service and that he could expect an attentive audience and sympathetic response to his predicament.

Like Captain Peirce, Henry Meriton had probably invested heavily in private trade. This was now at the bottom of the sea, his investment was lost and he must still have had outstanding debts to settle. A disaster of this magnitude would touch the feelings of his colleagues and they might be moved to offer financial help.

It was a shrewd step. By 17 January, the *Morning Chronicle and London Advertiser* was carrying a notice inviting donations 'for the benefit of Mr Henry Meriton, Second Officer'.[33] By then, over £130 had already been collected; some, like EIC director Mr Cuming and Captain Huddart, had donated £20 each. Additional donations could be handed in at the Jerusalem Coffee House or at a bank in Lombard Street.

Later on Sunday evening, both Henry Meriton and John Rogers went to speak to newspaper reporters. They seem to have done so separately. Unlike that new daily paper, *The Times*, many London papers were published every three days or so. The earliest that the disaster could be reported would be Tuesday 10th January. Even *The Times* chose to wait until then, probably because it was too late on Sunday evening to make the next day's edition. From variations in the accounts, it seems that Henry Meriton spoke to the *Morning Post and Daily Advertiser*.[34] These reports make no mention of John Rogers. The third mate, however, must have spoken to a reporter from the *Whitehall Evening Post*.[35] Its coverage included the fact that Rogers had escaped by clinging to the hen coop.

On Monday morning, after India House had opened its doors for business as usual, news of the disaster passed quickly throughout the building. Although shipwrecks were an occupational hazard, the circumstances of this one were especially shocking. Captain Peirce was a respected and experienced commander and his death, together with the drowning of so many young ladies, moved even the most hard-bitten of Company employees. The papers reported that 'not a dry eye could be found yesterday at India House'.[36]

News of the fate of the *Halsewell* also spread rapidly through the streets of London. It would only be a matter of hours before it would reach Kingston-upon-Thames. It was important that someone broke the news to Mrs Peirce before rumours reached her ears or, worse, she read about it in the papers. The ship's husband, Peter Esdaile, also had to be informed and a message was sent to his bank in Lombard Street. There, the Esdailes and Benjamin Hammet listened, stunned, to the news that their investment was lost. For Hammet, the loss was also personal. His friend, Richard, was dead and, now he felt obliged to carry the news to the bereaved family.[37] A frequent visitor, Benjamin Hammet was already a familiar face at Walnut Tree House. It would be better if he, rather than Peter Esdaile, carried out this painful duty, As soon as he had established the facts of the disaster, Benjamin Hammet set off, with a heavy heart, for Kingston.

PART FOUR

'OF WIDOW'D CONSORT
AND OF ORPHAN'D CHILD'

1786–1791

20
Ruin & Remorse

At Walnut Tree House in Kingston-upon-Thames, Mrs Mary Peirce was becoming accustomed, once more, to the absence of her husband. It had characterised most of their married life. Much more difficult to come to terms with had been the departure of her two eldest daughters. They had been gone for more than a week but still dominated her thoughts. She had even dreamed about them; dreadful nightmares in which the *Halsewell* had been lost.[1]

It was a surprise when a servant informed her that Sir Benjamin Hammet had come to call. He was an old friend of Richard's and she knew they shared business interests. His colleague, Peter Esdaile, had succeeded Mary's own father as managing owner of the *Halsewell*. Surely, Sir Benjamin must have known that Richard had sailed at the New Year? Why had he come to call now?

Mary Peirce was sitting with young Sophia on her knee, when Hammet was shown in. Immediately, Mary sensed something was wrong. As gently as he could, Sir Benjamin broke the news. It was devastating. Mary had lost her two eldest daughters, her husband and her fortune. Almost dropping the infant Sophia, Mary Peirce fainted. She was helped to bed and there, for several days, she would remain.[2]

Having carried out his painful duty, Sir Benjamin Hammet returned to town. The loss of the *Halsewell* affected him, too. The finances of his bank were tied up in a ship that was lying at the bottom of the sea. The body of his good friend, the captain, was missing and, now, he would need to take care of the widowed Mary. Overwhelmed by the enormity of it all, Sir Benjamin Hammet followed Mary's example and retreated to his own bed.[3]

At India House, the Court of Directors met in full session on Wednesday 11 January 1786. By then, they had received a letter from the Custom House in Poole, corroborating Meriton's news. Referring to this letter, the Chairman informed the Court of the total loss of the *Halsewell* and that 'one hundred and twenty-six persons have lost their lives, amongst whom are the captain, his two daughters and ten other female passengers'.[4] It was agreed that an investigation was required and a motion was passed instructing the Committee of Shipping to enquire into the causes of the disaster. Plans were also laid for the recovery of *Halsewell's* cargo. The Company's investment on the outward voyage was relatively small – *The Times* estimated it at no more than £6,000 – but it was worth salvaging nonetheless.[5] The ship was carrying silver coin. There were also valuable metals, including cannons and anchors, that might be recovered. One of the Company's pilot yachts was instructed to sail to Dorset, carrying equipment for diving on the wreck, provided it could be found.[6]

The East India Company had a long-standing reputation for generosity towards those who came to its aid. This was widely understood and perhaps explains why the Rev. George Ryves Hawker, Rector of Wareham, wrote to the Company so promptly. On the 9th, he petitioned them to 'recompense' the local people who had helped to rescue and shelter the survivors. He informed India House that 'The Crew have just left this town, where all their present wants have been supplied by the inhabitants with a liberality that does them honour'. He went on to single out the quarriers whose 'intrepidity and humanity' deserved the 'highest commendation and ample reward'. Then, in case his own contribution was overlooked, the Rev. Hawker added 'Mr Jones and myself promised them every exertion in our power to procure them the latter; had we not been there to have encouraged and directed them, many more had perished'.[7]

The Directors were not slow in showing their appreciation. On the 13th they wrote to Mr Garland, enclosing 100 guineas to be distributed to the quarrymen and, for himself, a china tea service bearing the East India Company's crest. On 20 January, the Rev. Hawker replied to India House, acknowledging receipt of the money.[8] He promised that it would be distributed in full, despite the fact that other expenses had been incurred in treating the injured and clothing the survivors. Still keen to remind the Directors of his own role in the affair, Rev. Hawker explained that, 'in consequence of an application I made to them', the local gentry had made generous donations which would cover these additional costs. He ended with a suggestion of his own. 'I have had it in contemplation to erect a small monument in the spot where the disaster happened.' It would remind people of the 'bounty of the India Company' and encourage 'the future protection of any unfortunate seamen who may experience the like calamity on this coast'. Given how the survivors of other wrecks were often treated, Rev Hawker may have had a point. He asked the Company to donate £20 towards this project. However, the Directors clearly felt they had done enough already and declined to respond. No such monument has ever been erected near Winspit.

On 21 of January, *The Times* reported that the quarrymen who had assisted the rescue were to be rewarded with two guineas each, while the generous landlords of Blandford would also receive appropriate gratuities.[9] Meanwhile, as they trudged towards London, the surviving seamen were offered assistance from people along the way. In Winchester, for example, transport and subsistence were provided by local officials.[10] No doubt, many other acts of charity went unrecorded.

In the week following the wreck, bedraggled crewmen from the *Halsewell* began to arrive in Leadenhall Street. Although the Company was under no obligation to offer them any support, these men, too, were paid a small sum, to tide them over while they recovered. As for Henry Meriton, he hoped that a position would soon be offered to him on another of the Company's ships. In the meantime, he needed to restore his financial affairs. The donations of well-wishers would help greatly but he knew that he also had a story to sell, one that people were curious to hear.

The wreck of the *Halsewell* became public knowledge on Tuesday 10 January. *The Times*, and at least four other London newspapers, reported versions of the event. It caused an immediate sensation and, within days, the news was spreading further afield through regional newspapers.[11] Across the nation, everybody, including members of the Royal Family, was

Mr Garland's tea set.
Langton Matravers
Museum.
© E. Cumming

gripped by the story. The death of so many beautiful young ladies, the self-sacrifice of Captain Peirce, the gruesome details of the rescue, all struck a chord with even the most impervious readers. The disaster, it seemed to many, had the hallmarks of a tragedy. No wonder people were fascinated.

In Leadenhall Street, close to India House, William Lane ran his publishing business. Lane had a nose for a bestseller. Within days, he had reached a deal with Henry Meriton and James Thompson to publish their story in what would be called *A Circumstantial Narrative of the Loss of the Halsewell*. Then, as more survivors began to congregate in London, Lane seized the opportunity to embellish Meriton's account with further sensational detail. On 14 January, he placed an advertisement in several papers inviting survivors to tell him their stories.[12] Further advertisements followed and, John Rogers must have seen them. He wanted his share of the limelight and any financial benefits that might accrue, so he, too, called on William Lane. Thereafter, John Rogers was to get equal billing with Henry Meriton. Both their names were on the title page when the *Circumstantial Narrative* went on sale on 25 January. William Lane's instincts had been sound; the publication was an instant bestseller. By the end of January it had gone through six editions, with many more to follow.[13]

Until the publication of the *Circumstantial Narrative* provided the definitive account, the public relied on newspapers for their information about the wreck. Each day, new snippets emerged but not all were accurate. At first it was reported that two Miss Templers had been on board.[14] Their address was given as Bedford Square, London, and it is likely that they were sisters of Charles Templer. In fact, they had not sailed with the *Halsewell*, though Meriton seems to have thought they had. It was a day or two before this mistake was corrected.

More facts were added. The *Halsewell* was of 758 tons burthen. She was carrying 70 lascars. The Company's loss was not £6,000 but £160,000.[15] In turn, this figure was disputed. Scattered among these dry statistics were more sensational details. Mrs Peirce had been in the act of suckling her youngest child when Hammet had imparted the 'shocking intelligence'. She had only just time to give the infant to an attendant before she 'sank lifeless to the floor'.[16]

The manner of death was also given full treatment. George Wilson, the Ship's Steward, was said to have had valuables with him worth £2,000. In the act of being rescued, half way up the cliff, he had let go of the rope and had fallen to the bottom where he had been 'dashed to pieces'.[17] A grim tally of corpses was begun. It was reported that George Schultz's body had been found, washed up near Christchurch, twenty miles to the east, carried there by currents and tides.[18] Each day, the public scanned their newspapers for the latest revelations.

The authorities at Christchurch Priory had also begun to keep a record. The Christchurch Burial Register shows that on 12 January, five bodies had been recovered from the shore near West Cliff. The names of three of them were unknown but the bodies of George Schultz and Charles Webber had been positively identified.[19] Over the following days more burials were recorded but few could be given names. On 16 January, *The Times* quoted from a letter sent from Christchurch and dated Thursday the 12th. It described the whole shore from Christchurch to Poole 'strewed with wreck'. Every day brings 'fresh intelligence of dead bodies being cast on shore'. The correspondent went on to condemn the behaviour of the local people, 'savage shore walkers' who stripped the dead bodies naked, leaving them 'without any discriminating mark, except of sex only'. Local gentlemen had tried to protect the bodies from the 'rapacity of these wretches' but with limited success.[20] It seemed that the Rev. Hawker's fears for the survivors may not have been idle fancy after all.

On 16 January, one newspaper reported that Captain Peirce's remains had been found.[21] Later, this turned out to be untrue. Then on Wednesday 18 January the body of Elizabeth Blackburn was discovered near West Cliff. Three days later, Mary Ann Peirce was found nearby. They were buried on the same day in the graveyard of the Priory.[22] Two local gentlemen, Mr Charles Bill of Wick and Mr Hooper of Longham were active in organising it and possibly paying their funeral expenses. In Purbeck, on the cliffs near the wreck, a mass grave was dug for the dozens of corpses that had been cast onto the rocks. No headstones would be raised for them. And there was still no sign of Captain Peirce's body.

While he continued to be missing, Mary Peirce remained confined to her bed. Her anguish manifested itself in 'frantic fits' and she 'declared her distraction would not abate till the body of her husband was found'.[23] Either to comfort her or because they believed it was true, somebody eventually told her that Richard Peirce had been recovered. This must have provided some sort of resolution for Mary; she could begin the grieving process at last.

Families were in mourning in other parts of the country, too. Word had reached West Monkton in Somerset and now Henry and Anne Paul knew that their two daughters were drowned. In the same village, the Jeane family received bad news. The death of Thomas Jeane, the promising young midshipman, was particularly unfortunate. He had escaped the sinking ship and had swum strongly to a rock. Although a wave had quickly washed him off, he had managed to regain it. There he held on against 'the assaults of the tempest' for seven hours, until finally, his strength giving out, he had slipped back into the sea.[24]

In Devon, James Templer learned that his youngest son, Charles Beckford Templer, had died.[25] Elsewhere, the Larkins, the Rayners, the Millers, the Cowleys and the Falconers were all mourning the loss of sons. Altogether, maybe one hundred and thirty families were affected. In one instance, there was, at least, a small consolation. Just before the ship went down, one of the officers gave a box of diamond rings to a seaman called George Woodgate. The officer was clearly intending to stay with the ship and wanted some of his personal valuables or private trade to be saved. The identity of this officer was not revealed but it may have been Thomas Burston. He had made clear his intention to stay with his relatives to the end. George Woodgate, however, had been rescued. Remarkably, he handed over the box of rings to Henry Meriton and, on 19 January, the *Morning Chronicle* reported that the rings had been returned to the owner's family.[26]

Throughout January and into February, as the press in London continued to report the *Halsewell* story, a number of issues began to emerge. There was the question of the behaviour of the crew, the

Gravestone of Elizabeth Blackburn.
© E. Cumming & Brian Sutton

seaworthiness of the ship and the leadership of its captain. Questioned, also, was the morality of sending young ladies overseas in search of husbands. All of these issues divided public opinion. Strong letters were sent to newspapers.

A number of correspondents speculated about the ship. Why had *Halsewell* leaked so badly and broken up so quickly? Was her design faulty? One reader suggested her ribs were to blame. Another that it was due to the 'badness of her bolts' which had allowed some of her planking to come loose.[27] Others thought that ship had 'bulged' because she was overladen. Excessive greed must have prompted Peirce and his officers to carry too much cargo in private trade. These criticisms were soon refuted by other readers. The *Halsewell*, they argued, was a fine ship and in good condition.

It was obvious to most people that responsibility for the disaster did not lie solely with the ship. It followed, therefore, that the performance of the captain and the conduct of the crew must have played a part. Why did it take so long to discover the water in the hold? On men-of-war, the carpenter's mate checked the hold for leaks every half hour. The fact that, on the *Halsewell*, this had not been done was evidence of neglect and bad seamanship. Or so it was argued in the *Public Advertiser*.[28]

Everyone recognised that Captain Peirce was one of the longest-serving commanders of the East India Company. Any mistakes he might have made could hardly be due to lack of experience. If blame was to be apportioned, perhaps it should lie with members of the crew. Right from the start, the newspapers had referred to 'a want of subordination' among some seamen. They can only have obtained this information from Henry Meriton and, perhaps, from John Rogers.

On 15 January, the *London Recorder* reported that the seamen 'absolutely refused to obey their officers'. When Thomas Burston and other officers threatened them with punishment, they were defiant and insolent. 'You be d-n'd. If you dare, d-n my eyes but I'll Loughborough you'.[29] They were referring, of course, to the Court of Common Pleas and the recent judgements by Lord Loughborough. Even though William Douglas had failed to gain redress, others had succeeded. If an officer tried to flog a seaman or put him in irons, he could find himself charged with assault. This is what the men on *Halsewell* were threatening and it must have made Thomas Burston hesitate.

In the face of such defiant behaviour, the authority of the officers were undermined. Yet the urgency of the situation required men to work the pumps and to go aloft. According to the same newspaper, Peirce had turned to an alternative source of manpower, the Company's recruits. There were almost a hundred of them and they were more amenable. It was reported that, ' *The soldiers assisted every way in their power, and actually mounted aloft, but were not sufficiently expert in the necessary business*'. This is hardly a surprise. It required more than just physical strength to manhandle and deploy the sails on an East Indiaman. High above the deck, in rough seas and freezing temperatures, the soldiers would have been of little use.

The news that some sailors had refused to obey orders outraged many commentators. It was intolerable that a few recalcitrant sailors could jeopardise the safety of the entire ship. Why were officers left without power to enforce their commands? A letter to the *Public Advertiser* expressed this concern in a colourful way: 'If I am attacked by a mad dog, who seizes the muzzle of a loaded gun which I have in my hand, the necessity of the case will justify me if I fire down his throat?' There were calls for the legal powers of officers to be increased: 'If there is no law in being to enable us to use the means of self-preservation which we have in our hands, I hope the wisdom of the Legislature will speedily provide one, for mutiny and mad dogs are dreadful things'.[30]

But not everyone shared this point of view. The *St James Chronicle* pointed out that the 'grievous sore' of indiscipline was a recent phenomenon. It was caused by 'the late misunderstandings between them [the seamen] and the Sea Officers.' This had shown that there is 'as much littleness among men in laced coats as among tarred jackets'.[31] It is not clear what the commentator is referring to here. Does it imply that some officers had behaved dishonourably recently? Did the writer have the William Douglas case in mind? We cannot say but it does hint at an underlying sense of injustice that may have provoked the crisis on the *Halsewell*. The writer concludes 'The truth is Jack Tars are not well treated and yet in their own line they are really very honest fellows'.

Although Meriton and Rogers were the source of the story about ill-discipline on *Halsewell*, they must have felt uneasy at the way it was now being reported. Perhaps, they feared it reflected badly on them and could jeopardise future promotion. Maybe, they thought it attributed too much blame to the crew as a whole. In any case, they tried to put the record straight. On 15 January both men wrote a letter to the *Public Advertiser*. It was published two days later. In the letter, they stated that 'not the least abusive language was made use of to any officer' nor was the 'invidious threat' made to 'Loughborough' anybody in authority.[32]

Meriton and Rogers were prepared to counter the more extreme versions of events but they did not refute them altogether. When the *Circumstantial Narrative* was published ten days later, it still accused many of the seamen of being 'remarkably inattentive and remiss in their duty'. Some had actually 'skulked in their hammocks' instead of helping to work the pumps. It seemed that the insubordination of some crew members remained a contributory factor to the disaster.

For the East India Company, discipline on their ships was a matter of great importance. No doubt, it featured in the Shipping Committee's reports into the causes of the disaster. Unfortunately, these reports have not survived. However, they must have exonerated Meriton and Rogers as the Court Minutes for Wednesday 1 February record that 'it does not appear to this Court that the ship Halsewell was lost through any neglect in Mr Henry Meriton second mate and Mr John Rogers third mate of that ship'.[33]

This did not satisfy everybody. One of the victims of the shipwreck had been William Rayner, the Purser's Assistant. His father, a legal practitioner at the Inner Temple, was an authority on Stamp Duty legislation. John Rayner was angry at the death of his son and felt the real causes of the disaster were in danger of being ignored. It was not good enough simply to blame the weather. There had been human failures as well. He made his views known in the preamble to the publication of his *Observations on the Statutes Relating to the Stamp Duties*. They were quickly picked up and reported in *The Times*.[34]

Mr Rayner repeated the charge of mutiny by the crew, quoting the evidence from *Circumstantial Narrative*. To this, he added the fact of the undiscovered leak; the fact that the ship was overladen and that she set sail in a storm. If all these factors were true, he argued, the finger of blame must be pointed at *Halsewell's* commander and his senior officers. It was their 'remissness, indiscretion and breach of duty' that had led to the disaster. Protesting that it was not his intention to 'calumnate the dead', he nonetheless concluded: 'We can no longer admire the heroism of the Captain in preferring instant death with his children' rather than a life of lingering misery and regret that he had not been 'more circumspect and less venturesome'. It was a telling criticism. The wreck was not 'solely due to stress of weather'; hubris had played its part.

John Rayner may have seen flaws in the character of Captain Peirce but this view was not universally shared. The East India Company's Committee of Shipping produced a further seven reports during February. On 21 February, the Court of Directors concluded that 'the loss of Halsewell does not appear to be imputable to any conduct in Captain Pierce (*sic*) or his sworn officers'.[35]

Such was the view of the Company but what is to be the verdict of history on Captain Peirce? There is no doubt that the weather conditions he faced were exceptionally challenging and beyond his control. But they were the same conditions that the *Ganges* and *Manship* managed to overcome. What complicated matters for *Halsewell* was the leak. During a storm, it is extraordinary that five feet of water could collect in the hold before anybody noticed. Why were regular checks not made, and why did Peirce not enquire? Ultimately, responsibility for this oversight must rest with him.

Having discovered the leak, it should still have been possible to deal with it, provided the ship had altered course and speed appropriately. That it could not do so, suggests a lack of manpower. When *Halsewell* left the Thames, she carried a full crew, sufficient to work the ship in almost any conditions. It follows, therefore, that a considerable number of seamen must have withheld their labour. If it is true that Peirce had to look to the military recruits for help, he must have been very short of manpower. Only this can explain why he also directed his officers to help work the pumps.

We will probably never know why some sailors were so uncooperative but the disaffection must have been too widespread for Captain Peirce to deal with during the crisis. One or two 'bad apples' could have been punished but asserting his authority in the face of general insubordination would take time. Time was a luxury he did not have. The ship was in danger and Peirce's priority had to be its survival. In the circumstances, his decision to cut down two masts and to turn back towards Portsmouth was a sensible one. His misfortune was that he could not find shelter. If *Halsewell* had not been so crippled, she might have tacked back to Weymouth Bay or been able to round Peveril Point. That she ended up on rocks, faced by cliffs, was a cruel act of the gods.

Despite the location, not everyone on *Halsewell* would die. Almost a third would be rescued. Many of those who drowned were trying to escape but Captain Peirce was not among them. He had chosen to stay in the roundhouse with his daughters. This behaviour is interesting. From the moment it became inevitable that *Halsewell* would hit the rocks, Captain Peirce seems to have become almost passive. By now, he had endured five days of extreme physical and mental stress; he was cold, he had had little sleep and it must have seemed that everything was against him. He felt responsible for the safety of his sister's children and his own, his financial investment was in jeopardy and his future was in ruins. Under this pressure, Richard Peirce seems to have entered a state of fatalistic paralysis. All he could do was to sit with his daughters and comfort them.

If, like Meriton, Captain Peirce had gone forward to investigate the situation, he might have seen the cave. Perhaps, this would have given him hope that his daughters could be saved. Instead of passively waiting for the end, he might have reassumed leadership and galvanised those in the roundhouse. Instead, he sat motionless, holding his daughters, while his despair infected those around him with fatal consequences. Yet, even at the end, there is a nobility about Richard Peirce. In deciding to stay with his daughters, he was consciously choosing to die with them.

It was this pathetic scenario, at the stern of the *Halsewell*, that captured the imagination of the general public. To them, questions of seaworthiness and maritime competence were of only limited interest. It was the anguish of the doomed passengers, the despair of the young ladies and the resignation and fortitude of the commander that people were moved by. The newspapers played on this with some relish. They stressed the accomplishments and the promise of the young lives so cruelly cut short. Captain Peirce's younger daughter, 'Miss Marianne' was 'very beautiful'. Her older sister had a 'great share of elegant attainment' and 'an astonishing skill in music; she could play any piece at sight'.[36] This love of the 'polite arts' was even extended to Captain Peirce himself. The *Morning Herald* reported that he had introduced the great portrait painter, Zoffany, to India.[37] We know that this was not actually true but it reinforced an impression of refinement and culture, over the vulgar imperative of commerce.

However, one awkward question remained. Why were so many young ladies on the ship? Were they really sailing to India to search for husbands? If so, their motivation can only have been mercenary. Only the prospect of great wealth could outweigh the risks of such a hazardous course of action. There was something very distasteful about such calculating behaviour. Some papers were quick to criticise. A mere ten days after the shipwreck, the *Hampshire Chronicle* carried the following comment:

> It is a dreadful thing to hear of seven young ladies being drowned – nor is it much less lamentable to think that beautiful women are now reckoned among the articles of our export trade to India, not one ship sailing now without a cargo on board; and they are literally going to market. On their arrival they are shewn as we shew a horse, and are

disposed of to the best bidder. This is a coarse description, but does not such an indelicate traffic deserve rebuke?

The correspondent continued by pointing out the risks inherent in this human export trade. A faultline of distrust would run through marriages arising from this indelicate traffic. The husbands would always suspect such wives of being little better than gold-diggers:

> When a lady carries her beauty, youth and accomplishments to a foreign market, when she decks herself out to attract the Nabobs and makes a venture of her own person among people that she never saw, exposing herself to the scrutiny of suspicious wealth and age (for wealth and age are always suspicious) she lowers herself from the rank which she can only preserve by delicacy.

Marriages based on such cynical foundations were doomed to end in regret. The writer concluded 'If she accomplishes her purpose in marrying a man of fortune, she finds him an imperious Lord, or a jealous dotard'.[38]

These were harsh words but, no doubt, they reflected widely held views. The number of unmarried women sailing to India had increased and there was little doubt that many hoped to return as wives. But not all. Miss Mansell, for example, had completed her education in England and was simply going back to her family in Madras. This was common practice. Even the mixed race or 'natural' sons and daughters of Company Servants were often sent to England to be educated. It was only to be expected that many would want to rejoin their families in India, at some point.

And what of the daughters of Richard Peirce and Ann Paul? Were they part of this indelicate trade? We know Eliza and Mary Ann Peirce were intending to stay with relatives and would join a social circle that was familiar to their father. It is likely that he had already identified certain suitable young men and there may have been some prior understanding that related to Eliza, at least. But there was nothing improper about this. The girls would continue to move in polite society, subject to all the usual rules and constraints. In the light of general criticism, perhaps Benjamin Hammet or even Mrs Peirce herself decided to put the record straight. On 1 February, the *Morning Chronicle and Daily Advertiser* carried the following paragraph:

> If the intended voyage of Captain Pierce and his daughters had been in the usual way of our young women, shipped off to India to a casual market for mercenary beauty, it would, in a family so wealthy as that of Captain Pierce, have been a transaction as blameable in its motive, as pitiable in its event. But this was not the fact, the young ladies were embarking for India, under specifick engagements that had existed for some time.[39]

The daughters of Captain Peirce may have been beautiful but they were not going to a 'casual market'. Whatever the behaviour of others, the Peirces were above such things, both morally and financially. They would not be marrying in haste. However, in hindsight, Mary Peirce's attempt to distance her family from the vulgar behaviour of others is not entirely convincing. In the years that followed, the younger daughters in both the Paul and Peirce families would, indeed, find, in India, young men with wealth and position. Evidently, despite the haughty denial, the temptation to secure a nabob for a husband remained difficult to resist.

All this discussion may have prompted some tut-tutting in fashionable drawing rooms but there was no mistaking the public's reaction to the final moments of the *Halsewell*. Captain Peirce began to assume a tragic stature. At the pinnacle of his career, he had chosen to die rather than abandon his daughters and the other young ladies in his care. Almost from the outset he was referred to as the 'unfortunate Captain Peirce'. Whether his misfortune was of his own making or was an act of God was open to debate but no-one could deny the scale of that misfortune. It prompted a creative response that was to be expressed in a variety of artistic forms.

21

'Every memorial of human sorrow' – the Arts

Poetry

An artistic response to the disaster was called for by the *Morning Herald*. On Friday 13 January 1786, it argued that 'Such a pathetic tale deserves every memorial of human sorrow'.[1] To illustrate this, the newspaper supplemented its coverage of the *Halsewell* story with an extract from a poem. The poem in question was *The Shipwreck* by the Scottish poet, William Falconer. It had first been published in 1762 and was hugely popular.[2] William Falconer had himself been shipwrecked twice so he had drawn on direct experience when composing the verses.

The circumstances of the *Halsewell's* fate and those of the ship in Falconer's poem had many similarities. The newspaper clearly thought Falconer had captured the drama of the final scenes: 'Mr Falconer, the author of the SHIPWRECK, has pictured the dissolution of the vessel with such accuracy, that we cannot forbear giving an extract on the subject'. The extract includes the moment when the ship hit a rock which:

> With deep convulsion, rends the solid oak.
> At length asunder torn, her frame divides,
> And crashing spreads in ruin o'er the tides.

The selection from Falconer's poem inspired others to emulate him. Four days later, the *Public Advertiser* printed a poem by a Mr Birch.[3] It, too, was entitled 'The Shipwreck' but with the subheading 'occasioned by the loss of the Halsewell, Indiaman'. Mr Birch's poetic

endeavours do not match those of William Falconer either in length
or quality but they are interesting for another reason. Written so
soon after the event, Birch's poem captures the immediate emotional
response to the news of the wreck. He starts with a quotation from
Virgil which roughly translates as 'Who could speak of such things
without weeping?' He then goes on to contrast the official, formulaic
grief shown on the death of a monarch with the spontaneous, heartfelt
and sincere emotion that has been prompted by the drowning of
'gallant Peirce' and his daughters

> With sighs the desolating tale we hear,
> And ev'ry cheek is moisten'd with a tear.

He stresses the scale of the disaster in rather pedestrian
hyperbole:

> An equal fate, not time itself can shew
> Of mighty ruin and extended woe!

For Mr Birch, responsibility for the disaster lies exclusively
with Fate. He blames the 'destructive deep' and the 'deceitful gale'.
But, in the face of such overwhelming forces, Captain Peirce remains
stoical,

> The hardy veteran to his fate resign'd

though his composure is threatened by the anguish of the young ladies.

> The fruitless cries of beauty in despair:
> Doomed in the keenest anguish to expire,
> The daughters helpless grasp their helpless Sire!

Birch ends by reminding the reader that, despite our 'mental
pain', we should know that the disaster is part of the divine plan. He
calls on Providence who 'directs the storm' to

Soothe the wild workings of affliction's breast
And teach our wishes that thy will is best.

It would be interesting to know if Mary Peirce saw this poem
or derived any comfort from it. She was still in the early stages of grief
and acceptance of her loss was yet to come.
Two weeks after it had printed Mr Birch's poem, the *Public
Advertiser* published another. This time, the author was anonymous
and female. *On the Late unfortunate SHIPWRECK by a Lady* appeared
on Saturday 28 January 1786.[4] By now, more information about the
shipwreck had emerged and was reflected in the content of this later
work.

Captain Peirce is introduced, sailing for 'India's coast' with his
'chosen band of kindred dear'. The intentions of the young ladies are
made explicit from the start. They are 'resolv'd for wedlock on that
distant shore'. However, unlike some in society, this poet does not
condemn them. She accepts it as a well-established practice.

Seven charming virgins follow custom's lore

The poet has learned that the ship was also carrying seventy
Lascars. This she attributes to Peirce's 'kindness' in helping them 'gain
their native home'. It is, of course, a poetic device. There was nothing
charitable about their presence on the *Halsewell*. Even if Peirce felt well
disposed towards this human cargo, he will have been adequately paid
for their passage.

Like Mr Birch, the 'Lady' employs classical allusions to explain
the causes of the disaster. The 'treach'rous gale' is the fault of those
'adverse gods', fierce Aeolus and roaring Neptune. But she also holds
the sailors accountable too. Sea monsters have whispered sedition in
their ears and they have become 'unruly Tars'.

They swear, they threat again, they won't obey

Faced with the intransigence of his crew, Captain Peirce is
forced to turn to the soldiers for help:

Ready they climb aloft, but skilless there,
They alter this for that, or wrongly veer.

Soon the inevitable happens, the ship approaches the rocks, and the poet turns her attention to the scene which her impatient readers eagerly await:

The hapless females round the Captain clung
While bellowing seas advance and billows flung

At this moment of high drama, Peirce is portrayed as 'distress'd yet firm'. He clasps his daughters 'fondly to his manly chest'.

For them, he life despis'd, resolv'd to go
With his dear daughters to the shades below.

The first mate decides to join the 'afflicted father' in self-sacrifice. 'Gallant Barston' (*sic*) declares:

With such a brother and such cousins dear
I die resolv'd.

To our twenty-first century ear, all this talk of 'manly chests' and embracing death verges on melodrama but it was not so for readers in 1786. What seems overly sentimental to our modern ear, spoke to the sensibilities of that age. Readers were genuinely moved and their emotions were to be tested further as 'The Lady' described the rescue attempts of the quarrymen:

Some draw up safe, some lose their hold again,
And dash'd to pieces, tumble in the main

For the onlookers, survivors and, indeed, for the reading public,

A freezing horror thrills through ev'ry vein

The poem ends, like Birch's, by exhorting the families of the dead to bear their woes with resignation. It is 'Heaven's all-wise behest' and we must trust in 'a future good, from present ills'. This was the conventional response to unexpected acts of God. Yet, for the reader, it was the 'freezing horror' that would leave the most lasting impression.

Although horror and sympathy continued to dominate people's emotions, over time other responses began to be reflected in verse. In October, the *Morning Chronicle and London Advertiser* published a poem 'on the HALSEWELL INDIAMAN, outward-bound'.[5] Its author was identified by the initials 'A.B.' From the first lines of blank verse, this poet makes his standpoint very clear. The doomed voyage of the *Halsewell* was not morally neutral. The East India Company as a whole and its servants in particular were motivated by greed:

> The freighted ship to spicy shores consign'd,
> Where Nature's laws to Luxury's give way;
> Where callous hearts make gold their idol god,
> And pageant Nabobs ape a Monarch's rule.

In these lines, A.B. articulates the popular criticism of those who seek their fortunes in the East. They are all condemned as 'nabobs' interested only in money and the trappings of wealth. Most are 'allured by gain' and voluptuousness but many seek power, as well. Through the 'terrific pow'rs of war' and the 'Conqueror's despotick sword', they seek to 'gratify ambition's boundless heights'. Although Captain Peirce is not yet mentioned by name, he is condemned by association. He is also guilty of complacency. With the Halsewell 'gliding majestic in the briny course',

> When all around seem'd placid and serene,

the 'advent'rous harden'd mariner' has allowed himself to become

> Blind to the dread quicksands of dim despair
> Ignorant of the gloomy book of fate,
> Mortality he conceives immortal.

Faced with such hubris, it is inevitable that the elements will turn on him. The anger of avenging deities, Boreas, Aeolus and Neptune, is aroused. The 'pleasing undulation of the tide' and the gentle winds that 'waft the lofty ship to foreign climes' are soon replaced by a 'raging swell'. At first the *Halsewell* is

> Proudly confident in her oaken strength

but soon

> The pumps give way, unable to resist
> The impetuous torrent of the leak.

The fall of her 'lofty mainmast' is 'an emblem of human frailty'. Bereft of her power, the *Halsewell* drifts towards the 'lofty cliffs' of Purbeck that

> Strike the spectator with terrific awe.

Stone quarried from here has built great buildings and 'towering structures'. Like the tower of Babel, they too 'raise man's vanity above himself'. But pride comes before a fall.

> On these deceitful rugged points of stone
> In the dead gloom of night, the Halsewell struck.

A.B. cannot resist pointing out the irony in the manner of Peirce's *nemesis*.

> Ah Pierce! he who o'er the wide world has roam'd
> In wat'ry course, in water met his doom.

Only now, at the moment of his downfall, is Peirce presented in a more sympathetic light.

A husband, kind, attentive, and sincere,
A father, noble and compassionate,
Who, to assuage a tender offspring's dread,
Plung'd unfearful into eternity!

As to whether Peirce's act of self sacrifice is sufficient to earn him redemption, A.B. is silent. That is for God to decide.

Thy ways are past human comprehension,
And make us mortals contemptible indeed.

With her husband's business ventures in ruins and with creditors beating a path to her door, Mary Peirce may have wondered if A.B. had a point. However, she is unlikely to have thanked him for expressing it.

Painting

Poetry was not the only medium through which people could respond to what had happened. If there was a public appetite for the horrific scenes that had occurred, that hunger was best satisfied through pictures. The *Morning Herald* was quick to recognise this. '*The fate of Captain Pierce and his unfortunate companions should be made the subject of a picture*.'[6] The paper even went so far as to suggest who might undertake this task. 'Copley should seize the subject; or Fusili, who possesses an enthusiastic mind, well adapted to scenes of horror.' Sensing a healthy market, other reputable artists thought themselves capable of supplying such works, too. The same day, the *Morning Post and Daily Advertiser* reported that 'Several designers are at work on a representation of the loss of the Halsewell; among the rest, we understand Mr Gainsborough is to be one'.[7] For an artist as celebrated as Gainsborough to consider embarking on a work of this nature gives some indication of how deeply affected he must have been. A week later, he was still giving it serious thought. The *London Chronicle* reported that 'Opie means to undertake the melancholy subject of the

Halsewell. Gainsborough, we find, is also meditating the same subject as Opie'.

It is not known if Gainsborough, Opie or Copley ever embarked on a painting of the wreck of the *Halsewell*. No such picture has been attributed to any of them. But other artists were already at work. The first to declare his intentions was Thomas Stothard. He was a student at the Royal Academy and was already attracting public attention. Since 1780, he had regularly contributed illustrations to the new literary periodical, *The Novelists' Magazine*. Other works of his had been reproduced as engravings by the publisher and engraver, Edmund Scott. In fact, it was probably Edmund Scott who commissioned Stothard to paint the final scene in the roundhouse of the *Halsewell*.

Scott was a successful businessman and understood the commercial potential of this subject. The public would want their own copies of Stothard's picture. It would have to be reproduced in large numbers and at a cost that people could afford. The only practical solution was to convert the picture into an engraving that could be printed. This would give Stothard the widest possible audience for his work and yield the greatest financial return.

Edmund Scott may also have suggested a move that would give Stothard's picture an advantage over any others. Through his links in the publishing world, he must have heard that William Lane was talking to Henry Meriton and other survivors. It was common knowledge that the *Circumstantial Narrative* was in preparation and would be published soon. Why not enlist Meriton's help with the picture too? Using Meriton's eye-witness testimony, Stothard could compose a picture that would have a claim to authenticity. In the days before photo-journalism, his picture would be the next best thing. Until the *Circumstantial Narrative* was published, other artists would have only their imagination to draw on.

Doubtless, Henry Meriton was pleased to be approached. It was flattering to have his assistance publicly acknowledged but, more importantly, he was probably paid for his contribution. Meanwhile the task of publicising the work got under way.

Edmund Scott understood marketing. On 28 January he placed an advertisement in several newspapers including the *Public*

Advertiser.[9] It announced his intention to publish a print, in memory of the late Captain Pierce and his daughters. It would be engraved by Edmund Scott from a picture by Mr Stothard. 'The Print to represent the above unfortunate Persons anxiously waiting the Return of Day, in hopes of being relieved from their distressed Situation.' Scott then inserted the unique selling point: 'The Picture will be painted from the particular Instruction of Mr Henry Meriton, Second Officer on board, who has obligingly undertaken to superintend the Design, and to give the ingenious Artist any further Instruction that may be necessary.' Measuring 14 inches by 12 inches, the print would be sold to subscribers for eight shillings, with half the cost to be paid in advance. Purchasers could place their orders at a number of approved distributors in London and also at outlets in Colchester and Bath.

There must have been an enthusiastic response from the public. On 15 February, the advertisement appeared again but, this time, additional distributors were listed in Portsmouth, Bristol and Liverpool.[10] The demand for Stothard's print was now on a national scale. By the time the print was actually available for collection, two more subscription agents had been added, in Canterbury and Alresford, Hants.

On the 1 April the *General Evening Post* announced that the print was, at last, ready for inspection.[11] Anticipation of what it would portray must have been at fever pitch because Scott felt it necessary to reassure the public about what it contained: 'Edmund Scott begs to assure the public that this picture is not designed to excite horror, as has been suggested; it represents a cabbin scene with the unfortunate sufferers, before the fatal catastrophe waiting in suspence and anxiety the return of day.' Finally, Scott took the opportunity to remind his readers of his eye-witness source by expressing 'his sincere thanks to Mr Meriton not only for his valuable instructions, but in the polite manner in which they were given'.

The picture that subscribers took possession of did not conform to the way shipwrecks were typically depicted. Instead, as advertised, Stothard had chosen the interior setting of the roundhouse. The scene is dimly lit from a single source of light, a lantern hanging from the ceiling. The confined space is filled with figures, most of whom are seated or lying down. The viewer's eye is drawn along two diagonals to a point where they converge, at the right of the picture. There, Captain Pierce is seated. He is almost completely obscured by his daughters and nieces who cling to him. Only his face is visible, lifted to gaze at the light from the lantern above. The symbolism is clear. In the darkness and impending peril, he is seeking the light of salvation.

Opposite him, but standing, are the two figures of Henry Meriton and John Rogers. Other less well-defined figures lie around the edges of the room or lean despairingly against the bulkhead. In the foreground, a woman sits alone, isolated in her own grief. Could this be Miss Mansell whom the *Circumstantial Narrative* described as being in 'hysteric fits upon the floor'? Next to her a mandolin lies abandoned and forgotten.

In 2007, the National Maritime Museum obtained Stothard's original oil painting. It already held a copy of one of Edmund Scott's engravings. A comparison of the two is interesting. In Stothard's painting, the combination of chiaroscuro and soft, vague brushwork lends the whole picture an aethereal, otherworldly quality. Nothing is clearly defined. With their pale, pinched faces, it is as if the people in the painting have become ghosts already.

The engraving by Scott brings everything into sharper focus. The musical instrument, which is only hinted at in the painting, is clearly visible in the engraving. So, too, is the panelling of the roundhouse. As a result, Scott is able to introduce a significant new dimension to the picture. The room is now tilted away from the vertical to suggest that the world these figures inhabit is already on the verge of collapse. The effect is to heighten the dramatic tension of the scene.

Although Edmund Scott had publicised Stothard's picture before any other relating to the *Halsewell*, his was not the first to go on sale. A week earlier, on 23 March, a portrait of Richard Peirce himself was published.[12] It showed the bust of Captain Peirce in profile. He is wearing a coat, unbuttoned to reveal a frilled shirt, and we see that he is of stocky build, with a thick neck. He stares ahead confidently and there is a hint of a smile about his mouth.

The inscription below tells us that the picture was by I. Cruikshank and based on a sketch by one of Peirce's own friends.

Halsewell sinking by R. Smirke
© *National Maritime Museum, Greenwich, London*

We can, therefore, assume it to be a reasonable likeness of the man himself. The Cruikshank in question is probably Isaac Cruikshank, the Edinburgh born artist who arrived in London in 1783. (He was later to be the father of the celebrated satirist George Cruikshank.) Although much of Isaac Cruikshank's later work was to be published by S.W. Fores, on this occasion it was William Maynard who did so.

A day after Cruikshank's portrait of Peirce went on sale, a new print of 'The *Halsewell* East Indiaman' was published. The publisher was the engraver Robert Pollard and his print was based on a painting by Robert Smirke.[13] Two years previously, Robert Smirke had painted the notorious wreck of the *Grosvenor* East Indiaman which had run aground on the coast of Africa. This new work was of the same dimensions and was clearly intended as a companion piece. In his haste to publish before Stothard, it is evident from Smirke's picture that he had not delayed to take advice from any of the survivors. Nevertheless, he more than compensates for any lack of factual accuracy by the dramatic composition of the scene. He depicts Captain Peirce and the young ladies on the open deck of the *Halsewell* in the final seconds before the ship sinks.

In Smirke's picture, Captain Peirce is shown standing up, on the listing deck. His two daughters cling to his waist, their backs turned towards the viewer and the approaching sea. Other ladies are huddled next to them, some resigned to their fate, others gesturing in despair. Peirce raises his face to the heavens and makes a dramatic gesture with his left arm. At the same time an enormous wave can be seen poised over his shoulder, just about to engulf them all. To his right, the ship's wheel is abandoned and a half-submerged sailor slides into the sea.

On the left side of the picture, lower on the sloping deck, Smirke has placed an Indian lady with a turban. She sits apart from Peirce and the group of English ladies yet she counterbalances them. She raises her right arm, mirroring the gesture of Peirce, but unlike him her gaze is downwards towards the sea that is already breaking over her feet. Above and behind her, on the poop deck is another group of figures. Near the broken mizzen mast, a man, woman and toddler cling to the railing. They are the archetypal family group, with echoes almost of the holy family. We know that they too will be sacrificed to the waves.[14]

By April 1786, fascination with the *Halsewell* showed no sign of waning. It was to be further sustained by the publication of yet more pictures. Most notable of these was a pair of illustrations by the artist and engraver, Robert Dodd. By 1786, Dodd was a well-established artist. In 1782 he had exhibited at the Royal Academy. The following year his painting, *Greenland Whale Fishing*, had attracted favourable notice. Dodd now turned his attention to the *Halsewell*.

His first picture was dated 3 April 1786 and was entitled 'Society at Sea'.[15] A sub-title explains that the picture depicts 'the recreation of the company on board the *Halsewell* in serene weather'. The right half of the picture shows the stern of *Halsewell*, with her name clearly revealed. On the stern gallery, we see Captain Peirce surrounded by seven young ladies. Peirce's right hand holds a book, probably a music score, which is draped over the railing. His other hand rests casually on the back of a chair on which one of his daughters is sitting. He smiles down at her. To his right, a young man, perched on the corner of the railing, plays a violin. The scene is demarcated by the ship's ensign which hangs loosely like an enormous curtain. There is clearly no wind at this moment and the motionless ensign prevents Peirce from seeing what may be on the horizon.

To the left of the picture we see two more representations of the *Halsewell*. In keeping with convention, she is shown simultaneously from two perspectives, broadside and head-on. Her sails and ensign hang limply. Only some clouds in the distance suggest that the serene weather may be about to change.

Dodd's second picture is in marked contrast to the first.[16] Day has become night and the balmy weather has now been replaced by a violent storm. As in the first picture, *Halsewell* presents her stern to the viewer. Although seen from further off, we can still read her name and discern the outline of agitated figures on her stern gallery. Enormous waves are crashing over *Halsewell's* deck and she is listing heavily to port. To the left of the picture, parallel to the ship, are the forbidding cliffs of Purbeck. At their base, injured and exhausted men are trying to clamber onto the rocks from the sea. One man still clings to a floating cage-like object. perhaps John Rogers and his hen-coop. Part way up the cliff we see the black entrance to the cavern where survivors are already gathering. Other more intrepid men are attempting to climb the vertical cliffs and one is shown in the very act of tumbling to his death. Unlike Edmund Scott, Robert Dodd has no qualms about presenting his public with the full horror of the situation.

A lengthy inscription along the bottom of the print tells us that the picture was both painted and engraved by Robert Dodd. It is dedicated to 'The Directors of the Honourable East India Company'. It is clear from the composition of this picture that Dodd had paid close attention to the account in the 'Circumstantial Narrative' by Meriton and Rogers. He was not the only artist to do so.

On 18 April, Samuel William Fores published a print at his Caricature Warehouse in Piccadilly. It was drawn by Thomas Rawlinson and aquatinted by P. Mercier.[17] Although more crudely drawn and hastily executed, its composition bears a striking resemblance to the work by Robert Dodd. Despite the date of publication, one can't help suspecting plagiarism and a rush to publish. In what was perhaps an astute marketing ploy, S. W. Fores dedicated this print 'to the survivors

Final moments on the Halsewell by Gillray after Northcote
© National Portrait Gallery, London

and relations of the unfortunate persons who perished in the Halsewell,
East Indiaman'.

Examination of the collections of the National Maritime
Museum, the National Portrait Gallery and of advertisements in
contemporary newspapers shows that several other pictures depicting
the wreck of the *Halsewell* were produced. Perhaps the most remarkable
appeared in June 1787, eighteen months after the event. It was painted
by James Northcote, engraved by James Gillray and published by
Robert Wilkinson.[18] Like Thomas Stothard, James Northcote focused
his attention exclusively on Captain Peirce and the young ladies. They
are shown, grouped in a most striking and theatrical pose, at the
moment when they about to be engulfed by a wave. Northcote has no
interest in the precise events of the wreck. He cares only to provoke our
reaction to the human tragedy and he uses melodrama to arouse what
Geoff Quilley has called 'an excessive sympathetic involvement with
its horrors'. Certainly these horrors made an impression on Northcote
himself. Having read Meriton's account, his sleep was disturbed for

a week by 'frightful dreams of their ghastly ghosts surrounding my bed'.[19] His powerful and dramatic picture reflects the emotional response of the general public better than any other.

Theatre

To see a shipwreck captured in a still image evoked one kind of response. To see that shipwreck re-enacted before your very eyes injected an immediacy that prompted a reaction of a very different order. This is what Philip James de Loutherbourg sought to achieve. In later years, he would become best known for dramatic paintings such as 'Lord Howe's Victory, or the Glorious First of June' and 'Coalbrookdale by Night', but in the 1780s, the theatre was his artistic milieu.

Born in 1740 in Strasbourg, the son of a Swiss miniaturist, Philip James de Loutherbourg showed prodigious artistic talent from an early age. He was elected to the French Academy in 1767 where he gained celebrity for his paintings of sea storms and battles. During several years spent touring Germany and Italy, he became interested in the theatre and ways of staging dramatic theatrical effects. He explored the use of light behind canvas to suggest the moon and stars and he tried out other devices to create the illusion of running water. He had already established a reputation for such special effects when he moved to London in 1771.[20]

David Garrick realised that De Loutherbourg could enhance the productions of the plays at his theatre in Drury Lane. From 1773, he, therefore, employed De Loutherbourg at £500 a year to supervise the scene-painting and to provide special effects. This he did with great success. For many years, the name of Mr De Loutherborg appeared in the publicity for plays at the Theatre Royal.

His work in the theatre provided opportunities for De Loutherbourg to experiment further with the use of light. By filtering light through coloured glass or gauze he could create the rosy glow of a sunset or the hazy light of a foggy dawn. By adding sound effects, De Loutherbourg found he could summon up a convincing storm.

Moving his lights behind screens enabled the tableau to become alive. It was as if he was animating nature itself.

London audiences were impressed by De Loutherbourg's work. His effects added such an exciting dimension to Garrick's plays that his employer may have feared they would steal the show. De Loutherbourg must have thought likewise. In 1781 he decided to launch a show of his own. It would be called the *Eidophusikon*.

The name *Eidophusikon* is constructed from Greek and means 'image of nature'. On 28 February 1781, the *Morning Chronicle and London Advertiser* carried an advertisement for De Loutherbourg's new 'exhibition'. It would consist of 'various imitations of natural phoenomena, represented by moving pictures, invented and painted by Mr De Loutherbourg in a manner entirely new'. The show would include music, specially composed to add atmosphere and to fill the intermissions during scene changes. The performance would begin at seven o'clock at Mr De Loutherbourg's 'large house' on Lisle Street, overlooking Leicester Square.[21]

The fact that De Loutherbourg felt able to charge as much as five shillings per ticket shows how confident he was that his show would be a hit. His instincts were sound and the upper classes of London flocked to his door. In a room that could accommodate an audience of no more than a hundred and thirty people, they saw what can best be described as either a very large picture, or a miniature stage. The framed picture was ten feet wide and six feet high. What distinguished it from a conventional painting was the fact that it had a depth of eight feet. This allowed De Loutherbourg to create a very different visual experience. Once the audience were seated, the lights would be dimmed, the show would begin and the scene would appear to come to life. Despite its small size, the scenes that played out on this miniature stage amazed the London audience.

In the course of the 'exhibition', they saw a view of London at dawn, becoming progressively illuminated by the rising sun. This was followed by the exotic location of Tangier, seen at midday in the blazing African sun, with the Rock of Gibralter visible in the distance. The third tableau showed Naples, at sunset, its buildings fading into the twilight. Next the audience watched the moon rise over the Mediterranean, with silvery light reflecting off the water and clouds. Then, in a dramatic climax, the scene became a violent storm. Horrified, the audience watched as a sailing ship appeared to battle against the rising waves before being shipwrecked on a rocky shore. Nobody had ever seen anything like this before. The effect was electrifying.

A reviewer wrote, 'This exhibition is one of the most curious that was ever invented". The 'wonderful effects', he enthused, were 'closer imitations of nature than any we have ever before beheld'. The room in which they occurred was 'fitted up in a theatrical stile with unparalleled taste'. Having described the various scenes, the critic concluded with a glowing verdict. This entertainment, he assured his readers 'forms one of the richest, though most peculiar, feasts for the eye and ear, that ever was prepared in this metropolis'.[22] With an accolade like this, it is no wonder that the *Eidophusikon* was sold out for weeks to come.

To the modern viewer, accustomed to CGI and films shown in 3D on enormous cinema screens, De Loutherbourg's efforts seem puny. Yet, for its time, the *Eidophusikon* was genuinely revolutionary. The recent invention of the Argand lamp provided a vital component. It was named after its inventor, the Swiss scientist Francois Pierre Aime Argand, and could produce as much light as ten conventional candles. Such a powerful light source, combined with mirrors, metal sheets and scrims or gauze, allowed De Loutherbourg to create his various illusions. The use of panels, like stage flats, gave a sense of enormous depth to the scene and mechanical winches could cause three-dimensional model ships to appear to glide over the surface of the sea.

Having excited his audience with these marvels, De Loutherbourg quickly found he had created an appetite for more. This posed a problem. The scenes were expensive to create and slow to construct. Keeping up with the demand for new sensational settings was a challenge. Nevertheless, De Loutherbourg opened his 1782 season with a new programme. This time, it included the cataract of Niagara Falls, a waterspout off the coast of Japan, and most dramatic of all, a scene from Milton's *Paradise Lost* in which Satan reviews his army of fallen angels on the banks of a fiery lake.

The audience was not disappointed and the revised *Eidophusikon* ran to packed houses from February to May. The following year, 1783, De Loutherbourg took *Eidophusikon* to Bristol for the Spring season.[23] This gave him breathing space to work on new material. In March 1784, he was back in London but now he had found a bigger venue. An exhibition room was fitted out at the Exeter Exchange on the Strand. It could cater for much larger audiences and would no longer be restricted to the wealthy nobility. Although he would reduce the cost of admission from five shillings to three, De Loutherbourg recognised that economics would work to his advantage.

This larger audience enjoyed two scenes in particular. The 'storm and shipwreck' and 'the Grand Scene' from Milton clearly appealed to the less refined tastes of this broader section of society. *Eidophusikon* was so popular that De Loutherbourg decided to open in December 1784 for a short winter season. In keeping with the time of year, the music would include extracts from the Messiah. There would be new items on the programme but the two 'favorite scenes' were retained.

During the first half of 1785, *Eidophusikon* continued its run at the Exeter Exchange. But by now it was becoming tired. Audiences were falling off and the struggle to introduce new and ever more sensational material was proving too much. By May, *Eidophusikon* seems to have run out of steam; no more advertisements for it were placed in the newspapers.

Ironically, the loss of the *Halsewell* in January 1786 seems to have thrown a lifeline to De Loutherbourg. The public's reaction to the news of the wreck was so powerful that he knew he must tap into it. He already had a 'storm and shipwreck' scene. He just needed to re-brand it as the wreck of the *Halsewell* and the punters would return.

On 30 January 1786, the *Morning Herald* carried a fresh advertisement for a revival of the *Eidophusikon*. Top of the bill would be the 'awful and pathetick scene' of the shipwreck, 'conveying a very striking idea of the late catastrophe of the Halsewell, East-Indiaman'.[24] For anyone wanting to experience vicariously the terror and pity of the last moments of Captain Peirce and his daughters, this show must have been irresistible. Just as in its hey-day, *Eidophusikon* played again to full houses.

The publication of the *Circumstantial Narrative* at the end of January gave De Loutherbourg the information he needed to adapt the show to reflect the actual events more closely. The model ship could lose her masts in the correct sequence and could run broadside against the cliffs before sinking. It was important for the audience to know that what they were watching was authentic. The advertisement in the *Morning Post* on the 10 February made it clear that 'particular attention is paid to the affecting narrative published under the directions of the chief surviving officers, at Mr Lane's, Leadenhall-street.'[25]

On 16 February, the *Eidophusikon* was able to go one better. This time, as well as giving an 'exact, awful and tremendous representation of this lamentable event', the performance would be attended by Mr Thompson, bookseller, who would sell copies of the Narrative. The public lapped it up and, perhaps, even some of *Halsewell's* survivors were persuaded to attend. One reviewer suggested that the 'awful and astonishing' effect of the storm scene was 'such a marvellous imitation of nature that mariners have declared, whilst viewing the scene, that it amounted to reality'.[26]

Feelings about the *Halsewell* were so powerful and so widespread that *Eidophusikon* ran almost continuously until 10 May. More immediate than any still painting, print or book, the *Eidophusikon* had proved to be the ideal vehicle for conveying the tragedy of the *Halsewell*.[27]

22
Rebuke, Rejection & Reckoning

At Walnut Tree House, Mary Peirce now started the painful process of coming to terms with her loss. On being told that Richard Peirce's body had been found, she had become calm, at last. However, the real truth about her husband may have been kept from her. As late as 13 February it was being reported that his body was still missing. In fact it would never be recovered.[1]

Even without his body, the death of Captain Peirce could not be allowed to pass without the consolation and dignity of a religious ceremony. If there could not be a funeral, there must, at least, be a service of remembrance. It would be held on Sunday 19 February at All Saints Church in Kingston-upon-Thames and the preacher would be the Rev. Matthew Raine, Fellow of Trinity College, Cambridge.

The Peirce family had lived in Kingston for about fifteen years. They were already well-known locally and now their name was recognised throughout the land. Not surprisingly, therefore, the service of remembrance was well-attended. The *General Evening Post* reported that the church was 'exceedingly crowded'. The entire Corporation of Kingston was present, dressed in mourning 'as a mark of their great respect to the deceased'. According to the same newspaper, Captain Peirce not only 'enjoyed the friendship of the opulent' but was a 'sure and liberal benefactor' to the poor.[2]

In his sermon, the Rev. Raine drew inspiration from the Epistle of James, chapter IV, verse 14: 'For what is your life? It is even a vapour that appeareth for a little time and then vanisheth away.' If he intended to offer comfort to the bereaved family, this was a challenging text to choose. His opening remarks were no less direct. We all know that life is short, he began, and possession of life's enjoyments is uncertain, yet few men actually live their lives in a manner which corresponds with this conviction. Instead we spend our time in pursuit of things of this world. People who engage 'in the pursuit of riches and power' simply do so more urgently and focus their attention on 'their separate interests'. They forget the frailty of their existence, which should teach them to bear misfortune with resignation. Raine now read the first lines of the verse from which he had taken his text: 'Go now,' says the Apostle, 'ye that say today or tomorrow we will go into such a city, and continue there a year, and buy and sell and get gain; whereas, ye know not what shall be on the morrow.' Sitting in her pew, near the front, one wonders how Mary Peirce received these words. There was no mistaking their aptness to her husband's situation. He had intended to be away at least a year and to 'get gain' before his return. As if it needed any reinforcement, Raine developed the theme. 'Let us suppose', he continued, 'a man engaged in some honest and laudable pursuit, by the success or miscarriage of which his family and himself are to be rendered happy and respectable, or to be sunk at once in wretchedness and distress. We see him then, with an eager and fond desire to accomplish his wishes, hazarding his all upon a single venture.' How often are such hopes ruined by some sudden and unlooked for loss. 'But the loss which diminishes fortune, may be repaired by industry.'

Mary Peirce certainly needed no reminding. Her husband had hazarded most of their wealth on this his last venture and she was still discovering the true financial implications of the disaster. She would have to devote much thought, effort and industry, if the loss was ever to be repaired.

Now, Matthew Raine turned his attention from individual to corporate ambition.

Let us conceive for a while, instead of one individual, or one family, a number of persons, on whom many families are dependent for support, employed together in [...] promoting the commercial prosperity of their country: that 'they go down to the sea in ships', as the Psalmist expresses himself, and that 'their business is in great waters'.

His congregation would have been in no doubt that this was a reference to the East India Company itself. Echoing the theme of so many poems and perhaps the paintings of Robert Dodd, Raine contrasts the gentle winds and high hopes of success at the start of a venture with the subsequent tempests, despair and destruction. Although he was less outspoken than many, Raine clearly shared the widely held view that the servants of the Company, 'enriched with merchandize', deserved to be taken down a peg or two.

Before Mary Peirce could feel too affronted or upset by these general remarks, the Rev Raine switched his attention to the specific event which was had led to that day's memorial service. Without mentioning Captain Peirce by name or even alluding obliquely to his drowned daughters, Raine invited the congregation to recall the 'melancholy event [...]which has been of late a subject of so general sorrow'. Perhaps with Smirke and Stothard in mind, he used the analogy of a picture to represent the event itself: 'In whatever point of view we place the gloomy picture, the contemplation of it fills the mind with a mournful horror.' Our thoughts of both the deceased and the bereaved excite in us feelings of regret and compassion, he continued.

Then addressing Mary Peirce and the congregation directly, Matthew Raine declared 'We cannot omit the mention of one, who, from the peculiar relation in which he stood to you, [...] has engaged your particular attention and concern'. And now, at last, the preacher paid tribute to Richard Peirce himself: 'If ever there was a man to whose memory a marked respect was due, to such respect his memory feels fairly entitled.' It was not for Peirce's undoubted professional abilities but for his virtues as a man and a Christian that the congregation should remember him. The 'ready bounty' with which he helped those in need and the warmth and sincerity of his friendships were conspicuous qualities in the man.

Looking down at the congregation from his pulpit, Raine acknowledged that his words of praise for Peirce were superfluous. 'You had frequent opportunities to contemplate his good qualities [...]You saw and you admired them.' Yet, it was the manner of his death that was most striking: 'He possessed a mind, fitted by religious cultivation, to meet death undismay'd.' This should be an 'unspeakable consolation' to those affected by his loss. Like Job and like Peirce, we too must try to bear misfortune with 'patient fortitude and pious resignation'. It is through humility and pious resolve than we can resist despair. Then, returning finally to his earlier theme, Raine warned his listeners against 'the height of wealth, prosperity and power' which lead only to 'arrogance of presumption and the selfish insolence of pride'.

With these words ringing in her ears, Mary Peirce was left to contemplate her future. She can have been in no doubt that Raine's condemnation of flaunted wealth and the arrogance which accompanied it was directed at those who made fortunes in the east. The clergyman had simply echoed the general view, regularly expressed in the newspapers and now surfacing in poems and pictures, that the 'nabobs' deserved their comeuppance. If what had happened to her husband was a moral rebuke delivered by the Almighty, then she would bear it with the fortitude and patience that was clearly expected of her. At the same time, though, she would do her best to restore her remaining family to their former position in society.

Matthew Raine probably felt his sermon had struck the right balance between compassion and condemnation. It seemed to have gone down well with the congregation and the papers reported that his 'whole discourse was delivered in such affecting language that [...] there was not a dry eye in the church.'³ He will have felt further justified when, a week later, he received a letter from the Corporation of Kingston. The bailiffs and freemen of the town had met at the Guildhall on Saturday 25 February and had passed a vote of thanks. Even more flattering was their request that he have his sermon published. It is unlikely that the Reverend Mr Raine felt that his exhortations to humility inhibited the publication of his own sermons. He was happy to oblige and by 25 March his sermon was with three firms of printers and on sale to the public at one shilling a copy.⁴

If the financial rewards from the sale of his sermon were of little importance to the unworldly Matthew Raine, the financial predicament in which Mary Peirce now found herself was of very great concern to her. The husband who had provided for her and her family was dead; their investments in the *Halsewell* were all lost and there were creditors to be paid. To make matters worse, Captain Peirce had died intestate.[5] It was an extraordinary omission for someone of Peirce's age and in such a hazardous profession. Was Matthew Raine correct? Had the pursuit of wealth really blinded him to any thoughts of mortality?

We would have a much better idea of the riches that Peirce might have secured if we knew the precise value of his investment. Sadly, these records have not survived. Although the Company required those privileged to carry private trade to submit a list of their 'sundries' and the purchase value of each investment, these documents were all destroyed in the nineteenth century. The best we can do is to make an educated guess.

Between 1768 and 1780, on their outward voyages, East India Company commanders declared on average between £2,000 and £2,500 worth of private goods. However, Huw Bowen has suggested that the actual value of their investment was often closer to £8,000 or £10,000.[6] In some cases it was far higher. In 1778 Captain Chisholme had carried £25,000 worth of goods on the *Gatton*. In addition, captains often exceeded their allocation of 80 tons by hiding other goods about the ship.

Although Richard Peirce was a respected commander, he was probably not above this kind of sharp practice. This was his final voyage and he needed to maximise his return. The newspapers may not have been exaggerating when they reported 'We are given to understand that the unfortunate Capt Pierce had the largest investments on board the Halsewell that perhaps has been known for some years'.[7] It is possible, therefore, that his losses amounted to at least £10,000. Whether any of this could be recovered would depend on the level of insurance cover. As far as the East India Company's own cargo was concerned, this seemed to have been taken care of. On 19 January 1786, the *Public Advertiser* reassured its readers that, 'Notwithstanding the late loss of the Halsewell East Indiaman, and even over-rating that loss at the highest possible value, the company have still a very considerable balance in their favour, by their constant custom of being their own underwriters.'[8] But had Richard Peirce been so prudent?

It is not known if Richard Peirce had insured any of his private trade but it would be surprising if none of it were. However, it would take time for any insurers to pay up and, in any case, we know that some of the goods that Peirce was taking to India were on a sale or return basis. Their owners would be demanding recompense as soon as they learned of the wreck. Mary's first priority was to raise some money quickly. She immediately began to consider which of their possessions she could sell. There was the china Richard had brought back from Canton, there were the paintings and prints he had collected and maybe even some of their furniture could be sold. Having engaged the auctioneer, Mr Willock, an advertisement was placed in the papers on 29 May.[9] It informed the public that 'sometime next month, the genuine household furniture, pictures, prints, fine Old China and various other effects of Captain Richard Peirce' would be sold at auction. A second advertisement appeared on 10 June announcing that the auction would take place on Tuesday 13 June and that the sale would include Peirce's 'library of books'.[10] It is a sign of Mary's desperation that she was prepared to part with so many possessions that must have had great personal and sentimental significance. We do not know how much money was raised by the auction but it was not sufficient to clear all her debts.

Five of her children were living with Mary Peirce, at Walnut Tree House. The eldest, Emilia was fourteen years old; the youngest, Sophia Jane, was barely a toddler and had not yet been weaned. In between them, came Thomas, who would be ten in June; then Louisa, aged eight; and next Frances who would be seven in May. How were they to be provided for?

It was common for the East India Company to make provision for the widows of men who had died in its service. Generally a widow would receive an annual pension of £80 a year with a further £16 for each of her children. Many such cases are recorded in the minutes of the meetings of the Court of Directors. We also know that survivors from the *Halsewell* received some assistance and that those who had helped to rescue them were similarly rewarded. One might expect, therefore, that the Company would offer financial help to the widow of one of its most respected and senior commanders. Perhaps it did. However, there is no record in the Court Minutes of any pension being granted and this might account for Mary Peirce's predicament.

There is another quarter from which help may have come. One of the key functions of the Society of East India Commanders was to look after the families of commanders who died in service. Since Richard Peirce was one of the founding members of this group, Mary Peirce probably petitioned the Society for assistance. Again, we cannot say if she was successful. Although some of the Society's records survive, none record whether any grant or pension was offered to Mrs Peirce. It is difficult to imagine, though, that they would have turned their backs on the widow of someone who had helped to create the Society in the first place.

Even if Mary Peirce did receive help from the Society or the East India Company itself, this was not enough to offset the debts that still burdened her. Thomas Bourne, the jeweller from Cheapside, was one of the creditors who were pursuing her. He was demanding £1,000 for his diamond-encrusted shoe buckles. Despite having sold many of her possessions, Mary could not or would not raise this kind of money. Her best hope was to stall Thomas Bourne and his ilk until she could find the necessary funds by some other means.

At this point, it is worth attempting to estimate what Mary Peirce's assets actually were. Sir Peregrine Fury owned Walnut Tree House where they lived. It cost them £80 a year in rent and a further £16 in land tax and poor rates. Together this was the equivalent, today, of about £13,500. In April 1785, Captain Peirce had insured the property with Sun Fire Insurance for £800. He had also insured his library of 'printed books' for £50, his plate for £200 and their 'wearing apparel' for £250. A year later, following his death, the policy was due for renewal. This time, Mary reduced the insurance on Walnut Tree house to £600. She also dropped the value of her plate and wearing apparel by £100 each. In today's terms that makes her clothes worth about £21,000. Interestingly, she held the value of the library at £50.[11] As this premium was paid a mere month before the auction was advertised, it seems to suggest that Mary was intending to sell only about half of her 'plate'. Regarding her husband's books, she must have had second thoughts. His library was added in the later advertisements as being for sale too.

An examination of the tax records at Kingston reveals that Mary Peirce had an interest in other property in the area.[12] She owned a house. Probably, this was where she and Richard had lived before upsizing to Walnut Tree House. This property was somewhere in Norbiton and was now occupied by a Dr Perkins at an annual rent of £14, equivalent to approximately £2,000 today. While this provided useful income to Mary, she had other property liabilities too. Since 1782, the Peirces had rented a small house from Sam Hollis for £3 per annum. It is not clear why they wanted it but there must have been a good reason because they still had possession of it in 1786.

In June the *Morning Chronicle and London Advertiser* reported that, a few months previously, Richard had bought land at the southwest corner of Richmond Park.[13] He had planted and enclosed it but there had not been time to build on it. Had the voyage been a success, perhaps the Peirces intended to build a fine house of their own there. Now the land lay neglected.

It is almost certain that Mary Peirce's property portfolio extended yet further. There was 17 Gower Street, the address that her husband had used when writing to Justice Buller at Christmas. Uncle Richard had also referred to Gower Street when making his will in July so it was probably still in Mary's possession. Furthermore, there was her own father's real estate to consider.

When Thomas Burston died in 1785, he had left property in Norfolk to his son-in-law, Richard Peirce.[14] Despite the absence of any will by her late husband, Mary must surely have expected this property to pass to her. Thomas Burston also had been involved in property in Kingston. At various stages he had rented houses or land in Market Place, High Row and from Thomas Fassot and Lord Spencer. In 1782 he paid a total of £38 in rents but after his death most of these were let go. In 1785, Mary Peirce's mother, the widow Mary Ann Burston, seems only to have rented property in West-by-Thames, near the White Hart. It cost £14 a year.

In October 1786, Mary Peirce took out a second insurance policy with the Sun Fire Insurance company. This time she paid £100 for house insurance, presumably for the house occupied by Dr Perkins. She also insured her 'utensils and stock' in her Rick Yard for £300, Wandry Barn for £60 and Home Barn and Stable for £140. The fact that Mary Peirce had these assets to insure shows that she was not left destitute. In today's terms the combined value of all this would be about £84,000. Nevertheless, Mary knew she would need to economise and it was essential to secure an income. Although she continued to live in Kingston until her death, within a year, Mary and her children had left Walnut Tree House. She could no longer afford its rent and the position in society that the house implied.

In the autumn of 1786, Mary received fresh bad news, although this time it did provide a crumb of financial comfort. Her late husband's uncle, Richard Peirce senior, had died. In his will he had named Mary as sole beneficiary and also executrix.[16] He does not seem to have left a fortune. Uncle Richard had no land to bequeath, just money owing to him from a life assurance policy with the Bathonian Society in Bath. Welcome though this legacy was, it did not significantly alter Mary's circumstances.

In the light of her new financial situation, Mary recognised that her best lifeline was her eldest son Richard. He was still in Calcutta and was now eighteen. If he could be found a well-paid post in the Company, he could provide support to his mother and siblings. But to gain a post in the Bengal Civil Service required patronage. Appointment to the position of writer was in the gift of Company Directors. Without the support of at least one sympathetic Director, this could not be achieved. Although several of the twenty-four Directors were former ship commanders themselves, it appeared that none of them felt inclined to help. Why this was so is not very surprising. Patronage was a tool for currying favour, gaining influence and rewarding past service. Now that her husband was dead, there was little incentive for any Director to use his influence on behalf of a widow who could offer nothing in return.

Fortunately an opportunity presented itself to alter this state of affairs. The annual election to the Court of Directors was due in April 1787. Company Directors were elected for a term of office lasting four years but these elections were staggered, so six places or a quarter of the Directorate was contested every Spring. The voters were those 'proprietors' or shareholders who held Company stock worth £1,000 or more. There were at least a thousand such proprietors but they tended to vote conservatively. Once they had elected someone as a Director, they often returned them again and again. John Manship, for example, had been elected in 1755 and would still be a Director half a century later.[17]

Although Directors came from all parts of the kingdom, including Scotland and Ireland, few were of humble origin. Before being elected, many had had successful careers in the worlds of trade, finance or shipping. Any new candidate would have a better chance of success if they came from a similar background. Fortunately, Mary Peirce knew somebody with the right credentials. He just needed to be persuaded to offer himself as a candidate.

Sir Benjamin Hammet may not have needed much persuasion. Besides a natural desire to help the widow of his old friend, Hammet would have regarded the position of Company Director as an appropriate career move. Since marrying into the Esdaile family, he had pursued a successful career in banking. He was a Member of Parliament and an Alderman of London. As a Director of the East India Company, his power and influence would be further enhanced. At the very least, he could use it to promote the career of the young Richard Peirce and alleviate the distress of his family.

In Bengal, Richard Peirce had now learned of the death of his father. The *Ganges* had arrived at Diamond Harbour at the end of June with news of the terrible storm she had survived. The non-appearance of *Halsewell* soon raised concern and its fate must have been confirmed by the next Company packet soon afterwards. Perhaps prompted by his mother, Richard Peirce wrote in early October 1786 to Alderman Hammet seeking his support. He sent his letter via the homebound fast packet ship, the *Severn* but, unfortunately, it came to grief in the Ganges estuary and Richard's letter was lost.

In November, he wrote again. 'The late unhappy misfortunes of my family, in which you have lost a valuable friend, and myself a tender and affectionate parent, have made me cast my eyes on you sir, as the man to whom I shall chiefly look up to for the protection of my unfortunate mother and sisters.' Justifying his request for Hammet's protection by appealing to his 'very long and sincere friendship for my poor father', he implored him not to 'forsake the widow and family of his friend after so severe a misfortune'.[18]

Richard need not have worried. By January 1787, Benjamin Hammet seems to have made up his mind and, at the beginning of March 1787, he announced his candidacy in the forthcoming election of Company Directors. On 2 March he placed advertisements in all the main London newspapers.[19] In his statement, he acknowledged the 'magnitude and consequence' of the Company. He then allied himself firmly with the faction of ship owners and their backers known as 'the shipping interest': 'I have ever maintained that the rights and privileges of the Proprietors, with the safety of private property, ought inviolably be preserved; and that a permanency of the shipping interest is indispensable with the security of the returns to this country.' This stance, he hoped, would go down well with the voters.

The challenge facing Hammet was considerable. Five of the six outgoing Directors intended to offer themselves for re-election. They were all formidable opponents and had already declared their intentions in a joint advertisement. Only Governor Johnstone was not standing again. In February, he had communicated this to the Court of Directors, and several independent candidates had promptly emerged, seeking to replace him. John Lewis had thrown his hat into the ring on 23 February, followed by Thomas Pattle and James Fraser. If Sir Benjamin Hammet were to secure a place, he would have to see off these rivals.

Hammet's campaign got off to a good start. To ensure the Proprietors knew of his candidacy, he placed advertisements in the chief newspapers on almost a daily basis. Unfortunately, so did his rivals. Over the following weeks, he conducted his campaign with commendable vigour, canvassing every proprietor in London in person. To his face, the proprietors were polite and appeared to be supportive. The campaign seemed to be going well. Then at the end of March came a setback.

On 30 March, many newspapers carried a notice, signed by twenty-two directors and former directors, in which they gave their backing to six of the candidates.[20] Proprietors were advised to vote for the five directors who were standing again and, significantly, for James Fraser, the independent candidate. This was a blow for Hammet. The opinion of the current Directors naturally carried

Benjamin Hammet
© *Somerset County Council.*

weight with the Proprietors. From now on, it would be an uphill struggle.

On 6 April, things took a turn for the worse. The *World and Fashionable Advertiser* carried a letter from 'A Proprietor' in which he urged fellow voters to be unanimous in re-electing 'your five old and faithful Directors'. Then he turned on the other candidates:

Let us be very minute in enquiring into the characters of the new candidates', he warned. 'I have seen candidates formerly who had defrauded the Company of considerable sums by contracts and jobs in India, and Captains who had cheated the public revenue and the Company of above £20,000 each voyage, who wished to get into the Direction to screen themselves. What has happened may happen again. Merchants or Independent Gentlemen, who have not been in India, are the most proper persons to be elected Directors.' The five former directors should not be subject to the 'threats and menaces of India Contractors and Smugglers.'[21]

It is not entirely clear what lay behind this outburst. Benjamin Hammet had not been to India himself nor do we know if he had benefited from any financial dealings over contracts. But it was common knowledge that he was intending to help the widow of a sea captain. Even if not a direct reference to Captain Peirce himself, some of the mud thrown in allegations of smuggling and cheating the revenue may have stuck, at least in the minds of the voters. It is also possible that other negative comments had been published about Hammet too because, at this eleventh hour, something prompted an intervention from Mary Peirce.

On 8 April, she wrote to several papers.

A paragraph having appeared in the public papers, which in its tendency, and published at the moment, might prejudice my good friend Sir Benjamin Hammet, in the opinion of the Proprietors of East India Stock, I think it my duty to declare in contradiction to the insinuation of such a paragraph, that I have experienced the most friendly and benevolent assistance from Sir Benjamin Hammet and that he has exerted every possible effort to obtain my son Richard, now in the East Indies, a situation there which would enable him to be a second father to my children.[22]

Then, by way of evidence, she included an extract from the letter that young Richard had written to Hammet in November. It was also a blatant attempt to play on the voters' emotions. Everyone remembered the death of the unfortunate Captain Peirce. Surely the Proprietors would respond sympathetically to this appeal from his son.

Finally, in case any further reinforcement was required, Mary quoted from a letter she had received from a friend, only days before.

Writing from Portsmouth, the author indicated his support for Hammet.

One of my friends has promised me to vote for Sir Benjamin. I sincerely hope he will succeed, as in that case he will have it in his power to do something handsome for my friend, your son Richard, and I dare say that Sir Benjamin does not want for inclination to do so. It is my ardent wish that the letters of recommendation from the Governor and Council at Calcutta, to the Directors here, will be successful. My son William had a letter also from your son, per the Ranger Packet.

Although the identity of the writer is not revealed, it is possible that the letter was from Daniel Garrett, the Portsmouth brewer. He was a family friend and, in a few years, Mary's daughter, Louisa, would marry one of his sons.

As the day of the ballot approached, Sir Benjamin Hammet wrote again to the papers to address the voters. He did his best to sound confident:

Having completed my Canvas, and called at the House of every Proprietor in London and Westminster [...] I cannot delay returning you my warmest thanks for the very flattering Prospects of Success which have been afforded me by your kind Assurances of Support.

On 11 April, the votes were counted. As expected the five former directors were all re-elected, with James Moffatt topping the poll on 744 votes. The sixth place went to Thomas Pattle who secured 558 votes. Despite his official endorsement, James Fraser only managed 553 votes. Well behind him came Sir Benjamin Hammet with 448 votes. John Lewis was last.[23]

Having fallen short by over one hundred votes, Hammet must have been disappointed, though he may not have been entirely surprised. To become a Director, candidates often spent years preparing the ground, assiduously courting proprietors and building up a circle of supporters who would campaign on their behalf. This campaign had been entered in haste, with little backing and no time to build up a groundswell of support. In the circumstances, to have secured almost

450 votes was actually quite creditable. But that thought will have been of little consolation to Mary Peirce. She still had nobody on the Directorship who would come to her aid.

However, as it turned out, Fate allowed Benjamin Hammet one more throw of the dice. In early November 1787, George Cuming, one of the Directors, suddenly died. There would need to be a by-election and the date was set for the 5th of December. Encouraged by his previous result, Hammet thought that, this time, he might have a real chance of success. He would not be competing against existing Directors who were 'out by rotation'.

On 12 November, he placed a fresh advertisement in the newspapers, soliciting the votes of the Proprietors once again.[24] Attributing his lack of success in April to the fact that he had been competing against 'other very powerful opponents, whose interests were also engaged long before I declared myself a candidate', this time, he assured the reader, he did not expect to experience the same 'difficulties'. He ended by reminding Proprietors how many of their votes had been cast for him before. He trusted it would not be 'considered too assuming in me to repeat my solicitations for your support'.

At first, Hammet appeared to have only one rival, Robert Mendham from Walbrook. Given his previous showing, Hammet probably expected that he could beat him. Then Robert Thornton entered the fray. It soon became clear just how serious an opponent he would be. On 21 November, the entire Directorate, including recently elected Thomas Pattle, threw their weight behind Robert Thornton. Advertisements quickly appeared in the press, advising Proprietors to vote accordingly.[25] Opposed by such a united front, Benjamin Hammet realised the game was up. He would have no chance against the unanimous voice of the Directors.

On 29 November, he published a notice announcing his withdrawal.[26] He would not continue against the 'influence of all those powers, which I trusted would be at least inactive, now combined in support of Mr Robert Thornton'. Then, in a slightly petulant tone, he added 'I cannot avoid saying, that the man who supports the measures of government, when they appear to be for the good of the Public....does not merit the opposition I have experienced'.

Although Hammet did not use this opportunity to describe the opposition he had faced, there are hints that he may have come in for strong personal criticism and smears. On the 1 of December the *Morning Chronicle* praised the 'upright and manly conduct' of Sir Benjamin Hammet in the face of 'mean and puerile scribblers' and the 'rancour of his unmerited adversaries'.[27] In the *Gazeteer and New Daily Advertiser*, another commentator wrote, perhaps with his tongue in his cheek, 'Sir Benjamin Hammet thinks it very hard that a gentleman who has devoted himself and his talents to Ministry as he has done, should not be made a Director! It is highly ungrateful in them, and ought to ruin them in the eyes of all sensible men. Not make Sir Benjamin a Director!' The writer then refers to a characteristic or 'pretension' of Hammet's that should have recommended him to the Proprietors. 'The pretension is, that he is the only candidate who ever honestly and candidly owned that he was influenced by a private motive, namely, the wish of being serviceable to the family of his deceased friend, Capt Pierce.' The implication is that the private motives of other aspiring and existing Directors were not so honourable. This was, of course, a commonly held view. What made the difference was that others kept their real motives to themselves whereas Hammet had brazenly exposed his.

As 1787 came to an end, Mary Peirce knew her attempt to influence her son's career had come to nothing. Worse than that, she may actually have alienated any residual support for her at Leadenhall street. From now on she would have no comfort from that quarter. Her friend, Sir Benjamin Hammet had spent much money campaigning for her. Now, he was poorer and they were both wiser.

During 1786, while Mary Peirce grappled with the repercussions from the loss of her husband, the East India Company had concerned itself with the loss of its ship. The *Halsewell* had sunk on rocks only yards from the shore. Her wooden hull had disintegrated but there was still a reasonable prospect that some of its contents might be recovered.

Within days of the disaster, one of the Company's pilot yachts had been dispatched to the scene. On board was salvaging equipment and, probably, one or more diving bells. However, the weather continued to be boisterous and it was considered too dangerous to bring the pilot yacht close in to the cliffs where *Halsewell* had struck. The only prudent course of action was to mark the spot and postpone the search to later in the year.

> The late severe weather has prevented any experiments being made hitherto upon the wreck of the Halsewell, East-Indiaman; but as the place is marked by buoys etc and the property on board her valuable, the divers will be at work as soon as the spring approaches.[28]

The diving equipment that the Company was intending to deploy was of a type that had been developed by Edmond Halley in the seventeenth century. Bell-shaped but constructed with wood, like a barrel, diving bells were rudimentary and primitive. They had to be supplied with air, either from lowered barrels or pumped from the surface through a tube. In order for divers to carry out their work, a diving bell had to be lowered from the mother ship onto the wreck, lying directly below. In the case of *Halsewell*, this posed a problem. The pilot yacht would have to anchor in shallow water over the rocky ledges which extended out from the cliffs. To operate safely, calm seas would be essential.

Diving bells worked best when the exact location of a wreck was known but, by now, little remained of *Halsewell* and her contents were scattered under the kelp and hidden in the gullies and fissures in the ledges. A more mobile method of seaching was required. The people who might have supplied it were the Braithwaite family. They had developed a diving 'machine' which allowed the diver much more freedom of movement, together with the ability to stay under water for hours at a time. During the previous summer, they had operated successfully, in similar conditions, off the Scilly Isles where the East India Company's packet ship, the *Nancy*, had been wrecked.[29]

No illustration of the Braithwaites 'machine' survives but it may have resembled a suit of armour, made from copper. A bellows pumped fresh air into the diver's helmet through a breathing tube. A second tube was used to communicate with the surface and to extract the 'foul' air. When the *Royal George* sank off Spithead in 1784, the Braithwaites worked on her, too, and just such a suit was described by an onlooker.[30] Many years later, the Braithwaites would dive on the *Earl of Abergavenny* when she went down off Portland but, in 1786, they were not available. They had moved their operations to warmer waters off Tangiers and were busily raising Spanish cannon at the behest of the Emperor of Morocco.[31]

In the absence of the Braithwaites, the Company did the best it could with its own resources. However, many of the smaller valuables were impossible to find, having disappeared into gaps in the rocks or been swept into deeper water. On the 10 June the *General Evening Post* carried a report from Poole that

The vessels that have been employed over the wreck of the Halsewell East-Indiaman, lost near Seacombe last winter, have had little more than their labour for their pains, so they have now desisted, as it appears there are large fissures in the rocks, into which the valuables have probably sunk, never more to be recovered.'[32]

Despite this gloomy assessment, the operation had not been a complete waste of time. In December 1786, the Company held an auction at the Old Antelope Inn in Poole.[33] Among the items salvaged from the *Halsewell* were listed 98 plates of copper, 196 pigs of lead, iron hoops, anchors, carriage guns, broken muskets and even Spanish hides.[34]

Having called off its own salvage operations, the Company then delegated responsibilty for further work to the local Collector of Customs. On 17 January 1787 the Court Minutes recorded that the Directors had 'Resolved that as Mr Lander of the Customs House at Poole is employed under a letter of Attorney from the Company to fish on the wreck of the Halsewell, it is unnecessary to accept the services of Mr Jostage or Mr Symington'.[35] The identity of the two rejected applicants is not known but it is possible that Mr Symington was the celebrated Scottish engineer whose pioneering vehicle, powered by a steam engine, was attracting widespread attention.[36]

A tourist to the area noticed

a number of boats employed in search of the wreck, which collected, during his stay, several pieces of copper, iron etc. He learned from the men, that an immense quantity of cargo had been, at different times, got up. Upon his arrival at Swanage, about three miles further, he purchased a variety of small articles, such as ribbons, perfumery etc and a few pair of silk stockings, but these he found very scarce, as a principal tradesman in Wareham, a neighbouring town, had bought all he could lay his hands on, amounting to many dozens, at about 4s. 6d. a pair, as well as ribbon equally cheap, which was selling at an immense profit.[37]

As with many travellers' tales, this story needs to be treated with some scepticism but there is no doubt that locals hoped more items of value would be recovered and some must have been tempted to try.

In 1789, other more illustrious tourists visited Purbeck. During August, while on holiday in Weymouth, King George III paid a visit to the Weld family at Lulworth Castle. The Royal family had been touched by the tragic events of three years before and decided to make an excursion to the cliffs at Seacombe. It was reported that the King and Princesses were particularly moved as they stood and surveyed the scene. In a poem commemorating the visit, William Holloway entreated the reader to 'See how, with sudden sympathy opprest, Melts ev'ry eye and beats each Royal breast, As yon rude rocks tremendous greet the view, And active fancy paints the scene anew'. Until even 'Britain's Sov'reign joins the gush of woe'.[38]

It would appear that not everyone shared such sympathetic emotions. By now, the directors of the East India Company had become irritated by the political manoeuvrings of Benjamin Hammet and Mary Peirce and this may have influenced their decision in the Court of Directors, the following year. Despite Hammet's failure to be 'serviceable' to her, Mary Peirce had clearly continued to petition the Court on behalf of her eldest son. But now she was without influence and could look to no-one for patronage. Her request fell on deaf ears. Court Minutes record that on 27 February 1789, the Court declined to appoint Richard Peirce as a Writer.[38] The door to preferment and reward had been firmly shut and Richard would have to make his way in the world by another route.

The next year, 1790, the Directors rebuffed Mary Peirce for a second time. With her creditors still hounding her, she decided to approach the East India Company for financial help. Her husband had taken a quantity of diamonds with him on the *Halsewell*. These had never been recovered so Mary decided to seek compensation for their loss from the Company. The justification for this claim is not recorded but the Court of Directors must have believed her case was worthy of their consideration. The request was referred to the Committee of Treasury but the outcome was not what Mary Peirce had hoped for. She was awarded £6-9s-9d, a nominal sum only. It was a clear signal that she should expect no further help from that quarter.[39]

The wolves now began to close in. For almost five years, Mary Peirce had held out against Bourne & Hawkins but she could stall them no longer. Time had run out. The jewellers had not given up on recovering the money for their missing shoe buckles or the 'large quantity of goods' they had sent on the *Halsewell*. In 1791, they resorted to litigation and Mrs Peirce was summoned to appear in court. In July, the case was brought before a special jury at the Court of King's Bench in Westminster Hall.[40] The key piece of evidence produced by the plaintiffs was a bond for £500, signed by Richard Peirce. Faced with this, Mary's only defence was to claim it was a forgery. This was not her husband's signature, she maintained, and the bond was a fake. It was a final gamble and it convinced no-one. Lord Justice Buller ruled in favour of the plaintiffs and Mary had no alternative but to pay.

1791 was probably the lowest point in the fortunes of Mary Peirce. She had relinquished Walnut Tree House and was living with her surviving children in a smaller property in Kingston. The East India Company had failed to come to her rescue. But all was not lost. Despite everything, Mary continued to believe that the best hope for her children and the salvation of her family lay in India. While she still had friends within the Company's maritime service, she would do all in her power to recover from the disaster that had shattered her family.

PART FIVE

'FRIENDS IN INDIA'

23
Husbands in Bengal

Despite the bereavements that both families had suffered, the Pauls continued, like Mary Peirce, to look towards India. They knew it offered the best prospect for their remaining daughter and, through her, a means of advancing the family as a whole.

Only two years after Amy and Mary's deaths, Henry and Ann sent their youngest child to Bengal. Martha Maria Paul was seventeen. By now, her older sister, Anne Graham, had been in India for five years and was firmly established in Calcutta society. In April 1788, Maria (as she preferred to be called) sailed for the East on the *Triton*. George Templer and William Cator were her guarantors but, on this occasion, the East India Company waived the usual £200 security fee.[1] No doubt, this gesture was prompted by compassion for the family. Perhaps for the same reason, the Company also suspended its recent ruling, prohibiting more than three 'ladies' from travelling on the same ship.

In India, where, in matters of the heart, nothing was gained by procrastination, Maria quickly accepted a proposal of marriage from George Frederick Cherry. Still only twenty-four, he had already spent eight years in India working as a linguist. His flair for languages was clearly precocious because, while still in his teens, he had been appointed as Persian translator to the Commander-in-Chief at Calcutta.[2] Persian was the language of the Mughal Court and essential for diplomacy in eighteenth-century India. It was also vital for espionage. In addition to his official duties, George Cherry was to play a covert role, monitoring the correspondence of Indian rulers and gathering intelligence about their intentions.

In 1787, the *Bengal Register* listed George Cherry as a Junior Merchant and Deputy Persian Translator at Nudea.[3] It did not record that George Cherry had also become a father. As William Dalrymple and others have shown, it was not uncommon, in these pre-Imperial times, for Europeans to form relationships with Indian women and to have children with them. These 'natural' children were generally acknowledged by their fathers and often sent to England to be educated. In 1780, George Cherry had a son by Bibi Fanee. Later, he would make provision for this boy in his will, though his name is not recorded and the child is only identified through his mother.[4]

On 5 March 1789, Maria Paul married George Cherry in Calcutta. Her parents must have breathed a sigh of relief at her safe arrival in India and, now, at her married status. They had another reason to be pleased. Their eldest daughter, Jane, and her husband, George Templer, had recently completed that voyage in the opposite direction. They had taken up residence nearby, at Shapwick, with their two children.[5] If the life expectancy of a man in Calcutta was two monsoons, the Templers had beaten those odds. Back in Somerset, their chances of living for many more years were greatly improved.

Meanwhile, in Bengal, young Richard Peirce's prospects were improving, too. Despite the earlier setback, he had gained promotion, at last. The Bengal Register listed his appointment as an Assistant at the Board of Trade.[6] This would ensure that his income would rise and he could offer more support to his family in England. Since the disappointment over the diamonds and with the impending court case, his mother would have to depend on him more and more. Fortunately, his younger brother, Thomas, would soon be able to share the burden.

Thomas Burston Peirce was only ten when his father drowned. By 1790, he was fourteen and old enough to start following in his father's footsteps. Ideally, the first rung of the ladder would be as a midshipman but appointment to such a post was the prerogative of the ship's captain. Luckily, Mary Peirce still retained some influence in that quarter. Although the *Halsewell* had been smashed to matchwood, long-established custom within the East India Company gave her owner, Peter Esdaile, the right to replace her. In 1790, the Company had given him the go-ahead and a new, much bigger ship had been built at Barnard's Yard. In October, that ship had been launched before a large crowd of well-wishers. Ceremonially breaking a bottle against her bows, Benjamin Hammet had named her the *Taunton Castle*.[7] It was an interesting choice of name. By 1790, Benjamin Hammet had been returned three times as member of parliament for Taunton. It was his home town and he had bought and restored its ruined castle. But the name of the ship may also have contained an oblique reference to Richard Peirce. Taunton was, possibly, his home town, too.

Earlier in October, the newspapers had reported that the man appointed to 'command the new ship built on the bottom of the unfortunate Halsewell" would be Captain James Urmston.[8] What the newspapers did not say, but was widely understood, was that Urmston's appointment was in the hands of Mary Peirce herself. Under normal circumstances, the choice of a new commander was decided by the outgoing captain, unless, of course, that captain was already deceased. In such cases, the privilege passed to his widow. Just as Richard Peirce had paid his predecessor for command of the *Earl of Ashburnham*, Mrs Peirce expected payment from James Urmston for the command of *Halsewell's* successor. It would have cost Urmston several thousand pounds but Mrs Peirce may have been willing to negotiate the price in return for a position for her youngest son. Captain Urmston was happy to oblige. Thomas Burston Peirce would sail on *Taunton Castle* as one of his midshipmen.

It was hoped that, in the fullness of time, Thomas Peirce would rise, like his father, to become commander of an East Indiaman. But this could take many years and Mary Peirce still had four surviving daughters to provide for. It was advisable for them to marry as soon as possible and, despite everything, India still offered the best prospects for a good match.

In 1792, Emilia Peirce made the voyage, the fate of her older sisters very much in her mind, but also buoyed by the prospect of seeing her brother again. Just as her cousins had done, Emilia joined in the round of social engagements and dances that kept the wheels of Calcutta society turning. There, she met William Fleming, a young army officer in the Bengal Artillery. Having permitted him to escort her to her pew on Sunday, Emilia was soon being led all the way to the altar. The wedding took place in January 1793 at the newly completed Anglican church of St John's.[9] The marriage was reported in various newspapers though, puzzlingly, Lieutenant Fleming's Christian name was given as John.[10] He may, of course, have had both first names but it was as William that he would be known to the family.

The next daughter in line was Louisa Harriet Peirce. She had been born in 1778 and, by 1794, was also ready for matrimony. Once again, the Company directors were petitioned. In February, permission to travel was granted and Louisa's sponsors put up the customary £200. In this case, the guarantors were Francis Magniac, a merchant from St John's Square, Clerkenwell, and Richard Barker of Tavistock Street, Bedford Square.[11] We can assume they were both friends of Mrs Peirce.

What happened next is unclear. Louisa may have travelled to India in March 1794 but, if she did so, she must have returned almost straight away. The voyage could take six months in each direction. What is known for certain is that Louisa Peirce married George Garrett in Portsmouth in March 1796.[12] It is possible that she met George in India and returned to England with him at once. More likely, is that they met in late 1793 or early 1794 and that, as a result, Louisa abandoned her travel plans. If so, one wonders what her guarantors thought of this decision. Mrs Peirce must have agreed. The Garretts owned the Portsmouth Brewery and had risen through trade but now they owned estates in Hampshire and were on the verge of entering the landed classes. It would be a comfort to Mary Peirce to have one of her married children living in England.

Perhaps, this outcome made it easier for Mary Peirce to bid farewell to her next daughter. It was now the turn of fifteen-year-old Frances Peirce to take to the high seas. In April 1795, just a year after her sister Louisa had done so, Frances petitioned the Court of Directors for permission to 'proceed to her friends in Bengal'. Once again, Francis Magniac offered himself as her guarantor. The second guarantor was a London surgeon, Benjamin Hollingsworth from St John Street.[13]

It should come as no surprise that Frances married, almost as soon as she stepped ashore, the wedding taking place at St John's, in October 1795.[14] The bride was barely sixteen while her husband, at thirty, was almost twice her age. He was Kennard Smith, commander of the East India Company's ship, *Minerva*. He had served on this ship for at least ten years, rising from the position of second officer. He may have already known Frances's father and, perhaps, had visited the Peirce family on his return from various voyages. If so, there could have had a prior agreement between him and Mrs Peirce, before young Frances boarded ship, but a whirlwind romance cannot be ruled out, either. This was Calcutta, after all.

Kennard Smith was a tough seaman who stood no nonsense from his crew. Once, in the face of a potential mutiny, he had drawn his sword and severely wounded the ringleader. Cowed by his decisive action, the other malcontents resumed their duties.[15] Kennard Smith was a disciplinarian and sailors challenged him at their peril. What the young teenager thought of her new husband is not recorded but she probably obeyed his wishes too, at least at the start.

In India, the climate had begun to take its toll on Mary Peirce's eldest son. Just as he was beginning to make headway in his career, Richard fell ill. By now he was supplying elephants to the East India Company and also working as an auctioneer.[16] The nature of his illness is not known but Richard understood that only a change of climate would give him a chance to recover. Unfortunately, he did not live long enough to put it to the test. On 19 November 1795, just as he was about to take ship for England, Richard Peirce died. He was only twenty-seven. The inscription on his mausoleum in South Park Street cemetery lamented the loss of 'a dutiful son and affectionate brother' whose 'amiable qualities' had 'endeared him to society'.[17]

News of the death of her eldest son came as a bitter blow for Mary Peirce. Since the loss of her husband, he had become the nominal head of the family but now he had been snatched from her, too. Further heartache was to follow within a year.

Meanwhile, the fortunes of her in-laws, the Pauls, continued to rise. Thomas Graham, the husband of their second daughter, Anne, was promoted to the Board of Revenue in Calcutta.[18] Not even his brother's financial mismanagement dented Thomas Graham's upward progress. In 1791, the bank of Graham, Mowbray and Skirrow collapsed but, while Robert Graham was once again forced to flee, Thomas seems to have avoided disgrace.[19] In 1793 he was elected to the Supreme Council of Bengal.[20] His brother-in-law, George Cherry,

The tomb of Richard Peirce junior in Calcutta.
© *Philip Browne*

was also making good progress and, in the same year, was appointed
Resident in Benares.[21] In this position, he became the East India
Company's chief representative in the area, with overall responsibility
for its affairs and its diplomatic relations with the local nawab.

With his sons-in-law doing so well, inevitably some of the
rewards percolated down to Henry Paul himself. In 1789, Henry and
Ann Paul left West Monkton and took up residence in Cossington
Manor near Bridgwater.[22] Although not particularly large or
ostentatious, Cossington Manor was a distinct step up. It was certainly

more appropriate for people of their rising status, even if it was gained by association, rather than by their own efforts.

In 1796 Capt Kennard Smith was given instructions to return to England with *Minerva*. Naturally, he did not want to be parted from his young wife so soon – she may already have been pregnant – so it is no surprise that, on the passenger list, we find the name of Mrs Frances Smith. Their arrival in England was reported in the *Oracle & Public Advertiser*.[23] Then on the 5th November 1796, the *True Briton* reported that Mrs Smith, wife of Kennard Smith, had died at the Smith's family home in Epsom.[24] Sadly, his young bride had died in childbirth.[25]

By the start of 1797, Mary Peirce had lost four of her eight children. Before she herself died, she would lose one more. In 1799, the Paul family also suffered further bereavements. Death from tropical illness, childbirth or even from drowning might be expected but the manner of George Cherry's death shocked everyone.

In 1796, he was enjoying his position as Resident at Benares. The local ruler was the Nawab of Oudh where, until recently, the incumbent had been Wazir Ali. He had displeased the East India Company by some of his actions and they had connived to have him replaced. His legitimacy was called into question and another more sympathetic candidate had been installed instead. By such means, the Company ensured that local potentates were amenable to its interests. Those who opposed them would be undermined. To ensure that he caused no further trouble, Wazir Ali was summoned to Calcutta where he suspected he would be detained.

Wazir was not happy about this challenge to his authority. He decided to take it up with the Company's representative, George Cherry. At breakfast time he arrived at the Resident's house, accompanied by a large retinue of followers.[26] George Cherry listened to his complaints but said that the decision to summon Wazir to Calcutta had not been his. He tried to play for time but it was to no avail. Incensed, Wazir drew his sword and struck George Cherry on the arm. In the ensuing melee, the ex-Nawab's supporters joined in and George Cherry was hacked to pieces. Following the massacre, Wazir Ali's forces then rampaged through Benares, causing much devastation. Having vented his anger, the former Nawab knew that retribution from the British forces must follow. He went on the run and took refuge in Nepal. It did not save him. He was soon betrayed and forcibly returned, a prisoner, to Calcutta where he spent his remaining days confined in a small cage. To the East India Company and its servants, this may have seemed an appropriate punishment but it probably provided little consolation to George Cherry's widow.

In January 1786, at the moment when Benjamin Hammet had informed Mary Peirce of the death of her husband, she had been in the act of suckling her youngest child. This infant was Sophia Sarah Jane and she was said to have been about six months old. By 1800, the infant was fifteen. The last of Mary Peirce's children, Sophia can have had little doubt about her destiny. It was pre-ordained. She, too, must travel to India and marry a servant of the East India Company.

Her future husband turned out to be George Poyntz Ricketts. In 1790, at the age of sixteen, he had been appointed to the position of Writer at the Company's offices in Calcutta. His Indian credentials were impressive.[27] Although his father, George Poyntz Ricketts senior, had been Governor of Barbados, the family had long been associated with the East Indies. Young George's maternal grandfather was William Watts. He had worked for Robert Clive and had helped to orchestrate the conspiracy that toppled Siraj ud Daula at the Battle of Plassey in 1757. He had received a reward of £114,000 for his efforts and was briefly Governor of Fort William. George's maternal grandmother was herself the daughter of a former Governor of Bengal. She had outlived four husbands – a salutary demonstration of the theory of two monsoons – and, by 1800, was one of the most celebrated widows in Calcutta, where she was known as the 'Begum' Johnston. George's brother was also employed in the Bengal Civil Service. In addition to her own relatives, Sophia Peirce would have several in-laws she could turn to for support. She was still almost a child. When the wedding bells rang at St John's on 20 February 1800, George Poyntz Ricketts was twenty-six. Sophia Peirce was fifteen.[28]

The wedding of Sophia and George Poyntz Ricketts now left Mary Peirce with only one child still unmarried. During the previous decade, her son, Thomas Burston Peirce, had spent much of his time at sea. He had shown early promise and had been rewarded with the rapid promotion they had hoped for. In the year of his youngest sister's marriage, Thomas was appointed captain of the *Taunton Castle*.[29] He was twenty-four and his elevation to this command may well have owed something to his mother's influence with Peter Esdaile. Now that he was commander of an East Indiaman, Thomas was in a position to consider marriage. At some point he was introduced to the sister of one of his fellow commanders, James Peter Fearon of the *Belvedere*. Anna Maria Fearon may have been living on Prince of Wales Island off the coast of the Malay peninsular. Certainly, that is where the marriage took place, in 1801. The witnesses were the Governor of Penang and J. P. Fearon.[30]

Three years later, Anna Maria Peirce gave birth to a daughter, Mary Ann.[31] In choosing the name, they may have had in mind the little girl's paternal grandmother. Unfortunately, any happiness that the birth of this child brought to the family was to be clouded by bad news. Her father, Thomas Burston Peirce, had become ill. It was soon evident that his condition was serious and he had no option but to relinquish command of the *Taunton Castle*. It was a severe setback. With his wife and baby daughter, Thomas Peirce settled at Castle House in Sidmouth in an attempt to recover his health. Even the benign Devon climate was not sufficient to save him and on 15 October 1806, Thomas Burston Peirce died.[32]

His mother, Mary Peirce was also nearing the end of her own life. In the twenty years since she had been widowed, Mary had lost three daughters and both her sons. Her brother-in-law and sister-in-law were also dead. In January 1803, three years after the death of his wife, Henry Paul passed away. He was 71 and had lived at Cossington Manor for the last fourteen years. The *Morning Post* (1803) included a brief tribute, describing him as 'deservedly regretted for his numerous unostentatious acts of charity'.[33] Mary's own health was now in decline. She was suffering from a lingering and painful illness, probably cancer. On 2 May 1807, her life finally came to an end.

The *Hampshire Telegraph* (1807) summed up her life as follows:

Perhaps modern history does not afford a more remarkable instance of what human nature can endure, than is to be found in the latter

part of this Lady's life; accustomed to the most elegant and liberal style
of life, surrounded by a numerous and engaging family, united to a
man, who occasioned more tears at his loss perhaps than any private
individual before or since the lamentable loss of the *Halsewell*: in the
midst of this transient scene of bliss did she hear of the beginning
of her misery, in the wreck not only of her fortune, but her friends,
her children, and her husband, all buried in the devouring ocean.
Like a true Christian did she bear up with unexampled fortitude
against her cruel fate, which has still continued in its most merciless
form, to invade her, by the loss of her two sons, the eldest in the
most promising situation in India, and the youngest commanding
the *Taunton Castle* East Indiaman, and a short time prior to this, her
favourite daughter died in childbed. To complete this scene of human
misery, for the last twelve months, this unfortunate sufferer had been
labouring under a complication of diseases, the anguish of which was
in no degree diminished by the calmness she evinced on bending with
pious resignation to the will of the Almighty. She has left three most
amiable daughters behind her, all married, who, together with the
widow of her youngest son, alleviated by their unremitting assiduity
and tenderness the latter moments of their much lamented relative.[34]

It is a touching and generous epitaph, creating an image of a
woman facing, with courage and dignity, the misfortunes that had
blighted the latter part of her life. And we have no reason to doubt
that Mary Peirce displayed these admirable qualities. But the notion
that the Peirce family was 'unfortunate', tragic figures against whom
fate had turned, is too simplistic and fundamentally inaccurate.

The 'unfortunate Captain Peirce' was unlucky only in one
respect. At the end of a long career, he was caught in a storm which
disabled his ship and caused its destruction. Given the circumstances
and sequence of events, it is unlikely he could have avoided that
outcome. Even then, he might have saved his own life. He was a
powerful swimmer and who is to say that he might not have gained the
shore, as so many others did? The decision to stay with his daughters
was his. He made the judgement that the women in his care would
have no chance of getting ashore and climbing the cliffs, and he was

probably correct. His only hope was that the *Halsewell* would stay intact until morning and that the gale would blow itself out. In his heart, he knew he was clutching at straws.

The fact that Richard Peirce made no will is bizarre but not unusual. Some people regard doing so as morbid and comfort themselves with the thought that there will be plenty of time to do so later on. Perhaps, Richard Peirce thought so too. By dying intestate, he made his widow's situation more difficult but it was not a catastrophe. Although the family's circumstances were reduced, they were not left destitute. Mary continued to maintain a property in Gower Street as well as in Kingston. Although widowhood placed some constraints on her participation in society, Mary's friends stood by her. If the East India Company was irritated by her political manoeuvrings, others, like Hammet and Magniac, were willing to come to her aid. A general feeling of sympathy and goodwill towards Mary Peirce remained throughout her life and would ensure she was not forgotten.

When we consider the life of her husband, it is difficult not to conclude that it was, in fact, a fortunate one. In a relatively short time, Richard Peirce achieved his ambition to command his own ship. This endowed him with status and influence. On seven occasions, he visited the East Indies where he encountered peoples, cultures and places utterly different from anything in his previous experience. He traded there with success and the profits from these endeavours enabled him to live in one of the grandest houses in Kingston. Had he survived that last voyage, his reputation and wealth would probably have led to his emulating his father-in-law by becoming a ship's husband. Later, perhaps as a champion of the 'shipping interest', he might have stood for election to the Court of Directors.

The scathing condemnation of the East India Company that was expressed so often and so vehemently, cannot fairly be directed at Richard Peirce. Others, like that 'piratical grandee' Thomas Rumbold, and even John Graham, lined their pockets through corruption and dubious dealing but there is no evidence that Richard Peirce did. The private trading and other perquisites that went with his position were officially sanctioned and carried no guarantee of financial success. Although he did well from his transactions, Richard Peirce never seems to have struck the jackpot as some other commanders did. At the same time, he avoided disaster.

On average, one ship in twenty was lost each year.[35] From his quarterdeck, Peirce saw several of his fellow commanders get into difficulties and he heard of many more. He understood the risks. Just as, today, economic migrants from Africa take their chances in crossing the Mediterranean, the East India Company calculated the odds and sailed east. For Richard Peirce, the roll of the dice was favourable. Despite encountering a number of violent storms, before 1786, it never looked as if he was about to lose his ship. That was not simply down to good luck. Peirce was a consummate professional who commanded his ship with energy, balanced with attention to detail. If disaster occurred, it would not be of his making.

He also enjoyed robust health. The rigours of life at sea and the climate in the East took a heavy toll on the crews of East Indiamen.[36] Commanders were not immune. Captain Williamson of the *Ganges* would die before he could return from India. Similarly, disease had cut short Thomas Burston Peirce's life but, apart from in 1778, illness never prevented Richard Peirce from carrying out his duties. He endured. The stocky figure in the sketch by Isaac Cruikshank looks resolute and unshakeable. There is steadfastness in his solid profile. This was the man who decided to remain with his daughters and refused to abandon his ship. Misfortune may have forced *Halsewell* onto the Purbeck rocks but Richard Peirce chose the manner of his final end.

Epilogue

The families of Captain Richard Peirce and Henry Paul never lost faith in India. Despite the toll it took in terms of their children's lives, they continued to believe that their best prospects lay in that subcontinent. They knew that service to the East India Company offered a route to advancement and wealth. For people of their social status, similar opportunities were scarce in England.

The best way to unlock these opportunities was through marriage. Over the ensuing decades, alliances with other families, associated with the East India Company, would weave the Peirces and the Pauls into a network where influence, favours and family loyalty worked to their advantage. For both families, the rewards were not instant. The widowed Mary Peirce struggled to maintain the social position her husband had achieved and her financial circumstances remained precarious after the deaths of her sons. Henry Paul was more fortunate. His move to Cossington Manor lifted him out of the class of yeoman farmers and secured his place among the minor gentry.

Those who reaped the greatest rewards were their children. They were now linked to the world of banking and high finance, to the army and the maritime service, to developers and diplomats. When Henry Paul's eldest daughter, Jane, returned from Calcutta with her husband George Templer, she was no longer an ordinary girl from a Somerset village. Now she could afford to live at Shapwick House and to eat from the finest Chinese porcelain, emblazoned with the Templer coat-of-arms. In 1790, her husband was elected M.P. for Honiton.[37] Two years later, he entered the world of merchant banking, partnering other 'nabobs' to set up the London and Middlesex Bank. Even when that bank collapsed, in 1816, and he was forced to sell Shapwick, all was not lost. At the age of 62, George returned to India, where the East India Company allowed him to assume his old rank.[38] In 1818 he was appointed Commercial Resident at Jungpore. When George died of a fever, the following year, Jane returned to England to live with her

Thomas Graham
© *Yale Center for British Art*

sister-in-law, Lady Anne de la Pole, at Shute Manor, near Axminster. There she remained until her death in 1847.[39]

The career of Anne Paul's husband, Thomas Graham, turned out to be even more successful than his brother-in-law's. By 1793, Thomas had become President of the Board of Revenue and a member of the Supreme Council in Calcutta.[40] A portrait by Thomas Hickey shows him seated near his desk.[41] He has his legs crossed and sits with an air of calm authority. The shrewd alertness of his gaze suggests a man who has already made his fortune and intends to keep it. In 1801, the Grahams returned to Scotland. At first they lived at Burleigh Manor but, following the death of Thomas Graham's half-brother, George, they inherited Kinross House.[42] By 1802, the former Anne Paul of West Monkton had become the mistress of one of the finest Georgian mansions in Scotland. In 1811, Thomas was elected MP for Kinross-shire, a seat he held until his death in 1819.[43]

Louisa Peirce who had stayed at home to marry George Garrett also found herself moving up the social scale. In 1805 her husband inherited the family business, the Portsmouth Brewery. Like his brothers, George also became heavily involved in raising and leading a local volunteer militia, the Portsmouth Royal Garrison Volunteers. In September 1820, on board the Royal Yacht at Spithead, he was knighted for his services.[44] Although he retained his house in Penny Street, next to the brewery, he and Louisa lived mainly at Gatcombe. It was there, in November 1825, that Louisa Garrett died.[45] George Garrett did not remain a widower for long. He had obviously kept in close touch with his sister-in-law Anna Peirce, widow of the late Thomas Burston Peirce. Both she and he had been married to the children of Captain Richard Peirce. Finally, in April 1828, they married each other.[46]

The youngest of the Peirce girls, Sophia Ricketts, also prospered. For fifteen years, she lived with her husband in India, mainly in Patna and Benares, as he gained promotion within the Bengal Civil Service. During that time, she gave birth to nine children, of whom eight would live to adulthood. In 1815, George Poyntz Ricketts died and, soon afterwards, Sophia decided to return to England. She lived in Cheltenham, the last surviving child of Captain Richard Peirce, until her death in 1830.[47]

The death of Sophia Ricketts marks the conclusion of this postscript. For forty-five years, the families of Peirce and Paul had been able to focus their attention on India, thanks chiefly to the courageous and adventurous spirit of their ten daughters. Despite tragic loss of life, the family had forged links in Bengal that would underpin their future. For several more generations, these friends would continue to open doors and smooth the path to preferment and promotion. The tragic event, in Dorset, on the night of 6 of January 1786, shocked the world. But even a disaster of such proportions could not break the spell that India had cast over the family of Captain Peirce. It would lure them and dominate their dreams for years to come.

Notes

Prologue. Pages 3-4
1. *Whitehall Evening Post*, No 5931, 17 May 1785
2. TNA, HO47/2/82, Judges Reports on Criminals. Letter from Capt Richard Peirce to Judge Buller, 13 Dec 1785.

Chapters 1 and 2. Pages 5-22
1. BL, APAC, B/102. Court Minutes, 30 November 1785
2. ibid.
3. *The Times*, No 334, Thursday 19 January 1786 [online] available at http://infotrac.galegroup.com/itweb/lancs?db=BBCN
4. BL, APAC, L/MAR/B/465/E/1-2 Pay Book of *Halsewell*.
5. BL, APAC, B/102. Court Minutes, 12 October 1785
6. BL, APAC, B/102. Court Minutes, 11 November 1785
7. *Morning Herald and Daily Advertiser*, No 324, 14 November 1781, p.3.
8. Joan Wakeford, *Kingston's Past Rediscovered* (Chichester, 1990). Also in Kingston Land Tax Returns, 1784. Microfilm 0992274.
9. TNA, HO47/2/82, Judges Reports on Criminals. Letter from Capt Richard Peirce, dated 13 December 1785.
10. Kingston Local Archives Service. Baptismal records of All Saints Church, Kingston-upon-Thames, 1741-1832. Microfilm 0991684.
11. BL, APAC, B/102. Court Minutes, 18 November 1785
12. Henry Meriton & John Rogers, *The Circumstantial Narrative of the Loss of the Halsewell (East Indiaman)* 20th edition (London, 1786), p. 27.
13. Henry Meriton, *The Circumstantial Narrative*, p. 17.
14. *Whitehall Evening Post* No 6000, 25-27 October 1785, p. 3. [online]
15. BL, APAC, B/102. Court Minutes, 18 November 1785
16. BL, APAC, B/102. Court Minutes, 16 November 1785
17. *Morning Herald and Daily Advertiser*, No 1595, 6 December 1785, p.3. [online]
18. Jean Sutton, *The East India Company's Maritime Service 1746-1834* (London, 2010), pp. 277-280.
19. BL, APAC, L/MAR/B/465 E(2) Pay Book of *Halsewell* 1782-84.
20. Holden Furber, *John Company at Work* (Boston, 1948)
21. Edward Cuming, *Three English East Indiamen Wrecked Off the Dorset Coast* (2003) CD-ROM.
22. TNA, KB122/596, p.51. Court of King's Bench Judgement Rolls.
23. BL, APAC, L/MAR/B/86C Journal of *Ganges* 1785-87. Meriton records that *Halsewell* 'fell down' to Gravesend on 16th November. *The Circumstantial Narrative*, p.2.
24. ibid.
25. BL, APAC, L/MIL/9/91
26. BL, APAC, B/102. Court Minutes, 21 February 1786, p. 806

27. *Public Advertiser*, No 16120, 23 January 1786, p.3 [online]
28. BL, APAC, B/102. Court Minutes, 13 December 1785
29. Jean Sutton, *The East India Company's Maritime Service 1746-1834* (London, 2010), p.66.
30. Henry Meriton, *The Circumstantial Narrative*, p.30.
31. *London Chronicle* No 4518, 3 November 1785, p. 432.
32. *Public Advertiser,* No 15013, 31 July 1782, p.7.
33. BL, APAC, B/102. Court Minutes, 21November 1785
34. *Hampshire Chronicle*, No 696, 16 January 1786.
35. *London Chronicle*, No 4548, 12 January 1786, p. 34.
36. BL, APAC, B/102. Court Minutes, 13 December 1785
37. BL, APAC, B/102. Court Minutes, 21 November 1785
38. B.A. Saletore, *Fort William Correspondence* Vol IX, 1782-85, p.280.
39. *Morning Chronicle and London Advertiser*, No 5200, 13 January 1786, p.3.
40. *Morning Chronicle and London Advertiser*, No 5222, 8 February 1786, p.3.
41. BL, APAC, L/MAR/B/86C Journal of *Ganges* 1785-87.
42. Sian Rees, *The Floating Brothel* (London, 2001) p. 56
43. TNA, HO47/2/82, Judges Reports on Criminals. Letter from Capt Richard Peirce, dated 27 December 1785.
44. BL, APAC, L/MIL/9/91
45. BL, APAC, L/MAR/B/363A, Journal of *Manship* 1785-86.
46. BL, APAC, L/MAR/B/86C Journal of *Ganges* 1785-87.
47. BL, APAC, L/MIL/9/91 Muster Roll of Recruits 1783-86, Embarcation Lists Volume 8: 1784-87.
48. *The London Chronicle*, No 4546, 5-7 January 1786, p 18.
49. *The London Chronicle*, No 4546, 5-7 January 1786, p 19.

Chapters 3 to 5. Pages 25-63

1. Bell & Daldy, *Notes and Queries*, 3rd Series, Vol. III, Jan. 10th, 1863, London: Bell & Daldy, p. 34.
2. TNA, PROB 11/1147. Will of Richard Peirce, gent. of Taunton, 1786.
3. Somerset Heitage Centre microfiche of parish records from West Monkton. Also LDS Film 0178046 Page 490 Ref 10282
4. SHC, DD/DP/7/9 and DD/DP/7/14
5. Meriton & Rogers, *The Circumstantial Narrative*, p. 21
6. BL, APAC, L/MAR/B/465 E (1 &2) Halsewell Ledger and Pay Book J
7. *Public Advertiser* No. 13245, 29 August 1778, p.2.
8. Sir Lewis Namier & John Brooke, *History of Parliament: House of Commons 1754-1790, Volume 2.* London, 1985, p.575.
9. *Morning Chronicle & London Advertiser*, No. 5203, 17 January 1786.
10. Anthony Farrington, *A Biographical Index of East India Company Maritime Service Officers 1600-1834*, London: British Library, 1999, p.614.
11. BL, APAC, N/1/1 f.130 Marriage of Capt Peirce & Ann Shiers in Calcutta, 1731.
12. TNA, PROB 11/765. Will of Robert Peirce, merchant of Brentwwod, 1748.

13. Anthony Farrington, *A Biographical Index*.
14. *Daily Gazeteer* , No. 5064, 11 July 1745 and No. 5073, 23 July 1745.
15. BL, APAC, L/MAR/B/438 CC(1 & 2) *Houghton* Ledger and Pay Book
16. BL, APAC, Court Minutes B75, p. 250.
17. Farrington, *A Biographical Index.*.
18. BL, APAC, L/MAR/B/438-I. Journal of the *Houghton*
19. BL, APAC, L/MAR/B/438-I. Journal of the *Houghton*.
20. Peter Earle, *Sailors: English Merchant Seamen 1650-1775*, London: Methuen, 2007, p. 70.
21. Thomas Twining, *Travels in India A Hundred Years Ago*, London: Osgood McIlvaine, 1893, p. 21
22. Twining, *Travels in India*, p.21
23. C. Northcote Parkinson, *Trade in the Eastern Seas 1793-1813*, Cambridge: Cambridge University Press, 1937, p. 74
24. Twining, *Travels in India*, p.22.
25. E.W. Sheppard, *Coote Bahadur*, London: Werner Laurie, 1956, p. 68.
26. William Hodges, *Travels in India*. London, J. Edwards, 1793, p.4
27. Thomas Twining, *Travels in India*, p. 53
28. William Hodges, *Travels in India*, p.9.
29. Stephen Taylor, *Storm & Conquest*, London: Faber & Faber, 2007, p.28.
30. Thomas Williamson, *The East India Vade-Mecum* London: Black, Parry & Kingsbury, 1810, p.143
31. Thomas Williamson, *The East India Vade-Mecum*, p.144
32. Thomas Williamson, *The East India Vade-Mecum*, pp. 146 & 150
33. Sutton, *The East India Company's Maritime Service 1746-1834*, p.98.
34. Defoe, *A General History of the Pyrates*, p. 124. A gallivat is a local vessel, of 40 − 70 tons burthen, from the Malabar coast. It sailed with a peak sail and was rowed with 30 or 40 oars. It carried about 100 men, including 20 fighting men, as well as rowers. It was fast and manoeuvrable, carried 4-8 swivel guns and, therefore, was often used by pirates. A Grab is a large coasting vessel of India, of 150 to 300 tons burthen, generally of two or three masts but without a bowsprit.
35. Sutton, *The East India Company's Maritime Service 1746-1834*, p. 63.
36. In the eighteenth century, one unpleasant treatment for syphilis was known as salivation. This involved rubbing an ointment of mercury on the sores and then heating the patient until his tongue was literally hanging out.
37. The National Archive holds the wills of several seamen from ships that Richard Peirce sailed on. See also Peter Earle, Sailors, chapter 5.
38. *The Annual Register for the Year 1809*, London: Baldwin, Cradock & Joy, 1821, p.638
39. BL, APAC, L/MAR/B/338CC(2)
40. Equivalent to £9,909 in today's terms (2015). Calculating the modern equivalents of sums of money in the eighteenth century is not straightforward. Other authors seem to vary considerably in their approach. I have taken, as my starting point, the calculations formerly provided by the Bank of England Inflation Calculator at http://www.bankofengland.

co.uk/education/Pages/resources/inflationtools/calculator/flash/default.
aspx.

Chapter 6. Pages 64-81

1. Jean Sutton, *Lords of the East*, London: Conway Maritime Press, 2000, p. 72

2. Northcote Parkinson, *Trade in the Eastern Seas 1793-1813* (Cambridge, 1937) p. 193

3. Sutton, *The East India Company's Maritime Service 1746-1834*, p. 24

4. Richard Cavendish, 'The Coronation of George III' in *History Today*, Volume 61, Issue 9, 2011 available at http://www.historytoday.com/ richard-cavendish/coronation-george-iii

5. A third officer was entitled to carry three tons in private trade. See Sutton, *The East India Company's Maritime Service*, p.278.

6. BL, APAC, Court Minutes B77

7. BL, APAC, Court Minutes B77, p. 264. 13 Jan 1762.

8. Sutton, *The East India Company's Maritime Service 1746-1834*, p. 70.

9. BL, APAC, L/MAR/B/473 A (14 Nov 1761-30 Aug 1763) Journal of the *Horsenden*.

10. The East India Company permitted £3,000 of silver to be carried to exchange for gold. If Captain Stewart had already accounted for his allowance on his own ship, this may have been a ploy to exceed his quota.

11. BL, APAC, Court Minutes B77, p. 272. 13 Jan 1762.

12. Farrington, *Catalogue of East India Company ships' journals and logs, 1600-1834*, London: British Library, 1999, p.327

13. Sutton, *Lords of the East*, p.98.

14. Twining, *Travels in India*, p. 45.

15. Sutton, *Lords of the East*, p.109.

16. Sutton, *The East India Company's Maritime Service 1746-1834*, p. 69

17. Paul Van Dyke, *The Canton Trade*, Hong Kong: Hong Kong University Press, 2007, p. 51

18. Van Dyke, *The Canton Trade*, p. 62

19. Van Dyke, *The Canton Trade*, p. 61

20. Northcote Parkinson, *Trade in the Eastern Seas 1793-1813*, p.58

21. Van Dyke, *The Canton Trade*, p. 148

Chapters 7 and 8. Pages 82-101

1. TNA, CUST 47/229 and 47/246

2. *St James Chronicle or British Evening Post*, No 492. 28 April 1764

3. BL, APAC, L/MAR/B/497 E(1) Ledger of the *Pacific*.

4. Stephen Taylor, *The Caliban Shore: The Fate of the Grosvenor Castaways*, London, Faber & Faber, 2004.

5. Sutton, *The East India Company's Maritime Service 1746-1834*, p. 277

6. BL, APAC, L/MAR/B/497A Journal of the *Pacific*.

7. John Harland, *Seamanship in the Age of Sail*, London: Conway Maritime Press, 2009, p.49

8. Northcote Parkinson, *Trade in the Eastern Seas*, p.248
9. BL, APAC, Court Minutes B80, 23 Jan 1765. p. 366
10. BL, APAC, Court Minutes B80, 13 Mar 1765, p.418
11. BL, APAC, Court Minutes B77, 2 April 1762, p.351
12. BL, APAC, L/MAR/B/497A
13. Nick Robins, *The Corporation That Changed The World*, London: Pluto Press, 2012, p. 79
14. BL, APAC, Court Minutes B82, 23 March 1767, p.456
15. Namier & Brooke (eds), *History of Parliament: the House of Commons 1754-1790*, p. 245
16. Robert Harvey, *Clive The Life and Death of a British Emperor*, London: Hodder & Stoughton, 1998, p.41
17. John Lodge and Mervyn Archdall, *The Peerage of Ireland* Volume 2, Dublin: James Moore, 1789, p.60. Also mentioned in Alfred Spencer (ed), *Memoirs of William Hickey 1790-1809, Volume 1, p.33.*
18. Robins, *The Corporation That Changed The World*, p. 91 (HC raises dividend.)
19. London Metropolitan Archive. Microfilm. Marriages: St Dunstan's in the East. 1767. Also [online] 'England Marriages, 1538–1973 ,' index, FamilySearch (https://familysearch.org/pal:/MM9.1.1/V5KD-N3T : accessed 21 January 2015), Richard Peirce and Mary Burston, 25 Sep 1767; citing Saint Dunstan In The East, London,London,England, reference ; FHL microfilm 396189, 942 B4HA V. 69, 942 B4HA V. 84-85, 942 B4HA V. 86-87.
20. *London Evening Post* No. 6226. 26 Sept 1767, p.1.
21. TNA PROB 11/1015 Will of Thomas Pearce 1776.
22. Sutton, *Lords of the East*, p. 53
23. C. Northcote Parkinson, *Trade in the Eastern Seas*, p.191
24. *Public Advertiser,* No 10506. 2 July 1768, p.2.
25. BL, APAC, Court Minutes B84, 27 July 1768.
26. 'England Births and Christenings, 1538-1975,' index, FamilySearch (https://familysearch.org/pal:/MM9.1.1/NTWH-C9L : accessed 21 January 2015), Richard Pearce, 30 Sep 1768; citing Lynn, Norfolk, England, reference item 1; FHL microfilm 1,526,838.
27. BL, APAC, L/MAR/B/542 C. Journal of the Earl of Ashburnham.
28. Northcote Parkinson, *Trade in the Eastern Seas*, p.157
29. Alfred Spencer (ed), *Memoirs of William Hickey 1790-1809*, London: Hurst & Blackett, 1925, p.358
30. *St James Chronicle or British Evening Post*, No. 1223. 29 Dec 1768, p.1.

Chapters 9 and 10. Pages 102-18

1. BL, APAC, L/MAR/B/542 C, Journal of the *Earl of Ashburnham* (26 Oct 68 – 4 Sep 70)
2. Spencer, *Memoirs of William Hickey*, Volume 1 (1749-1775), p. 153
3. Northcote Parkinson, *Trade in the Eastern Seas*, p. 219
4. Robert Laurie and James Whittle, *The Oriental Navigator or directions for*

   sailing to and from the East Indies, London: Laurie & Whittle, 1794, p. 389
5. Laurie and Whittle, op. cit. p.336
6. Laurie and Whittle, op. cit. p.488
7. Alexander Dalrymple, *Strait of Malacca by Capt R Peirce*, Plate 2, London: Dalrymple, 1779, held at the British Library,
8. Dalrymple, *Strait of Sincapore*, London: Hydrographical Office, 1780 held at the British Library
9. Laurie and Whittle, op. cit. p.468
10. Sutton, *The East India Company's Maritime Service*, p.66
11. Wathen, *Journal of a Voyage in 1811 and 1812 to Madras and China*, p.196
12. Sutton, *The East India Company's Maritime Service*, p.71
13. Farrington, A Biographical Index of East India Company Maritime Service Officers : 1600-1834.
14. James Horsburgh, *India Directory*, Volume 2, London: Parbury, Allen & Co, 1827, p. 293

Chapter 11. Pages 119-37

1. *Morning Post & Daily Advertiser* No. 4037. 10 Jan 1786, p.2.
2. Bell & Daldy, *Notes & Queries*, 10 Jan 1863, pp.34-35
3. TNA, CUST 47/269 & 47/243
4. Kingston upon Thames Records Officer. Kingston Land Tax Returns. 1782
5. BL, APAC, L/MAR/B/542 I (2) *Earl of Ashburham* Pay Book
6. *Whitehall Evening Post* No 3616. 30 May 1769, p.3.
7. Robins, *The Corporation That Changed the World*, p.92.
8. Robins, op.cit. p.95
9. Robins, op. cit. p.99
10. Kingston-upon-Thames London Family History Centre, All Saints Church Parish Records 1741-1812, Microfilm 0991684
11. BL, APAC, L/MAR/B542D *Earl of Ashburnham* Journal 24 Oct 1771 – 14 Sep 1773
12. On quiet days, seamen were often kept occupied with routine tasks such as making nippers and gaskets. A nipper is a length of rope about 6 feet long that is used to tie the ship's cable to the voyol – an essential part of the process of raising the anchor. A gasket is a short plaited cord, used to furl or tie up the sail to the yard.
13. *Middlesex Journal or Chronicle of Liberty* No 427, 24 Dec 1771, p.3.
14. BL, APAC, Court Minutes B87, 27 Dec 1771
15. BL, APAC, Court Minutes B87, 31 Dec 1771
16. *Public Advertiser* No 11871, 23 Apr 1773, p.2.
17. *London Chronicle* No 1936. 13 May 1769. Also [online] London Lives. *Old Bailey records.*
18. *London Chronicle* No 1969. 29 July 1769, p.100.
19. *London Evening Post* No 6692, 9 Oct 1770, p.1.
20. Northcote Parkinson, *Trade in the Eastern Seas*, p. 246
21. Laurie & Whittle, *The Oriental Navigator*, p.112.
22. Alexander Dalrymple, *General Collection of Nautical Publications*, Volume 1

(London, 1783), p. 5

23. *Middlesex Journal or Universal Evening Post* No 638, 1 May 1773, p.1.

24. From his cell in Madras, Richard Green wrote aggrieved letters to England, protesting his innocence. On the 15th July 1772, he appeared before George Stratton JP, charged with forging testimonials purporting to be from a variety of noble patrons. Deciding that the Rev Green was a crank rather than a hardened criminal, the judge released him on a technicality. By September 1774, Richard Green had returned to his father's house in Fleet Street. After a spell in the King's Bench Prison, he married a Mary Fuller of Golden Square and then, putting notoriety behind him, disappeared into respectable obscurity.

25. Spencer, *Memoirs of William Hickey* Volume 1 (1749-1775), p.223

26. Wathen, op.cit. p. 208

Chapters 12 to 14. Pages 138-81

1. Robins, *The Corporation that Changed the World*, p.113.

2. Robins, op cit., p. 114.

3. *London Chronicle*, No 2427, 30 June 1772

4. BL, APAC, L/MAR/B542 J(2) *Earl of Ashburnham* Pay Book.

5. *London Evening Post* No 8063, 2 December 1773, p.3.

6. *Public Ledger* No 4301, 6 October 1773

7. Kingston Land Tax returns 1773.

8. London Metropolitan Archive. Memorandum Book Ms 31376.

9. Sutton, *Lords of the East*, p. 61

10. Keith Feiling, *Warren Hastings* (London, 1966), pp. 81 & 135. A lakh is 100,000 rupees, worth about £10,000 in 1774. See Marshall, P. J., p. 164.

11. *Public Advertiser* No 14599, 18 June 1776, p. 2.

12. *London Evening Post* No 5935, 9 November 1765, p.1.

13. Kingston-upon-Thames London Family History Centre, All Saints Church Parish Records 1741-1812, Microfilm 0991684

14. BL, APAC, Court Minutes, B/91. May 1775, pp.17 & 59

15. Kingston-upon-Thames London Family History Centre, All Saints Church Parish Records 1741-1812, Microfilm 0991684

16. Kingston Land Tax returns 1777, worth £175,000 today.

17. Farrington, *Catalogue of East India Company ships' journals and logs*, p.294.

18. *Public Advertiser* No 13259, 12 April 1777, p.1.

19. *Morning Chronicle & London Daily Advertiser* No 2619, 11 October 1777, p.1.

20. Kingston-upon-Thames London Family History Centre, All Saints Church Parish Records 1741-1812, Microfilm 0991684

21. *London Chronicle* No 3373, 18 July 1778, p.64.

22. *London Packet or New Lloyd's Evening Post* No 1361, 26 August 1778, p.4.

23. *Public Advertiser* No 13245, 29 August 1778, p.2.

24. Sutton, *Lords of the East*, p.18

25. Holden Furber, *John Company At Work* (Boston, 1948), chapter 8.

26. Sutton, *The East India Company's Maritime Service*, p. 138.

27. Farrington, *Catalogue of East India Company ships' journals and logs*, p.294.
28. Sutton, *Lords of the East*, p.29.
29. *London Chronicle* No 3373, 18 July 1778, p.64.
30. BL, APAC, Court Minutes, B/94. 22 July 1778, p.149.
31. *London Packet or New Lloyd's Evening Post* No 1361, 26 August 1778, p.4.
32. *Diary or Woodfall's Register* No 493, 25 October 1790, p.2.
33. BL, APAC, L/MAR/B/465 A-B, Journal of *Halsewell* 1778-1782.
34. West Monkton Parish Records, Somerset Heritage Centre, Taunton. Jane was baptised at West Monkton church on 16 September 1760..
35. Anne De Courcy, *The Fishing Fleet: Husband-hunting in the Raj*. (London, 2013), p. 3.
36. BL, APAC, Court Minutes, B/94. 7 November 1778, p. 458.
37. BL, APAC, Court Minutes, B/94. 11 November 1778, p. 345.
38. BL, APAC, Court Minutes, B/94. 18 November 1778, p.349.
39. Farrington, *A Biographical Index*, p.241.
40. BL, APAC, Court Minutes B/94 6 November 1778, p. 458.
41. Major A. Annand, 'Major-General Lord Macleod, Count Cromartie, First Colonel, 73rd Macleod's Highlanders' in *Journal of the Society for Army Historical Research*, Vol 37, No 149, March 1959, p. 25.
42. Henry Davison Love, *Vestiges of Old Madras 1640-1800*, volume 3, (London, 1913), p. 169.
43. Major Annand, op.cit
44. The Paul girls were said to be very beautiful. Mr Strangways of Shapwick described Jane and Ann as the most beautiful women ever married in India. Referred to [online] at http://www.jjhc.info/grahamthomas1819.htm
45. Mildred Archer, *India and British Portraiture 1770-1825*, London: Philip Wilson Publishers, 1979, p.107 and National Galleries Scotland [online] at www.nationalgalleries.org/collection/artists-a-z/W/5849/artist_name/George%20Willison/record_id/2823
46. Elijah Bridgman & Samuel Villiams, *The Chinese Repository* Volume V, May 1836– April 1837, Canton, p. 150.
47. Hosea Morse, *The East India Company Trading to China 1635-1834*, Volume Two, (Oxford, 1926), chapter 34.
48. Northcote Parkinson, *Trade in the Eastern Seas*, p.5.
49. Hosea Morse, chapter 34.
50. Kingston-upon-Thames London Family History Centre, All Saints Church Parish Records 1741-1812, Microfilm 0991684
51. Laurie & Whittle, *The Oriental Navigator*, p.547.
52. Spencer, Memoirs of William Hickey 1790-1809, volume IV, p. 101. Also Anjali Sengupta, *Cameos of Twelve European Women in India 1757-1857*, India: Rddhi, 1984, p. 60. Also P. Thankappan Nair, *Hicky and His Gazette*, S&T Book Stall, 2001, p. 196

Chapters 15 and 16. Pages 182-216

1. *St James Chronicle or British Evening Post* No 3107, 30 Jan 1781, p.4.
2. *St James Chronicle or British Evening Post* No 3117, 22 Feb 1781, p.3.

3. BL, APAC, B/97. Court Minutes, 7 November 1781, p. 427
4. BL, APAC, B/98. Court Minutes, 16 October 1782, p.501
5. BL, APAC, B/98. Court Minutes, 29 May 1782, p. 124
6. Wakefield, *Kingston's Past Rediscovered*, p.79 and Kingston Land Tax Returns. Microfilm 0992274.
7. *Gazeteer and New Daily Advertiser* No 16525, 11 Dec 1781, p.1.
8. *Morning Herald and Daily Advertiser* No 393, 1 Feb 1782, p.3.
9. BL, APAC, L/MAR/B465A-B, *Halsewell* Journal, Aug 1778-Feb 1782
10. J. Debrett, *The Parliamentary Register*, Vol. VI, London: Debrett, 1782, p.19
11. *Public Advertiser* No 15013, 31 July 1782, p.4.
12. *Morning Herald & Daily Advertiser* 553, 7 Aug 1782, p.3. Also online at www.historyofparliamentonline.org/volume/1754-1790/member/mayne-robert-1724-82
13. *St James Chronicle or British Evening Post* No 3352, 31 Aug 1782, p.1.
14. *Morning Post and Daily Advertiser* No 3116, 22 Jan 1783, p.2.
15. BL, APAC, L/MAR/B465E(2) *Halsewell* Pay Book 1782-84
16. SHC. West Monkton Parish records on microfilm. Anne Paul was baptised at West Monkton Church on 3 July 1765.
17. Online at www.historyofparliamentonline.org/volume/1790-1820/member/graham-thomas-ii-1752-1819
18. BL, APAC, B/98. Court Minutes, 25 September 1782, p.461
19. BL, APAC, L/MAR/B465A-B, *Halsewell* Journal, Aug 1778-Feb 1782
20. *London Chronicle* 3761, 9 Jan 1781, p.1. and online Wikipedia.
21. Rees, *The Floating Brothel*, p.133
22. *The Oriental Navigator*, p. 98
23. Penelope Treadwell, *Johann Zoffany: Artist & Adventurer*, London: Paul Holberton Publishing, 2009, p.330
24. Treadwell, *Johan Zoffany*, p. 334
25. Spencer, *Memoirs of William Hickey* Vol.1, p.155.
26. Treadwell, *Johan Zoffany*, p.339
27. BL, APAC, N/1/2/467 Ecclesiastical Records, St John's Church, Calcutta, 1783.
28. Online at http://kolkataonwheelsmagazine.com/article-details/dacres-lane.html
29. *Calcutta Gazette*, 4 March 1784 in W. S. Seton-Karr, *Selections from Calcutta Gazettes*, London: Longman, Green, Roberts, Longman & Green, 1864, p.31
30. Spencer, Memoirs of William Hickey Vol 3, pp 163-4 and 205 and Feiling, *Warren Hastings*, p.327 and Suresh Chandra Ghosh, *The Social Condition of the British Community in Bengal 1757-1800*, Leiden, Netherlands: E. Brill. 1970, p. 44
31. Spencer, *Memoirs of William Hickey* Vol.4, p.358
32. Thomas H. Brooke, *A History of the Island of St. Helena*, London: Black, Parry & Kingsbury, 1808, pp.259-267
33. *Morning Chronicle and London Advertiser* 5659, 30 June 1787, p. 3.

34. The London Metropolitan Archive, Sun Fire Insurance, 1785 SUN 1 327
03\05\79 BN, Policy 502993, 4 April 1785. £800 is equivalent to £112,000
today.

35. St Thomas Hospital, Minutes of Court of Governors, LL Ref:
LMTHMG553030016, 3 Aug 1785.

36. Kingston-upon-Thames London Family History Centre, All Saints Church
Parish Records 1741-1812, Microfilm 0991684

37. BL, APAC, Court Minutes B/102, 11 Nov 1785, p. 522 and Farrington,
Catalogue of East India Company Ships

38. SHC, West Monkton Parish Records. Amy was baptised in August 1767
and Mary in May 1769.

39. BL, APAC, Court Minutes B/102, 30 Nov 1785, p. 570

40. National Maritime Museum, Capt [Richard] Pierce Etch'd by J
Cruikshank from an Original Sketch by a Friend of the Captains, Repro
ID: PU2961, Object ID PAD2961, 23 Mar 1786.

41. Alexander Dalrymple, *A Collection of Views of Land in Indian Navigation*.
London: Hydrographical Office, 1783, p.5 and in *Memoir of the Chart of the
Natunas, Anambas and adjacent islands*, London: Hydrographical Office, 1786

Chapters 17 to 19. Pages 217-62

1. Henry Meriton and John Rogers, *A Circumstantial Narrative of the Loss of
the Halsewell (East Indiaman) Capt. Richard Pierce* 20th edition (London,
1786), p.30. Hereafter *Meriton, A Circumstantial Narrative*.

2. Meriton, *A Circumstantial Narrative*, p. 27.

3. Dennis Kincaid, *British Social Life in India, 1608-1937* (London, 1973)
pp.69-71.

4. Meriton, *A Circumstantial Narrative*, p. 27.

5. Meriton, *A Circumstantial Narrative*, p. 28.

6. BL, APAC, L/MAR/B/86C Journal of *Ganges*, 1785-87.

7. *Morning Herald*, No 1632, 18 January 1786, p.2.

8. *Public Advertiser*, No 15013, 31 July 1782, p.4.

9. Meriton, *A Circumstantial Narrative*, p. 3.

10. Alan Villiers, *Captain Cook, the Seamen's Seaman* (London: 1967), p. 231.

11. Alfred Spencer (ed.), *Memoirs of William Hickey* (London, 1923), Vol 1, p
141, hereafter Hickey, *Memoirs*. For storms & seasickness: Vol 1 p141; Vol
2 p. 217; Vol 3 p. 19; Vol 4 p. 434

12. BL, APAC, L/MAR/B/542D Journal of *Earl of Ashburnham* 1771-73

13. John Harland, *Seamanship in the Age of Sail* (London, 1985), p238

14. Alan Villiers, op.cit. p. 246.

15. John Harland, op.cit. p 304

16. Meriton, *A Circumstantial Narrative*, p. 8.

17. William Falconer, *The Poetical Works of William Falconer*. (London, 1800),
p.53. See the section concerning the cutting down of masts, that annotates
Canto II of Cooke's edition of 'The Shipwreck' poem.

18. Meriton, *A Circumstantial Narrative*, p. 6.

19. Meriton, *A Circumstantiential Narrative*, p. 6.

20. Hickey, *Memoirs* Vol III, p. 21.
21. Hickey, *Memoirs* Vol III, p.22
22. William Falconer, *William Falconer's Dictionary of the Marine* (London, 1780), p. 518. Also [online] available at http://southseas.nla.gov.au/refs/falc/0518.html (accessed 20 Jan 2015)
23. Hickey, *Memoirs* Vol III, p.20.
24. Trinity House [online] available at http://www.trinityhouse.co.uk/lighthouses/lighthouse_list/portland_bill.htm (accessed 8 May 2012)
25. Burial Register, St Nicholas Church, Worth Matravers. Dorset History Centre. Ref: PE/WMT RE 1/3 MIC/ R/83
26. Hickey, *Memoirs* Vol III, p. 22.
27. *Hampshire Chronicle*, No 697, 23 January 1786
28. Rev Morgan Jones, letter to the *Hampshire Chronicle*. Dorset History Centre, D/135942
29. A local story survives that this lascar was the ship's cook. When discovered by locals, near the stile, they mistook him for the devil and murdered him. This account was told to me by Reg Saville, curator of Langton Matravers Museum.
30. Rev Morgan Jones, ibid.
31. Meriton, *A Circumstantial Narrative*, p.24.
32. *General Evening Post*, No 8149, 26 January 1786, p.2.
33. *Morning Chronicle and London Advertiser*, No 5203, 17 January 1786, p.2.
34. *Morning Post and Daily Advertiser*, No 4037, 10 January 1786, p. 2.
35. *Whitehall Evening Post*, No 6030, 10 January 1786, p.4.
36. *London Chronicle*, No 4547, 10 January 1786, p. 31, and *Public Advertiser*, No 16110, 11 January 1786, p.2.
37. *General Evening Post*, No 8144, 17 January 1786, p.1.

Chapter 20. Pages 265-78
1. *Morning Chronicle & London Advertiser* No 5199, 12 Jan 1786, p.3.
2. *Daily Universal Register* No 331, 16 Jan 1786, p2.
3. *Morning Chronicle & London Advertiser* No 5203, 17 Jan 1786, p.2.
4. BL, APAC, B/102, Court Minutes, 11 Jan 1786, p.677 and BL, APAC, E/1/78 letter from J Lander, dated 7 January 1786.
5. *The Times*, 16 Jan 1786
6. *General Evening Post* No 8143, 14 Jan 1786, p.1.
7. BL, APAC, E/1/78 letter 13 from Rev Geo Ryves Hawker to Thomas Southcomb, 9 Jan 1786.
8. BL, APAC, E/1/78 letter 33 from Rev Geo Ryves Hawker to Thomas Morton, 20 Jan 1786. A surviving piece from Mr Garland's tea service is held at Langton Matravers Museum.
9. *The Times*, 336, 21 Jan 1786.
10. HRO, Ref: Q10/3/2 *Account of Treasurer's Disbursements*.
11. *Hampshire Chronicle* 696, 16 Jan 1786 and *Western Flying Post or Sherborne & Yeovil Mercury* 1928, 16 Jan 1786.
12. *Morning Post and Daily Advertiser* 4041, 14 Jan 1786, p.1.

13. The *Circumstantial Narrative* ran to at least 24 editions. This was a time before the laws of copyright and at least one 'bootleg' version was also published by W. Bailey: *An Interesting and Authentic Account of the Loss of the Halsewell East-Indiaman, with All Its Dreadful Circumstances.*
14. *The Times*, 11 Jan 1786
15. *The Morning Chronicle & London Advertiser* No 5200, 13 Jan 1786, p.2.
16. *Daily Universal Register* No 331, 16 Jan 1786, p.2.
17. *The Morning Chronicle & London Advertiser* No 5199, 12 Jan 1786, p.3.
18. *The Times*, 2 Feb 1786
19. The gravestone of Charles Webber and George Schultz still stands in the grounds of Christchurch Priory. The lettering is very worn but just decipherable. Close by is the headstone of Elizabeth Blackburn. It has not been possible to locate the grave of Mary Ann Peirce.
20. *The Times*, 16 Jan 1786
21. *The Times*, 16 Jan 1786
22. *General Evening Post* 8151, 31 Jan 1786, p.4.
23. *Morning Post & Daily Advertiser* 4042, 16 Jan 1786, p.2.
24. Meriton & Rogers, *Circumstantial Narrative*, p. 28
25. There are memorials to Charles Beckford Templer in Teigngrace Church and Shute Church, both in Devon.
26. *Morning Chronicle & London Advertiser* 5205, 19 Jan 1786, p.3.
27. *London Chronicle* 4549, 14 Jan 1786, p.46.
28. *Public Advertiser* 16118, 20 Jan 1786, p.3.
29. *London Recorder or Sunday Gazette* 132, 15 Jan 1786, p.2.
30. *Public Advertiser* 16120, 23 Jan 1786, p.2.
31. *St James's Chronicle or British Evening Post* 3879, 14 Jan 1786, p.4.
32. *Public Advertiser* 16117, 19 Jan 1786, p.2.
33. BL, APAC, B/102, Court Minutes, 1 Feb 1786, p. 739
34. *The Times* , 20 April 1786.
35. BL, APAC, B/102, Court Minutes, 21 Feb 1786, p.805
36. *Hampshire Chronicle* 697, 23 Jan 1786.
37. *Morning Herald* 1628, 13 Jan 1786, p.3.
38. *Western Flying Post or Sherborne & Yeovil Mercury* 1928, 16 Jan 1786.
39. *Morning Chronicle and London Advertiser* 5216, 1 Feb 1786, p.3.

Chapter 21. Pages 279-97
1. *Morning Herald* No 1628, 13 Jan 1786, p.2.
2. William Falconer, *The Shipwreck*, London: W. Miller, 1804   In 1769 Falconer had the extraordinary misfortune to be shipwrecked for the third and final time. This time he did not survive.
3. *Public Advertiser* No 16115, 17 Jan 1786, p.4.
4. *Public Advertiser* No 16125, 28 Jan 1786, p.2.
5. *Morning Chronicle and London Advertiser*, No 5438, 18 Oct 1786, p.4.
6. *Morning Herald* No 1628, 13 Jan 1786, p.2..
7. *Morning Post & Daily Advertiser* No 4040, 13 Jan 1786, p.2
8. *London Chronicle* No 4551, 19 Jan 1786, p.2.

9. *Public Advertiser* No 16125, 28 Jan 1786, p.1
10. *Morning Herald* No 1656, 15 Feb 1786, p.2
11. *General Evening Post* No 8178, 4 April 1786, p.1.
12. National Maritime Museum, *Capt (Richard) Pierce etched by I Cruikshank from a drawing by a friend*, 23 March 1786. Ref: PAD2961.
13. *Morning Herald* No 1688, 24 March 1786, p.4.
14. For an interesting analysis of Stothard's painting and other depictions of the *Halsewell*, see Chapter 6 'Commerce, Luxury and the Moralisation of Shipwreck' in *Empire to Nation* by Geoff Quilley (2011)
15. National Maritime Museum, Robert Dodd, *Society at Sea*, 1786. Ref: PAG7004
16. National Maritime Museum, Robert Dodd. *To the Directors of the Honbl East India Company this print representing the loss of their ship Halsewell.* 1786. Ref: PAH7421
17. National Maritime Museum, Thomas Rawlinson & S.W. Forbes, *To the survivors and relations of the Unfortunate Persons who perished in the Halsewell East Indiaman*, 18 April 1786. Ref: PAH0503
18. National Portrait Gallery, James Northcote & James Gillray, *The Loss of the Halsewell*, 4 June 1787. Ref:D13063
19. Stephen Gwynn, *Memorials of an Eighteenth Century Painter* (London, 1898) quoted in Quilley, *Empire to Nation*, p. 148.
20. *Encyclopaedia Britannica* [Online] at www.britannica.com/EBchecked/ topic/349376/Philip-James-de-Loutherbourg
21. *Morning Chronicle & London Advertiser* No 3677, 28 Feb 1781, p.1.
22. *Morning Chronicle & London Advertiser* No 3677, 28 Feb 1781, p. 3.
23. *Felix Farley's Bristol Journal* No 1796, 29 March 1783, p.1.
24. *Morning Herald* No 1642, 30 Jan 1786, p.1.
25. *Morning Post & Daily Advertiser* No 4063, 10 Feb 1786, p.1.
26. C. Baugh, *Garrick and Loutherbourg* (Cambridge, 1990) quoted in Willis, *The Glorious First of June.*
27. The literary and visual works referred to in this section are among some of the first artistic responses to the wreck of the *Halsewell*. They were not the last. In 1790, William Lane published a longer poem, *Monody on the Death of Captain Pierce, and those unfortunate young ladies who perished with him, in the Halsewell East Indiaman.* In 1796, the composer, Augustus Kollmann, wrote an instrumental piece for piano and strings, called *The Shipwreck or the Loss of the East Indiaman Halsewell.* At the Cecil Higgins Art Gallery in Bedford, J.M.W. Turner's painting of the *Loss of an East Indiaman* (c.1818) is now thought to represent the *Halsewell.* In December 1853, the *Halsewell* featured in a short story, *The Long Voyage*, written for the magazine, *Household Words* by Charles Dickens. Even today, the *Halsewell* continues to affect and inspire us.

Chapter 22. Pages 298-318

1. Daniel Lysons (Rev), *Environs of London Vol 1: The County of Surrey*, London: T.Cadell, 1792, p. 245.

2. *General Evening Post* No 8159, 18 Feb 1786, p.3.
3. Ibid.
4. *Morning Post & Daily Advertiser* No 4087, 23 March 1786, p.1.
5. TNA, Court of Kings Bench Judgement Roll KB122/596, p.51.
6. Huw Bowen, 'Privilege and Profit' in *International Journal of Maritime History*, Vol XIX, No 2 (Dec 2007), p.59
7. *General Advertiser (1784)* No 2854, 14 Jan 1786, p.2
8. *Public Advertiser* No 16117, 19 Jan 1786, p.3.
9. *Morning Chronicle & London Advertiser* No 5309, 29 May 1786, p.4
10. *Morning Chronicle & London Advertiser* No 5326, 10 June 1786, p.4
11. London Metropolitan Archive, Sun Fire Insurance, 1786 SUN 1 336 24/8/79 ML, Policy 517852, 26 April 1786.
12. Kingston Records Office, Kingston Land Tax Returns1786
13. *Morning Chronicle and London Advertiser* No 5659, 30 June 1786. It is possible that the land referred to was that owned by Thomas Fassot. In the Poor Rate book for 1786, it is described as being 'near the Park Wall' and rented to Peirce for £9.)
14. TNA, PROB 11/1129/344 (Kingston, Surrey, 1785) Will of Thomas Burston.
15. London Metropolitan Archive, Sun Fire Insurance, 1786 SUN 1 340 24/9/79, Policy 523405, Oct 1786
16. TNA, PROB 11/1147 (Whoford, Taunton, 1786) Will of Richard Peirce
17. Huw Bowen, *The Business of Empire* (Cambridge, 2006), p. 126.
18. *Public Advertiser* No 16501, 10 April 1787, p.3.
19. *Public Advertiser* No 16468, 2 March 1787, p.1
20. *World & Fashionable Advertiser* No 77, 30 March 1787, p.1
21. *World & Fashionable Advertiser* No 83, 6 April 1787, p.1.
22. *St James Chronicle or British Evening Post* No 4073, 10 April 1787, p.4.
23. *World and Fashionable Advertiser* No 88, 12 April 1787, p.2.
24. *General Evening Post* No 8423, 13 Nov 1787, p.4.
25. *World and Fashionable Advertiser* No 269, 23 Nov 1787, p.1.
26. *World* (1787) No 274, 29 Nov 1787, p.1.
27. *Morning Chronicle & London Advertiser* No 5791, 1 Dec 1787. Also *Gazeteer & New Daily Advertiser* No 18400, 1 Dec 1787, p.2
28. *General Evening Post* No 8149, 26 Jan 1786, p.1.
29. Stevens, Todd & Cumming, Ed. *Ghosts of Rosevear and the Wreck of the Nancy Packet.* (St Mary's, Isles of Scilly, 2008).
30. *Parker's General Advertiser and Morning Intelligencer* No 2108, 11 Aug 1783, p.2
31. *General Evening Post* No 8231, 29 August 1786, p.3.
32. *General Evening Post* No 8208, 10 June 1786, p.1.
33. *Public Advertiser* No 16404, 18 Dec 1786, p.4.
34. Edward Carson, The Ancient and Rightful Customs (London, 1972), p. 118. Carson also lists 54 barrels of red wine, 5 hogsheads of porter and 3 trunks of stationery.
35. BL, APAC, B/104, Court Minutes, 17 Jan 1787, p.884

36. *General Evening Post* No 8213, 18 July 1786, p.4.
37. *Morning Chronicle & London Advertiser* No 5400, 5 Sept 1786, p.2.
38. BL, APAC, B/108, Court Minutes, 27 Feb 1789
39. BL, APAC, B/112, Court Minutes, 22 Dec 1790
40. TNA, Court of Kings Bench Judgement Roll KB122/596, p.51

Chapter 23 & Post Script. Pages 321-36
1. BL, APAC, B/106, Court Minutes, 1 March 1788, p. 1068.
2. *The Bengal Calendar for the Year 1789.* London: John Stockdale, p. 5.
3. op.cit.
4. TNA, PROB 11/1348. Will of George Frederick Cherry, Calcutta, 1800.
5. R. Thorne (ed) *The History of Parliament: the House of Commons 1790-1820*, London: Boydell & Brewer [online] URL: http://www. historyofparliamentonline.org/volume/1790-1820/member/templer-george-1755-1819 Date accessed: 18 September 2014.
6. *The Bengal Register for 1790*, p. 131.
7. *Diary or Woodfall's Register* No 520, 25 October 1790, p.2.
8. *London Chronicle*, No 5325, 5 October 1790, p.8.
9. BL, APAC, IOR, N/1/4/155, Ecclesiastical records of Bengal.
10. *Gentleman's Magazine* Volume 12, October 1793, p. 955.
11. BL, APAC, B/118, Court Minutes, 5 March 1794, p. 855.
12. *Lloyd's Evening Post*, No 6013, 9 March 1796, p.6.
13. BL, APAC, B/121, Court Minutes, 13 May 1795, p. 37.
14. *Sun*, No. 1096, 31 March 1796, p.4.
15. Parkinson, *Trade in the Eastern Seas*, p. 378.
16. *The Bengal Register for 1795*, p. 118.
17. *Oracle and Public Advertiser* No 19-330, 26 May 1796, p.4.
18. Mildred Archer, *India and British Portraiture 1770 – 1825* (London, 1979), p. 215.
19. William Hickey, *Memoirs* Volume 4, p. 57.
20. William Hickey, *Memoirs* Volume 4, p. 77.
21. William Hickey, *Memoirs* Volume 4, p. 213.
22. Robert Dunning, A History of the County of Somerset, Volume 8, 2004, pp.42-50. [online] URL: http://www.british-history.ac.uk/report. aspx?compid=15106 Date accessed: 18 September 2014.
23. *Oracle & Public Advertiser* No 19-391, 4 August 1796, p.2.
24. *True Briton* No 1206, 5 November 1796, p.4.
25. *Hampshire Telegraph*, No 400, 8 June 1807, p.4.
26. *Lloyd's Evening Post* No 6529, 1 July 1799, p.3.
27. Sir John Maclean, *The Family of Poyntz*, 1886, quoted in [online] http://homepages.rootsweb.ancestry.com/~poyntz/india_old2.html Date accessed: 14 September 2014.
28. *Gentleman's Magazine*, Vol 20, October1800, p. 1001.
29. *The Albion and Evening Advertiser* No 352, 23 October 1800, p. 2.
30. Nordin Hussin (2002) 'Social Life in Two Colonial Port Towns 1780-1830' in *Malaysian Journal of Tropical Geography*, Vol 33, No 1-2.

31. 'England Births and Christenings, 1538-1975,' index, FamilySearch (https://familysearch.org/pal:/MM9.1.1/N5FM-XZQ : accessed 29 January 2015), Mary Ann Peirce, 20 May 1804; citing , reference ; FHL microfilm 918,886.

32. *Trewman's Exeter Flying Post*, No 2244, 23 October 1806, p.4.

33. *Morning Post* No 10709, 29 January 1803, p.4.

34. *Hampshire Telegraph*, No 400, 8 June 1807, p.4.

35. Peter Earle, *Sailors*, p. 109.

36. Op.cit., p.130.

37. *The History of Parliament* [online] available at http://www.historyofparliamentonline.org/volume/1790-1820/member/templer-george-1755-1819 (accessed 12 November 2014)

38. *The Templer Family from Somerset, Devon & Dorset* [online] available at http://www.templerfamily.co.uk/html/george_templer_of_jungpore.html (accessed 12 November 2014).

39. Ibid.

40. *The History of Parliament* [online] available at http://www.historyofparliamentonline.org/volume/1790-1820/member/graham-thomas-ii-1752-1819 (accessed 15 Nov 2014)

41. Mildred Archer, *India and British Portraiture 1770 – 1825*, Philip Wilson Publishers, p.215.

42. Graham Family website [online] available at http://www.jjhc.info/grahamthomas1819.htm (accessed 14 November 2014)

43. *The History of Parliament* [online] available at http://www.historyofparliamentonline.org/volume/1790-1820/member/graham-thomas-ii-1752-1819 (accessed 15 Nov 2014)

44. *The Morning Post* No 15456, 29 September 1820, p.3.

45. *Hampshire Telegraph and Sussex Chronicle* No 1363, 21 November 1825.

46. *The Morning Post* No 17887, 14 April 1828, p.4.

47. *Bristol Mercury* No 2105, 24 August 1830, p.4.

Bibliography

Abbreviations

APAC	Asia, Pacific and Africa Collections, British Library
BL	British Library, St Pancras
BRO	Bath Record Office
DHC	Dorset History Centre, Dorchester
DCM	Dorset County Museum, Dorchester
HRO	Hampshire Record Office, Winchester
IOL	India Office Library, British Library
KRO	Kingston-upon-Thames Record Office, Surrey
LMA	London Metropolitan Archive
NMM	National Maritime Museum, Greenwich
SHC	Somerset Heritage Centre, Taunton
TNA	The National Archive, Kew

Manuscript Sources

Contemporary published works

Bell & Daldy (1863) *Notes & Queries*, 3rd series, Volume 3. London: Bell & Daldy

Bridman, Elijah & Villiams, Samuel (1837) *The Chinese Repository* Volume V, May 1836– April 1837. Canton.

Brooke, Thomas (1808) *A History of the Island of St Helena*. London: Black, Parry & Kingsbury.

Dalrymple, Alexander (1783) *A Collection of Views of Land in Indian Navigation*.

Dalrymple, Alexander (1783*) A General Collection of Nautical Publications*, Volume 1. London: Bigg.

Dalrymple, Alexander (1786) *Memoir of the Chart of the Natunas, Anambas and adjacent islands.*

Debrett, John (1782) *The Parliamentary Register*, Vol. VI, London: Debrett, 1782

Defoe, Daniel (1724) *A General History of the Pyrates* (1999 edition, edited by Michael Schonhorn) New York: Dover Maritime Publications.

Eastwick, Robert. (1841) *A Master Mariner: Being the Life and Adventures of Captain Robert William Eastwick*. (1891 edition, edited by Herbert Compton) London: T. Fisher Unwin

Falconer, William. (1798) *The Poetical Works of William Falconer*. London: C. Cook

Falconer, William. (1780) *William Falconer's Dictionary of the Marine*. London: T. Cadell

Fay, Eliza (1986) *Original Letters from India*: with introduction by M. M. Kay. London: The Hogarth Press.

Foote, Samuel. (1778) *The Nabob; a comedy in three acts.* London: T. Cadell.

Gwynn, Stephen (1898) *Memorials of an Eighteenth Century Painter (James Northcote).* London: T. Fisher Unwin.

Hodges, William. (1793) *Travels in India during the years 1780, 1781, 1782, & 1783.* London: J. Edwards.

Horsburgh, James (1827) *India Directory or Directions for Sailing to and from the East Indies, Volume 2.*. London: Parbury, Allen & Co.

House of Commons (17??) *The Reports of the Secret and select committees, to enquire into the causes of the war in the Carnatic; and the state of justice in the provinces of Bengal, Babar and Orissa. 1782*

Ives, Edward. (1773) *A Voyage from England to India in the Year MDCCLIV.* London:

Kindersley, Mrs Jemima (1777) *Letters from the Island of Teneriffe, Brazil, the Cape of Good Hope, and the East Indies.* London: J. Nourse. Also available [online] at http://travel-letters.org/kindersley/

Kirby, Major Charles. (1867) *The Adventures of an Arcot Rupee*, Volume One. London: Saunders, Otley And Co.

Knight, Charles. (1853) *Knight's Tourist Companion through the Land we Live in.* London: Nattali & Bond.

Lane, W. (1786) *Monody on the Death of Captain Pierce, and those unfortunate young ladies who perished with him in the Halsewell East Indiaman.* London: W. Lane

Laurie, Robert & Whittle, James (1794) *The Oriental Navigator or directions for sailing to and from the East Indies*, London: Laurie & Whittle

Lodge, John & Archdall, Mervyn (1789) *The Peerage of Ireland.* Dublin: James Moore

Lysons, Rev Daniel (1792) *The Environs of London: Vol 1 the County of Surrey.* London: T. Cadell.

Maurice, Thomas. (1821) *Memoirs of the Author of Indian Antquities.* Part 1. Second edition. London: Messrs. Rivington.

Meriton, Henry and Rogers, John. (1786) *A Circumstantial Narrative of the Loss of the Halsewell (East Indiaman) Capt. Richard Pierce*, 20th ed. London: William Lane.

The Annual Register, for the year 1809. (1829) London: Baldwin, Craddock & Joy.

The Bengal Calendar, for the year 1787; including a list of HEIC civil & military servants on the Bengal establishment. Calcutta: John Hay

The Bengal or East-India calendar for the year 1795. London: John Stockdale

The London calendar, or, court and city register for England, Scotland, Ireland, and America, for the year 1784.

The London Directory for 1768.

Twining, Thomas. (1893) *Travels in India A Hundred Years Ago.* London: Osgood, McIlvaine & Co.

Wathen, James. (1814) *Journal of a Voyage in 1811 and 1812 to Madras and*

China. London: Nichols, Son & Bentley.

Williamson, Captain Thomas. (1810) *The East India Vade-Mecum*. London: Black, Parry and Kingsbury.

Other works

Archer, Mildred (1979) *India and British Portraiture 1770 – 1825*. London: Philip Wilson Publishers.

Black, Jeremy (2006) *George III America's Last King*. London: Yale University Press.

Blechynden, Kathleen (1905) *Calcutta Past and Present*. (Reprinted 2003) New Delhi: Sundeep Prakashan.

Bowen, H.V. et al (eds) (2002) *The Worlds of the East India Company*. Woodbridge: Boydell Press.

Bowen, H. V. (2002) 'So Alarming an Evil: Smuggling, Pilfering and the East India Company 1750-1810' in *International Journal of Maritime History*, vol XIV, no. 1 (2002).

Bowen, H. V. (2006) *The Business of Empire: The East India Company and Imperial Britain, 1756-1833*. Cambridge: Cambridge University Press.

Bowen, H. V. (2007) 'Privilege and Profit: Commanders of East Indiamen as Private Traders, Entrepreneurs and Smugglers, 1760-1813' in *International Journal of Maritime History*, vol XIX, no. 2 (December 2007).

Bowen, H. V. et al (2011) *Monsoon Traders: The Maritime World of the East India Company*. London: Scala Publishers Ltd.

Bulley, Anne (1992) *Free Mariner: John Adolphus Pope in the East Indies 1786-1821*. London: British Association for Cemeteries in South Asia (BACSA).

Carson, Edward (1972) *The Ancient and Rightful Customs*. London: Faber and Faber.

Cavendish, Richard (2011) 'The Coronation of George III' in *History Today*, Volume 61, Issue 9, 2011 available [online] at http://www.historytoday. com/richard-cavendish/coronation-george-iii

Chatterton, E. Keble (1914) *The Old East Indiamen*. (Re-published 1971) London: Conway Maritime Press.

Cotton, Sir Evan (1949) *East Indiamen: The East India Company's Maritime Service*. London: Blatchford Press.

Dalrymple, William (2002) *White Mughals: Love and Betrayal in Eighteenth-Century India*. London: Harper Collins.

De Courcy, Anne (2013) *The Fishing Fleet: Husband-hunting in the Raj*, London: Phoenix.

Dunning, Robert (2004) *A History of the County of Somerset*, Vol 8. London: Victoria County History and [online] at http://www.british-history.ac.uk/ vch/som/vol8/pp1-7

Earle, Peter (2007) *Sailors: English Merchant Seamen 1650-1775*. London: Methuen.

Edwardes, Michael (1976) *Warren Hastings: King of the Nabobs*. London: Hart

Davis.

Farrington, Anthony (1999) *A Biographical Index of East India Company Maritime Service Officers 1600-1834*, London: British Library.

Farrington, Anthony (1999) *Catalogue of East India Company ships' journals and logs, 1600-1834*, London: British Library.

Feiling, Keith (1954) *Warren Hastings*. London: Macmillan.

Foster, Sir William (1924) *The East India House: its History and Associations*. London: Bodley Head.

Fowler, Frederick (1980) *Edward Miller, Organist of Doncaster: His Life and Times*. Doncaster: Doncaster Museums & Arts Service.

Furber, Holden (1948) *John Company At Work: a study of European expansion in India in the late Eighteenth Century*, Boston: Harvard University Press.

Hackman, Rowan (2001) *Ships of the East India Company*. Gravesend: World Ship Society.

Harland, John (2009) *Seamanship in the Age of Sail*, London: Conway Maritime Press.

Harvey, Robert (1998) *Clive: The Life and Death of a British Emperor*. London: Hodder & Stoughton.

Hayter, Alethea (2002) *The Wreck of the Abergavenny: The Wordsworths and Catastrophe*. London: Macmillan.

Hood, Jean. (2003) *Marked For Misfortune*. London: Conway Maritime Press.

Hussin, Nordin (2002) 'Social Life in Two Colonial Port Towns: Dutch Melaka and English Penang 1780-1830'. In *Malaysian Journal of Tropical Geography*, Vol 33, No 1-2.

Keay, John (1991) *The Honourable Company*. London: Harper Collins.

Kincaid, Dennis (1973) *British Social Life in India, 1608-1937*. London: Routledge & Kegan Paul.

Lavery, Brian (1991) *Building the Wooden Walls*. London: Conway Maritime Press

Love, Henry Davison (1913) *Vestiges of Old Madras 1640-1800*, volume 3, London: John Murray.

Marshall, P. J. (1976) *East Indian Fortunes: The British in Bengal in the Eighteenth Century*. Oxford: Oxford University Press,

Morse, Hosea Ballou (1926) *The Chronicles of the East India Company Trading to China 1635-1834*, Vol 1 & 2. Oxford: Clarendon Press.

Namier, Sir Lewis & Brooke, John (1985) *History of Parliament: House of Commons 1754-1790*, Volume 2. London: Boydell & Brewer.

Parkinson, C. Northcote (1937) *Trade in the Eastern Seas 1793-1813*. Cambridge: Cambridge University Press.

Quilley, Geoff (2011) *Empire to Nation: Art, History and the Visualisation of Maritime Britain 1768-1829*. New Haven & London: Yale University Press.

Rees, Sian (2001) *The Floating Brothel*. London: Hodder Headline.

Robins, Nick (2006) *The Corporation That Changed the World*. London: Pluto Press.

Saletore, B.A. (1959) *Fort William – India House Correspondence* Vol IX, 1782-

85. Delhi: National Archives of India.

Sengupta, Anjali (1984) *Cameos of Twelve European Women in India 1757-1857*, India: Rddhi.

Sheppard, E. W. (1956) *Coote Bahadur: A Life of Lieut Gen Sir Eyre Coote.* London: Werner Laurie.

Spear, Percival (1975) *Master of Bengal: Clive and His India.* London: Thames & Hudson.

Spear, Percival (1963) *The Nabobs: A Study of the Social Life of the English in Eighteenth Century India.* Oxford: Oxford University Press.

Spencer, Alfred (ed.) (1923) *Memoirs of William Hickey*, Four Volumes, New York: Alfred A. Knopf.

Stevens, Todd & Cumming, Ed (2008) *Ghosts of Rosevear and the Wreck of the Nancy Packet.* St Mary's Isles of Scilly: Todd Stevens & MIBEC Enterprises.

Sutton, Jean (2000) *Lords of the East: The East India Company and its Ships 1600-1874.* London: Conway Maritime Press.

Sutton, Jean, (2010) *The East India Company's Maritime Service 1746-1834: Masters of the Eastern Seas.* Woodbridge: The Boydell Press.

Taylor, Stephen (2004) *The Caliban Shore: The Fate of the Grosvenor Castaways.* London: Faber and Faber.

Taylor, Stephen (2007) *Storm and Conquest.* London: Faber and Faber.

Treadwell, Penelope (2009) *Johann Zoffany: Artist & Adventurer*, London: Paul Holberton Publishing.

Van Dyke, Paul (2005) *The Canton Trade: Life and Enterprise on the China Coast, 1700-1845.* Hong Kong: Hong Kong University Press.

Villiers, Alan (1967) *Captain Cook, the Seamen's Seaman.* London: Penguin Books.

Wakeford, Joan (1990) *Kingston's Past Rediscovered.* Chichester: Phillimore.

White, Jerry (2013) *London in the Eighteenth Century.* London: Vintage Books

Wild, Antony (1999) *The East India Company: Trade and Conquest from 1600.* London: Harper Collins

Yule, Henry & Burnell, A. C. (1886) *Hobson-Jobson: The Anglo-Indian Dictionary.* (Reissued in 1986.) Ware: Wordsworth Editions.

Other Media

Cumming, Edward (ed) (2003) Three English East Indiamen Wrecked Off the Dorset Coast. CD-ROM. ISBN 0-9542104-3-3

British Library, India Office Collections, B/75-132 Minutes of the Court of Directors.

British Library, India Office Collections: L/MAR/B/542D Journal of the Earl of Ashburnham 1771-73

British Library, India Office Collections: L/MAR/B/542 I (2) Earl of Ashburham Pay Book

British Library, India Office Collections: L/MAR/B/86C Journal of the Ganges,

1785-87.
British Library, India Office Collections: L/MAR/B/465 A-B, Journal of
    Halsewell 1778-1782
British Library, India Office Collections: L/MAR/B/473 A (14 Nov 1761-30
    Aug 1763) Journal of the Horsenden.
British Library, India Office Collections: L/MAR/B/438-I. Journal of the
    Houghton
British Library, India Office Collections: L/MAR/B/438 CC(1 & 2) Houghton
    Ledger and Pay Book
British Library, India Office Collections: L/MAR/B/363A, Journal of Manship
    1785-86.
British Library, India Office Collections: L/MAR/B/497A Journal of the
    Pacific.
British Library, India Office Collections: L/MIL/9/91 Muster Roll of Recruits
    1783-86

Dorset History Centre. Burial Register, St Nicholas Church, Worth Matravers.
    Ref: PE/WMT RE 1/3 MIC/ R/83 Rev Jones entry in parish records of
    storm

The National Archive, HO47/2/82 Judges Reports on Criminals.

British Banking History Society [online] available at http://www.banking-
    history.co.uk
Sir John Maclean, The Family of Poyntz, 1886, quoted in [online] http://
    homepages.rootsweb.ancestry.com/~poyntz/india_old2.html Date
    accessed: 14 September 2014.
The Templer Family from Somerset, Devon & Dorset [online] available at
    http://www.templerfamily.co.uk/html/george_templer_of_jungpore.html
    (accessed 12 November 2014)
Trinity House [online] available at http://www.trinityhouse.co.uk/lighthouses/
    lighthouse_list/portland_bill.htm (accessed 8 May 2012)

Index

Lightning Source UK Ltd.
Milton Keynes UK
UKOW06f0839190216

268718UK00012B/237/P